Video Field Production

VIDEO FIELD PRODUCTION

SECOND EDITION

Ron Whittaker
Pepperdine University

Mayfield Publishing Company
Mountain View, California
London • Toronto

Library of Congress Cataloging-in-Publication Data
Whittaker, Ron.
    Video field production / Ron Whittaker.—2nd ed.
        p.   cm.
    Includes bibliographical references (p.   ) and index.
    ISBN 1-55934-444-X
    1. Video recordings—Production and direction.
PN1992.94.W47   1995
791.45'0232—dc20

95-24592
CIP

Manufactured in the United States of America
10   9   8   7   6   5   4   3   2   1

Mayfield Publishing Company
1280 Villa Street
Mountain View, California 94041

Sponsoring editor, Holly J. Allen; *production editor,* Merlyn Holmes; *copyeditor,* Robert deFreitas; *text designer,*
Detta Penna; *cover designer and art manager,* Susan Breitbard; *cover photographs from upper right,* © Robert Brenner/
PhotoEdit, David Toy/Bay Area Video Coalition, Jeanne M. Schreiber; *illustrators,* Robin Mouat, Susan Breit-
bard, and Judith Ogus; *manufacturing manager,* Amy Folden. The text was set in 11/12 Adobe Garamond by
Thompson Type and printed on 50# Saybrook Opaque, an acid-free paper, by Quebecor Printing Book Group.

Many of the photos were shot, scanned, and manipulated by the author. The following photographs were used
with permission: 1.1: © Robert Brenner/PhotoEdit; 2.1: Jay Blakesberg for KRON-TV; 2.2 and 5.11: © David
Toy; 4.5 and 4.8: Leo Kadehjian; 5.21: Miller Fluid Heads (U.S.A.), Inc.; 6.7: Greater Houston Partnership;
7.1 © Ken Staniforth/Fox Broadcasting Company. Additional photos were provided by 3M Company;
Aerospatiale; Air Products and Chemicals, Inc.; *AKG;* Ampex/Nagra Andrew Corporation (Bernard J. Surtz);
Amway Corp.; Band ProFilm/Video Inc.; Boeing Corp.; BTS; Canon USA; Century Precision Optics; *Cinema
Products;* CNN; Colortran; Conus Communications; Denny Mfg. Co., Inc.; *Dynatec;* Echolab Inc.; *EMC²;*
Grass Valley Group; Griffolyn; Robert Herco; Hitachi Denshi America, Ltd.; Hollywood Radio and Television
Society; Hubbard Communications; Ikegami Electronics, Inc.; Kurta Corporation, Phoenix (IS/ADB Graphics
Tablet); Lowel-Light Mfg.; Lynx Video Ltd.; Magnetic Media Division; Micro-Trac Corp.; Miller Fluid Heads
(USA) Inc.; NCR Corporation, Stakeholder Relations Div.; NEC America/Broadcast Equipment Div.; *Newstar;*
Nikon Electronic Imaging; Nurad; Panasonic Broadcast (Division of Matsushita Electronic Corp. of America);
Panasonic Professional/Industrial Company AV Systems; Panther Corp. of America; Pepperdine (University)
Sports Information; Pioneer Electronics; Pixar; Porta-Pattern; Prime Ticket © Barbara White; *Professional Video
Services; Erik Rimer (Makeup);* Sharp Electronics Corp. Professional Products Div. (World globe graphic devel-
oped by Tom Rzoncer and Scott McNulty, Griffin Bascal Advertising); Sony Corp. of America; Smith-Victor
Corp.; Stata Vision (Ed. Tutle); Steadicam; Studio Eleven; Sure Brothers Inc.; Tektronix, Inc.; *Telex Communi-
cation;* Tiffen Manufacturing Corporation; Toshiba; Travellers; Truevision, Inc.; Union Carbide Corp.; Vinten
Equipment Corp.; Westinghouse Corporate Video Services.

BRIEF CONTENTS

Contents

⧙ Audio   **184**

12   Editing Techniques   284

13   Directing and Multiple-Camera Field Production   313

PREFACE

MUCH HAS HAPPENED in television since the first edition of *Video Field Production* was published. To keep pace with these changes and their implications, it was necessary to completely rewrite large portions of the book. The second edition is more streamlined, less hardware oriented, and more concept oriented.

As video and audio technologies have become simpler and more reliable, the technical expertise needed to use them has been reduced. If the scenario ended there, life would be much easier for those of us working in television production. Unfortunately, this is not the case. At the same time our equipment was becoming simpler and more reliable, other developments were taking place. The number of media outlets vying for our attention dramatically increased. Added to the competition from standard, over-the-air broadcasting, we now have scores of direct-broadcast satellite channels and many new C-band and Ku-band satellite channels. In many broadcast markets there has been at least a five-fold increase in the number of cable channels available.

For production people there is an important plus to these developments. As each of these new services is introduced, the need for programming increases. This situation provides new opportunities for people with an aptitude for producing new programming. At the same time, to successfully compete in the highly competitive, 50-plus channel world we now live in, production personnel must demonstrate much more creativity, sophistication, and all-around production savvy than ever.

There has been rapid change in another area. Sophisticated production and postproduction equipment is available to many more people. Whereas a decade ago tens of thousands of dollars separated broadcast quality camcorders and consumer camcorders, today TV stations and even networks regularly use footage shot with consumer-type S-VHS and Hi8 equipment—the type you can purchase at almost any major electronics outlet. Video and audio editing and special effects, which for years had been reserved for those who could afford expensive dedicated editing equipment, have now moved out of professional postproduction houses to the desktop computer.

Digital electronics, which were only briefly mentioned in the first edition of this book, have become a central part of professional audio and video production. The terminology has also changed. When the first edition was written, phrases such as "video server," "W-VHS" and "morphing" had not been heard of. Finally, we have entered the realm of HDTV production. The implications of this new high-resolution medium have required many revisions to *Video Field Production.*

Video Field Production is written for community college, college, and university students who fall into two groups: (1) those who desire to work in some phase of video production and (2) those who need a solid understanding of video production to assist them in such allied fields as advertising and public relations. The text does not assume the reader has had a basic course in studio production; it starts at the beginning and tries to quickly establish a broad-based understanding of the audio and video media. Technical material is included only when it is seen as important to an understanding of larger issues. (You'll note that the footnotes are often used to expand on the technical aspects of the text discussion.)

The order of the chapters and their content has been changed from the first edition. They are now presented in an order consistent with the production process, and with the approach of many production courses. Even so, the chapters may be covered in any sequence. Institutions that require prerequisite courses such as audio production, broadcast news, or media law may want to quickly review related text chapters to allow more time to develop such topics as composition or editing. The instructor's manual that accompanies this text includes suggestions for changing the order of chapters. It also offers ideas for going beyond the text material in each chapter.

When I started teaching video production after twenty years as a producer-director, I found a chasm between the real world of video production and the approach of many textbooks. In addition to the ever-accelerating technological change and the difficulty most schools have in keeping pace with the latest production equipment, some problems lie with spokespersons for the television field. Corporate presidents and station managers often advise students to "simply get a well-rounded, liberal education and let us take care of teaching you how to use the equipment." Although it may seem like good advice, when faced with an abundance of applicants for entry-level production positions, those further down the corporate ladder (the ones who actually do the hiring) typically require more exposure to the field. Not only do they look for experience, they often request a resumé reel of production segments. Resumé reels, the kind students typically develop while taking production courses, go beyond the applicant's statement of good intentions (no matter how enthusiastic), and provide a type of "proof of performance." Resumé reels enable employers to sort out good prospects from what may be a torrent of applicants. Hiring a person who can initially demonstrate sufficient knowledge of production reduces expensive on-the-job training—not to mention reducing the possibility of costly production mistakes. Given the realities of a competitive profession, when students acquire a solid understanding of the many facets of audio and video production, they will more easily attain internships, employment, and professional advancement.

A number of people who helped create this revision of *Video Field Production* should be acknowledged. First, my wife, Alana, a successful model in her own right, "volunteered" to be a model for many photos. I also owe a debt of gratitude to those who reviewed the manuscript. Dr. Michael Jordan of Pepperdine University offered suggestions for the chapter on legal and ethical issues. Those who reviewed the full manuscript and offered suggestions included David P. Kintsfather, Kutztown University; Bill Lyon, SUNY College of Cortland; John MacKerron, Towson State University; Donald G. Wylie, San Diego State University; Fred Owens, Youngstown State University; Francis R. Filardo, SUNY College at Brockport; Edward L. Wells, University of Florida; and Dana Hawkes, Palomar Community College.

Ron Whittaker, Ph.D.
Malibu, California

About the Author

Ron Whittaker, Ph.D., is a professor of broadcasting at Pepperdine University in Malibu, California. He has worked as a producer-director for three television stations, as a radio and television news commentator, and as a reporter and photographer for two Illinois daily newspapers. Professor Whittaker has published more than 100 articles on television production and has served as a video production editor-writer for three broadcast magazines.

Video Field Production

CHAPTER 1

VIDEO FIELD PRODUCTION TODAY

Video Field Production—live or videotaped television production done outside a studio. Also called on-location production, remote video production and electronic field production (EFP). Electronic news gathering (ENG) is a part of video field production.

DURING TELEVISION'S EARLY years, production was rarely done outside the studio. It's easy to see why. A typical remote telecast required thousands of pounds of equipment, a gaggle of engineers and days of preparation. Today, the story is quite different. Most local stations now do a major part of their production on location, and network and cable news services switch to Bonn, London or Rome almost as easily as they switch from one studio camera to another.

The shift to non-studio production was primarily made possible by revolutionary advances in electronic technology in the 1970s and 1980s. Cameras that used to take two strong men to hoist onto a sturdy tripod can now be transported in a briefcase. The original 20-pound, 2-inch-wide videotapes have been replaced with videocassettes—some of which are small enough to fit into a shirt pocket. Reliable microwave, fiber optic and satellite links are rapidly moving us into an era when the nation and even the world are, in effect, one large TV studio.

Beyond the major advances in technology is an even more important reason for the dramatic shift from studio to on-location production. The authentic look of an on-location setting has proven itself to be more interesting to audiences. The preference was first noticed in the late 1970s when "minicams" started replacing TV news film and stations started doing many more stories from the field (see

Figure 1.1). Even in dramatic production, audiences show a clear preference for the authenticity of the actual location represented—be it Malibu or Manila—rather than a studio or Hollywood simulation.

The Extra Demands of On-Location Shooting

Technically, video field production isn't nearly as cumbersome and difficult today as it was when it took one or more large trucks just to haul the necessary equipment. But even though field production is technically easier today, it is much more demanding in other ways. Today's TV audiences are sophisticated in their expectations. Successful on-location productions now require much more in the way of overall production knowledge, creativity and general programming savvy.

The Special Needs of Video Field Production

Field production demands great flexibility in both equipment and personnel. The on-location director does not have ready control of lighting, sound, video, power, and so forth, the way a studio director does. In the field, many more things *can* go wrong, and more things *do* go wrong.

Nevertheless, most problems encountered in the field are not actually caused by "technical difficulties" (as convenient as that term can be in explaining things that go wrong). An examination of the circumstances behind these difficulties often shows that the problems could have been solved, or at least sidestepped, if personnel had more thoroughly understood the television medium and the wide range of options it offers.

Developing the ability to consistently produce good programming under a variety of on-location conditions is one of the goals of this book. Before you can reach this goal, you have to focus on another one: gaining a thorough understanding of the basic concepts behind good video field production—concepts that any serious student or video professional should know.

Some of the equipment discussed in this text will not be available in many schools and small production facilities. Even so, it is important to understand the equipment and techniques that are an integral part of larger production facilities. For one thing, you may suddenly be confronted with an internship or job opportunity where such knowledge is essential. In the professional arena, camerapersons, writers, directors, producers, and even on-camera talent find that having a solid understanding of the tools and techniques of the whole production process can make a major difference in the quality and success of productions. In television production, as in most of today's high-tech areas, knowledge is power.

Figure 1.1   Today, ENG (electronic newsgathering) cameras routinely take viewers anyplace in the world where news is being made. This "instant visibility" has profoundly impacted decision-making at every level of our society—from local politics to international relations.

An Overview of the Field Production Process

What follows is a bit of a whirlwind tour of the field production process. Like most quick tours, no one will expect you to grasp everything. Even so, you should end up with an idea of the basic structure of the production process. Keep in mind that most of the things introduced here will be explained more fully in later chapters.

The following overview includes elements associated with elaborate on-location commercials or major on-location dramatic productions. Depending on the project, many of these elements will be scaled down, combined, or eliminated altogether in smaller productions. They are covered here so that a comprehensive view of the entire production process can be introduced.

Production Personnel and Their Responsibilities

The person who is typically in charge of the entire production is the **producer.** He or she develops the program concept, lays out the budget for the production, and coordinates advertising or financial support. From the beginning, this person is the team leader, the person who works with the writers, decides on the key talent, hires the director, and guides the general direction of the production.

In smaller productions the producer will take charge of more mundane things: supervising the crew call, handling location arrangements and looking after the details of the crew and the cast (including seeing that talent release forms are signed allowing legal distribution of the final result). In small productions, the director (discussed below) may also handle the producer's responsibilities. In this case the combined job title becomes **producer-director.**

Depending on the production, there may also be a **field producer** who assists the producer by taking charge of specific on-location (field) segments. Some productions may also have an **associate producer,** who sets up schedules for the talent and crew, and who, in general, assists the producer throughout the production.

On a major production, one of the producer's first jobs is to hire a **writer** and commission a **script,** the written plan or blueprint for the production. Television writers range from those who create the scripts for 90-minute dramatic productions to staff members who write the material for short videotaped segments in newscasts. Besides spoken words, the writers may include in their scripts descriptions of scenes and locales, music, video and audio effects, and descriptions of the actions of talent.

The principal talent for the production will normally be the next thing considered by a producer. **Talent** includes actors, reporters, hosts, guests, and off-camera narrators—anyone whose voice is heard or who appears on camera. Sometimes this general category is broken down into three subcategories: **actors,** who portray other people in dramatic productions, **performers,** who appear on camera in non-dramatic roles, and **announcers,** who read narration, and are heard but not seen.

In a large production the producer will be responsible for hiring a **director** (Figure 1.2). The director is normally in charge of working out preproduction details, coordinating the activities of the production staff and on-camera talent, working out camera and talent positions, selecting the camera shots during the production, and overseeing postproduction work. In short, the director is responsible for handling the details in transforming the script into the final TV production.

Depending on the size of the production, one or more **production assistants** **(PAs)** may be hired to help the producer and director. During rehearsals, production assistants keep notes on production needs and changes, and notify the personnel involved.

Other production personnel include the **lighting director (LD)** who designs the lighting plan, arranges for the lighting equipment needed, and sets up and checks the lighting. On some productions there will be a **set designer** who, in collaboration with the producer and director, designs the set and supervises its construction, painting and installation. Next, there may be a **makeup person** who,

Figure 1.2 The director is primarily responsible for minute-by-minute decisions throughout the production process. Here a director "calls the shots" during a live newscast.

with the help of makeup, hair spray, etc., sees that the talent look their best (or, if a dramatic roll calls for it, look their worst!). Elaborate productions will have a **wardrobe person** who is responsible for seeing that the talent has clothes or costumes appropriate to the needs of the production.

The **audio director** or **audio technician** arranges for the audio recording equipment, sets up and checks microphones, monitors audio quality during the production and then **strikes** (disassembles and, if necessary, removes) the audio recording equipment and accessories after the production. The **microphone boom/grip operator** observes rehearsals and decides on the proper microphone and its placement for each scene. The **videotape recorder operator (VTRO)** arranges videotape recording equipment and accessories, sets up the videotape recording, performs recording checks, and monitors video quality. The **continuity secretary (CS)** carefully makes notes on continuity details as each scene is shot to ensure that details remain consistent between scenes. Once production concerns are taken care of, the continuity secretary is responsible for releasing the actors after each scene or segment. The **slate person** handles and updates identifying information on the **slate** used at the beginning of each camera "take" (taped segment) and coordinates sound and picture recording for the start of each take. The **CG operator** (character generator operator) programs opening titles, subtitles and closing credits into the device which electronically inserts this text over the picture during the production.

Camera operators (Figure 1.3) arrange the camera equipment pickup and delivery, set up the cameras and ensure their technical quality, and work with the director, lighting director and audio technician in blocking (setting up) and shooting each shot. Depending on the production, there may be a **floor manager** or **stage manager** who is responsible for coordinating activities on the set. He or she may be assisted by one or more **floorpersons,** or **stagehands,** who may be assigned various responsibilities on the set.

After shooting is completed, the **editors** take the videotapes and meld the segments together, adding music, video and audio effects to create the final product.

Figure 1.3 To ensure video quality, camera operators must work closely with the director, lighting director and audio technician during the rehearsal phase of production.

Although editors are at the end of a long list of production personnel, the importance of editing to the success of a production is far greater than most people realize. As you will see, an editor can make or break a production.

The Three Phases of Production

The production process is commonly broken down into three phases: preproduction, production and postproduction.

The Preproduction Phase

There is an axiom in TV production: *The most important phase of production is preproduction.* In **preproduction** the basic ideas and approaches of the production are developed and set in motion. It is in this phase that the production can be set on a proper course, or misdirected to such an extent that no amount of time, talent, or editing expertise can save it.

The Prime Directive: Hit the Target Audience   In order for the program to be successful, the needs, interests, and general background of the **target audience** must be studied and kept in mind throughout each production phase. Successful television and film directors such as Richard Colla stress that not only must you aim

Figure 1.4 After the basic script for a production is approved, rehearsals can start. In this photograph, camera shots and microphones are checked prior to a taping; the cue cards at the right will remind the interviewer of the basic points to be covered.

your production at your target audience but, in order for your program to have value and a lasting effect, the production must in some way affect the audience emotionally. All of these goals must be kept in mind as the script is developed (and, often, repeatedly revised).

Setting Things in Motion   During preproduction, not only are key talent and production members chosen, but all the major elements for the production, such as locations, sets and costumes, are planned. Because things such as scenic design, lighting and audio are interrelated, they must be carefully coordinated in a series of production meetings.

Once the basic elements of the production are determined, location permits can be acquired, sets can be constructed, and the necessary equipment can be commissioned.

Rehearsals   After the basic structure of the production is established, **rehearsals** can start. For a simple on-location segment, a rehearsal may only involve a quick check of talent positions so that camera moves, audio, and lighting can be checked. In contrast, a complex, fully scripted production may require many days of rehearsals. These generally start with a **table reading** or **dry rehearsal,** where the talent sits around a table with key production personnel and reads through the script. Suggestions made at this time may be passed back to the writer. A script often goes through several revisions at this point before everyone is satisfied.

Once everyone is satisfied, a **dress rehearsal** can take place (Figure 1.4). The

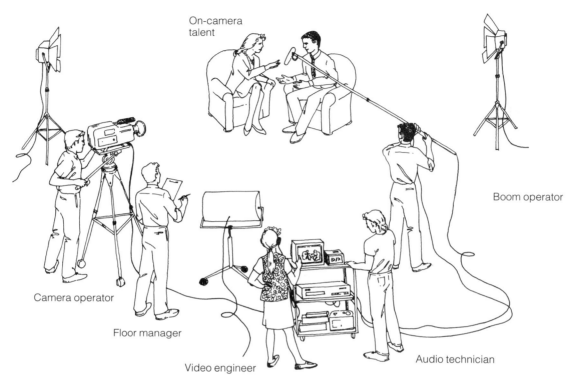

Figure 1.5 Several of the crew members discussed in the text are shown in this behind-the-scenes diagram of an on-location dramatic scene. Audio is recorded on a DAT (digital audio tape) machine by the audio technician. In addition to running the videotape recorder, the video technician monitors video quality with the help of a high-resolution color monitor, a waveform monitor and a vectorscope. (The function of each of these will be discussed later in the text.)

term comes from the fact that the talent is "dressed" in the appropriate wardrobe and all production elements are in place. Dress rehearsals represent the final opportunity for production personnel to solve remaining production problems.

The Production Phase

The **production phase** is where everything (it is hoped) comes together in a kind of "final performance." Productions can be either broadcast live or recorded on videotape (Figure 1.5). With the exception of news shows, sports remotes, and some special-event broadcasts, productions are typically recorded on videotape for later broadcast or distribution. Recording the show or segment provides an opportunity to fix problems by either stopping the tape and redoing the segment, or making changes during editing.

Figure 1.6 In its most basic sense, editing is the process of rearranging and joining together the recorded video and audio segments in a production. However, as computer-controlled editing techniques and postproduction special effects have become more sophisticated, editing has gone far beyond these activities and is now a primary focus of production creativity.

The Postproduction Phase

All after-production tasks such as striking sets and lights, dismantling and packing equipment, handling final financial obligations and evaluating the effect of the program are part of the **postproduction phase.** Even though postproduction may actually include many after-production duties, most people associate postproduction with videotape editing.

In its most basic sense, editing refers to the process of rearranging and joining together the recorded video and audio segments of a production. However, as computer-controlled editing techniques and postproduction special effects have become more sophisticated, editing has gone far beyond this and is now a major focus for production creativity (Figure 1.6).

Complex TV productions are typically assembled—some would go so far as to say "created"—during this critical postproduction phase. Editing offers the opportunity to rearrange program segments, alter camera shot sequences, and try out a variety of audio and video options. Changes in the audio at this point may include adding narration, sound effects, and background sounds; filtering out noise; and rerecording dialogue that is unclear or requires modification. This audio postproduction phase is called **audio sweetening.**

CONFUSING THE MEDIUM WITH THE MESSAGE

Armed with the latest digital effects, the editing phase of production can add much in the way of "razzle-dazzle" to a production. Today it is easy to become entranced with the impressive technology and sophisticated production and postproduction techniques that are available. At the same time we should not lose sight of the fact that television, in essence, is only a medium of communication, albeit the world's most powerful and influential mass medium to date. As important as production techniques are in producing television programming, they should be considered only as essential tools for accomplishing the greater purpose: the effective communication of ideas and information.

History books will dutifully record the impressive and even revolutionary technological advances in television that we are now witnessing. Although technology is important, when all is said and done, a far more significant issue will be what those history books say about how we made use of our powerful communications tools. This, in large measure, will be determined by people like you.

CHAPTER 2

SCRIPTS, BUDGETS AND PREPRODUCTION

"**I HAVE THIS** great idea for a TV show!"

The common response to that statement is, "Okay, get it down on paper and we'll take a look at it."

Once you can get it down on paper, you can at least communicate your idea to a producer and to key production personnel. Developing a **production outline** or **treatment**—a clear and succinct summary of your idea—that everyone can understand, and agree on, is the first step in preproduction. We'll go into more detail on this later.

Even though you have a clear idea of what you want to get across in a production, at times it seems as if there is a "moat full of alligators" between the idea as initially conceived and the result as eventually perceived. Successfully navigating the moat depends on an understanding and mastery of the full range of available production tools and procedures. In this chapter we are going to look at the whole creative sequence, including

- script form and content
- defining the needs and interests of the target audience
- the role of treatments, program proposals and storyboards
- budget considerations
- the preproduction and production phases
- script conventions and formats
- elements of scriptwriting

Figure 2.1   A production may take the form of a lecture, panel discussion, drama, variety show, news program, demonstration, or even an animated sequence.

Productions can vary from 10-second news bits to 90-minute documentaries or dramas. For the purposes of this discussion we'll look at the steps involved in a major video production. This category can include an elaborate commercial, an hour-long, single-camera, film-style documentary with re-enacted segments, or a dramatic feature. Once these production phases are understood, they can be appropriately scaled down to fit other, more basic types of productions.

FORM AND CONTENT

A script should be viewed as having two fundamental attributes: form and content.[1] The **form** of a script refers to its basic design, genre and logical construction. Specifically, a script may reflect a production that takes the form of a lecture, panel discussion, drama, variety show, news program, demonstration or an animated sequence (Figure 2.1).

---

[1] Many of the ideas in this section were suggested by Richard Colla, an accomplished film and television director.

Content, which includes *goals* and *visions,* not only includes the substantive or meaningful part of the script, but also embodies the production's affective (emotional) attributes. In a production our **goal** relates to what we want the audience to experience, feel, or gain. Our **vision** relates to how we get to our goal—how we personally use the tools of the trade to translate the goal into an audio and visual experience for the viewer. Our vision reflects our personal production approach. It will probably mirror our own perspective and viewpoint.

It is primarily within the realm of content—goals and visions—that engrossing and effective productions are separated from those that are mediocre and dull. And it is primarily within the realm of content that we can make our own personal, creative contributions. Although there are definite rules for the successful operation of production equipment, there are no rules for program content—guidelines, but no hard-and-fast rules. The bottom line for content is simply, Does it do what it's supposed to do? Or, more specifically, Does it work?

Capturing and Holding Viewer Attention

Nothing much matters in television if we are not able to capture and hold viewer attention. It would be nice if an audience could be captivated solely by the depth, profundity and worthiness of program content. Although these things certainly help, the success or failure of our productions ultimately depends on the effect of content on an audience, in particular, the *emotional response* of the audience to our production. Although you might at first assume this applies only to dramatic production, when you fully analyze audience-engaging principles (that is, what works, what doesn't, and why), you will see that on some level this principle applies to all types of television content. Although people may try to evaluate a production logically, it is their basic emotional reaction which sets the course for their evaluation.

Audience-Engaging Principles

What types of production content emotionally engage an audience? First, and foremost, we and our audiences have an interest in other people, especially in "experiencing the experiences" of other people. We are particularly interested in people who lead interesting lives: dangerous, romantic, fast paced, prestigious, wretched, or engrossingly spiritual (Figure 2.2). Part of this phenomenon involves gaining new insights and being exposed to new points of view, in short, learning new things.

We also like content which reinforces our existing attitudes, and we tend to react against ideas which run contrary to our beliefs. Production people, therefore, must be prudent in presenting ideas that challenge widely held beliefs, even when

Figure 2.2   What types of production content engage an audience? First and foremost, audiences have an interest in people, especially in "experiencing the experiences" of other people.

there is ample evidence to support an alternative view.[2] At the same time, we know that for a democracy to be successful the media have a social responsibility to bring to light corruption and impropriety.

Audiences also like new things and things that generate excitement. This is undoubtedly why danger, intrigue, sex, fear, violence, action and even horror do so well at the box office. They all stir the adrenaline, rouse us from our complacency, and make us sit up and take notice. Of course, there is sometimes a rather blurry line between honestly presenting these things and unduly emphasizing and exploiting them for the sake of grabbing and holding an audience. Beyond a certain point audiences will sense they are being exploited and manipulated, and will resent it.

With this background established, we can now turn to some of the "nuts-and-bolts" aspects of scripting.

---

[2] A number of years ago a TV station in a large East Coast city did an undercover segment which very clearly documented a popular law official taking a bribe. Audience reaction was immediate and negative—*against* the TV station. A subsequent analysis revealed that many audience members were angry at the station for upsetting their beliefs in a person who was for them a law-and-order hero. Likewise, when President Nixon was forced to resign after the Watergate cover-up, some people put the entire blame on the media for exposing the scandal.

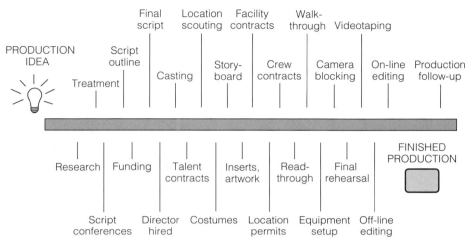

Figure 2.3 The 15 phases of production outlined in the text are expanded in this typical, step-by-step outline for a dramatic production. Depending on its size, a production may involve only a few steps, or dozens of preproduction, production and postproduction elements.

Timing, Budgeting and Scheduling

In addition to the form and content already discussed, the script is also used to determine three other things about a production: timing, budgeting and scheduling. **Timing** refers to how long the total production is, including time allotted to the individual scenes and program segments. As the term suggests, **budgeting** refers to the process of costing-out (determining the cost of) the various components of the production. **Scheduling** refers to breaking down scenes and shots into a convenient and cost-efficient sequence and creating a production timetable. (In single-camera, film-style production the most convenient and cost-efficient arrangement for shooting will seldom follow the sequence of events presented in the script.) We'll cover many of these considerations in more detail as we move through 15 steps in the production process.

The 15-Step Production Sequence

Figure 2.3 illustrates one way of outlining the production process. Again, remember that these steps are appropriate for a fairly elaborate production and they will have to be scaled down for smaller productions.

Step 1: Identify the Goals of the Production

First, and foremost, *there must be a clear formulation of the goals and purposes of the production.* The best way to achieve this is to ask some questions. What is the production primarily intended to do? Is it to instruct, inform, entertain, or possibly to generate feelings of pride, or social, religious or political need? Possibly its purpose is to create a desire in the audience to take some action. If there is no clear agreement on the purpose of a production, it will be impossible to evaluate success. (How do you know if you've arrived at your destination, if you don't know what your destination is?) Most productions, of course, have more than one goal. We'll elaborate on some of these later.

Step 2: Analyze Your Target Audience

You must clearly define and investigate your target (intended) audience. Based on such things as age, sex, socioeconomic status and educational level, programming preferences of television audiences differ. These preferences are also different in different areas of the United States (North, South, urban, rural, and so on). These regional variations can in part be seen by differences in the local programming that is broadcast in different parts of the country, and sometimes by the films and network programming that some local stations refuse to air.

Compared to standard broadcast television, institutional television, which includes corporate and educational video (Chapter 15), has different needs and expectations. Here, too, there are demographic characteristics, such as age, sex and education which will influence the production's form and content. But in institutional television the producer and script writer have to be keenly aware of the audience's experience, education, needs and expectations. To underestimate the education or experience and inadvertently talk down to members of your audience insults them. To overestimate education or experience and talk over everyone's head is probably even worse; you lose them and they can become totally frustrated with the presentation. But, whatever type of television script you are writing, the better you know the needs, interests and expectations of your audience, the greater the probability of your success.

Step 3: Review Similar Productions

Investigate similar productions done in the past. How will your proposed production differ from the successful and unsuccessful efforts that have been done before? (If you are going to make mistakes, at least make some new ones!) Review whatever similar productions you can find. Take into consideration differences in time, place and audience.

Step 4: Determine Value and Marketability

Determine the overall value of the production to a sponsor or underwriter. Obviously, underwriters or advertisers want some sort of return on their investment. Although costing-out a production will be discussed later, here we want to make sure we can justify production expense in terms of some sort of gain or return on the investment. To do this, several questions must be asked. First, what is the probable size of the audience? In determining this we must know whether it will be a one-shot presentation or whether production expenses can be recouped over time by presenting it to other audiences.

Generally, the larger the audience the more marketable a production will be to an underwriter or advertiser. At the same time, simple numbers don't tell the whole story. Let's say an advertiser has a product intended for young people, athletic shoes or jeans, for example. In this case, a production that draws a large percentage of this age group will be more valuable than a production that has a larger overall audience, but with a lower percentage of young people.

Once the potential value of a production to an advertiser or underwriter is determined, its value must be balanced with the projected cost of producing and presenting the production. This balance is the return on the investment—the infamous "bottom line," or payback. In commercial television this payback is generally in the form of increased sales and profits. However, return on investment may take other forms, such as the expected moral, political, spiritual, or public relations benefit derived from the program.

Step 5: Develop a Treatment or Production Outline

Next, *commit the idea to paper.* There are several sub-steps to this process; they span the interval from the initial proposal to the final shooting script.

After the initial decisions are made as part of the previous steps, the producer generally commissions a written **program proposal,** called a treatment in dramatic production. It may be just a couple pages or, in the case of a dramatic production, it may be 30 or more pages. A program proposal is written as an aid in presenting and getting agreement on the focus and direction of the production. It may also be used to interest key people, especially financial backers, in supporting the production. A program proposal or treatment should cover the focus of the production or, in the case of a dramatic production, the basic storyline. Also included are the locations and talent required, and sometimes even a key scene or two. In non-dramatic productions the approximate lengths of the segments and basic production needs are also included.

Anyone who reads the program proposal should be able to get a clear idea of the whole production. If there is disagreement on the program concept, it will be much easier to change elements at this stage rather than after the complete script is written.

After the program proposal is approved, a full script is requested. At this point the remaining research is commissioned. If the script called for someone watching TV in a 1960s **period piece**—a production that takes place during a specific historic era—we would need to check on what television shows were being broadcast at that time.

Generally, the first version of the script is considered a **first draft,** the first of several revisions. Throughout this process, a number of story or script conferences

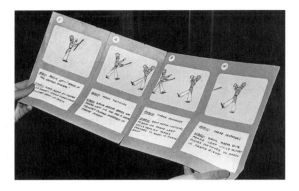

Figure 2.4 A storyboard consists of drawings of key scenes with corresponding notes on dialogue, sound effects and music. Storyboards are especially useful in conveying basic production concepts to advertisers and underwriters. Although storyboards can be drawn by hand, today there are numerous computer programs that make the process much easier.

typically take place as the script is revised and developed. In these conferences such things as audience appeal, pace, or problems with special interest groups are debated and alternative ideas are considered. In an institutional production, the specific goals of the production will be reviewed (and possibly sent on for approval to those higher up), and questions about the most effective way of presenting specific concepts will be decided. If the director is on board at this time, he or she may be a part of these conferences (See Step 7).

Finally, a script version emerges that is more-or-less acceptable to everyone. However, even the version of the script used to start a production may not be final. In some instances revisions on a scene continue right up to the moment it's shot. Not infrequently, writers sit on the set of a major motion picture and crank out revised pages on almost a minute-by-minute basis. Each revision is issued on a different colored paper so that the cast and crew will not confuse it with an earlier version.

Depending on the production, a storyboard may be requested. A **storyboard** (Figure 2.4) consists of drawings of key scenes with corresponding notes on dialogue, sound effects and music. Storyboards are common in short productions, such as commercials and public service announcements, but somewhat less common in dramatic productions. The ideas of set designers and costumers, as well as the angles and shots envisioned by the director, all go into these drawings. Storyboards are especially useful in conveying basic production concepts to advertisers and underwriters.

Step 6: Develop a Production Schedule

Next, *a tentative production schedule is developed.* Often, broadcast or distribution deadlines will dictate the production schedule (the written timetable listing the time allotted for each production step). If a corporate video production must be completed in time for an international conference, for example, you will need to outline a realistic production schedule that can ensure the completion of the production on time. Missing the deadline could even make the production worthless to the corporation which, in turn, wouldn't contribute much to your job security.

Figure 2.5 One of the advantages of video field production is the opportunity to travel to exotic locations. Cities that encourage TV and film production have film commissions that supply photos and videotapes of interesting shooting locations in their area.

Step 7: Commission Key Personnel

From here on, the various production steps will overlap and in many cases take place simultaneously. About this point *key, above-the-line production personnel are brought on board.* **Above-the-line personnel** include the writer, producer, production manager and director, in general, the creative team. (**Below-the-line personnel** primarily include the technical staff.) A promotion director may be assigned to document and publicize the various phases of production.

Step 8: Select Locations

Next, *locations are selected.* In a major production a **location manager** will be hired to find locations that are as similar as possible to those described in the script. More and more frequently, as audiences expect authenticity in productions, footage is being shot at the actual locations depicted (Figure 2.5). Cities that encourage TV and film production have film commissions that supply photos and videotapes of interesting shooting locations in their areas. These commissions will provide information on usage fees and the people who need to be contacted. They generally also assist in getting the necessary permits, licenses and bonds (See Step 9).

Often—especially in high-budget productions—it is necessary to arrange for modifications of on-location settings. These alterations might include rooms that have to be repainted or redecorated, signs that have to be changed, and so on.

Step 9: Decide on Talent, Wardrobe and Sets

Decisions are made on talent, wardrobe (costuming) and sets. Depending on the type of production, talent interviews, auditions and casting may take place at this point. Contracts are then negotiated and signed. (If you are lucky enough to be able to afford well-known actors, these will have probably been decided early in the preproduction process and contracts negotiated at that point.) Once final decisions are made on actors, the selection of wardrobes can start.

During this phase, set design and construction will also get underway. After a set designer is engaged, he or she will review the script, possibly do some research, and then discuss initial ideas with the director. If the designs are accepted, sketches of the set or sets can be made and plans drawn up. After approval, construction can begin.

Rehearsals, from initial walk-throughs to the final dress rehearsal, can then be scheduled. Even though sets are not finished, the talent can start reading through the script with the director to establish pace, emphasis and rudimentary blocking. When the sets are finished, final blocking and dress rehearsals can take place.

Step 10: Engage Remaining Production Personnel

Decisions are made on remaining staff and production facility needs. In this phase arrangements are made for key technical personnel, equipment and facilities. If necessary, this includes the rental of equipment and production facilities. Transportation, catering from food and refreshment trucks, and on-location accommodations for overnight stays must also be arranged.

If unions are involved, their contracts will include job descriptions and specific responsibilities. Working hours, including graduated pay increases for overtime hours, will also be spelled out. In addition, unions often set minimum standards for transportation, and the quality of meals and accommodations.

Step 11: Obtain Permits, Insurance and Clearances

In major cities and in many foreign countries it is not possible to just go to the location of your choice, set up your tripod, and start taping. *Necessary access permits, licenses, security bonds and insurance policies must be arranged.* Except for spot news and short documentary segments, permits are often required. Many semipublic interior locations, such as shopping malls, also require filming[3] permits. Depending on the nature of the production, liability insurance and security bonds may be necessary in case an accident is directly or indirectly attributed to the production. In some locations the controlling agency will limit exterior production to certain

---

[3] Although production personnel generally make a distinction between "taping" (with video equipment) and "filming" (with a motion picture camera), government agencies generally do not.

areas and to specific hours. If there is a street scene and traffic will be affected, it will be necessary to arrange for special police patrols.

Included in this category are a wide variety of clearances. They range from permission to use prerecorded music to reserving satellite time. If clearance cannot be obtained, alternatives must be explored quickly.

Step 12: Determine Supporting Production Elements

As this work progresses, *program inserts can be selected and second unit work started.* During this phase arrangements can be made for shooting and acquiring VTR or film inserts, still photos and graphics. If possible, existing **stock footage** is secured (generally for a fee) from film or tape libraries located around the country. If suitable footage is not available or it does not meet the needs of the production, a second unit may have to be hired to produce needed segments. **Second unit** work refers to production done away from the main location by a separate production crew. It generally does not involve the principal on-camera talent. If part of a dramatic production calls for a specific building in Chicago, for example, a second unit can shoot the necessary Chicago exteriors, while the interior shots, which are supposedly taking place within the Chicago building, are actually shot in New York, where the actors are living.

Initial decisions on music are made at this point. Copyright clearances and royalties must be worked out for music and visual inserts. (These will be covered further in Chapter 14.)

Step 13: Start the Production Sequence

The production goes into rehearsal and shooting. Depending on the type of production, rehearsals may take place either minutes or days before the actual shooting. Productions shot live-on-tape (without stopping except for major problems) must be completely rehearsed before taping starts. This stage includes early walk-through rehearsals, camera rehearsals and one or more dress rehearsals.

Productions shot single-camera, film-style, are taped one scene at a time (Figure 2.6). Rehearsals generally take place right before each scene is taped.

Step 14: Begin the Editing Sequence

After shooting is completed, *tapes are reviewed by the producer, director and videotape editor, and editing decisions are made.* For major productions this has traditionally been done in two phases.[4]

First, is **off-line editing,** using copies of the original tapes. Off-line editing

---

[4] More and more often, as digital, nonlinear editing equipment moves into postproduction, the off-line phase is being bypassed (See Chapters 11 and 12).

Figure 2.6   Productions shot single-camera, film-style, are taped one scene at a time. Rehearsals generally take place right before each scene is taped. Here reflectors are being used to direct the sun into the shaded area of a porch during the taping of a dramatic sketch.

decisions are typically made by editing a copy of the original footage, generally on one of the smaller videotape formats. Using this edited tape and an **EDL** (edit decision list) as a guide, the production then moves to **on-line editing,** where much more sophisticated (and expensive) equipment is used to create the **edited master,** the final edited version of the tape. During this final editing phase all necessary sound sweetening, color balancing, and special effects are added.

Step 15: Postproduction Follow-up

Although most of the production crew will be finished once production *wraps* (finishes) there is still much in the way of follow-up work to be done. Final *bills have to be paid, financial statements totaled, and the success or failure of the production determined.* Broadcast television has ratings; in institutional television there may be tests, evaluations, or simply informal viewer feedback to consider.

Planning the Script

Having outlined this overview of the production process, let's back up and examine the key element in the production process: the script.

There are semi-scripted shows and fully scripted shows. In the first category are interviews, discussions, ad-lib shows, and many demonstration and variety shows. The scripts for **semi-scripted shows** resemble a basic outline, with only the show segments and their times indicated on the script. This type of show puts considerable pressure on the director and talent to keep things on track as the show progresses.

As the name suggests, the scripts for **fully scripted shows** list the complete audio and video for each second. In the fully scripted show, overall content, balance, pace and timing can be carefully worked out before production starts. Unpleasant surprises are thereby minimized.

The Concrete-to-Abstract Continuum

Documentary and hard news pieces should be reasonably concrete; that is, they should (ideally) present information so clearly that the possibility for misunderstanding is eliminated. This type of script will be quite different in approach and structure from the script for a feature, soft news piece, music video, or a dramatic production. In the latter cases it is often desirable to not be too concrete but, rather, to allow room for personal interpretation.

Let's look at two examples. An instructional video on the operation of a computer would need to be as concrete as possible. Given the nature of computers and computer programs, information would have to be presented in a highly structured, step-by-step fashion. Although the material should be presented in a creative, interesting and possibly even humorous way, the success of the production would rest on each member of an audience getting the same, clear idea of a specific sequence of operational procedures. If members of the audience walk away from the production confident that they can operate the computer program covered, the production is a success. Indeed, the success of the production would be easy to evaluate when these people were subsequently confronted with the operation of the program.

In contrast to this very concrete production would be a feature piece on aerobic dance or new fashions. Given the fact that the audience has undoubtedly seen scores of television segments on fashion, the first challenge would be how to approach the segment in a fresh, creative, attention-getting way. Considering this challenge, actually doing the piece would probably be the easy part. Unlike computers or stereo components, fashions are not sold on the basis of technical specifications but, rather, appeal largely to the ego and the emotions. So, in doing the fashion piece, we are not as interested in communicating facts as generating some excitement about new fashions and creating an emotional response.

Likewise, a soft news piece on aerobic dance would not emphasize facts, as much as action. Its purpose would be to communicate something of the feelings surrounding exercise—the feelings that go along with having a trim, fit body.

Structuring the Script

Once the intent and focus of the production are established and the characteristics of the audience are known, the various program elements can be selected and arranged.

In scripting content, a logical and linear sequence is, of course, the most natural approach, especially when information must be presented in a concrete, step-by-step fashion. An example would be the instructional computer piece already cited. Often, however, it is desirable to abandon a structured, linear presentation, which sometimes can be pretty boring and predictable. In some productions the technique of using flashbacks, or presenting **parallel stories** (two or more stories running concurrently) is used to stimulate interest. The primary consideration is a sequence that will provide aural and visual variety and offer the most interesting variations in pacing. A production outline can be helpful in organizing these elements.

Working Around Weaknesses in Interviews

For better or worse, interviews are the mainstay of many, if not most, non-dramatic productions. Because of this, and because of the difficulty involved in making most interviews interesting, they merit special attention.

Within limits, the credibility and authenticity involved in getting information directly from a believable source is better than having a narrator present the same information. Even if sources for interviews are not highly effective speakers, at least you are getting information right from the horse's mouth, so to speak. This fact, alone, tends to offset presentation weaknesses. Even so, needed video and audio variety can be introduced into interview-centered programming by regularly switching to new speakers in new locations. Unless the person being interviewed on camera is an unusually gifted speaker, or is recounting a highly dramatic, engaging event, interviews should be broken up into short segments and intercut with related material. You will probably also want to select only the most cogent elements from the interview.

Keep in mind that once we see what someone looks like on camera, very little can be gained by holding the same shot while the person continues to talk. Interest and pace can be increased by staying with the audio track while cutting in related B-roll footage. **B-roll** footage typically consists of shots of people, objects or places referred to in the basic interview footage, the **A-roll.** This will be covered in more detail in Chapters 11 and 12.

Organizing and Writing an Interview-Based Production

Turning reels of interview footage and B-roll material into a coherent production during the editing phase is a formidable task. Experienced writers (with good memories) may need only to review the interview and B-roll footage while making periodic notes on topics and time codes. Writers who prefer a more systematic approach start out by getting a transcript of the interviews typed up on a computer. This is especially valuable if there are numerous, lengthy interviews which need to be broken up and rearranged. Once on computer disk, word or phrase searches can be done to quickly locate key words or topics in the various interview segments. These segments can then be condensed, rearranged and assembled right on the computer screen to provide the most logical flow. Most word processing programs allow for multiple windows on the screen. Using this approach the interview transcript can be searched and reviewed in one window while the script is written in another. It then becomes simply a matter of cutting and pasting text from one computer window to another. Whenever it's necessary to explain or amplify points, or to establish bridges between segments, narration can be written. This will generally be read by an announcer over B-roll footage (Figure 2.7).

Once the script is finished, a videotape editor can use the written text and associated time-code references to locate the beginning and ending points of the needed segments.

Matching Production Techniques to Content

In writing the script, you must be aware at each moment of the most effective way to express your ideas. Sometimes you can best do this by asking yourself some questions. What technique will best illustrate a necessary point: a narrator, a short clip from an interview, an electronically animated sequence, a graph, or a still photo? As you pull the elements together, think of yourself as watching the show and try to visualize exactly what's going on at each moment. It is said that the great musical composers can hear each instrument in their heads as they write. In the same way effective script writers should be able to visualize scenes as they write their scripts.

Figure 2.7   Off-camera announcers typically provide narration for news and documentary pieces. Here an announcer records a voice-over audio track for a production segment.

Pacing the Production

In establishing the pace of the production, there should not be long, slow periods or even long periods of fast pacing. Either will tire an audience. Except for short, fast-paced montages, scene segments should be at least three seconds in length.[5] Conversely, only a scene with plenty of action or intensity will be able to hold an audience for more than a minute. (Five- to 10-second scenes are closer to the norm.)

The most important parts of your production are the beginning and ending. To capture and hold attention, productions must engage the audience quickly. And to leave an audience with a positive impression, your production must have an effective ending. In between, you have to keep interest from drifting by varying pace, emotional content and presentation style.

---

[5] We assume that you want the audience to fully grasp the content of a scene. There are times, especially in commercials, when the object is to convey only a fleeting impression. In this case you may elect to have a scene last only a second, or even a fraction of a second. To make sense—and not just be frustrating—the latter will need to be within the context of material that has already been introduced and that the viewer understands.

Basic Scriptwriting Guidelines

Although a complete guide to writing the various types of scripts used in television is beyond the scope of this chapter, some basic principles can be outlined. First, it should be emphasized that writing for the visual media is different from writing for print. Those writing for publication enjoy advantages that their counterparts in television don't have. For one thing, a reader can go back and reread a sentence. If a sentence is not understood in a television production, it is lost; or worse, the listener is distracted for some time trying to figure out what was said. With the written word the reader is guided by such things as chapter divisions, paragraphs, subheadings, italics and boldface type. And in print the spelling of sound-alike words can indicate their meaning.

Since narration should be read in a conversational style, the standard rules of punctuation sometimes aren't followed. Commas and ellipses (three dots) are commonly used to designate pauses. Often, complete sentences are not used . . . just as they aren't used in normal conversation. Although such usage is inconsistent with proper written form, the overriding consideration in writing narration is clarity.

The way we perceive information also complicates things for the script writer. When we read, we see words in groups or thought patterns. This process helps convey meaning. When we listen, information unfolds one word at a time. This means that to make sense out of the sentence we must retain the first words in memory and add them to all subsequent words, until the sentence or thought is complete. If the sentence is too complex or takes too long to make its point, meaning is missed. Even worse, the listener's normal reaction in such cases is to dwell on the troublesome sentence to try to figure it out, thereby missing subsequent points.

Video scripts are written in what has become known as the *broadcast style*. With allowance for sentence variety, this means that video scripts use short, concise, direct sentences. All unnecessary words are weeded out. Do not say "at this point in time" when you mean "now." In writing for the ear it is especially important to eliminate verbal "fog." In writing the script remember that the active voice is preferred over the inactive voice; nouns and verbs are preferred over adjectives; and specific words are preferred over general words. Avoid dependent clauses at the beginning of sentences. Attribution should come at the beginning of sentences ("According to the Surgeon General . . .") rather than putting it at the end of the sentence, which is common to newspaper writing.

Since viewers are used to having the video relate to the audio, the basic guideline *correlate audio and video* should be kept in mind. If viewers are seeing one thing and hearing about another, they can become confused. Watch out, however. This can lead to the "see Dick run" approach. If you can clearly see what is happening on the screen, it can be annoying to then be told exactly what you are seeing.

Guarding Against Information Overload

Although the purpose of many TV scripts is to impart information, if the script is packed with too many facts, the viewer will become confused, lost and frustrated. The average individual can absorb only a limited amount of information at a time. It is better to cover effectively a little bit of important material than to inundate viewers with a torrent of information they can't possibly retain.

Not only is the amount of information important, but so is the pacing of that information within the presentation. You need to give the viewer a chance to process each idea before moving on to the next point. The best approach in dealing with crucial information is to first signal the viewer that something important is coming up. Next, present the information as simply and clearly as possible. And, finally, reinforce the point through repetition or with an illustration or two.

In summary, here are six rules to remember in writing for television:

1. Assume a conversational tone through the use of short sentences, informal words and contractions.

2. Avoid complex sentence structure including beginning sentences with dependent clauses.

3. Provide adequate logical structure; let viewers know where you are going, which points are key concepts, and when you are going to change the subject.

4. After making an important point, expound on it; then illustrate it.

5. Pace the presentation of important ideas; give your audience a chance to digest one concept before moving on to another major point.

6. Don't try to pack too many facts into one program.

Video Protocol

Some people argue that, unlike writing, video and film don't have any standardized grammar, that is, conventions or structure. This is debatable. Although paragraphs, subheadings and chapter divisions aren't as apparent in television as they are on the printed page, nevertheless the TV audience has become somewhat adept at picking up the meaning of various audio and video transition devices.

The slow **lap-dissolve,** where two sources momentarily overlap, often signal a transition. They can be used to signal a change in time or place. Fade-ins and fade-outs, which apply to both audio and video, can be likened to the beginning and ending of book chapters. They consist of a two- or three-second transition from a full signal to black and silence. These transitions normally signal a major division in a production. Often they indicate a passing of time. Traditionally, **teleplays** (television plays) and **screenplays** (film scripts) start with fade in and close with fade out.

In the process of scriptwriting, a number of other phrases and abbreviations are commonly used. First, there are those that describe camera shots.

Cuts or **takes** are instant transitions from one video source to another. Put in grammatical terms, shots can be likened to sentences; each shot is a visual statement. In describing shots in scriptwriting, remember that cutting from a static scene to a scene with motion accelerates tension and viewer interest. Conversely, cutting from a scene with fast-paced movement to a static scene can bring about a sudden collapse of tension.

A **cover shot, master shot,** or **establishing shot** are all designations for a wide shot (**WS**) or long shot (**LS**) that gives the audience a basic orientation to the geography of a scene. In the relatively low resolution medium of NTSC television they are visually weak, simply because important details aren't easy to see. Cover shots should be used only long enough to orient viewers to the relationship between major scene elements. Thereafter, they can be momentarily used as reminders or updates on scene changes. In the video column of video scripts the shorthand designation LS is normally used. Occasionally, the abbreviations **XLS,** for extreme long shot, or **VLS,** for very long shot, will be seen.

Except for dramatic shock value, a long shot would not be immediately followed by a close-up. The transition is too abrupt. A medium shot or medium long shot should come in between.

Other shot designations you will find in scripts include

MLS (medium long shot) or **FS** (full shot). With people, this is a shot from the top of their heads to their feet.

MS (medium shot). When applied to talent an MS is normally a shot from the waist up.

MCU (medium close-up). On a person, a shot cropped between the shoulders and the belt line.

CU (close-up). A head and shoulders shot. A relatively straight-on CU is the most desirable for interviews. Changing facial expressions, which are important to understanding a conversation, can easily be seen. CUs are also commonly used for insert shots of objects when important details need to be shown.

XCU (extreme close-up). On people this is generally reserved for dramatic impact. The XCU shot may show just the eyes or mouth of an individual. With objects an XCU is often necessary to reveal important detail.

2-S and **3-S** (**two-shot** and **three-shot**) designates a shot of two or three people in one scene.

Subjective shot indicates that the audience (camera) will see what the character sees. Often, it indicates a hand-held camera shot that moves in a walking or running motion while following a character. Subjective camera shots can add drama and frenzy to chase scenes.

Camera angles are also sometimes indicated on scripts. Included are bird's eye view, high angle, eye-level, and low angle. A **canted shot** or a **Dutch angle shot** is tilted 25 to 45 degrees to one side, causing horizontal lines to run up or down hill. Although a writer occasionally feels it necessary to indicate camera shots and angles on a script, this is an area that is better left to the judgment of the director. Even so, in dramatic scripts you may find the terms *camera finds,* to indicate that the camera moves in on a particular portion of a scene; *camera goes with,* to indicate that the camera moves with a person or object; *reverse angle,* to indicate a near 180-degree shift in camera position; and the term *widening,* to signal a zoom or dolly back. The terms *various angles* and *series of cuts* indicate a variety of shots, generally on some specific subject matter.

In addition to these basic script terms, there are a number of other abbreviations used in scriptwriting. (See the sample scripts later in this chapter.)

EXT and **INT** (exterior [outside] and interior shot).

SOT (sound-on-tape). This term indicates that the voice, music, or background sound will be from a videotape audio track.

SOF (sound-on-film).

VTR (videotape).

VO (voice over). This term refers to narration heard over a video source. It can also refer to narration heard at a higher level than a source of music or background sound.

OSV (off-screen voice). The voice indicated on the script is from a person who is not visible.

MIC or **MIKE** (microphone).

POV (point of view). Dramatic scripts will often note that a shot will be seen from the point of view of a particular actor.

OS shot (over-the-shoulder shot). The picture shows the back of one person's head and possibly one shoulder; these are also designated as O/S and X/S shots.

ANNCR (announcer).

KEY (the electronic overlay of titles and credits over background video).

SFX or **F/X** (**special effects**). These may be audio special effects (audio FX) or video special effects—effects that alter reality and are created in the production process.

Script Formats

There are two basic script formats used in production: the general video script (which includes scripts for news, documentaries, commercials and public service announcements) and the dramatic (film-style) script.

News, Documentary and Commercial Scripts

Unlike dramatic scripts (discussed below) there is no real consistency in the format of video scripts. Most are divided into audio and video columns. Some script layouts call for the columns to be equal; most allot more room for the audio column. To facilitate reading by the talent, the audio text should be double-spaced. Instructions in the audio or video column should be single-spaced.

A sample news script is shown in Figure 2.8. Note that the left column describes the video that corresponds to the audio in the right column, which is being heard at the same time. Both columns can include technical notes, such as times, segment titles and computer file names. The various members of the production staff will add their own production-related notes to their copies of the script.

Unlike film scripts, capitalization in video scripts is not standardized. The announcer's words are often written in upper- and lowercase and the instructions in all capitals. However, announcers who have become used to reading news wire copy in "all caps" often prefer that the parts of the script intended for reading be printed in capital letters.

Dramatic Scripts

Dramatic scripts are either written in the shot-by-shot or master-scene style. Both are patterned after traditional film scripts. In a **master scene script** each new scene or setting is typically described in a paragraph of text. Note at the beginning of the scene in Figure 2.9 that Sandy's apartment is described in some detail. This is particularly important for the location manager, the set designer and the wardrobe manager, all of whom are responsible for creating the setting.

The **shot-by-shot script** is almost identical to the master scene style except that camera shots are numbered within the scenes and basic camera shots and directions are added. Because some directors feel that deciding on the shots is their job and not the job of the script writer, many writers feel it's safer (not to mention easier) to write in terms of master scenes.

Figure 2.9 shows three pages (part of one scene) from *The Theta Experiment,* a 90-minute dramatic production. Since it was written in the master scene style, the director has written in his own notes on shot numbers and descriptions.

Note in Figure 2.9 that many words and phrases are capitalized. In traditional film scripts the first time characters appear in a scene their names are capitalized. Unlike video scripts where abbreviations are used, such as CU, ECU, LS or MS, these terms are spelled out in film-style dramatic scripts and put in all caps: CLOSE-UP, EXTREME CLOSE-UP, LONG SHOT, MEDIUM SHOT. The bibliography at the back of this text suggests a number of books which will go into much more detail on the intricacies of script writing.

(*text continues on p. 36*)

11 PM News - 10/29/95   <u>Selma Fed. Records Fire—Page - 7</u>
Writer: P. Smith

Studio - Jacobs   FIRE OFFICIALS SAY THE BLAZE THAT RAVAGED THE

                         FEDERAL RECORDS STORAGE FACILITY IN SELMA

                         VALLEY IS NOW UNDER CONTROL.

Server - video only: MORE THAN 40 FIREFIGHTERS BATTLED THE FLAMES
(<u>file:</u> fedfire.01)
                         THAT ERUPTED LATE WEDNESDAY NIGHT. TV-3'S JOHN

                         JACOBS ASKED FIREFIGHTER JENNIFER CARRY IF THE

                         BLAZE MAY HAVE BEEN THE WORK OF AN ARSONIST.

                         ========================
Server - video+audio   ((<u>In cue:</u> "Well, it's a bit too early to tell yet but there seems to be . . .))
(<u>file:</u> fedfire.07)
                         <u>Server Segment:</u> 1:12

                         ((<u>Out cue:</u> . . .and so as firefighter Jennifer Carry says, it's really too

                         early to tell about arson. This is John Jacobs for TV-3."))
                         ========================

Studio - Jacobs   BECAUSE THE FIRE INVOLVED FEDERAL RECORDS,

                         THE F-B-I HAS BEEN CALLED IN TO INVESTIGATE.

                         EARLIER THIS AFTERNOON TV-3'S SANDRA PARKS

                         ASKED BUREAU CHIEF TIM RAY ABOUT THE F-B-I'S

                         INVOLVEMENT.

                         ========================
Server - video+audio   ((<u>In cue:</u> "The FBI's arson unit was called in this morning. . . ."))
(<u>file:</u> fedfire.04)
                         <u>Server Segment:</u> 0:42.

                         ((<u>Out cue:</u> ". . . and that aspect of the work will start Thursday at the
                         scene of the fire. This is Sandra Parks for TV-3."
                         ========================
                                                                              ((MORE))

Figure 2.8   Typical news script format

INT. SWANK APARTMENT-DAY

1A-WS

Sandy leads the way into a large, plush apartment which has a warm, almost sensual atmosphere. To one side of a large bookcase and tapestry-lined living room is a modern kitchen area. A snack bar divides the two areas. On the opposite side of the living room there is a glass wall with a sliding glass door leading to a large balcony. Sunlight floods the apartment. Steve looks around.

          STEVE
This is where you live?

2C-MS, Steve

          SANDY
This is it.

          STEVE
By yourself?

Sandy moves into the kitchen area.

3A-WS

          SANDY
Except for Oliver, my cat. He's around here somewhere. Can I get you a drink or a sandwich or something?

Steve's attention has just been captured by Sandy's large collection of books. As he walks over to the bookcase, he glances at his watch.

4C-MS, Steve

          STEVE
Well, it has been a while since breakfast.

Sandy opens a cabinet and starts pushing some cans around.

5 B- 2 SHOT

          SANDY
What have I got? Not much. I seem to be getting low on things.
          (pushing more cans around)
You're probably not too big on cat food. Here's some tuna fish. How about tuna sandwiches?

Steve pulls out a book and flips through it.

          STEVE
Puss and Boots?

6C-MS, Steve

          SANDY
Chicken of the Sea.

          (continued)

Figure 2.9   Film-style dramatic script

<u>continued:</u>

                              STEVE
                    Sure; why not.

Sandy starts getting things out of the refrigerator.

                              SANDY
7B - 2 shot   What do you like in it. . .mayonnaise,
                    onions. . .all that?

                              STEVE
                         (starting to read a page in a book)
                    It doesn't matter. Don't go to any trouble.
                    (beat) As I remember you were ready to
                    graduate before you dropped out.

8 cut in
        The SOUND OF ELECTRIC CAN OPENER brings Oliver, A LARGE
        TOMCAT, out of bedroom.

                              SANDY
9B-MS, Sandy   I got a job. Money was kind of a concern at
                    first. (quieter) But money's not the problem
  ↓   any more.

        Steve is lost in a book. Sandy starts mixing the tuna in
        a bowl. She is obviously fighting fatigue.

Slowly   SANDY (cont'd)
tighten   You know, I'm afraid I won't last much longer.
                    I haven't slept for. . .it seems like days. I
to MCU   generally try to sleep until early afternoon. . .
                    (almost to herself) when I can.
                         (no answer)
                    Hello, are you there?

                              STEVE
10 C MLU,   I'm sorry. You have quite a collection on
   STeve   Eastern mysticism. Some of these I haven't
                    seen before. Where did you get them?

                              SANDY
                    Here and there. I've done a bit of traveling.

                              STEVE
                    I'd like to take down some of these titles?

11 B
MCU   Sandy suddenly stops her work. A look of desperation
Sandy   comes over her.
                                        (continued)

Figure 2.9   (*continued*)

continued:

                    SANDY
          I've got to tell you about some things. There
          are some. . .problems. . .a number of
          problems, in fact. . .and I guess you're about
          the only person who would. . .maybe understand.

Her change of tone gets his attention. He looks over at
her, puts the book on the shelf, and walks over to the
kitchen.

12 C
2 shoT

                    STEVE
          Well, from my experience with the other
          subjects, it really shouldn't be much of a
          problem; just a session or two at most. . .

                    SANDY
          It goes far beyond the experiments. That was
          just the start.

                    STEVE
          Well, even so. . .

13 B - MCU
   Sandy

                    SANDY
          (interrupts) Since you were sort of
          responsible for this mess, I need you to
          promise that you won't leave until this gets
          straightened out.

                    STEVE
          (defensively) If you hadn't run out. . .

                    SANDY
          (interrupts) Okay, I ran out, but you didn't
          tell me what kind of stuff we were messing
          with. . .what might happen. . .

14 CU,
   Steve

                    STEVE
          Well, I guess if we knew the outcome of every
          experiment. . .

15 B cu,
   Sandy

                    SANDY
          (interrupts) Look, I'm too tired to play
          games. Just. . .just help me get this mess
          straightened out.

                    (MORE)

16

          SHOT OF TWO OF THEM as seen through the viewfinder of a
          single-lens reflex camera. A 5,000 mm lens gives an
          extreme telephoto perspective. ANOTHER ANGLE shows the
          man in the LAU tee-shirt with a camera trained on the
          apartment from the window of a nearby building.

Figure 2.9 *(continued)*

COSTING-OUT A PRODUCTION

Once the script is written and there is a basic idea of what the production will entail, we must confront the major question that underlies all television production in the real world: how much is it going to cost? Even if you have no interest in producing *per se,* the better grasp you have on this issue, the better your chances of success. It would be a waste of your time to come up with ideas—impressive as they might be—if they have little chance of being produced.

Of course, to-the-penny production costs won't be known until all of the production steps previously outlined are completed. Even so, no production company—at least none that expects to stay in business very long—will commit itself to a production without some idea of cost.

Various systems have been devised to **cost-out** a production. First, expenses should be divided into categories. It has been traditional to think of expenses as falling into two broad categories: above-the-line and below-the-line. Although the "line" involved can at times be a bit blurry, above-the-line expenses generally relate to the performing and producing elements: talent, script, music, office services, stock footage, etc. Below-the-line elements refer to (1) the physical elements involved (sets, props, makeup, wardrobe, graphics, transportation, production equipment, studio facilities and editing) and, (2) the technical personnel required (the stage manager, engineering personnel, VTR operators, audio operators, and general labor).

To accurately cost-out a production it is necessary to go beyond just the above-the-line and below-the-line designations and divide production into at least 13 categories. An example of the cost categories in a major production would be

1. Preproduction
2. Location and travel
3. Studio, set and construction
4. Props and wardrobe
5. Equipment rental
6. Videotape, audiotape
7. Production crew
8. Producer, director, writer, creative
9. On-camera talent
10. Insurance, shooting permits, contingencies
11. On-line, off-line editing
12. Advertising, promotion, publicity
13. Research and follow-up

Many of these categories would be omitted for smaller productions.

Renting vs. Buying Equipment

Note that one of the categories covers rental equipment. It is often more economical to rent equipment rather than buy it. There are several reasons:

■ Production equipment (especially cameras and recorders) tend to become outdated rather quickly. It is not unusual to spend $50,000 on a top-notch CCD camera. If you do, you assume that you will be able to depreciate the cost over a number of years (Tables 2.1 and 2.2). If you were able to pay cash for a $50,000 camera and use it for 10 years, the cost would break down to $5,000 a year, plus repair and maintenance costs. But even though the camera might still be reliable after five or more years, compared to the newer models it would probably seem a bit primitive. Parts for repair might even be hard to get.

If the equipment were rented, several production facilities would probably end up using it. This means that the initial investment could be written off by a rental company more quickly, making it possible to more rapidly replace the equipment with newer models.

■ Second, when equipment is rented, it is the rental company rather than the production facility that's responsible for repair, maintenance and updating. If equipment breaks down during a production, many rental companies will replace it within a few hours without additional cost.

■ Next, rental can represent an income-tax advantage. When equipment is purchased it has to be depreciated (written off) over a number of years. Sometimes this time span exceeds the practical usefulness of the equipment. This means that the facility may be faced with having to sell the used equipment in order to recoup some of its initial investment. (Colleges often get used equipment in this way, since donated equipment represents a tax write-off.) Rental expenses can be immediately written off of taxes as part of a production expense. Although rules governing income taxes regularly change, deducting the costs of rental equipment has for some people represented a route to a quicker, simpler (and in many cases a greater) tax deduction.

■ Finally, when equipment is rented there is greater opportunity to obtain equipment that will meet specific needs. Once equipment is purchased, there is pressure to use it, even though at times other makes and models might be better suited to the specific needs of a production.

Even for Hi8 or S-VHS equipment the cost of rental (which may be only $50 a day) might make sense if it's only going to be used for a few days.

APPROACHES TO ATTRIBUTING COSTS

Once the cost for a production is projected or determined, you may need to justify it, either in terms of expected results or cost-effectiveness (generally compared to

Table 2.1   Purchase of Video Camera

Purchase Price = $50,000

Period	Now	Year 1	Year 2	Year 3	Year 4	Year 5
Price	$50,000					
Loan Balance	36,750	29,400	22,050	14,700	7,350	
Down Payment	13,250					
Principal Payments		7,350	7,350	7,350	7,350	7,350
Interest Payments		4,778	3,822	2,867	1,911	956
Prop. Taxes		500	500	500	500	500
Insurance		500	500	500	500	500
Maintenance		500	500	500	500	500
Depreciation		7,143	7,143	7,143	7,143	7,143
Total Expense	13,250	13,628	12,672	11,717	10,761	9,806
Cash over Five Years = $71,834						

Tables 2.1 and 2.2 illustrate the cost differences between renting a $50,000 video camera and purchasing it with standard financing. The total cash required over five years for purchasing the camera is calculated by adding the initial investment, the yearly principal and the expenses paid out. This includes a 13-percent interest charge on the balance of the loan at the end of the year. Note that the total cash invested over this period is $71,834. But this figure does not take into consideration depreciation—a major tax deduction. (Depreciation is figured on a straight-line basis and is amortized over seven years.) When this is considered, the total expense to purchase the camera drops to $47,549.

Table 2.2   Rental of Video Camera

Rental Fee = $600/day

Period	Now	Year 1	Year 2	Year 3	Year 4	Year 5
20-Day Rental		$12,000	$12,000	$12,000	$12,000	$12,000
Interest		0	0	0	0	0
Prop. Taxes		0	0	0	0	0
Insurance		500	500	500	500	500
Maintenance		0	0	0	0	0
Depreciation		0	0	0	0	0
Total Expense		$12,500	$12,500	$12,500	$12,500	$12,500

In Table 2.2 the cost for renting or leasing the same $50,000 camera is broken down. In this case there is no initial investment, and the yearly costs are merely the sum of the rental ($600 per day) for 20 days, plus insurance. This adds up to $62,500 over five years. Although the expenses to buy are substantially less, there are two additional considerations. First, the sizable amount of cash required to purchase the camera may mean the difference between being able to go into production and not being able to. Second, depending on existing tax laws, it should be possible to deduct a sizable portion of the monthly rental fees.

other productions or production approaches). There are three bases on which to measure cost-effectiveness: cost per minute, cost per viewer, and cost per measured benefits.

Cost per Minute

The cost per minute is relatively easy to determine; you simply divide the final production cost by the duration of the finished product. For example, if a 30-minute production costs $60,000, the cost per minute would be $2,000.

Cost per Viewer

Cost per viewer is also relatively simple to figure out; you simply divide the total production costs by the actual or anticipated audience. In the field of advertising, CPM, or cost per thousand, is a common measure. If 100,000 people see a show that costs $5,000 to produce, the CPM would be $50. On a cost-per-viewer basis this comes out to be only five cents per person.

Cost per Measured Results

The last category, cost per measured results, is the most difficult to determine. For this we must measure production costs against intended results. In commercial television we might sell 300,000 packages of magic beans after airing a 60-second magic bean commercial.[6] If our profit on 300,000 packages was $100,000 and we spent $100,000 producing and airing the commercial, we would begin to question whether the ad was a good investment.

Of course, once produced, most ads are aired more than once. This means that the cost of future airings simply centers on buying air time. If the cost of TV time was $10,000 and we sold 300,000 packages of magic beans each time we aired the commercial, we would then show a profit of $90,000 with each airing, at least until people got very tired of seeing our bean commercial.

Of course, figuring the return on an investment is often not this simple. What if we are also running ads in newspapers and on radio, and we have big, colorful magic bean displays in stores? We can lump all advertising costs together in determining the effect of advertising on profits, but then it becomes difficult to determine the cost-effectiveness of each medium.

The returns on other types of productions may be even harder to determine. How do you quantify the return on investment on a public service announcement (PSA) designed to get viewers to stop smoking, to preserve clean air and water, or

---

[6] Although you may recall that Jack did very well with his beanstalk after he planted the magic beans, if he wanted to advertise them on TV today, it's doubtful he could get FDA approval.

to "buckle up for safety"? Even if before-and-after surveys are done to measure changes in public awareness on these issues, it can be almost impossible to factor out the influence of a particular type of public service announcement from the host of other voices the public regularly encounters on these issues. Apart from doing in-depth interviews with viewers, we may have to rely largely on "the record." If we find that a series of 60-second TV spots increases magic bean sales by 300,000, we might safely assume that a 60-second PSA might also have at least some influence on smoking, clean air and water, and buckling seat belts.

It is the producer, of course, who is primarily concerned with these issues, in addition to the general above-the-line considerations such as financing, selecting key actors or talent, coordinating advertising and guiding the overall project. Beyond this point, the director takes over to handle all the production and postproduction details.

With some of the major preproduction concerns covered, our next step is to become familiar with some of the tools we'll be using in the production process. To understand these we'll need to start with the basics of the medium itself.

CHAPTER 3 THE MYSTERIES OF LUMINANCE AND CHROMINANCE

IN ORDER TO have full creative control in video production, you need to have an understanding of the television process. We'll start with the basic building blocks of television pictures: fields and frames.

FIELDS AND FRAMES

Early experiments with motion pictures found that if a sequence of still pictures was presented at a rate of about 16 or more per second the individual pictures would blend together, giving the impression of a continuous, uninterrupted image. It was also discovered that if the individual pictures varied slightly to reflect changes over time, the illusion of motion would be created when the pictures were presented in an uninterrupted sequence. Two human perceptual attributes create the illusion of motion under these conditions: persistence of vision and the phi phenomena. Without their combined effect on perception there would be no "motion" in motion pictures or in television.

Although early silent films used a **frame,** or picture, rate of 16 and 18 per second, when sound was introduced this rate was increased to 24 per second. This was necessary, in part, to meet the quality needs of the added sound track. Unlike broadcast television, which has frame rates of 25 and 30 per second, depending on the country, film has for decades maintained a worldwide, 24 frame-per-second sound standard.

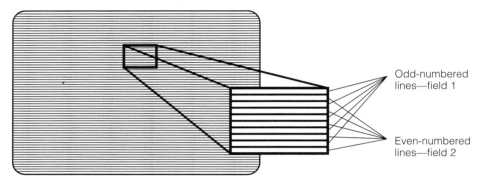

Odd-numbered
lines—field 1

Even-numbered
lines—field 2

Monochrome television screen

Figure 3.1   A TV image consists of hundreds of horizontal lines of video information. A complete TV picture, or frame, is made up of two fields. One field is composed of all the even-numbered lines; the other, the odd-numbered lines.

The NTSC (National Television Standards Committee) system of television used in the United States reproduces frames at a rate of approximately 30 per second.[1] A motion picture camera records a sequence of completely formed pictures on each frame of film. In a video camera each frame is composed of hundreds of horizontal lines. Along each of these lines there are thousands of points of brightness and color information. This information is electronically discerned by the TV camera, and then later reproduced on a TV display, in a top-to-bottom, left-to-right, sequence.

To reduce flicker and brightness variations during the scanning process, each complete television picture is typically divided into two interleaved segments. The odd-numbered lines are scanned first, and then the even-numbered lines and filled in. The term **interlacing** describes the alternating, odd-even line approach to scanning the total number of lines in each complete picture. Each of these half-frame passes (either the odd- or even-numbered lines) is called a **field;** the completed (two-field) picture is called a frame (Figure 3.1). Once a complete frame is scanned, the whole process starts over again. The slight changes between successive pictures that are associated with movement in the original subject matter are "fused together" by our perception, giving the illusion of continuous motion.

Today, rather than using an interlaced approach to scanning, some TV sets, video cameras and computer monitors use a **progressive** or **non-interlaced** scanning approach where the fields (odd and even lines) are combined and reproduced

---

[1] Although 30 frames per second is typically cited as the frame rate in NTSC television, this actually holds only for black and white television. When the NTSC color standard was adopted in the 1950s, the rate was changed to 59.94 frames per second to accommodate the needs of the color signal. This slight frames-per-second difference becomes significant in editing. However, to simplify things, the rate of 30 per second will be used throughout the text unless the difference is critical to the discussion.

at the same time in their proper sequence. Progressive scanning has a number of advantages, including the ability to more easily interface with computer-based video equipment.

The Camera's Imaging Device

The lens of the television camera forms an image on a light-sensitive **target** inside the camera in the same way a motion picture camera forms an image on film. But instead of film, television cameras commonly use solid-state, light-sensitive receptors called **CCDs** (charged-coupled devices), which are able to detect brightness differences at different points in the picture. The surface of the CCD (sometimes referred to as a **chip**) contains from hundreds of thousands to millions of pixel points, each of which can respond to the amount of light focused on its surface. The differences in image brightness detected at each of these points on the surface of the CCD are changed into electric voltages, which are "read out" by the camera's electronics on a line-by-line basis. We'll go into this more thoroughly in Chapter 4.

World Television Standards

There are a number of broadcast television standards (technical approaches to broadcasting the picture and sound) in the world. Unfortunately, they are incompatible with each other. This means that a program produced in one country can't be automatically viewed in another country without converting it to the appropriate technical standard. Since television programming is one of the largest and most lucrative exports for the United States, television producers and syndicators should be familiar with the differences in world television systems. (Many film and TV productions done in the United States do not even start to make money until they go into foreign distribution.)

Although there have been 14 different broadcast standards in use at different times throughout the world, today (excluding HDTV), three basic systems serve the vast majority of countries.[2] The difference between these international standards centers primarily on the number of horizontal lines in the picture, the broad-

---

[2] It should be noted, however, that significant differences exist even within these three basic standards and these differences can make TV signals incompatible with others within the same group or classification.

cast channel width (electronic bandwidth of the signal), and whether an AM- or FM-type signal is used for the audio and video.

Historically, the number of lines used in broadcast television has ranged from the United Kingdom's 405-line monochrome system to the 819-line system used in France. With both of these systems now phased out (and excluding high definition systems to be discussed below), the world has been left with two basic line standards: 525 and 625.

Aspect Ratios

Although the number of scanning lines may have varied, all of the systems of television had the same 4:3 aspect ratio. The **aspect ratio** is the width-height proportion of the picture. The 4:3 ratio was consistent with motion pictures that predated the wide-screen aspect ratios used in Cinemascope, Vista-Vision and Pan-avision films. As we will see, HDTV's 16:9 aspect ratio more closely conforms to these wide-screen processes.

The NTSC Broadcast Standard

The National Television Standards Committee's (NTSC) 525 lines,[3] 30 frames-per-second system is shared primarily by the United States, Canada, Greenland, Mexico, Cuba, Panama, Japan, the Philippines, Puerto Rico, and parts of South America. Because 30 frames consists of 60 fields, the NTSC system of television is referred to as a "525-line, 60-field" system. The NTSC's 60-field system originally based its timing cycle on the 60-hertz (cycles per second) electrical system used in these countries. Since other countries in the world use a 50-hertz electrical system, it was logical for them to develop systems of television based on 50 fields per second.

The PAL and SECAM Television Systems

More than half of the countries in the world use one of two 625-line, 25-frame systems: the **SECAM** (Systèm Électronique pour Couleur avec Mémoire) or the **PAL** (Phase Alternating Line) system. SECAM is used in France and most of the countries in and around the former Soviet Union. PAL is used throughout most of Western Europe, except in France.

The extra 100 lines in the PAL and SECAM systems add significant detail and clarity to the video picture, but 50 fields per second (compared to 60 fields in the NTSC system) means that a slight flicker can sometimes be noticed. Even so, since

---

[3] Although it is, technically, a 525-line system, we only see about 480 active lines on the TV screen. The remaining lines, which are between video frames and not displayed, are used for information such as closed captioning for the hearing impaired.

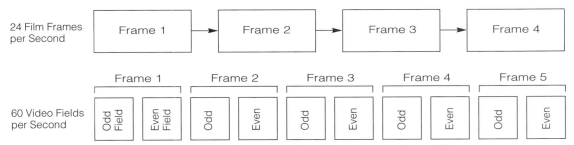

Figure 3.2 Several technical approaches are used to convert the 24-frame-per-second rate of film to the 30-frame-per-second rate of video. Whatever approach is used, a four-to-five conversion ratio must be achieved; that is, to maintain comparable speed between the two media, four frames of film must be translated into five frames of video. Figure 3.2 illustrates what takes place each 1/6th second (or during each four-film-frame interval) of the conversion process.

25 frames per second is very close to the international film standard of 24 frames per second, film is more easily converted to the PAL and SECAM video systems. With NTSC television, things are more difficult: the 24 frame-per-second film rate must be converted to 30 frames per second. Figure 3.2 illustrates one way this is done.

Standards Conversion

The presence of different broadcast television standards means that the exchange of international programming is made more difficult.[4] A videotape made in the United States cannot be played in England, for example, without going through electronic **standards conversion.** Whereas this used to be a major problem, with today's digital technology the process of converting from one international standard to another has been greatly simplified. **Multistandard** TV sets and VCRs now available readily switch from one standard to another.

High-Definition Television

It was hoped that as the world moved to high-definition television (HDTV), nations could agree on a single, worldwide television standard. It appeared that this was going to be possible in the late 1980s when many nations agreed on a proposed 1,125-line, 60-field HDTV standard. However, after technical, political, and economic concerns surfaced, the 200 national leaders attending a world conference on

---

[4] Historically, the problem of incompatibility between international broadcast standards was, in many cases, deliberately created. With some countries well within the television broadcast signal area of a neighboring country, some leaders decided on an incompatible system to make it difficult for their people to be exposed to "undesirable viewpoints."

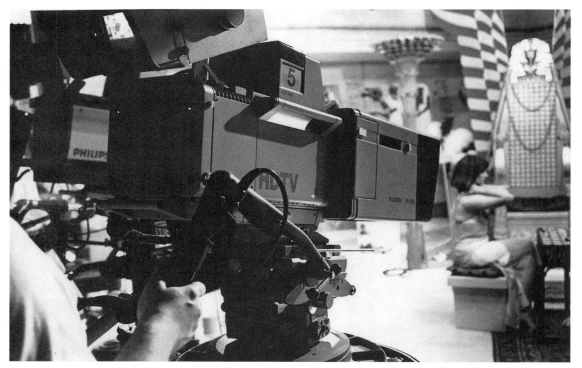

Figure 3.3   Even before HDTV broadcast standards were established for the United States, many producers saw the system's advantages and started recording programming in high definition. Once a production is recorded in this system, it can be either transferred to film, or converted to any one of several broadcast standards for over-the-air transmission.

broadcasting backed away from the initial agreement.[5] Now, the dream of a single, worldwide television standard has all but disappeared.

In the early 1990s, two types of high-definition standards were being debated: a production standard and a broadcast standard. Preferring not to wait until the mid-1990s when this debate was finally resolved in the United States, many producers decided to take advantage of HDTV and started doing productions using a 1,125-line, 60-field standard (Figure 3.3). Once a production is recorded in this system, it can be either transferred to film, or converted to any one of several broadcast standards for over-the-air transmission.

---

[5] Even a name for the new, high-definition process was a subject for debate. In the United States some wanted to call it "advanced television," or ADTV. Others preferred just HD. At the same time, the term, HDVS, for high-definition video system was being used in some applications. To add to the confusion, other countries had their own favorite designations. For the sake of consistency in subsequent discussions, we'll stick to the first widely used term, HDTV.

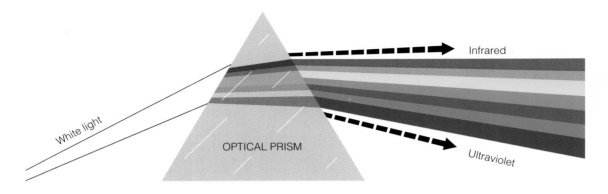

Infrared

White light

OPTICAL PRISM

Ultraviolet

Color Plate 1

White light is actually a mix of all colors from red to violet. As shown here, a prism can separate the various colors from white light. In somewhat the same way, a color TV camera separates component colors out of a color picture.

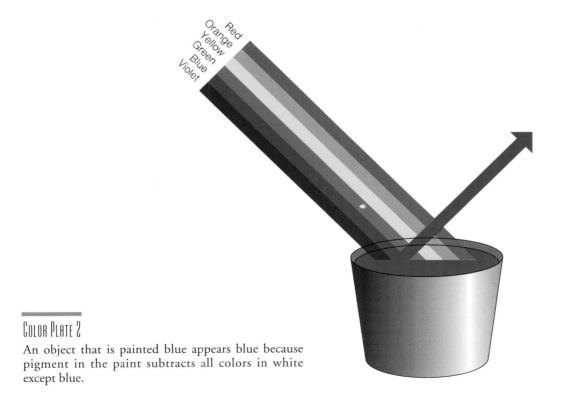

Red
Orange
Yellow
Green
Blue
Violet

Color Plate 2

An object that is painted blue appears blue because pigment in the paint subtracts all colors in white except blue.

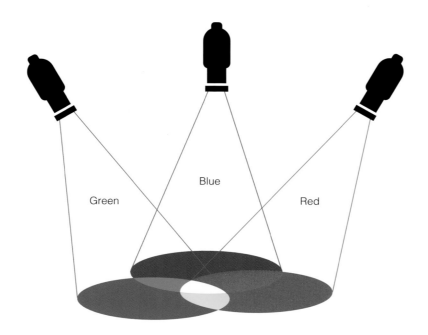

Color Plate 3

If lights with red, blue, and green filters were projected onto a white screen, the principles of additive color would govern the result. Note that when two primary colors overlap, the result is a secondary color (magenta, cyan, or yellow).

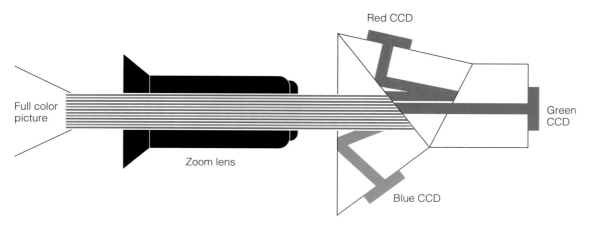

Color Plate 4

Dichroic filters within a video camera's prism block divide the light from the lens into three primary colors. A color picture can thereby be defined in terms of percentages of these three colors.

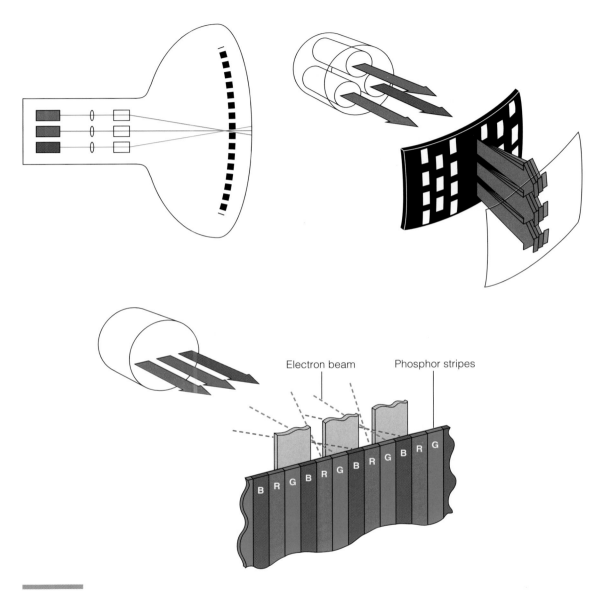

Electron beam   Phosphor stripes

B R G B R G B R G B R G B R G

Color Plate 5

The most common type of TV screen is based on a vacuum tube. Although the workings vary somewhat between manufacturers, all are based on the principle of one or more electron beams (guns) hitting red, blue and green phosphor dots. As the beam scans back and forth across the inside surface of the television tube, it causes the microscopic red, blue and green areas to glow in proportion to respective areas in the original scene. By studying the illustrations, you can see how the angle of the electron beam causes it to hit specific color areas. An aperture grill, commonly called a shadow mask, keeps the electron beam(s) from hitting the wrong phosphor areas.

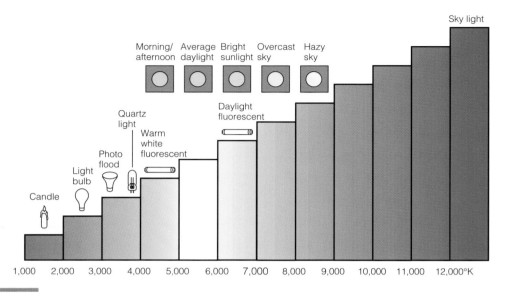

Sky light

Morning/ Average Bright Overcast Hazy
afternoon daylight sunlight sky sky
daylight

Quartz
light
Warm
white
fluorescent

Daylight
fluorescent

Photo
flood

Light
bulb

Candle

1,000 2,000 3,000 4,000 5,000 6,000 7,000 8,000 9,000 10,000 11,000 12,000°K

COLOR PLATE 6

The color temperature of light ranges from a candle flame at about 1,000 degrees Kelvin to more than 10,000 degrees Kelvin for the light of a clear blue sky. Although the human eye will more or less automatically correct for different color temperatures, unless color correction takes place within video cameras, the resulting picture may be either too red or too blue.

COLOR PLATE 7

Indoor and outdoor color temperatures vary by more than 3,000 degrees Kelvin. When these multiple sources are mixed within a single video setup, uniform color balance becomes impossible.

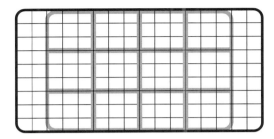

Figure 3.4   Instead of the raster (TV image) being three units high and four wide (4:3) as it is in NTSC, PAL and SECAM television, the aspect ratio of HDTV is 16:9. The difference between the two aspects ratios is illustrated by the white lines.

When the United States adopted a 1,125-line (1,080-active-line[6]) standard for HDTV, based on 60 fields per second,[7] many European countries were moving toward a 1,152-active-line standard, based on 50 hertz. At this point the FCC had set up a time schedule for the eventual phasing-out of NTSC television in the United States in favor of HDTV.[8]

How much better is an HDTV system? Compared to standard NTSC television, HDTV is able to reproduce six times the detail and ten times the color information. When projected on a 16- by 9-foot screen, and observed from a normal viewing distance, the picture detail in HDTV appears to equal what is normally attained by projected 35mm motion picture film.

Even so, since video and film are inherently different media, the question of their relative "quality"—a word that can mean many things to many people—has been a subject of active debate, one that can't be decided by purely technical criteria. Suffice it to say that when the film and video media are compared in a broadcast situation, the difference between video and film is based more on the respective production approaches than on any inherent quality differences between the media.[9]

One other element to consider in television systems is the aspect ratio, the numerical ratio between width and height. Instead of the raster (TV image) being three units high and four wide (4:3), as it is in NTSC, PAL and SECAM television, the aspect ratio of HDTV is 16:9 (Figure 3.4).

---

[6] The number of active (visible) lines on a TV screen is always less than the total number of transmitted lines. Because the number of inactive lines was reduced, the 1,080 active lines are actually more than the number of lines in the M-240, 1,125-line HDTV standard that was originally proposed.

[7] See footnote number 1 in this chapter.

[8] The original FCC schedule for a switchover to HDTV called for the HDTV standard to be set in 1995, and the HDTV-only era to begin in 2010.

[9] One of the original weaknesses of video cameras was their limited brightness range. By 1995, video cameras had been developed that had an 11 f-stop exposure (brightness range) latitude, compared to film's 9-1/2 stop latitude. This meant that video cameras could capture more shadow detail than normal film stocks. When transferred to video for broadcast, the sharpness of film (all other things being equal) is also slightly inferior to that of video. Because so many people prefer the slightly "softer" look of film, there are processes available that give video the "film look," right down to the motion artifacts created in the 24-to-30 frames per second film-video conversion.

Converting Wide-Screen Formats

The conversion of 16:9 HDTV images to the standard 4:3 aspect ratio is done in basically the same way as the conversion of wide-screen films to NTSC television. There are three approaches.

- First, the sides of the picture can be cut off. This is shown in Figure 3.5b. If the original HDTV (or wide-screen film) is shot with the narrower 4:3 cutoff area in mind—a procedure referred to as **shoot-and-protect**—losing the information at the sides of the picture may not be a problem.

- Second, if the production is done without considering the standard broadcast aspect ratio, and important visual information appears at the extreme sides of many scenes, the entire production may have to go through a process called **pan-and-scan.** This involves a technician reviewing every scene and programming a computer-controlled imaging device to electronically pan the 4:3 window back and forth over the larger, wide-screen format. In Figure 3.5 this would be like someone moving the 4:3 frame to the left and right over the larger 16:9 area so the most important information within a 4:3 area would be captured. Information outside this area is simply discarded.

- Finally, if the full HDTV frame contains important visual information, as in the case of written material extending to the edges of the screen, panning-and-scanning will not work. In this case a **letterbox** approach can be used (Figure 3.5c). But there is a problem with this approach: it results in blank areas at the top and bottom of the frame. Often, letterbox is reserved for the opening titles and closing credits of a production with the remainder of the production being panned-and-scanned.

Since many directors feel that pan-and-scan introduces pans that are artificial and not motivated by the action, they insist on the letterbox conversion approach. Originally, producers feared that audiences would object to the black areas at the top and bottom of the letterbox frame. (More than one person who rented a film in the letterbox format brought it back to the video store, complaining that there was something wrong with the tape.) However, today the letterbox format is commonly seen, and fairly well accepted.

For short segments of a production, there is another way of handling the 16:9 to 4:3 aspect ratio difference. You have probably seen the opening or closing of a film on television horizontally "squeezed" to accommodate the titles and credits (Figure 3.5d). The effect is especially noticeable when people are a part of the scene—people who, as a result, suddenly become rather thin. The narrowing effect is caused by an anamorphic lens used on the film camera which routinely compresses a wide-screen format into the standard 4:3 film ratio. Normally, when this film is projected in a theater, the compressed image is stretched back to its original, wide-screen ratio.

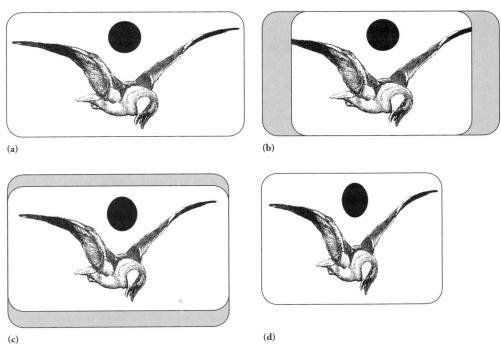

(a)   (b)

(c)   (d)

Figure 3.5   This series of drawings illustrates three approaches to converting a 16 × 9 aspect ratio to 4 × 3. View (a) shows an image in a full 16 × 9 aspect ratio. One way of converting the 16 × 9 image to 4 × 3 (b) results in a loss of the edges of the image. In (c), another approach to conversion is illustrated—shrinking the 16 × 9 image so that it all fits within the 4 × 3 space. However, this results in a dark area at the top and bottom of the frame. This type of conversion, called letterbox, is preferred by some directors because it preserves the full 16 × 9 image. View (d) illustrates the way the conversion process is typically handled in feature films: reproducing the 16 × 9 image with compressed horizontal dimensions. Note that the ball at the top of the frame, which was perfectly round in the original image, is now oval-shaped. This approach, which involves simply projecting the compressed wide-screen film image as it appears on the 35mm film, is often used during the titles and credits when a wide-screen feature film is shown on TV. The final approach to format conversion, pan-and-scan (not illustrated), could be likened to moving the 4 × 3 frame to the left and right within the larger 16 × 9 area as necessary throughout a production. This approach is discussed in more detail in the text.

DIGITAL AND ANALOG TECHNOLOGY

Since the difference between digital and analog electronics is significant in making production decisions, people preparing for the field should be familiar with each.

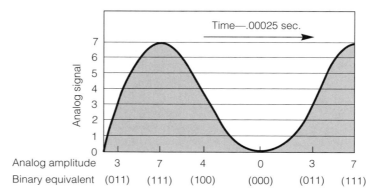

Figure 3.6   In the analog-to-digital (A/D) conversion process binary numbers are assigned to the amplitude of the analog signal. Thousands of times each second an A/D converter translates characteristics of the analog signal into binary numbers. Note in this figure that an amplitude of 3 equals 011, an amplitude of 7 equals 111, etc. Using this process, any analog signal can be converted into a string of computer-type numbers.

Analog Signals

Analog audio and video signals vary smoothly and continuously from one value to another (Figure 3.6). Although this seems as if it would be the most accurate way of representing data—and, in a sense, it is—unfortunately, the analog process has major limitations. Whenever an analog signal is amplified—a process that must be repeated over and over again in audio and video production—some amount of electronic **noise** is inevitably introduced into the signal. With audio, this takes the form of a subtle hiss, or hum; in video, noise typically resembles a subtle snow-pattern in the background of a picture.

Although limited re-amplification with good equipment will normally not produce discernible noise, if the analog signal has to be re-amplified or reproduced many times, the noise problem can quickly compound itself to the point of significantly degrading the audio or video signal. This problem becomes a major issue in copying analog audio- and videotapes. With each subsequent copy or generation, the quality of an analog tape drops appreciably. This situation changed with the introduction of digital technology.

Digital Signals

Digital electronics was introduced to broadcasting during the mid-1980s. By the early 1990s, television equipment manufacturers had moved toward digital electronics in all phases of video production, including audio- and videotape machines, cameras, switchers and editors.

Since most audio and video starts out as an analog signal, the trick is to convert it as soon as possible to digital data. As illustrated in Figure 3.6, digital signals are based on assigning numbers to amplitude and frequency characteristics of an analog signal. The numbers correspond to the original attributes of the signal and their values won't change, no matter how much the signal is amplified.

Digital signals consist of strings of binary numbers, which are simply strings of zeros and ones. For example, a value of 3 may be equal to the binary number 011. Note in Figure 3.6 that binary numbers are assigned to the amplitude of the signal at various points. In this case, an amplitude of 3 equals 011. If a mathematical reading can be obtained from the varying state of the analog signal thousands of times each second, the continuously changing analog signal can be turned into a long sequence of binary numbers. In fact, thousands of times each second an analog-to-digital converter "checks" the status of the analog signal and translates that status into a binary number.

Sampling Signals   The process of regularly "checking" the status of analog signal and converting it into binary numbers is called **sampling.** In professional audio recording, a sampling rate of 48,000 is used, which means that the audio recorder samples the value of analog signal 48,000 times each second.

For example, a 440-hertz tone will go through 440 cycles per second, and during each second the tone is sampled 48,000 times. Each time the tone is sampled its amplitude at that precise moment is assigned a binary number. Therefore, the analog 440 cycles (hertz) in one second can be translated into a string of 48,000 binary (digital) numbers. The device which converts analog signals to digital information is called an **analog-to-digital (A/D) converter.**

Since the zeros and ones in a digital signal are simply equivalent to "on" or "off" electrical states, the binary numbers are virtually immune to signal interference, system noise, and general distortion. However, since the binary numbering system is based on two instead of 10, many more numbers are needed to express values. For this reason, **bit speed,** or the number of bits of information (zeros and ones) that can be transmitted per second, becomes a major concern. In order to handle digitized audio and video signals, digital equipment must be capable of handling massive amounts of data per second, far more information than is required with analog signals.

Quantization   There is one other term that is used in digital electronics: quantization. While sample rate refers to the number of times per second that the analog signal is electronically plotted, **quantization** refers to the manner in which the signal is digitized. Figure 3.7 illustrates 4, 8 and 16 quantization levels. Note that the 4-levels sample shows a crude "stairstep" effect. We could say that the resolution of this sampling rate is quite low. In the A/D converter, sound values must be moved up or down to the nearest "step," since there can be no in-between state in digital electronics. As we move up to 16-level quantization the accuracy or resolution of the sound increases, but so do the demands on our numbering system. At

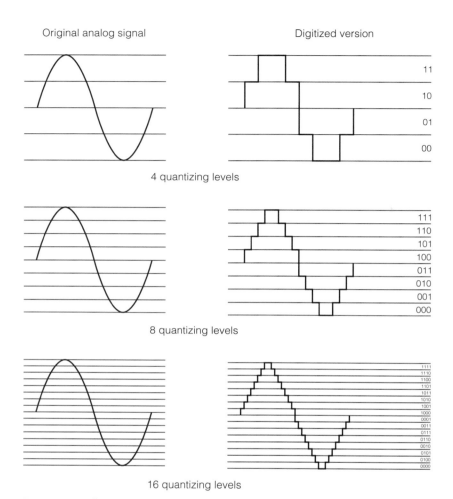

Figure 3.7   The more quantization levels in the analog-to-digital conversion process, the smoother transitions in loudness will be. At 16 quantizing levels, loudness transitions become imperceptible.

this level, binary numbers have 65,536 possible combinations of ones and zeros. Once we arrive at 16-levels quantization, we have arrived at the resolution of today's compact disc and digital audiotape systems. At this level we can no longer hear the stairstep digital values; our ears perceive a seamless web of smoothly varying sounds.

Manipulating Digital Signals   We now come to one of the most significant advantages of digital signals. Once in the form of numbers, digital information can be mathematically manipulated in many ways. For example, the signals can be expanded or compressed by simply multiplying or dividing the binary numbers that form their base. In audio this opens the door to manipulating time: segments can be shortened or lengthened. In the process the frequency or pitch of the audio signal can be corrected. In fact, it is possible to speed up an audiotape of a voice to almost twice the normal speed and not encounter a high-pitched "chipmunk" effect. If the original speech was clear and distinct, the speech will remain intelligible. Digital manipulation of audio is often used to disguise a person's voice in order to hide his or her identity.

In video, the digital numbers can be mathematically manipulated to expand, shrink, and reverse a picture. By linking the mathematical possibilities, a video picture can be made to rotate and spin, or can take the form of objects of various sizes and shapes.

Maintaining Video Quality

Video pictures that suffer from significant video-level or color-balance problems will be rejected by stations and distribution services. Therefore, it becomes the duty of production personnel to work together throughout the production process to maintain video and audio quality.

Although today's cameras and videotape equipment include much automatic circuitry, these automatic controls cannot recognize good video, only video that meets rudimentary technical specifications. Two pieces of equipment are critical to monitoring and controlling the basic video signal: the waveform monitor and the vectorscope. The **waveform monitor** graphically displays and measures the brightness or luminance level of the video; the **vectorscope** measures the color (chroma) information. Although these are generally separate instruments, in some cases both can be displayed on a single TV monitor or computer screen. Many desktop editing systems feature both displays as part of the editing program.

The Waveform Monitor

In critical professional video work, waveform monitors are used as scenes are being taped. During postproduction they are also used to monitor and maintain video quality and scene-to-scene consistency. Although some people think waveform monitors are reserved for engineers, they actually aren't any more mysterious than the gauges in an automobile.

By looping the video signal from a camera through a waveform monitor, the output of the camera can be electronically graphed on the face on the waveform monitor screen. The dark areas of the video picture are represented near the zero

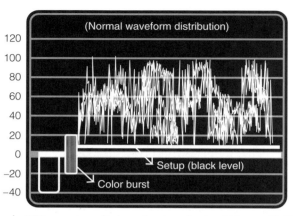

Figure 3.8   Just as the VU meter in audio is used to keep levels within specified limits, video limits must be kept within a limited range to ensure video quality. The blackest areas of a video picture should drop down to the 7.5 (setup) point on the waveform monitor, and the white areas should (for normal video) reach 100. The color burst signal indicates only the presence of a color signal; it reveals nothing about the accuracy of colors.

point of the waveform scale and white areas appear near the top. The scale along the side of the waveform monitor is calibrated in units of amplitude called IRE (Institute of Radio Engineers) units (Figure 3.8).

Dull, black objects, such as black velvet, reflect about 3 percent of the light falling on them. This minimal level of reflectance is considered **TV black** or **reference black.** On most camera control units (**CCUs**) where the basic camera adjustments are made, there is a black level or setup adjustment for establishing the black level of the picture.[10] On a waveform monitor the reference black level should appear at the 7.5 IRE point (Figure 3.8). Most professional video cameras have a black level control which automatically sets this level when the lens is capped (covered) and a button is pushed on the CCU.

Reference white is created by subject matter that reflects about 70 percent of the light falling on its surface. Reference white should register at the 100 mark on the waveform monitor.

White Level Considerations   Camera underexposure (insufficient light on the target) results in low video levels. On a waveform monitor this is immediately obvious since the peak video level may come up only to 50 or so IREs. (In the next chapter we'll see examples of video level problems.) If analog video is initially left at a low level and then raised or boosted later in the video recording or transmission process, the resulting picture may look grainy because of **video noise.** If the target of the camera is significantly overexposed (too much light), the waveform monitor will

---

[10]Although CCUs are built into field cameras, most professional cameras allow for an external CCU that offers a greater array of camera setup controls.

show a video signal significantly above 100. Left uncorrected, this will cause significant distortion in the video picture.

Healthy Sync   Before we leave the discussion of the waveform monitor, we should briefly mention the information displayed below the 7.5 black level point. In this "blacker-than-black" area there are some important timing signals referred to as **sync,** which is short for synchronizing pulses. These are the high-speed timing pulses which keep all video equipment "in lock step" during the process of scanning lines, fields and frames. The pulses dictate the precise point that the electronic beam starts and stops while scanning each line, field and frame. Without these pulses, electronic chaos would instantly break out with each piece of video equipment. A single source of sync from a master **sync generator** is used to supply a common timing pulse for all equipment that must work in unity within a production system or facility. On a waveform monitor the bottom line in the sync should be at −40 (the very bottom of the waveform scale) and the top should extend to the baseline, or the zero point on the scale. Too much sync will push the black level of the video too high, thus graying out the picture; too little and the black level will cut into the sync and the picture will roll and break up.

Although a waveform monitor cannot be used to evaluate the color quality of a picture, it does indicate whether a color signal is present. A **color burst** signal (refer to Figure 3.8) indicates whether video equipment is generating a basic color timing signal.

PRINCIPLES OF TELEVISION COLOR

Although a thorough understanding of the electronics of television is not necessary to produce effective television segments, a knowledge of the physics of color can frequently add to the effectiveness of a production and help eliminate production problems. Color television is primarily based on the physics of additive color. Problems in understanding additive color often center on confusion with the better-known subtractive color process, which governs the mixing of paints and pigments. The two are, in a sense, exactly opposite.

First of all, recall that white light is composed of all colors of light (Color Plate 1). These colors can be separated and manipulated by the subtractive and additive color processes.

Subtractive Color

The color of an object is determined by the colors of light it absorbs and the colors of light it reflects. When white light falls on a piece of red paper, the paper appears red because it subtracts (absorbs) all colors of light except red. The same process governs the color reflectance of an object of any other color. If you paint an object blue, you simply add a kind of filter to the surface of that object which absorbs all

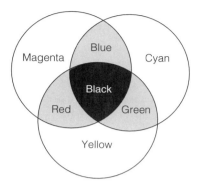

Figure 3.9 The principle of subtractive color governs the interaction of paints and pigments. Note that when the three primary colors are mixed, the result is black. The mixing of the same colors in the additive color process produces white (Figure 3.15).

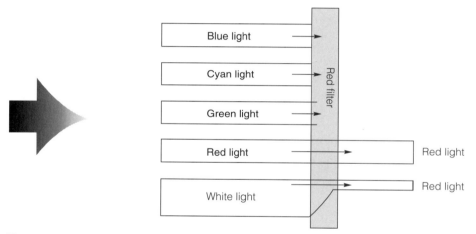

Figure 3.10 Contrary to what is widely believed, a color filter does not change the color of light, but subtracts dissimilar (complementary) colors. A cyan filter placed to the right of the red filter in the illustration would absorb the remaining red light.

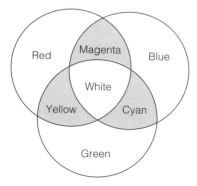

3.11 If slide projectors were equipped with red, blue and green filters and the light from these primary colors were projected onto a white screen, the color interactions would result. Note that when two primary colors overlap the result is a secondary color (magenta, cyan or yellow). When either three primaries or a primary and secondary color overlap, the result is white.

colors except blue (Color Plate 2). The light that is absorbed (subtracted) is transformed into heat. This explains why a black object, which absorbs all of the colors of light hitting it, gets much hotter in sunlight than a white object, which reflects all colors.

When the primary subtractive colors of magenta, cyan and yellow pigments are mixed together, the result is black—or, because of impurities in the pigments, a dark shade of something resembling mud. All color is essentially absorbed (Figure 3.9). When a colored filter or gel is placed over a camera lens or light, the same type of color subtraction takes place. For example, a pure red filter placed over a camera lens will absorb all colors of light except red (Figure 3.10).

Additive Color

Thus far we have been talking about the effect of mixing paints or pigments that absorb (subtract) light. When colored lights are mixed together, the result is additive rather than subtractive. Thus, when the additive primaries (red, blue and green light) are mixed together the result is white (Figure 3.11). This can easily be demonstrated with three slide projectors if a pure color filter is placed over each of the three projector lenses—one red, one green, and one blue (Color Plate 3). When all three primary colors overlap (that is, are added together) the result is white light. Note in Color Plate 3 that the overlap of two primary colors—for example, red and green—creates a secondary color, in this case, yellow.

The standard color wheel (Figure 3.12) is the key to understanding many issues in color television. If any two colors exactly opposite each other on the color wheel are mixed, the result is white. Again, note that instead of canceling each other as they did with subtractive colors, these complementary colors combine for an additive effect. (One definition of "complementary" is "to make whole.")

By extending this additive concept slightly it should be obvious that, by combining the proper mixture of red, blue and green light, any color can be produced. Therefore, in color television, only three colors (red, blue and green) are needed to produce the full range of colors in a color TV picture.

The full-color image "seen" by the color TV camera lens goes through a **beam splitter** (which can be either a **prism block** or **dichroic mirrors,** depending upon the camera design) which separates the full-color picture into its red, blue and green components (Color Plate 4). Note that all red light within a color scene is split off and directed to one of the three light-sensitive camera CCDs.[11] Likewise, all of the green light in the picture is directed to the green receptor, and the blue light is transmitted to the blue CCD. Since each color can be broken down into some percentage of red, blue or green, every color can be expressed in terms of some relative proportion of each of these primary colors.[12]

---

[11] Although a few HDTV and special purpose cameras use camera tubes instead of CCDs, to simplify the discussion we'll use the term CCD throughout the text.

[12] There are few highly saturated (deep or pure) colors that cannot be accurately reproduced by the TV system.

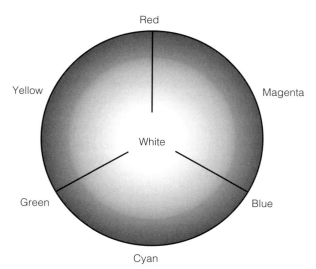

Figure 3.12 This additive color wheel is the key to understanding and predicting a wide variety of color issues in television. The primary colors are at the end of the three lines; the secondary colors fall in between. Colors directly opposite each other (such as green and magenta) are referred to as complementary colors.

This takes care of color; but how does a color camera detect pure black or white? Since white is the presence of all colors, the camera's CCDs respond to pure white as the simultaneous presence of all three colors. Black is simply the absence of all three colors.

How the Eye Sees Color

You might assume from the above that in color television "white" would result from an equal mix of the three primary colors. Unfortunately, it's not that simple. For one thing, the human eye does not see all colors with equal brightness. The eye is much more sensitive to yellowish-green light than to either blue or red light. Due to the greater sensitivity of the eye to the green-to-orange portion of the color spectrum, an equal, percentage of red, green and blue mix of colored light will not appear white. Because of this, and because of the nature (and limitations) of the color phosphors used in TV sets, the actual color mix used in color television ends up being about 30 percent red, 11 percent blue and 59 percent green.

A Little Simple Algebra

In the equation A + B + C = 100, if the values of A and B are known, it is easy to figure out "C." In the same way in the television process it is not necessary to know the values of all three primary colors, only two. If a TV camera were focused on a white card and the red channel registered 30 and the green channel registered 59, you would know that the missing factor (blue) would have to be 11, since 30 + 59 + 11 = 100.

TV transmission process can, therefore, work with only two color signals, and color cameras can be made that have only two pickup devices. And, there are many color TV cameras that have only one CCD. In a sense, one CCD can be made to do double or even triple duty. To do this, CCDs are made with **stripe filters,** on the surface of the target, which contain microscopic stripes that can detect the presence of specific colors. Thus, two more colors can be derived from a single CCD "chip."

Most consumer cameras have only one CCD; most professional cameras have three. In between, there are industrial grade cameras that rely on two CCDs. (The latter type of equipment is also referred to as **prosumer** equipment, a term that combines the words professional and consumer.)

All things being equal, three-CCD cameras will perform better than two-CCD cameras, and two-CCD cameras will perform better than one-CCD camera. Reducing the number of CCDs below three is simply a cost and space saving measure.

THE COLOR TV RECEIVER

As we've noted, the process of re-creating a color picture from a camera's signal is a matter of illuminating microscopic dots inside a color picture tube or on the surface of a color LCD. The three colors generated by the TV camera can be combined to generate the black and white or **luminance** component of a TV signal. It should be noted that the eye sees picture detail much more in terms of differences in luminance (brightness) than in differences in color. It is for this reason that the detail carrying capacity, or **resolution** of the luminance signal, is much more important than the resolution or sharpness of any of the three primary colors. We'll discuss resolution in more detail later.

The inside of the picture tube or color LCD display has small dots or stripes that will either glow *red, blue,* or *green* when electronically activated. The intensity or brightness of each of the primary colors varies with the voltage applied; this voltage, of course, reflects the characteristics of the original camera image. Therefore, by simultaneously controlling the intensity and percentages of each of the three primary colors, virtually any color can be created on a TV screen (Color Plate 5).

With this basic information covered, we can better understand the principles that govern the setup and use of key elements in the production chain. In the next chapter we will examine one of the most important components of a TV camera: the lens.

4 CAMERA LENSES AND THEIR EFFECTS

THE CAMERA LENS is the first and most essential element in creating a video image. Camera lenses can also provide a savvy video producer-director with a wide range of creative controls. Before we can understand how some of these creative controls work, we must cover some basic information about lenses starting with the most basic of lens attributes: focal length. As you will see, the focal length of a lens affects the appearance of subject matter in several ways.

LENS FOCAL LENGTH

Focal length is commonly defined as the distance from the optical center[1] of the lens to the **focal plane** (CCD or target) of the camera, when the lens is focused at infinity. This distance is generally measured in millimeters (mm). In the case of lenses with fixed focal lengths, we can talk about a 12mm lens, a 25mm lens, a 100mm lens, and so forth. Taking a 25mm lens as an example, the distance between the optical center of the lens and the image it creates on the camera target will be exactly 25mm when the lens is focused at infinity (Figure 4.1). Any object in the far distance is considered to be at infinity (∞).

---

[1] Although the optical center of the lens is commonly given as a point of reference, strictly speaking, this applies only to relatively simple lens designs. Depending on the complexity of the lens, this (nodal) point may be within the lens, at the back of the lens, or with some special purpose lenses, even outside the lens.

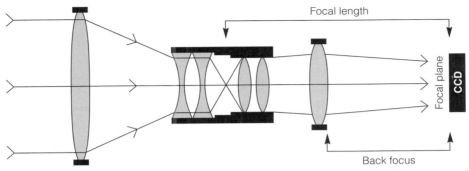

Figure 4.1 The most basic lens attribute, focal length, is defined as the distance from the optical center of the lens to the camera target. Although the effective focal length will change as the lens is zoomed, the critical back focus (the distance from the back of the lens to the target or CCD, or charge-coupled device, of the camera) will not.

When a lens is focused on objects closer than infinity, this lens-to-camera target distance must be increased to keep the image in focus. With many lenses, focusing is done by rotating the front part of the lens. In so doing, optical elements of the lens slowly move away from the camera's light-sensitive target. The closer the subject matter is to the lens, the greater this distance must be to keep it in sharp focus. Because the lens-to-target distance varies with many lenses as they are focused,[2] a single reference point for defining "lens focal length" is needed; that standard reference point is infinity.

Fixed Focal Length and Zoom Lenses

Cameras use both fixed focal length lenses and zoom lenses. A fixed focal length lens is referred to as a **prime lens** and is manufactured to operate at a particular, set focal length, such as 12mm, 25mm, or 100mm. With prime lenses, the focal length cannot be varied. These lenses are sometimes preferred by camera operators in film and HDTV because of their exceptional optics and predictable results. Several high-end consumer-type cameras use a VL lens mount which accepts hundreds of high-quality lenses designed for 35mm cameras. In general, prime lenses are available in a far greater range of specifications than the standard zoom lenses found on typical video cameras. Not all video cameras can accept prime lenses, however.

Unlike a prime lens, which is designed to operate at only one focal length, the focal length of a **zoom lens** can be continuously varied from a wide-angle to a telephoto perspective (Figures 4.2 and 4.3). The primary characteristic of visual perspective is angle of view.

---

[2] Many of the newer zoom lenses use *internal focus*. With this type of lens focus is handled by optics inside the lens, rather than by rotating the lens to change the distance between lens elements and the camera target. Since the front of the lens is not rotated, attachments to the lens (such as rectangular lens hoods) do not annoyingly shift position during focusing. Other advantages include faster focus, closer focusing distances and fewer image aberrations.

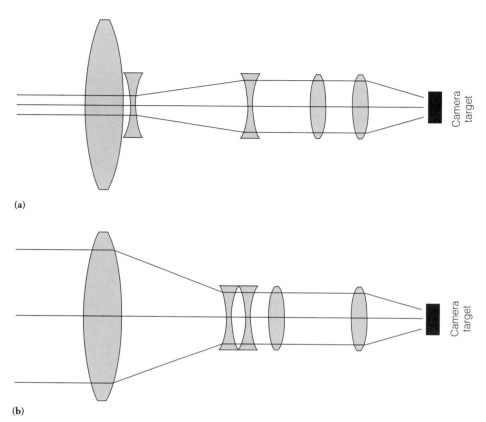

(a)

(b)

Figure 4.2   As you change the focal length of a zoom lens, the spacing between groups of internal glass elements is altered. In the top drawing (a) the lens is zoomed in full (to its maximum focal length); in the bottom drawing (b) the lens is in a wide-angle (minimum focal length) position. Note how the angle of view of the lens changes in each case. These drawings have been greatly simplified. Figure 4.3 shows the true complexity of a typical zoom lens.

Angle of View

Angle of view is generally associated with lens focal length.[3] A zoom lens used at a long focal length (roughly 50mm or greater, depending on the target size) will have a narrow angle of view (Figure 4.4). This means that from a particular vantage point the lens will see an angle of only a few degrees. Since this limited angle of view must still fill the full camera target area, this type of lens seems to magnify objects and bring them closer, in the same way a telescope seems to bring distant objects closer to an observer.

---

[3] In the interest of accuracy, we must explode a commonly held myth at this point. Strictly speaking, it is the optical design of the lens that determines the angle of view and not focal length. With a specific zoom lens, however, there will be a direct relationship between the effective focal length of the lens and angle of view. Since most video cameras use a single zoom lens, the apparent relationship between focal length and angle of view is valid. This direct relationship will not hold for prime lenses of different optical designs.

Figure 4.3   The true complexity of a professional zoom lens is illustrated in this cutaway photo. As the lens is zoomed, groups of glass elements move forward and backward at different speeds in relation to each other. Because of their complexity, sophisticated zoom lenses had to await the development of high-powered computers.

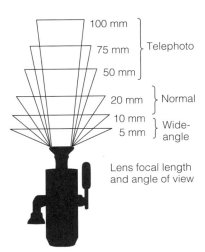

Figure 4.4   The focal length directly affects the angle of view of a lens. Note that as the focal length increases, the angle of view decreases. For cameras with 1/3-inch CCDs, the same effect would be achieved in each case with focal lengths slightly less than those shown. For cameras with 2/3-inch CCDs, lens focal lengths would be slightly greater for each angle represented.

When the same zoom lens is used at a short focal length (roughly 10mm or less, depending on the target size) the angle of view will be much wider. Note in Figure 4.4 that for a particular zoom lens there is a direct relationship between focal length and angle of view. When you double the focal length, you double the size of an image created on the target by the lens.

Figure 4.5   Although some zoom lenses have zoom ratios of 65:1 and beyond, a more typical range for portable electronic field production cameras is 15:1. These photos illustrate the effect of a 15:1 zoom lens used at its wide-angle and telephoto settings.

Zoom Ratio

The term **zoom ratio** is used to define this focal-length range. For example, if the maximum range through which a particular lens can be zoomed is between 10mm and 100mm, it is said to have a 10:1 (ten-to-one) zoom ratio (10 times the minimum focal length of 10mm equals 100mm). In practice, zoom lenses are typically defined by two numbers. The first is the zoom ratio, the second the minimum focal length. So a 10 × 12 (ten-by-twelve) zoom lens would have a minimum focal length of 12mm and a maximum focal length of 120mm (10 × 12 = 120).

Although the zoom lenses on most hand-held field cameras have ratios in the range of 10:1 and 18:1, some lenses used with large, tripod-mounted field cameras can have zoom ratios that exceed 60:1. In the latter case a camera covering a football game could zoom out and get a wide shot of the field, and then by zooming in, fill the screen with a football sitting in the middle of the field. A range that is more typical of EFP cameras is shown in Figure 4.5.

Figure 4.6 Although electric, servo-controlled zoom lenses can provide a smooth zoom at varying speeds, manually controlled zoom lenses are often preferred for sports coverage. For one thing, they can be adjusted much faster between shots, enabling the camera operator to quickly move from one shot to another. Here, a zoom lens with a hand crank is being used to cover a baseball game.

The Zoom vs. the Dolly

Unless you are zooming in on a flat object like a map or a wall, you will find that a zoom gives a much different effect than the one created by the camera actually moving (dollying) toward or away from a subject. A zoom is a slightly artificial move, similar to optically enlarging a portion out of the middle of a still photo. When a camera is dollied, it moves past objects, and the effect is the same as if you walked toward or away from a subject. Many videographers[4] prefer the more natural effect of a dolly, even though it is more difficult to achieve.

Motorized Zoom Lenses

Zoom lenses were originally operated by push rods and hand cranks, and it took skill to smoothly zoom in or out on a subject. Today, zoom lenses are typically controlled by built-in, variable-speed electric motors. These electric zooms are often referred to as **servo-controlled.** Although servo-controlled zoom lenses can provide a smooth zoom at varying speeds, manually controlled zoom lenses are often preferred for sports coverage (Figure 4.6). A manually controlled zoom can be adjusted much faster between shots, enabling the camera operator to quickly move from one shot to another.

---

[4] The term *videographer,* as used in this book, refers to a professional video cameraperson—normally, a person who shoots video to meet vocational or avocational needs.

Supplementary Lenses

Although most videographers end up working within the limits of the zoom lens supplied with their cameras, it is possible to modify the focal length of most lenses, including the zoom ratio of a zoom lens, by using a positive or negative **supplementary lens.** A positive supplementary lens—commonly referred to as a **wide-angle converter**—will increase the angle of view of a zoom lens. For example, when added to a 14 × 8.5 zoom lens a 0.8× wide-angle converter will change the normal 8.5 to 199mm range of the lens to a 7 to 98mm range.[5]

Conversely, a negative supplementary lens—also called a **range extender** or a **lens extender**—will increase focal length and narrow the angle of acceptance. A 2× negative supplementary lens can change a 100mm fixed focal length lens into a 200mm lens, or it can change a 12–120mm zoom lens into a 24–240mm zoom lens. (With some zoom lenses, 2× range extenders are not "supplementary"; they are built in.) Wide-angle or positive supplementary lenses are attached to the front of a lens; negative supplementary lenses can go either in front of, or behind the lens.

DISTANCE, SPEED AND PERSPECTIVE CHANGES

Varying the focal length of a zoom lens alters more than just the size of the image on the camera target (CCD). Three other things are also affected: the apparent distance between objects in the scene, the relative size of objects at different distances, and the apparent speed of objects moving toward or away from the camera.

Compressing Distance

A long focal length lens, coupled with a great camera-to-subject distance, appears to compress or reduce the apparent distance between objects in front of the lens (Figure 4.7). To cite a common example, sports fans become used to the fact that a shot of a pitcher and batter taken with a very long lens from the stands behind center field makes the pitcher look only a few feet away from the batter. In contrast, if the same shot were made from just a few feet behind the pitcher with an extreme wide-angle lens, the spatial relationship (distance) between the pitcher and the batter would be greatly exaggerated.

---

[5] In addition to wide-angle converters, there are also wide-angle adapters. The latter, however, do not allow you to use the full capabilities of a zoom lens. To compensate for the actual reduced focal length, wide-angle adapters must be used either with zoom lenses that have a macro mode, or with lenses that have readily accessible back focus adjustments.

Figure 4.7 The distance of the women from the fountain is exactly the same in each of these photos; only the camera distance changes. When the camera backs up and a telephoto lens is used, the distance between the woman and the fountain seems to dramatically diminish.

In actual fact, the spatial alteration that accompanies wide-angle and telephoto lenses (or zoom lenses used in the wide-angle or telephoto position) is not a function of focal length, but camera-to-subject distance.[6] When using a wide-angle setting you must get much closer to the subject matter to fill the screen. Conversely, to maintain the same size image on the screen with a telephoto lens you must back up a great distance.

The Case of the Wandering Billboards

A number of years ago a court case was reportedly launched by a group opposed to the construction of more billboards along an interstate highway. Advertisers defended the new billboards, saying that existing billboards had been placed far enough from each other that new ones would not create a cluttered appearance. Since the highway in question was in a remote area, the judge asked that photos be introduced as evidence. Both sides employed photographers who understood the apparent effect of subject-to-camera distance on spatial relationships.

As luck would have it, both photographers selected approximately the same group of billboards for their example. The photographer who was hired to show how close together the existing billboards were backed up a great distance and used a very long lens; consequently, the distance between billboards was greatly compressed making them appear as if they were already crowded together. The photog-

---

[6] Be aware that many books erroneously state that focal length directly affects perspective, the apparent speed of objects moving toward and away from the camera, and depth of field. Actually, focal length is not directly related to any of these.

rapher representing the advertisers moved in close to the first billboard and used a wide-angle lens, which made the billboards appear to be almost miles apart.

Seeing the dramatic difference between the photographs and possibly believing "the camera never lies," the judge reportedly assumed that some sort of fraud had taken place and disallowed all photo evidence.

Changes in the Apparent Speed of Objects

In addition to affecting the apparent distance between objects, changes in camera-to-subject distance, coupled with changes in lens focal length, also influence the apparent speed of objects moving toward or away from the camera. By moving away from the subject matter and using a long focal length lens (or a zoom lens used at its maximum focal length) the apparent speed of objects moving toward or away from the camera will be reduced. One of the closing scenes in the famous film *The Graduate* demonstrated how this technique can be effectively used. As Dustin Hoffman was running desperately down the street toward the church to try to stop a wedding, a lens with a very long focal length was used to convey what the character was feeling: that even though he was running as fast as he could, it seemed as if he were hardly moving and that he would never make it to the church in time.

Conversely, moving in close to subject matter with a wide-angle lens increases the apparent speed of objects moving toward or away from the camera.

Perspective Changes

The use of a wide-angle lens combined with a limited camera-to-subject distance also creates another type of perspective distortion. If a videographer uses a short focal length lens in shooting a tall building from the street level, the parallel lines along the sides of the building will appear to converge toward the top of the frame, making the building appear to be much narrower at the top. The building will also appear to be leaning backwards. (Compare Figure 4.8 with Figure 4.5.) The same wide-angle lens (or zoom lens used in an extreme wide-angle position) will also result in apparent distortion when photographing a face at close range. Unless this type of distortion is desired, the solution is to move back and use the lens at a normal to telephoto setting.

What's "Normal"?

Although, when it comes to human behavior, psychologists have been debating this question for decades, with lenses, what's *normal* is comparatively easy to determine. A good rule of thumb has been supplied by photographers who use 35mm still cameras. With a 35mm camera, a 45 to 50mm lens is considered normal because this is approximately the diagonal distance from one corner of the film to the other.

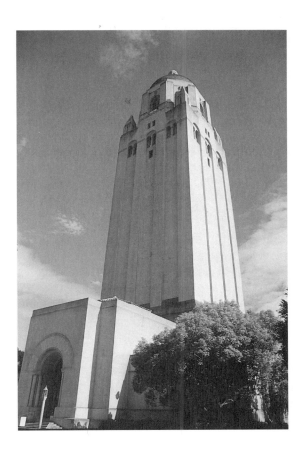

Figure 4.8   If a videographer uses a short focal length lens in shooting a tall building from the street level, the parallel lines along the sides of the building will appear to converge toward the top.

Using the same rule, a normal focal length for a video camera can be defined as the distance from one corner of the target area to the opposite corner. If the diagonal distance on the target of a video camera is 20mm, then a lens used at 20mm on that camera will provide a normal angle of view under normal viewing conditions.

Fish-Eye Lenses

Extreme wide-angle prime lenses, called **fish-eye lenses,** can cover an angle of acceptance of 180 degrees or more. These extreme wide-angle lenses can greatly distort images, especially when shooting up or down on an object. This distortion can represent an interesting, creative effect or a gross distortion of truth. If a relatively straight-on camera-to-subject angle is selected in using this type lens, distortion will be minimized. Super wide-angle lenses can be quite useful, especially when shooting in small, cramped areas.

Figure 4.9   Telephoto lenses, which allow the videographer to remain at a distance, are useful in photographing wildlife. Because of the image magnification involved, telephoto lenses (or zoom lenses used in the telephoto position) require a steady tripod.

Super Telephoto Lenses

Super-long lenses, such as those used for getting spectacular close-ups of wild animals, are generally of a fixed focal length—sometimes 2,000mm or more (Figure 4.9). The angle of view of a 2,000mm lens, for example, would be a mere 0.3 of a degree on most video cameras.[7] Telephoto lenses are available that fill the TV screen with objects miles away. But, since these lenses are relatively "slow" (they don't transmit much light) it is difficult to use them under low light conditions. Also, shooting over such distances means that things such as atmospheric haze, heat rising from the ground, and so forth, will distort the image.

Super telephoto lenses are normally from 3 to 4 feet long and, therefore, hard to work with. To solve this problem, compact **catadioptric lenses** were designed. The catadioptric lens works on the same principle as a reflecting telescope. An internal reflector "folds" the light path, thereby greatly reducing the overall length and weight of the lens. Catadioptric lenses are exclusively fixed focal length lenses.

Focal Length and Image Stability

Because of the great image enlargement that results from using a long telephoto lens, the slightest movement of the camera is greatly magnified or exaggerated. When using a long lens—either zoom, catadioptric, or fixed focal length—the camera must be mounted on a very steady tripod and shielded from wind and vibration. As we will see, focus is also critical with these lenses.

---

[7] For those of you who are familiar with 35mm camera lenses, a 250mm focal length on a standard video camera would be equal to using a 1,350mm lens on a 35mm camera.

Except for special effects, fast-breaking news stories and possibly home videos, it is never a good idea to shoot without a tripod. Although image shake and bobbing may not be apparent in the small camera viewfinder, when the footage is shown on a full-sized TV screen, the result can look quite amateurish. The regular use of a tripod is one of the major distinguishing characteristics that separates professional video work from that of amateurs.

IMAGE STABILIZERS

In 1962, a type of lens housing was introduced that can compensate, within limits, for camera vibration and unintentional camera movement. The original device, called an **image stabilizer,** was based on a gyroscopically controlled mechanism that resists short, fast movements by shifting lens elements in the opposite direction.

Today, there are two variations on the original image stabilizer design. The simplest, **digital stabilization,** electronically "floats" an active picture frame within a slightly larger target area. As the camera moves, the smaller frame shifts within the larger target area in an attempt to compensate for the movement. If, for example, the camera moves slightly (and, we'll assume, unintentionally) to the right, the digital frame will move in the opposite direction, in effect, canceling the movement on the camera's target. Although the technique is effective in canceling limited camera movement, the usable target image area is reduced, and image resolution and clarity are sacrificed.

Optical image stabilization, the approach preferred by many videographers, typically incorporates two parallel, floating optical surfaces within the lens, which act as a kind of flexible prism. When the camera moves, the movement is electronically detected and a voltage is generated which shifts the prisms (glass lenses) in relation to each other. This alters the angle of light passing through the prism and shifts the image on the target in the opposite direction of the camera movement. Since the full target image is used with optical image stabilization, no loss in image quality results.

With all types of stabilizers the camera operator must learn to "compensate for the compensation." When the camera is intentionally panned from left to right, there is typically a short delay as the camera initially tries to compensate for the move. Once beyond a certain point, the stabilizer can't compensate for the movement and the image starts to move as intended. However, at the end of the pan, the image may continue to move for a moment until the system comes back into balance. This means that the camera operator may have to end the pan a moment early and allow the camera to complete the move.

Once such things are taken into consideration, stabilization devices can be relied on to reduce or eliminate undesirable camera movement—the type of movement associated with such things as vibration from a helicopter, or the motion associated with a moving vehicle. These devices are also useful in reducing the shakiness of hand-held cameras in news and documentary work.

LENS MOUNTS

Many of the special purpose lenses we've discussed require that the existing camera lens be replaced with another type. With many types of video cameras—especially the consumer-type cameras—the zoom lens is permanently mounted to the camera body and can't be removed. However, as we've noted, some video cameras allow you to change lenses to meet specific needs. These lenses can be removed either by unscrewing them (in the case of *C-mount* lenses) or by turning a locking ring (in the case of the *bayonet* mounts).

With cameras using C-mounts the lenses are screwed into a finely threaded cylinder about 25mm in diameter. The C-mount was the first type of lens mount used with small video cameras because it can take advantage of a wide array of 16mm motion picture camera lenses. Although at least one prosumer video camera uses C-mount lenses, this type of mount is primarily used by industrial-type video cameras, including closed circuit surveillance cameras.

Many professional video cameras use some type of bayonet mount. This mount is faster to use than the C-mount, since the lens can be removed from the camera without going through many rotations. Earlier we mentioned the VL bayonet mount, which makes it possible to use Canon-type lenses from 35mm cameras. Nikon has a similar video camera mount for its extensive line of 35mm lenses.

Whenever a lens is removed from a camera there is a risk that specks of dust will find their way inside the camera to the prism block or target. Dirt settling at either of these points is often clearly visible in the camera's video. Lens changes should be done as quickly as possible and in relatively dust-free environments. Specks of dust can be removed from the lens or inside of the camera with the help of a clean camel's hair brush and light puffs of air from an ear syringe.

LENS SPEED

Cats and owls can see in dim light better than we can in part because the lenses of their eyes allow more light to enter. We could say that the speed of the lenses in their eyes was "faster" than ours. **Lens speed** is defined as the maximum amount of light that the lens can transmit.

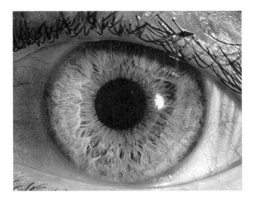

Figure 4.10 Like the pupil of an eye, which automatically adjusts to varying light levels, camera lenses have an iris that controls the amount of light going through the lens. Under low light conditions the iris (pupil) of our eyes opens up almost completely to allow in the maximum amount of light. In the bright sunlight the pupil contracts to avoid overloading the light-sensitive rods and cones in the back of our eyes. In the same way, the amount of light falling on the light-sensitive target of a TV camera must be carefully controlled with the aid of an iris in the middle of the lens (Figure 4.11).

Figure 4.11 Like the iris in the eye (Figure 4.10) the iris in a camera lens is designed to control the amount of light going through the lens. As we will see in Chapter 5, the iris setting is critical in maintaining video quality.

Like the pupil of an eye, which automatically adjusts to varying light levels (Figure 4.10), camera lenses have an **iris,** which controls the amount of light that can go through the lens. Under very low light conditions the iris (pupil) of our eyes opens up almost completely to allow in the maximum amount of light. In the bright sunlight the pupil contracts in an effort to avoid overloading the light-sensitive rods and cones in the back of our eyes. In the same way, the amount of light falling on the light-sensitive target of a TV camera must be carefully controlled with the aid of an iris in the middle of the lens (Figure 4.11). Too much light and the picture will become overexposed and washed out; too little, and detail in the darker areas of the picture will be lost.

Although an iris can be smoothly adjusted from a very small opening to the point of being wide open, certain specific points within this range are marked according to degrees of light transmission. These points are called **f-stops.**[8] Contrary to what you might first assume, the smaller the f-stop number the more light the lens transmits. Conversely, high f-stop numbers mean that little light is being transmitted through the lens. The following illustrates this relationship.

Occasionally we see that f-stops are not illustrated. Examples would be f/1.2, f/3.5 and f/4.5. These are midpoint settings between whole f-stops, and on some lenses they represent the **maximum aperture** (speed) of the lens. Figure 4.12 shows the aperture settings for a series of f-stops. We've noted that the speed of a lens is equal to its maximum (wide-open) f-stop. In the f-stop scale shown above, f/1.4 would be the speed of the lens represented. Fast lenses are expensive because they contain many large, glass elements and are difficult to design and build.

When an iris setting is opened up one f-stop (from f/8 to f/5.6, for example), it represents a 100-percent increase in the light going through the lens. Conversely, if the lens is stopped down one stop (as from f/1.4 to f/2.0), the light is cut by 50 percent. Put another way, when you open up one stop you double the light; when you stop down one stop you halve the amount of light going through the lens. Once the f-stop range is understood, it will be obvious which way a lens iris should be adjusted to compensate for a picture that is either too light or too dark.

Cameras with automatic exposure controls use a small electric motor to automatically open or close the iris according to varying light conditions. On professional cameras the f-stop settings are visible on the lens barrel. On many consumer cameras the numbers are not shown. Even so, a knowledge of the camera's iris and how it affects such things as exposure and depth of field (to be discussed later) is important to image and quality control. Although cameras with automatic exposure control can have an advantage in situations such as fast-breaking news, where there is no time to properly set up the camera, in other situations this automatic mode will not provide the best video.

---

[8] "F" stands for "factor" and, traditionally, it has been based on the mathematical ratio of focal length divided by the diameter of the iris opening. This is not valid for today's complex lenses, however. Many of today's "f-stops" are actually "t-stops," which are based not on this mathematical relationship, but on the actual amount of light transmitted by the lens.

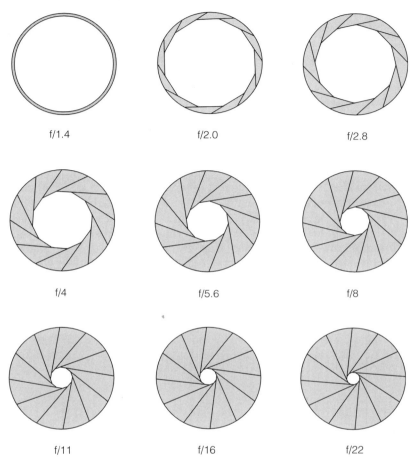

f/1.4   f/2.0   f/2.8

f/4   f/5.6   f/8

f/11   f/16   f/22

Figure 4.12   The size of the iris opening in a lens is given a number called an f-stop. All lenses set at a particular f-stop will transmit the same amount of light to the camera target. Contrary to what you might think, the larger the opening, the smaller the f-stop *number* will be.

The Effect of Supplementary Lenses on F-stop

Earlier we talked about the role of supplementary lenses and range extenders in multiplying focal length. Since f-stops are based on the relationship between focal length and lens aperture, when the lens focal length is altered through the use of one of these supplementary lenses, the f-stops on the lens are no longer accurate.

When attempting to use a range extender under low light conditions, you may suddenly find that the image is underexposed because of the increase in focal length and resulting loss of light through the lens.

LENS COATINGS

When transmitted through a lens, some light is lost as a result of reflections from the surfaces of the 10 to 30 glass elements that make up the lens. To reduce this problem the surfaces of lens elements are coated with a micro-thin, antireflection coating. This **lens coating** typically gives the glass elements a light blue appearance and greatly reduces the amount of light lost because of surface reflections. Although lens coatings are much more resilient than they used to be, they are still relatively easy to permanently scratch. Once a lens is badly scratched, its sharpness is diminished and the image contrast is reduced. A scratched lens is quite costly to repair; in fact, it is generally less expensive to replace the lens than to try to repair it.

Since it is easy for an object to come in contact with a camera lens, remember to always use a lens cap when the camera is being transported and any time the camera is not being used. A lens cap not only guards against the lens being scratched, but also keeps out dirt, which also reduces sharpness and contrast.

CLEANING LENSES

Although small quantities of dust on a lens will not appreciably affect image quality, fingerprints or oily smudges are a different matter. If not promptly removed, the acids in fingerprints can permanently etch themselves into the lens coating.

A lens should not be *routinely* cleaned; it should be cleaned only when dirt or dust becomes noticeable. Each time the lens is cleaned there is the risk of tiny abrasive particles present in the tissue creating microscopic scratches in the lens coating.

To clean a lens, first remove any surface dirt by blowing it off with an ear syringe or brushing it off with a clean camel's hair brush. Next, dampen a lens tissue with lens cleaner and gently rub the lens in a circular motion. While rubbing, turn or roll the tissue slightly so that any dirt will not be rubbed over the lens surface. Don't put the lens cleaner directly on the lens where it can easily seep behind lens elements. Never clean a lens with silicon-treated lens tissues or the silicon-impregnated cloth commonly sold for cleaning eyeglasses. The residue may permanently discolor the lens coating.

Figure 4.13 Although use of a video camera in rain is discouraged, news stories often have to be shot under adverse weather conditions. Camera "rain jackets" such as this cover all but the very end of the camera lens.

Condensation on the Lens

Condensation or rain drops on the lens can distort or even totally obscure an image. When a camera is taken from a cool area into warm air, the lens frequently fogs up. This is a special problem in cool climates when camera equipment is brought inside after being outside in the cold for some time. Even though moisture may be wiped off the lens, it may continue to fog up until the temperature of the lens equals the surrounding air. (Condensation can also take place within the camera and cause major problems. For this reason, most cameras have a "dew indicator" which detects moisture or condensation within the camera and/or VCR and shuts down the unit until the moisture has evaporated.) To control the effects of condensation, you should allow 30 minutes or so warm-up time when you bring a camera from a cold to a warm environment.

Although use of a video camera in rain is definitely discouraged, news stories often have to be shot under adverse weather conditions. Camera "rain jackets" are available that cover all but the very end of the camera lens (Figure 4.13).

Depth of Field

F-stops directly affect depth of field, which is one of the important creative tools available to a videographer. **Depth of field** is defined as the range of distance in front of the camera that is in sharp focus.[9] Theoretically, if a camera is focused at a

---

[9] Depth of field should not be confused with depth of focus, which is the tolerance associated with the distance from the back of the lens to the focal plane or target area of the camera.

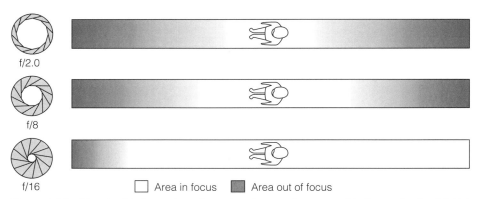

Area in focus   ▓ Area out of focus

Figure 4.14   Note in this figure that when a lens is opened up to a wide f-stop, depth of field is minimized; when the lens is stopped down to a small f-stop (bottom illustration), the depth is great. This effect is shown in another way in Figure 4.16.

specific distance, only objects at that exact distance will be sharp; objects in front of and behind that point will be, to varying degrees, blurry.

In actual fact, areas in front of and behind the point of focus may be acceptably sharp. The term "acceptably sharp" is subjective. A picture doesn't just abruptly become unacceptably blurry at a certain point in front of or behind the point of focus. The transition from sharp to out of focus is gradual. For practical purposes, the limits of sharpness are reached when details become objectionably blurry. This will vary according to the medium. What is acceptably sharp in standard NTSC television will be much greater than what is acceptable in HDTV. In the latter case the superior clarity of the medium will more readily reveal sharpness problems.

F-stop and Depth of Field

The larger the f-stop *number,* the smaller the iris *opening,* and the greater the depth of field (Figure 4.14). Therefore, the depth of field of a lens used at f/11 will be greater than when the same lens is used at f/5.6, and depth of field at f/5.6 will be greater than at f/2.8.

Depth of Field and Focal Length

Although depth of field also appears to be related to lens focal length, it is only an apparent relationship. As long as the same image size is maintained on the target, all lenses at a specific f-stop will have about the same depth of field, regardless of focal length. A wide angle lens appears to have a much greater depth of field than does a telephoto lens because, by comparison, the size of the image on the camera's target is much smaller. The smaller (compressed) image size created by the wide-angle lens simply hides the blur and brings it into the area of acceptability. If you

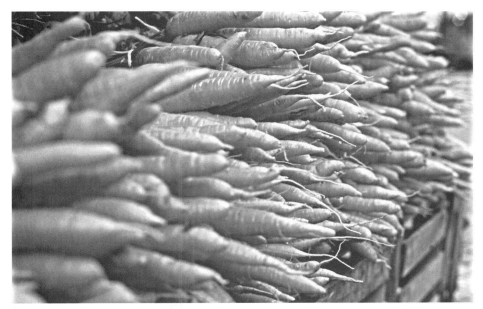

Figure 4.15 This wagon load of carrots illustrates the use of limited depth of field for this lens when used at f/2.8. Rather than a disadvantage, using "selective focus" to guide viewer attention can represent a creative production tool.

were to enlarge a section of image area out of the wide-angle shot exactly equal to the image area created by the telephoto lens, you would find the depth of field would be the same.

Because wide-angle lenses (or zoom lenses used at wide-angle positions) are good at hiding a lack of sharpness, they are a good choice when accurate focus is a problem. (Of course, when you use a wide-angle lens setting you may need to move much closer to the subject matter to retain the same-sized screen image. This means you are, in a sense, right back where you started; you've lost the sharpness advantage you seemingly gained by using the wide-angle lens.)

With a telephoto lens or zoom lens used at a telephoto setting, focus has to be much more precise. In fact, when zoomed in fully (at maximum focal length) the area of acceptable sharpness may be less than one inch—especially if the lens is used at a wide aperture (low f-stop number). This can represent either a major problem or a creative tool in effective composition. In the latter case it can force a viewer to concentrate on a specific object or area of a scene. (Our eyes tend to avoid areas of a picture that are not clear, but are drawn to areas that are sharply focused.) The term **selective focus** is used to describe the process of using limited depth of field to intentionally throw areas of the picture out of focus (Figure 4.15). This technique is widely used in film and is associated with the so-called "film look," which many people find desirable. We'll discuss this concept and how it can be used in more detail in the chapter on composition.

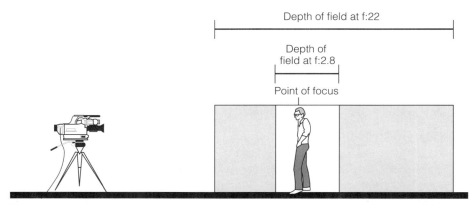

Figure 4.16   The total depth of field at any f-stop extends one-third of the way in front of the point of focus and two-thirds of the way behind it.

Depth of Field Limits

As you will note from Figure 4.16, the area of sharp focus does not extend equally in front of and behind the point of focus. At average subject-to-camera distances the total area of acceptable sharpness extends about one-third of the way in front of the point of focus and two-thirds behind it.[10] Not only does the depth of field increase as the iris closes and diminish as the iris opens up, but the transition rate from sharpness to out of focus is also more gradual at small f-stops and more rapid at wide f-stops.

FOCUSING A LENS

It might seem that focusing a lens is a simple process of just "getting things clear." True, but a few things complicate the issue.

It should be apparent from the preceding discussion that a zoom lens must be focused after first zooming in on a close shot. Since focusing errors will be the most obvious at this point, focusing will be easier and more accurate. Once focused, the lens can be zoomed back to whatever focal length is needed. If the scene contains a person, you will want to focus on the catchlight or gleam in one eye. There are two reasons for this: the person's eyes are normally the first place we look in viewing a

---

[10] Even though the 1/3, 2/3 ratios are commonly given, they vary slightly, depending on lens aperture (f-stop) and camera-to-subject distance. Although the ratios are true at a distance of between 15 and 20 feet (a common working distance for zoom lenses), the ratio shifts toward 20 percent in front of the point of focus and 80 percent in back at greater distances, and is about 50 percent at very close distances.

scene, and this small, bright spot is easy to focus on. If you do not zoom in and focus, but try to focus while holding a wide shot, you will inevitably find when you later zoom in that the picture will go out of focus because the focus error, which wasn't noticeable before, will suddenly be greatly magnified (Figure 4.17).

Follow Focus

In video production we are often dealing with moving subjects. A person may quickly move outside the limits of depth of field unless the lens can be quickly refocused. Professionals know which way to turn the focus controls to keep a moving subject in sharp focus. (Non-professionals end up throwing a slightly blurry image totally out of focus for a few seconds when they first turn the focus adjustment the wrong way.) The technique of **follow focus** is used to subtly refocus the camera to accommodate subject movement.

Auto-Focus Lenses

Although auto-focus lenses can be helpful in following moving subjects, you will encounter problems unless you fully understand their features and limitations.

First, auto-focus devices generally assume that the area you want in sharp focus is in the center of the picture. This is often not the case,[11] especially if you are trying for interesting and creative composition. Second, many auto-focus mechanisms can be fooled by subject matter, such as reflections, and flat, monochrome areas with no detail. Third, most auto-focus lenses have trouble determining accurate focus when shooting through such things as wire fences or glass. And, finally, auto-focus devices, especially under low light, can keep readjusting or searching for focus as you shoot.

Because of these problems, auto-focus has not been widely accepted by professional videographers. If the feature is present on a camera, it is generally turned off and reserved for fast-breaking news stories, where constant refocusing would be a major problem.

The Macro Lens Setting

Most zoom lenses have a **macro setting** that enables the lens to attain sharp focus on an object only a few inches or even a few millimeters from the front of the lens. (With some lenses the subject matter can even be at a "zero distance," that is,

---

[11] An example of the latter problem happened when one videographer was taping a speaker standing a few feet from a background curtain. As the individual spoke he nervously bobbed to the left and right. Each time he momentarily moved to one side of the frame the camera refocused on the background, throwing the speaker completely out of focus. Because of low light, the iris of the lens was wide open and depth of field was minimal, which made the constant in-and-out-of-focus effect quite noticeable.

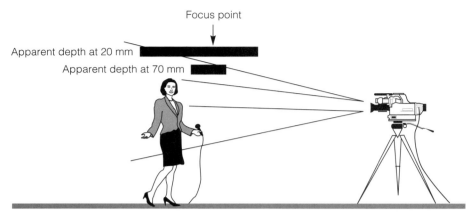

Figure 4.17   This drawing illustrates why a zoom lens should be focused by first zooming in all the way. Note that at 20mm (when the lens is zoomed out) the image looks fine; the depth of field of the lens keeps the woman in focus. However, when the lens is zoomed in to 70mm for a close-up, the depth of field diminishes, and the woman appears to go out of focus. Actually, the image does not go out of focus when the lens is zoomed in; the process of zooming in optically enlarges the image and makes the already existing blur noticeable and, for the first time, objectionable.

touching the front element of the lens.) Although lenses differ, to reach the macro position on many lenses a button or lever on the barrel of the lens is pushed to allow the zoom adjustment to travel beyond its normal stopping point. Many newer lenses are called *continuous focus lenses*. These are internal focus lenses that can be smoothly and continuously adjusted from infinity to a few inches without manually having to shift the lens into a macro mode.

Videographers often forget about the macro capability, but it offers many dramatic possibilities. For example, a flower, a stamp, or a portion of a drawing or snapshot can be made to fill the TV screen (Figure 4.18). A tripod or camera mount is a must when using the macro setting. Since depth of field extends only a few millimeters at this super-close range, focus is extremely critical.

Lens Shades

In the same way that our eyes must be shaded from a strong light in order to see clearly, the camera lens also has to be shielded from direct light. A **lens shade** or **lens hood** is designed to protect the image from offending glare or loss of contrast (Figure 4.19). Even if a strong light striking the lens does not create obvious evidence of lens flare, it may reduce the contrast of the image. Since most lens flare problems are apparent in the video viewfinder, the effect of a lens shade (or, in an emergency, a piece of dark paper taped to the barrel of the lens) can be clearly seen.

When selecting a lens shade, you will want to make sure that it extends as far out as possible without becoming visible around the edges of the picture when the

Figure 4.18 Most zoom lenses have a macro setting that enables the lens to attain sharp focus on an object only a few inches or even a few millimeters from the front of the lens. A tripod or camera mount is a must in using the macro setting. Since depth of field extends only a few millimeters at this super-close range, focus is critical.

Figure 4.19 In the same way that our eyes must be shaded from a strong light in order to see clearly, the camera lens has to be shielded from direct light. A lens shade or lens hood is designed to protect the image from offending glare and loss of contrast. Many zoom lenses have built in lens shades in the form of recessed lens mounts.

zoom lens is used in its wide-angle position. Many zoom lenses have built-in lens shades in the form of recessed lens mounts.

In addition to lens shades, there are a number of other attachments that fit over the front of a camera lens.

FILTERS

Glass filters consist of a transparent, colored gel sandwiched between two precisely ground (and sometimes coated) pieces of glass. Filters can be placed in a circular holder that screws over the end of the camera lens, or is inserted into a filter wheel behind the camera lens (to be discussed later). Gelatin filters are much cheaper than glass filters. These small, square sheets of optic plastic are used in front of the lens in conjunction with a matte box, which is illustrated later in the chapter.

Ultraviolet Filters

News photographers often put an **ultraviolet (UV) filter** over the camera lens to protect it from the adverse conditions often encountered in ENG work. (A damaged filter is much cheaper to replace than a lens.) Protection of this type is particularly important when the camera is used under adverse weather conditions, such as during storms. By screening out ultraviolet light, the filter also slightly enhances image color and contrast.

Using Filters for Major Color Shifts

Although general color correction in a video camera is done through the combination of optical and electronic camera adjustments, it is sometimes desirable to introduce a strong, dominant color into a scene. For example, when a scene called for a segment shot in a photographic darkroom, one camera operator simulated a red darkroom safelight by placing a dark red glass filter over the camera lens. (Darkrooms haven't used red filters to print pictures for decades, but since most audiences still think they do, directors continue to support the myth.) Obviously, the camera must be color balanced (Chapter 5) before the filter is placed over the lens, or else the camera's white balance system will try to cancel out the effect of the colored filter.

Neutral Density Filters

Occasionally, it is desirable to control the amount of light passing through a lens without stopping down the iris. For example, under bright sunlight conditions you may want to keep a relatively wide f-stop and use selective focus to reduce depth of field so that you throw distracting objects in the background and foreground out of focus. Although using a higher shutter speed is, perhaps, the best solution (see Chapter 5), the use of a **neutral density** or **ND filter** will achieve the same result. An ND filter is a gray filter that reduces light by one or more f-stops without affecting color. Professional video cameras normally have one or more ND filters included with their internal tungsten-to-daylight color correction filters.

Polarizing Filters

Most of us are familiar with the effect that polarized sunglasses have on reducing reflections and cutting down glare. Unlike sunglasses, the effect of professional **polarizing filters** can be continuously varied and go much further in their effect. Not only can these filters enable the camera to see much more clearly through the surface reflections of glass and water, they can darken a blue sky, thus providing a dramatic effect—especially in the presence of clearly defined clouds. Once its many applications are understood, a polarizing filter can become a videographer's most valuable filter (Color Plate 5).

Special Effect Filters

Although there are scores of special effect filters available, we'll just highlight four of the most popular: the star filter, the diffusion or soft focus filter, the fog filter and the low-contrast filter.

Star Filters You've undoubtedly seen TV scenes in which "fingers of light" projected out from the sides of shiny objects—especially bright lights (Figure 4.20). This effect is created with a glass **star filter,** which has a microscopic grid of crisscrossing parallel lines cut into its surface. Star filters can produce four-, five-, six-, or eight-point stars, depending on the lines engraved on the surface of the glass. The star effect varies with the f-stop used. It should be noted that star filters slightly reduce the overall sharpness of the image, which may or may not be desirable.

Soft Focus and Diffusion Filters Sometimes you may want to create a dreamy, "soft focus" effect. This can be done by using **soft focus** or **diffusion** filters. These filters, which are available in various levels of intensity, were regularly used in the early cinema to give starlets a soft, dreamy appearance and to hide signs of aging. A similar effect can be achieved by shooting through very fine-screen wire placed close to the lens or by shooting through a single thickness of a nylon stocking. The f-stop used will greatly affect the level of diffusion.

Fog Filters A certain amount of "atmosphere" can be added to dramatic locations by suggesting a foggy morning or evening. Without having to rely on nature or artificial fog machines, **fog filters** can create somewhat of the same effect (Figure 4.21).

Figure 4.20   Star filters can produce four-, five-, six-, or eight-point stars, depending on the lines engraved on the surface of the glass. The effect varies with the f-stop used.

General Considerations in Using Filters

Whenever a filter is used with a video camera, the black level of the video, as seen on a waveform monitor, is raised slightly. Because of this, it is advisable to automatically or manually re-adjust camera setup or black level whenever a filter is used.

Also remember that unlike electronic special effects created during postproduction, the optical effects created by filters during the taping of a scene cannot be undone. To make sure there are no unpleasant surprises, it is best to carefully check the results on location with a high-quality color monitor.

CAMERA FILTER WHEELS

Professional video cameras have one or two **filter wheels,** located behind the lens, which can hold a number of filters. Individual filters can be rotated into the lens light path as needed. Typically, a filter wheel will contain (1) two or more color correction filters, often with built-in neutral density properties, (2) a fluorescent light filter, which can reduce the blue-green effect of fluorescent lights, (3) one or

Figure 4.21 A certain amount of "atmosphere" can be added to dramatic locations by using a fog filter. Without having to rely on nature or artificial fog machines, fog filters can create somewhat the same effect.

more special effects filters, including the previously discussed star filter, and (4) an opaque "cap," which blocks all light going through the lens. Although filter wheels are located behind the lens, some filters, such as polarizing filters, must be mounted in front of the camera lens to be most effective.

MATTE BOXES

As shown in Figure 4.22, a **matte box** is a small bellows device mounted on the front of the camera. In addition to acting as an adjustable lens hood, matte boxes are designed to hold filters. As we noted earlier, instead of using circular glass filters, comparatively inexpensive four-inch-square colored gelatin filters (gels) can be inserted into the back of the matte box, just in front of the lens.

Matte boxes can also hold small cutout patterns or masks. For example, a keyhole-shaped pattern could be cut out of a piece of cardboard and used to give

Figure 4.22 A matte box is a small bellows device mounted on the front of a camera. In addition to acting as an adjustable lens hood, matte boxes are designed to hold filters.

the illusion of shooting through a keyhole (although in this day and age there are very few keyholes we can see through). The f-stop and focal length used and the distance of the mask from the lens affect the sharpness of the keyhole outline. Many of the effects formerly created by matte boxes are now more easily and predictably achieved electronically with a special-effects generator.

In Chapter 5 we'll look at the camera itself, the next step in changing the optical image into an electronic signal.

5 CAMERAS AND MOUNTING EQUIPMENT

FROM THE LENS and its accessories we turn to the camera and its associated equipment. In this chapter, we examine charge-coupled devices (CCDs), video levels, resolution, color quality, the camera viewfinder, camera mounting equipment, and camera prompters.

CAMERA CCDS

The very heart of a video camera is its imaging device. In most cases this means one or more CCDs. As we noted in the discussion of the color process in Chapter 3, the light from the camera lens either goes directly to a CCD imaging device or is directed through a prism block to two or three CCDs. The more pixels (light-sensitive points) there are in the target area, the higher the resolution or clarity of the CCDs. The most common CCD sizes are 1/2 inch and 2/3 inch. Less commonly used are 1/4-inch, 3/4-inch, and one-inch CCDs.

VIDEO RESOLUTION

Video **resolution** is a measure of the ability of a video camera to reproduce fine detail. The higher the resolution, the sharper the picture will look. The standard

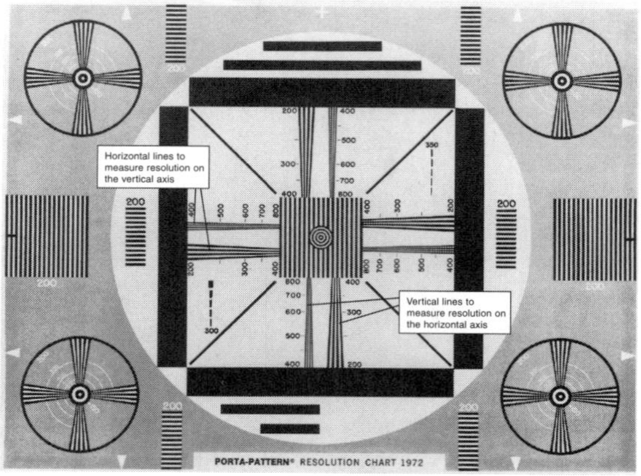

Figure 5.1 Resolution charts are used to measure the amount of detail a camera can reproduce. By filling the camera viewfinder with a resolution chart and observing the point where the lines appear to lose definition and blur together, the limits of sharpness for a camera can be determined. Note that vertical and horizontal resolution are measured separately.

NTSC broadcast TV system can potentially produce a picture resolution equal to about 300 lines of horizontal[1] resolution on a test pattern (see Figure 5.1). This is equal to the limits of what viewers with 20-20 vision can see when they watch a TV screen at a normal viewing distance. "Normal" in this case translates into a viewing distance of about eight times the height of the TV picture. So, if the TV screen is 16 inches high—a so-called 25-inch picture tube—the normal viewing distance would be about 10 feet. HDTV, with its higher resolution, makes possible both larger screens and closer viewing distances.

Determining Resolution

Charts that contain squares or wedges of fine black lines on a white background can indicate the limits of sharpness. Within a particular area of one of these **resolution charts** there are black and white lines of fixed width (Figure 5.1). Numbers such as 200, 300, etc., appear on the chart next to the corresponding line densities. By exactly filling the camera viewfinder with the resolution chart and observing the point on the chart where the lines appear to lose definition and blur together, we can establish the limits of resolution. High-quality NTSC cameras can resolve about 900 lines, HDTV cameras well over 1,000. Obviously, a high resolution monitor has to be used in this test.[2]

---

[1] Since vertical resolution is limited by the number of active TV scanning lines, which is set by the specific TV standard being used, measures of resolution commonly refer to horizontal resolution, or the detail that can be discerned along the horizontal axis of a picture.

[2] Although this is a quick method of determining camera resolution, the only technically precise method involves using an oscilloscope to measure depth of video modulation.

Color Resolution

The resolution we've been discussing is based on the sharpness of the black and white (luminance) component of the TV image. As we mentioned previously, it was discovered early in experiments with color TV that the human eye perceives detail primarily in terms of differences in brightness (luminance differences) and not color. When NTSC color television was developed, an ingenious and highly complex system of adding a lower-resolution color signal to the existing black-and-white signal was devised. Using this system, color information can be added to the existing monochrome signal without having to greatly expand the information-carrying capacity of the basic luminance signal.

Minimum Light Levels for Cameras

Television cameras require a certain level of light (target exposure) to produce good-quality video. This light level is measured in foot-candles and lux. A **foot-candle,** which is a measure of light intensity from a candle at a distance of one foot (under very specific conditions) is the unit of light intensity used in the United States. Other countries are on the metric system and use **lux** as the basic unit of light intensity. A foot-candle is equal to about 10.74 lux.

Although they will produce acceptable pictures under much lower light levels, most professional video cameras require a basic light level of 150 to 200 foot-candles (about 2,000 lux) to produce an optimum-quality picture. At this level of illumination the camera lens can be used at about f/8.[3]

As the light level increases, the iris of the lens is stopped down (changed to a higher f-stop number) to maintain the same level of exposure on the camera target.

Under low light conditions video can quickly start to look dark, with a complete loss of detail in the shadow areas. To help compensate, professional cameras have built-in, multiposition, video **gain selector** switches that can amplify the video signal in steps from 3 up to about 28 units (decibels or dBs).[4] Using video gain circuits, some cameras can produce acceptable video under less than one-half lux, which is equivalent to the light level found in a dimly lit room (Figure 5.2). But the greater the boost, the greater the loss in picture quality. Specifically, video noise increases and color clarity diminishes.

---

[3] Technically, most lenses are sharpest when they are stopped down (closed down) about 1/3 to 1/2 of the way from their maximum aperture. This range also affords reasonable depth of field.

[4] Consumer-type cameras typically have a switch with only one level of video gain.

Figure 5.2 Using video gain circuits, video cameras can produce acceptable video under less than one foot-candle of light. For situations that require video under even less light, light amplifiers are available, the most refined of which can produce video using only the light from stars (a light level of about 1/100,000 lux).

Night Vision Modules

For situations that require video under even less light, **night vision modules** use electronic light multipliers to amplify the light going through a lens. The most refined of these light amplifiers can produce clear, sharp video at night using only the light from stars (a light level of about 1/100,000 lux). Under conditions of "no light," most of these modules emit their own invisible infrared illumination, which is then translated into a visible image.

In recent years camera operators covering news have found night vision devices useful in covering night-time stories where any type of artificial lighting would call attention to the camera and adversely affect the story being covered.

Exceeding Maximum Brightness Levels

Ideally, video cameras should be operated under light levels that will not require special amplification. Under conditions of adequate light, camera exposure is controlled by the lens iris—either automatically by the camera itself, or manually by

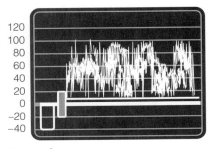

Figure 5.3   A well exposed scene results in video with a full tonal range and a waveform pattern evenly distributed between 7.5 and 100 on the waveform scale. In contrast, the series of illustrations that follow show various video level problems.

an experienced camera operator observing the image in the viewfinder.[5] When video quality is a major consideration, camera levels should be adjusted and maintained with the help of a waveform monitor. As noted in Chapter 3, video levels normally should be evenly distributed between 7.5 and 100 on the waveform scale, with parts touching both 7.5 and 100 (Figure 5.3). If the white level stops below 100 (Figure 5.4), the camera's iris should be opened to a wider f-stop; if the white level extends beyond 100 (Figure 5.5), the iris should be closed down. Maintaining video levels in this way is not unlike riding audio gain with a VU meter.[6]

The human eye can cope with differences in scene brightness of thousands-to-one; color film can successfully reproduce brightness differences of several hundred-to-one. As we've noted, the best of today's CCD cameras can cope with brightness ranges that exceed what's possible with typical motion picture film. Even so, limitations in the NTSC TV transmission and reception process mean that optimum results are obtained (on a typical home TV set) when the brightness range of video is held to between 20:1 and 30:1. This means that **TV white,** or the lightest part

---

[5]   Experienced camera operators doing electronic news gathering (ENG) frequently rely on this approach while taping fast-breaking news stories under difficult lighting conditions. Under such conditions automatic exposure circuitry can be adversely influenced by bright areas in the scene and render important subject matter very dark.

[6]   There are instances in which, to achieve a certain video effect, you may not want video to cover the full range from 7.5 to 100. Although this may be highly desirable from an artistic standpoint, a problem arises when automatic level circuitry is later used and these levels are expanded to the 7.5 to 100 range. One solution is to "plant" insignificant objects in a scene which (to automatic equipment and engineers schooled in maintaining "proper" video levels) represent 7.5 (TV black) and 100 IRE units (TV white). A light in an otherwise gray and murky scene could represent TV white and a black, possibly indistinguishable, foreground object could represent TV black.

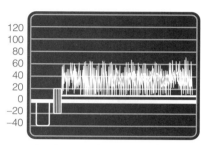

Figure 5.4   Underexposed video is evident on a waveform monitor because the average white level falls considerably below 100. Note how much darker this picture is compared to Figure 5.3. Opening the camera iris two to three f-stops solves the problem.

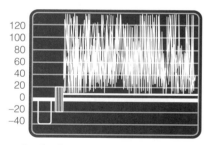

Figure 5.5   Overexposure is apparent in two ways: the video levels exceed 100 on a waveform monitor (causing major video problems) and the video looks washed out without adequate blacks. The solution is to close down the camera iris until the overall white level comes down to 100 as shown in Figure 5.3.

of the picture, can't be more than 30 times brighter than **TV black,** or the blackest area of the picture.

An example of exceeding the acceptable brightness ranges is illustrated in Figure 5.6a. The brightness range encountered in this setting caused the subject to be plunged into darkness. If the camera iris had been opened up several f-stops to correctly expose the subject, the bright background would then have driven the video levels far beyond an acceptable point, causing major video problems. The only solution was to reduce the excessive brightness range through the use of

Figure 5.6   Any bright object in a scene (such as this window) can result in a tonal compression of the gray scale. In this case the solution is relatively simple: just add front (fill) light to make the level of illumination on the subject equal to the light coming through the window.

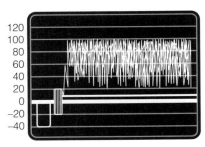

Figure 5.7   Some cameras try to compensate for overly bright areas (reflections from water, bright backgrounds, windows, lights, etc.) by clipping video levels that exceed 100 on a waveform monitor. Unfortunately, this results in white areas that are chalky and without discernible detail. Another unsatisfactory way automatic circuitry handles this brightness problem is illustrated in Figure 5.8.

supplementary lighting (Figure 5.6b). An excessive brightness range within a scene, therefore, can result from subject matter that is too light or bright or by subject matter lit by uneven lighting, or a combination of both.

To try to compensate for an excessive brightness range in a scene, the automatic circuitry in cameras will respond in one of two ways: it will cleanly **clip** or cut off the top of the video range at 100 (as shown on a waveform monitor), or it will **compress** (push down) the white-to-black range to keep it within the normal 7.5 to 100 range.

Although clipping the top end off of the video scale (Figure 5.7a) solves the problem of an excessive brightness range, much important detail in the lighter areas

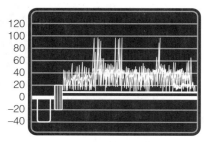

Figure 5.8   The automatic exposure circuitry built into cameras can cause problems when a scene contains bright areas, such as reflections from water, background windows, lights, etc. When the automatic circuitry closes down the camera iris to compensate for these bright areas, other areas of the scene suffer. In particular, skin tones go dark (Figure 5.6).

of the picture will be lost. Specifically, these light, clipped areas will lack detail and have a chalky, burned-out appearance (Figure 5.7b). The effect will be evident on the waveform monitor because the top of the pattern will look flat and cleanly lopped off instead of being jagged, as in a normal distribution (Figure 5.3b).

The second way of handling excessive video levels, compressing the gray scale, also creates undesirable effects. This gray scale compression means that most of the subject matter in the picture will be reproduced much darker than normal (Figure 5.8). And, as shown in Figure 5.6a, if the bright area influencing the video is large enough, the tonal range will be compressed to the point that many important tones will go completely black.

CAMERA COLOR BALANCING

Continuous Automatic White Balance

Consumer-type cameras typically have automatic white balance, which continuously monitors the video and attempts to adjust color balance.[7] A sensor within the

---

[7] We are speaking here of automatic white balance handled by the camera itself, sometimes referred to as *full-time auto white balance,* not the process of putting a white card in front of the camera and letting the camera "automatically" set the white balance.

camera averages the light within the scene and automatically adjusts the camera's internal color balance to zero out any generalized color bias. As with all automatic circuitry, however, automatic color balance is based on certain assumptions that may or may not be valid. In this case the assumption is made that when all colors and light sources in the scene are averaged, the result will be white or neutral (colorless) gray. Variations from this state are compensated for by the color balance circuitry. A problem arises if there are strong, dominant colors within the scene or, with some cameras, if the camera and the subject matter are illuminated by different light sources. Although automatic color balance circuitry will work reasonably well under the proper conditions, it cannot be relied on to consistently produce professional results. For that there is no substitute for a knowledgeable camera operator equipped with a white card.

White Balancing on a White Card

Since we know from Chapter 3 that red, blue and green must be present in certain proportions to create white, it is relatively easy to white balance (color balance) a professional camera to produce accurate color. With the camera zoomed in full frame on a pure white card, the operator can push a white balance button, and the camera's chroma channels will be automatically adjusted to produce pure white. Focus is not critical; but the card must be placed full frame within the dominant light source of the scene. This process is referred to as **white balancing** the camera.

Whenever the dominant light source in a scene changes in any way, professional cameras must be white balanced. Going from sunlight to shadow will necessitate white balancing the camera again, as will moving from outside light to inside light. Not to do so risks having colors in general, and skin tones in particular, change from scene to scene. This may become particularly bothersome during editing when you attempt to intercut scenes which won't match.

You can also "lie to the camera" during the white balancing process to create interesting effects. A warm (golden) color bias in a scene can be created by white balancing the camera on a light blue card; a rose-colored scene results from color balancing on a light cyan card. (In an effort to compensate for the colors presented as "white," the camera's white balance circuitry will push the camera's color balance toward the complement of whatever color is in the card.)

Although white balance can be electronically altered to some degree in postproduction, starting out with proper color balance at the camera is always best. Since proper color balance involves the interrelationship of three colors, it is not always possible to adjust just one color later in the production process without affecting the others.

Professional cameras also have black-level and black-balance adjustments. These are typically set by capping the lens, so that no light enters, and allowing automatic circuitry to appropriately balance the three colors for optimum black, while, at the same time, establishing the overall video level for black.

Color Reproduction is Subjective

Even though there is an impressive array of equipment to accurately measure color, color, as humanly perceived, is quite subjective. In fact, when it comes to judging color, the human eye can be quite easily fooled. To explain this problem, we'll need to look at the two primary standards of illumination: sunlight and incandescent light.

Sunlight contains a roughly equal mixture of all colors of light. The color of light is measured in degrees Kelvin (K).[8] On the Kelvin scale, the lower the color temperature, the redder the light is; and the higher the color temperature, the bluer the color is.

Compared to sunlight, which has a color temperature of about 5,500° K, the light from a standard 100-watt light bulb is only about 2,800° K. The light from the standard portable lights used in video field production measures 3,200° K (The color temperature of light will be discussed in more detail in the chapter on lighting). Through a process called **approximate color consistency,** the human eye can automatically adjust to color temperature changes in the 2,800° to 5,500° K range (Color Plate 6).

For example, if you look at a white piece of paper in sunlight, you should have no trouble verifying that it is white. When you take the same piece of white paper inside under the illumination of a normal incandescent light, it still looks white. By any scientific measure, however, the paper is now reflecting much more in the way of light yellow. A yellow (3,200° K) light falling on a white object creates a yellow object. But, by *knowing* the paper is white, your mind says, "I know that the paper is white." So, through approximate color consistency, you mentally and unconsciously adjust your internal color balance to make the paper seem white. In so doing you are able to shift all of the other colors slightly, so you also perceive them in their proper perspective. Although we make such color corrections for "real-world scenes" around us, we tend not to make them when viewing television or color photos. In the latter case we generally have a color standard within our view, such as sunlight or some artificial light source.

Since we know that human color perception is quite subjective, it is crucial that we rely on some objective, scientific measure or standard, so that video equipment can be accurately and consistently color balanced. That measuring instrument, which was introduced in Chapter 3, is the vectorscope. In a sense a vectorscope is a color wheel with the information electronically filled in. Note in Figure 5.9 that the face of a vectorscope has six small boxes inside the circle. These represent the three additive primary and the three additive secondary colors.

If a color camera is focused on a test chart that contains these six primary and secondary colors, or if a tape machine is playing back a tape of an electronic color test pattern consisting of vertical bars of red, blue and green (the primary colors), and magenta, cyan and yellow (the secondary colors), each of the six colors or hues

---

[8] The proper designation for this is in question. Some sources indicate that the word *degrees* is not necessary when used with Kelvin. Others insist that *degrees* is not a proper term at all, and that *units* should be substituted.

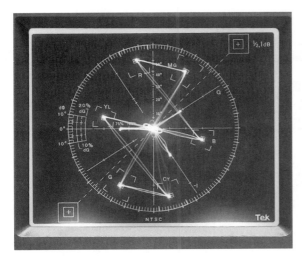

Figure 5.9 The vectorscope plots color in terms of hue and amplitude. Note the six small boxes inside the circle. These show the ideal positions of the three additive primary and the three additive secondary colors from a color test chart. The distance the plotted colors appear from the center of the display represents the purity of the colors.

should appear within its appropriate box. Primary and secondary colors that fall outside of their designated areas on the vectorscope will not be accurately reproduced. All six colors can be shifted together in one direction or the other by electronically shifting a color phase control. However, if some of the colors fall inside their designated areas and some don't, the task becomes more difficult, since each of the primary and secondary colors will have to be individually adjusted.

In addition to hue (color), the vectorscope also shows the amplitude or **saturation** (purity) of each color. Color saturation, which is measured in percentages, is indicated by how far out from the center of the circle the color is displayed.

Good Color vs. Real Color

You might assume that television viewers want to see colors reproduced as accurately and faithfully as possible. Studies have shown, however, that color preferences lean toward exaggeration. Viewers prefer to see skin tones healthier than they actually are, as well as greener grass, and a bluer sky. In terms of the vectorscope, this preference does not mean that hues are inaccurate, only that they are "stronger" and more saturated.

CAMERA SHUTTER SPEEDS

In addition to the focus, iris and color balance adjustments on camcorders, most video cameras have an adjustment for **shutter speed.** Unlike the shutters used in still cameras, the shutters used in CCD cameras are not mechanical. These speeds

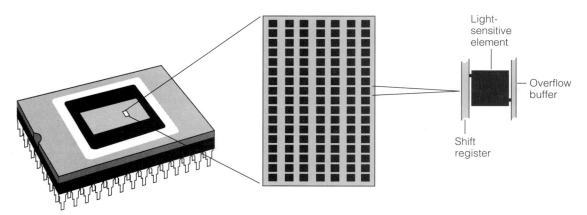

Figure 5.10   Most TV cameras rely on CCDs (charge-coupled devices) to convert the light from the camera lens into an electronic signal. On the top of the chip there is a small window called the target, which is 1/2-inch, 1/3-inch, or 2/3-inch across (measured diagonally). Within this area there are from a few hundred thousand to several million light-sensitive points (pixels). If too much light hits a pixel, the voltage overflows the shift register and is drained off into the overflow buffer.

simply represent the time that the light-induced charge is allowed to build before being transferred out of the shift register, that is, the electronic memory bank of the CCD (Figure 5.10). With speeds as high as 1/10,000 second in CCD cameras, most any movement can be "frozen" without blur or smear.

By setting a CCD camera at its "normal" shutter speed of 1/60 second, the sampling is done at the maximum time allowed by the field rate of the TV system. This represents the maximum exposure possible with normal scanning. But, under very low light conditions—especially where little or no action is involved—some video cameras have a provision to let the light-induced charge build for double and quadruple the normal time. Although this results in much brighter video, if there is any action, a pronounced stroboscopic effect will be obvious. This will be discussed in more detail later.

As the light level increases and there is a need to freeze action or reduce exposure, faster shutter speeds can be selected. Most professional CCD cameras have speeds of 1/60 (normal), 1/100, 1/250, 1/500, 1/1,000 and 1/2,000 second. Some go beyond this to 1/4,000, 1/8,000 and 1/10,000 second. The higher speeds, 1/1,000 and above, make possible clear slow-motion playbacks and freeze-frame still images (Figure 5.11).

Shutter Speeds and F-Stops

Just as in traditional still photography, with CCD cameras there is a direct relationship between shutter speed and f-stop. Each time the shutter speed is doubled, the lens must be opened up one f-stop to provide the same net exposure. This means

Figure 5.11 With speeds as high as 1/10,000 second in CCD cameras, almost any movement can be "frozen" without blur or smear. Most professional CCD cameras have speeds of 1/60 (normal), 1/100, 1/250, 1/500, 1/1,000 and 1/2,000 second. Some go beyond this to 1/4,000, 1/8,000 and 1/10,000 second. The higher speeds (1/1,000 and above) make possible clear slow-motion playbacks and freeze-frame still images.

that each of the combinations shown (1/100 at f/11, 1/2,000 at f/2.8, and so on) represents the same exposure or video level. The relationship between shutter speed and CCD exposure is illustrated in Table 5.1.

Shutter Speed and Stroboscopic Effects

A stroboscopic effect can occur in CCD cameras when very high (above 1/250 second) and very low (below 1/60 second) shutter speeds are used.

It is possible for cameras to reduce their CCD sampling rate to below 1/60 second. This allows the effect of the light to build in the CCD beyond the normal scanning time. In the process, fields and frames are omitted at regular intervals. If no movement is involved, the loss of frames will go unnoticed. However, with movement, the loss of frames results in a discontinuity in action and a jerky, stroboscopic effect. Besides the (somewhat questionable) special effect this pro-

Table 5.1   **Typical Relationship Between CCD Shutter Speed and Exposure**

CCD shutter speed:	"normal"	1/100	1/250	1/500	1/1,000	1/2,000	1/4,000	1/8,000	1/10,000
Corresponding f-stop:	16	11	8	5.6	4.0	2.8	2.0	1.4	1.2

vides, there are occasions—primarily very low light news and documentary situations—where imperfect video is better than no video at all.

Switching to the other end of shutter speed range, when shutter speeds shorter than 1/250 second are used, action tends to be cleanly frozen into crisp, sharp, still images. Without the slight blur that helps smooth out the transition between successive frames, we may notice a subtle stroboscopic effect when we view rapid action. Even so, the overall effect of the faster shutter speeds is to make images clearer, especially in slow-motion playbacks.

A final note on shutter speeds. When taping under fluorescent lights it is advisable to stick to a 1/60-second (normal) shutter speed. Using a higher shutter speed typically results in a flickering effect in the video as the CCD exposure interval interacts with the normal flicker of fluorescent lights.

The Camera Viewfinder

We now turn to the next major component of the video camera: the viewfinder. Most video cameras make use of the actual electronic camera image for their viewfinder image. The viewfinder can be the flat, LCD type, or the type that relies on a miniature TV picture tube and a magnifying eyepiece.

Although color viewfinders have been gaining in popularity, a black-and-white viewfinder image is sometimes preferred over color for three reasons: the resolution or clarity of a monochrome image is greater than color which, among other things, makes focusing easier; the black-and-white viewfinder requires less power (a black-and-white, tube-type viewfinder draws almost as much power as the rest of the camera); and the electronics of a black-and-white viewfinder take less space. Offsetting these advantages, however, is the fact that, by showing us color, a color viewfinder is a much more accurate representation of the image we are going to end up with.

Viewfinder Status Indicators

To help camera operators keep track of everything they need to know while shooting, EFP camera manufacturers have added an array of **status indicators** to viewfinders. There are many different types of indicators.

First, there are miniature colored lights around the edges of the video image. Red, yellow and green are common colors. Sometimes they even blink to capture the camera operator's attention. Next are the indicators that are superimposed on the viewfinder video. Boxes, bars and lines are common configurations. Some of the viewfinder messages may even be in plain English (or the language of your choice) superimposed over the image. For example, the superimposed message, "tape remaining: 2 min.," is hard to misinterpret. Some camera manufacturers use circuitry that superimposes **zebra stripes** in bright areas of the viewfinder video. These stripes, which show areas of maximum white in the picture, act as an aid in setting video levels. Finally, some cameras have small speakers built into the sides and, with the help of a voice synthesizer, announce such things as "low battery," or "tape remaining: five minutes."

Since every manufacturer uses a slightly different approach to status indicators, videographers need to study the camera guide to determine what a camera is trying to communicate at any one time. The time spent becoming familiar with the meaning of these status indicators will more than pay for itself in avoiding later disappointments and failures.

Viewfinder status indicators can include the following 15 items:

1. a tally light (indicating that tape is rolling or that camera is "on the air")
2. a low battery warning
3. minutes of tape remaining
4. color balancing may be needed
5. low light; insufficient exposure
6. low-light boost (gain selector switch) circuit in operation
7. indoor/outdoor filter in place
8. zoom lens setting (indicating how much further you can zoom in or out)
9. auto/manual iris status
10. audio level meter
11. tape footage counter
12. "zebra pattern" for monitoring and setting video levels
13. superimposed masks for safe area, and 4:3 and 16:9 aspect ratios
14. the presence of customized camera setup profiles (to accommodate specific types of subject matter)
15. camera warm-up diagnostics

Accommodating Left- and Right-Eyed People

With cameras that use side-mounted viewfinders, the viewfinder can often be flipped from one side of the camera to the other for operators preferring to use either left or right eyes. Sometimes, to accommodate cramped shooting conditions, it may also be desirable to move the viewfinder from one side of the camera to the other. When the viewfinder is flipped, the image will end up being upside-down unless the top-to-bottom electronic scanning is reversed. A reversal switch on these cameras takes care of this and occasionally explains why an unsuspecting camera operator finds the viewfinder image upside-down.

Cameras employing the liquid crystal (LCD) viewfinders are useful for shooting over the heads of crowds, or for ground-level angles. They also represent a definite advantage when you must hold a shot for a long time (for example, in taping a lengthy speech). Holding your eye to a standard viewfinder for a long time can be quite fatiguing. These flat, LCD viewfinders can also be used to compose shots that you, yourself, want to be in, after the camera is mounted on a tripod and the viewfinder is reversed 180 degrees so you can see it. It is also possible to get this type of viewfinder in the form of an "add on" which can be attached to a camera with a standard viewfinder. The main disadvantage of the flat, LCD display is that the image loses contrast and brightness when used in bright light, which can make the camera hard to focus.

Once you get used to their operation, viewfinder goggles, which resemble virtual reality goggles (Figure 5.12), allow even greater flexibility. This type of viewfinder can be used to supplement a standard side-mounted viewfinder. Since the viewfinder is connected to the camera by a long cable, you can easily hold the camera over your head, place it flat on the ground, or even shoot backwards with the camera mounted on your shoulder. Although this type of viewfinder offers several important advantages, it can restrict your vision of things going on around you while you are shooting.[9]

For critical, professional work the best "viewfinder" is an external monitor, typically, a bright, 3- to 5-inch AC/DC color monitor; however, any high-quality, color TV monitor will do. Even though this type of **stand-alone monitor** requires extra power and limits your mobility, it's the only sure way to check subtle lighting effects and critically evaluate such things as depth of field.

Camera Safe Areas

Because of overscanning and other types of image loss between the camera and the home receiver, a small area around the sides of the TV camera image is cut off before being seen. To compensate for this, directors must assume that up to 10 percent of the viewfinder picture may not be visible on the home receiver. Important visual information—especially written material—must be kept in the inner 90 percent of the picture. This area is referred to by various names: the **safe area, essential area** or, somewhat inaccurately, the **safe title area**[10] (Figure 5.13).

---

[9] Although only one eye is needed for a side-mounted (eyepiece-type) viewfinder, news videographers generally operate their cameras with both eyes open, so they can be aware of what's going on around them (or what might be coming toward them).

[10] Although often used in this context, originally, the term *safe title area* was defined as the inner 80 percent of the picture.

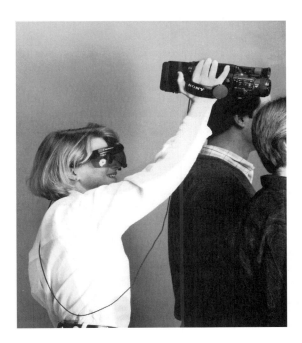

Figure 5.12 Once you get used to their operation, viewfinder goggles, which resemble virtual reality goggles, allow great flexibility. Since the viewfinder is connected to the camera by a long cable, you can easily hold the camera over your head, place it flat on the ground, or even shoot backwards with the camera mounted on your shoulder.

Figure 5.13 Because of overscanning and other types of image loss between the camera and the home receiver, a small area around the sides of the TV camera image is cut off before being seen. Therefore, important visual information must be kept at least within the inner 90 percent of the picture. Some production personnel insist that important written information be confined to an even safer area—the inner 80 percent of the picture. Both areas are illustrated.

Adjusting the Viewfinder Image

Because the image in the camera's viewfinder is actually the image from a miniature TV screen, it is subject to brightness and contrast variations. In addition, with tube-type viewfinders, there may also be electrical focus problems and the occasional lack of proper image centering. Remember that adjusting the viewfinder image in no way affects the video coming from the camera itself. However, adjustments to the camera video will affect the viewfinder image.

Viewfinders should accurately reflect the nature and quality of the video coming from the camera. To make sure that the contrast and brightness of the viewfinder are set correctly, the camera's built-in, electronically generated color bars (if available in the camera you are using) should be switched on and examined in the viewfinder. The viewfinder brightness and contrast controls can be adjusted until a full, continuous range of tones from solid black to white are visible. If the camera doesn't have a built-in test pattern, the quality of the camera video must first be verified, with the help of a test pattern and a reliable external video monitor, before the viewfinder controls are adjusted.

Checking Viewfinder Accuracy

Although CCD-type viewfinders normally remain stable over time, the accuracy of a tube-type camera viewfinder can drift so that it does not accurately show the output of the camera. It is relatively easy to check on this. First, a video monitor has to be found that has itself been perfectly aligned with the help of a test pattern. The output of the camera in question is then hooked up to the monitor and the camera is focused on a test pattern so that the outermost edges of the test pattern just fill the viewfinder image. Any discrepancy between the viewfinder image and the monitor image should then be obvious. Viewfinder alignment may have to be adjusted with the help of an engineer or technician.

Occasionally the electrical focus will also drift out of adjustment on a tube-type viewfinder. This will obviously make optical focusing difficult until it is corrected, generally with the help of a test pattern and screwdriver-equipped engineer.

Since wearing glasses while using a camera viewfinder can present problems, many side-mounted, eyepiece-type viewfinders have a control in the eyepiece to adjust image magnification. This is referred to as **diopter correction.** If this isn't built in, viewfinder magnification eyepieces can be purchased to eliminate the need for eyeglasses while using the camera.

CONVERTIBLE CAMERAS

Although many cameras are designed strictly for either field production or studio work, some manufacturers have seen the value of making **convertible cameras,** or cameras that can be quickly altered to serve the special needs of each application. Convertible cameras are designed to be modified in several ways (Figure 5.14).

Figure 5.14 Although many cameras are designed strictly for either field production or studio work, some manufacturers have seen the value of making convertible cameras, or cameras that can be quickly altered to serve the special needs of each application. Convertible cameras are designed to be quickly modified in several ways.

Modifying the Lens

The lenses associated with studio production are generally larger and more technically sophisticated than the lenses used on field cameras. The zoom lenses on many studio cameras have **shot boxes** that can electronically memorize several preselected zoom speed and focal length settings. When you push one of the buttons on the shot box, the zoom lens moves smoothly to a preselected shot at a programmed speed. This level of sophistication is seldom needed in the field.

Modifying the Viewfinder

The camera viewfinders associated with studio cameras are generally much larger and more technically versatile than those used on field cameras. For example, most studio camera viewfinders can be switched to a special effects feed from the control room switcher. This ability makes it possible for camera operators to take a direct role in setting up a special effect involving their cameras.

Adding Communication Links

Compared to field cameras, studio cameras also require much more elaborate intercom or PL (private line) communications links so that constant communications can be maintained with the director and other production personnel. Production communications will be discussed in more detail in Chapter 8.

Adding a CCU and an External Power Supply

The final major change in converting cameras from field to studio use involves the camera control unit or CCU. When more than one camera is used at the same time in an on-location production (Chapter 13) or when convertible cameras are configured for studio work, which generally involves two or more cameras, their video signals must be carefully matched; otherwise there will be distracting luminance or color shifts when switching from one studio camera to another. Individual remote CCU panels are normally used for each camera to set and maintain black level, white level, overall color balance, etc. This video adjustment process is referred to as **shading.** Normally, all of the CCUs will be grouped together in a central location so that cameras can be easily compared and adjusted simultaneously.

A related aspect of the studio/field conversion relates to the camera power supply. Whereas the studio camera CCU and its associated cable carries the power for the camera (along with the video signals, PL line communications, and so on), the field camera generally gets its power directly from an attached battery.

SETUP CARDS

Digital cameras have made possible removable **setup cards** or **smart cards,** which are about the size of a commemorative postage stamp. These cards, which are miniature, solid-state memory banks, are used to record all of the alignment, color balance and setup parameters associated with a camera. Once the main camera is set up and the information stored on the card, the card can be removed and inserted in other cameras and the information instantly transferred. Not only does this make it possible to set up all cameras so that they will match, but a special "look" can be programmed into the cameras. For example, each camera can be made to emulate a certain type of film stock.

It is also possible with either smart cards or internal camera circuitry to enhance skin characteristics by smoothing out skin tones and eliminating minor imperfections. The latter, which affects only skin tones in the picture, reduces the need for makeup.

CONNECTING CABLES

The various signals going into, and out of, the camera are carried by multiconductor cables. Early camera cables were almost 2 inches in diameter and carried more than 100 wires. Today's camera cables are typically either triax (three-conductor video cable) or optical fiber (We'll discuss optical fiber in Chapter 10).

Although today's camera cables are only a fraction of their earlier size and weight, one thing hasn't changed. When tabulations on equipment failure are done, these cables and their connectors remain a major weak link. This is not surprising. During production, cables are regularly flexed, pulled, twisted, stepped on and even knotted. Unfortunately, if only one wire breaks, or one pin in a connector is bent and doesn't make contact, the camera will be lost from service. This may mean that the entire production comes to a halt. On location, without standard test equipment, solving such problems can be difficult.

Before trying to make cable connections with any equipment, carefully observe the male and female pin connections. Some connectors may look similar but will have slightly different pin configurations. Trying to force dissimilar connectors together can easily result in bent or broken pins.

Camera Power Sources

Power for cameras and portable videocassette recorders comes from two sources: AC adapters and battery packs. **AC adapters** plug into a wall outlet and convert the 120 volts of alternating current (AC) into the regulated 12-volt direct current (DC) required by most field cameras.

Whenever possible, use an AC adapter to power a camera. Then you don't have to worry about batteries going dead in the middle of a segment. When an AC outlet is not near, however, you will need to rely on the camera or recorder's rechargeable battery pack.

Some types of batteries can suffer from a "memory effect." If the battery is regularly recharged after only limited use, it then may become impossible to fully discharge the battery. (The battery will, in effect, "remember" previous stopping points.) This type of battery should be fully discharged periodically and immediately recharged. Batteries of this type should not stay in a fully discharged state. Since battery types differ and some do not suffer from a "memory effect," you should pay particular attention to the charging and discharging recommendations of your particular battery type.

Camera Mounts

With few exceptions, anything that calls attention to the medium (for instance, a visible microphone boom, a bobbing camera, or unmotivated camera movements) should be avoided. Viewers have enough problems quickly grasping the meaning of the visual "message" without intrusive elements of the "medium" distracting their attention. But there are exceptions.

Figure 5.15   With a shoulder mount the weight of a camcorder can be equally distributed over the front and back of the mount, making it unnecessary to support the weight of the unit with the hands. This natural balance makes it much easier to operate the camcorder's controls.

Occasionally in dramatic productions a less-than-steady hand-held camera is used to represent the point of view of an actor. And, of course, electronic field production (EFP) and electronic news gathering (ENG) differ in terms of what is technically acceptable. In news, where a shaky, hand-held segment is better than no segment at all, it is often necessary for the camera to be mobile enough to "stay with" a breaking story. If moving subjects are being photographed, the fact that the camera is somewhat less than steady may not be too noticeable, especially if the camera is not zoomed in too far.

Whatever the application, keep unwanted camera movement to a minimum. To facilitate smooth pans and tilts, various types of camera mounts have been devised.

Shoulder Mounts

With a **shoulder mount** the weight of a video camera or a **camcorder** (camera and recorder combination) can be equally distributed over the front and back of the mount, making it unnecessary to support the weight of the unit with the hands (Figure 5.15). Instead, the hands can lightly steady the unit on the shoulder, making it relatively easy to operate camera controls.

Figure 5.16 One of the most sophisticated types of body mounts consists of an elaborate harness with a camera arm attached to a number of stabilizing springs. The spring-balanced arms of these camera stabilizers can, within limits, absorb and cancel the motion of a camera operator who is walking, going up a flight of stairs, or even running.

Figure 5.17 For light-weight cameras, smaller, lighter mounts offer many of the same advantages of the large Steadicam (Figure 5.16). These small, light-weight camera mounts, coupled with a good image stabilizer can (with practice) provide amazingly steady video, even while the operator is running with the camera.

Body Mounts

One of the most sophisticated types of body mounts consists of an elaborate harness with a camera arm attached to a number of stabilizing springs (Figure 5.16). Although there are several types, the Steadicam has become the most popular. The spring-balanced arms of these camera stabilizers can, within limits, absorb and cancel the motion of a camera operator who is walking, going up a flight of stairs, or even running. An attached high-intensity video monitor is viewed at a distance of 2 to 3 feet to allow for maximum camera movement.

The major disadvantage of the "studio version" of the Steadicam—apart from its relatively high cost—is that it is heavy. Sustained shooting can tire out the most hardy camera operator.

For light-weight cameras, smaller, lighter (and cheaper) mounts have been devised, which offer many of the same advantages (Figure 5.17). A camera mount of this type, coupled with a good image stabilizer, can with practice provide amazingly steady video, even while the operator is running with the camera.

Figure 5.18   Although setting up a tripod may seem like a tedious process, steady shots are the mark of a professional. Because each leg of a tripod can be separately adjusted for height, it is possible to level a tripod on a hillside, stairs, or uneven ground. Some tripods have a bubble- or LED-type indicator, which can be used to level the tripod and camera.

Tripods

Although some commercials and music videos feature frenetic camera movement (to try to hold attention and generate interest through screen movement), the constant bobbing and weaving of camera shots is not only the mark of an amateur, but it can quickly become tiring to viewers. Therefore, except for fast-breaking news stories, or to create a momentary dramatic effect, always mount the video camera on a tripod. Although setting up a tripod may seem like a tedious process, steady shots, with a minimum of panning, tilting and zooming, are the mark of a professional.[11]

---

[11] To prove this to yourself, view some good motion pictures and documentaries, preferably some that have won awards for excellence in cinematography.

When you use a tripod, make sure that the adjustable legs lock securely. More than one camera has bitten the dust when a tripod collapsed as a result of the adjustable legs not being securely locked.

Because each leg of a tripod can be separately adjusted for height, it is possible to level a tripod on a hillside, stairs, or uneven ground (Figure 5.18). Some tripods have a bubble- or LED-type indicator that can be used to level the tripod and camera.

Tripod Dolly

Tripods can be locked into three-wheeled bases and then rolled from one shooting position to another. (Recall that when a camera is rolled directly toward and away from the subject it is called a *dolly;* and when moved to the left or right it is called a *truck.*) The simple tripod dolly does not allow for smooth trucks and dollies the way a studio camera pedestal does. But, even if the tripod wheels are not used to vary shots while taping, just having a way of rolling the camera from place to place is a convenience in itself. Once the tripod is in position, the wheels can be locked to keep it from moving.

Monopods

A **monopod** or **unipod** is a kind of "one-legged tripod" (admittedly, a contradiction in terms). Monopods are often used by still camera operators covering outdoor sporting events. They are ideal for steadying and holding the weight of a camera, while allowing for rapid changes in camera position. The height of a monopod can be adjusted so that it will bring the viewfinder to eye level. Although a monopod is not as mobile as a shoulder mount, it does offer more stability.

Camera Jibs

With the advent of lightweight video cameras, the large, heavy camera cranes used in previous decades have given way to **camera jibs,** which are much smaller, lighter and easier and faster to maneuver (Figures 5.19 and 5.20). All operations, including panning, zooming and focusing, are remotely controlled by a single operator seated in front of a video monitor. Because of the speed at which camera jibs can glide along the floor or swoop into the air, they have added new levels of energy and ebullience to television production.

Improvised Camera Supports

Often, it is not possible to use one of the professional camera supports mentioned. But since steady camera shots are so important to professional-looking productions, support can often be improvised.

Figure 5.19 With the advent of light-weight video cameras, the large, heavy camera cranes used in previous decades have given way to camera *jibs* that are much smaller, lighter and easier and faster to maneuver. All operations, including panning, zooming and focusing, are remotely controlled by a single operator seated in front of a video monitor.

Figure 5.20 Because of the speed at which camera jibs can glide along the floor or ground, or swoop into the air, they have added new levels of energy and ebullience to television production.

A wheelchair or even a shopping cart can be pressed into service as a dolly. An assistant, taking directions from the camera operator, can push it in any direction, including pulling it backwards. To minimize the effects of small bumps, the zoom lens can be kept in a wide-angle position.

Pan Heads

When the camera is mounted on a tripod, the quality of the **pan head,** the device that attaches the camera to a tripod or dolly, is extremely important for smooth pans and tilts.

Friction Heads

Friction heads are the least expensive type of pan head. By turning the **pan handle** of the tripod clockwise until it is tightened down, both the vertical and horizontal movement of the pan head can be locked (Some friction heads have a separate control for locking the panning movement). Friction heads are adequate for simple locked-down camera work. Even though the larger friction pan heads incorporate a counterbalancing spring to control movement, really smooth pans and tilts can be difficult with friction heads. Fortunately, there's a better way.

Fluid Heads

Fluid heads are the most widely used type of head for general field production work (Figure 5.21). The internal parts of fluid heads move through a heavy, viscous liquid that dampens movement and helps ensure smooth pans and tilts.

Although used less often, two other types of camera heads should also be mentioned.

Cam Heads

Cam heads are generally reserved for studios and large studio-type cameras mounted on pedestals. These pan heads make use of several cams or cylinders to control and smooth out the pan and tilt movements.

Gear Heads

Gear heads (sometimes called *geared heads*) have long been the number one pan head choice in 35mm motion picture work. More recently they have been used in single-camera HDTV productions Two large wheels at the back of the pan head can be turned or spun to bring about extremely smooth and carefully controlled pans and tilts. Since the camera is supported entirely by the two gear chains, a pan handle isn't needed. Gear heads take experience to operate, and they do not lend themselves to covering fast-moving or unpredictable subject matter.

CAMERA PROMPTING DEVICES

People who work in front of the camera use various prompting methods to aid them in their on-camera delivery. Many news reporters working in the field simply rely on hand-held note cards or a small notebook containing names, figures and basic facts. Reporters typically memorize their opening and closing on-camera comments for a field report and then speak from notes or even read a fully written script while continuing with off-camera narration.

Figure 5.21   Although various types of pan heads have been devised for camcorders, the type that has found the most favor among ENG and EFP camera operators is the fluid head. The internal parts of fluid heads move through a heavy, viscous liquid that dampens movement and helps ensure smooth pans and tilts.

Some on-camera people prefer large posterboard cue cards with the script written out with a bold black marker. But this approach has definite limitations. Not only does the use of cue cards require the aid of an extra person, a **card puller,** but the talent must constantly be looking slightly off to the side of the camera to see the cards.

Some field reporters have mastered the technique of fully writing out the script, recording it on an audio cassette machine, and then playing it back in a small earphone while simultaneously repeating their own words on camera. Although this technique demands practice, concentration and reliable audio playback procedures, once mastered, it can result in highly effective on-camera delivery.

A camera **prompter** (originally referred to as a TelePrompTer, after the original manufacturer) is the most relied on form of prompting, especially for long on-camera segments. There are two types of camera prompters: hard copy and soft copy.

Hard-Copy Prompters

Hard-copy prompters use long rolls of paper or clear plastic. When paper is used, the on-camera script is first typed in large letters in short lines, typically two to four words in length. The paper is attached to two motor driven rollers and the image is picked up by a video camera.

Most prompters rely on a reflected image of the words on a mirror in front of the camera lens. Figure 5.22 illustrates how this works. The video image from the monitor is reflected into a half-silvered mirror mounted at a 45-degree angle. The image of the text as seen by prompter camera is electronically reversed left to right so that the mirror image will appear correct. Since the mirror is only half-silvered, it ends up being a two-way mirror. First, it reflects the image from the video

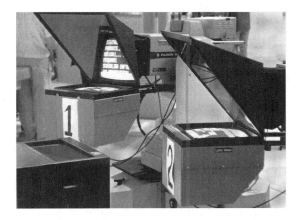

Figure 5.22 Most camera prompters rely on a reflected image of the words on a mirror in front of the camera lens. Being semitransparent, the mirror allows much of the light from the scene being photographed to pass through its surface and go into the camera lens. When the talent looks at the prompter mirror to read the text, it appears as if the person is looking right at the camera lens, and, therefore, at the audience.

prompter screen, allowing the talent to see the slowly moving text. Second, being semi-transparent, the mirror allows much of the light from the scene being photographed to pass through its surface and go into the camera lens. When the talent looks at the prompter mirror to read the text, it appears as if the person is looking right at the camera lens and, therefore, at the audience (In order not to give the appearance of constantly staring into the camera lens, most on-camera people who use prompters periodically glance at their scripts especially as a way of emphasizing facts and figures).

The script is then scrolled by at a carefully controlled speed while the talent reads the text. The speed of the prompter is regulated with a hand-held control by either a prompter operator or the talent.

Outside in bright sunlight two motor-driven rolls of clear plastic with black lettering are occasionally used. Since the clear plastic is illuminated from behind, the lettering can be clearly seen, even under the brightest of conditions.

Soft-Copy Prompters

Soft-copy prompters bypass the hard-copy—paper or plastic—version of the script and use a video screen to directly display the output of a computer. This has several advantages. First, because the text is a direct, electronically generated image, it is sharp and easy to read. Revisions are easy to make without the legibility problems involved in crossing out words or phrases on paper and penciling in last-minute corrections. When computerized word processing is initially used, the extra step of typing up a special prompter script is not required. Once the script is entered into the computer, it can be electronically reformatted and displayed in a standard prompter format (narrow lines with large bold letters). Lastly, if a color video prompter monitor is used, text can be color-keyed to set off the words of different speakers, or special instructions to the talent, which are not meant to be read aloud. In the field laptop computers are commonly used.

When using cue cards or any type of on-camera prompting device there is always the important issue of the compromise involved in the camera-to-subject distance. If the camera is placed close to the talent, which makes it easy to read the prompter, the constant left-to-right reading eye movement can be distracting to an audience. Moving the camera back and zooming in reduces this problem by narrowing the left-to-right motion of the eyes but, at the same time, the extra distance makes the prompter harder to read.

Now that we've covered the camera and its components, we can turn our attention to the subject matter in front of the camera.

CHAPTER 6

COMPOSITION AND GRAPHICS

IN PAINTING, AN understanding of paint, brushes and canvass is considered fundamental. In videography an understanding of cameras, lenses, VCRs and editing equipment is fundamental. In any medium, those who do not get beyond a basic understanding of the tools of the trade never distinguish themselves. At best, they will be considered good technicians. Only when an individual can master the basic tools and then use them to express meaningful ideas in creative and even artistic ways will the work be considered praiseworthy or even exemplary.

Have you ever wondered why certain paintings endure over the centuries and become priceless, while others fall into oblivion? Although art critics have been trying to explain that for centuries, most agree that the difference hinges on an elusive element called artistic talent. Although we don't know all of the factors of talent, we do know that, in the case of art, it goes far beyond a familiarity with the basic elements—paint, brushes and canvass. As we pointed out in Chapter 2, this talent involves an ability to effectively use the medium to create an emotional experience in the viewer (Figure 6.1).

FORM VS. CONTENT

If a scene in a production is striking, dramatic or humorous, we tend to overlook minor technical weaknesses. On the other hand, a scene can be well-exposed, in sharp focus, have perfect color balance and be well lit (in other words, have good

Figure 6.1   Have you ever wondered why certain paintings endure over the centuries and become priceless, while others fall into oblivion? In both art and videography the elusive attribute called *talent* goes far beyond a familiarity with the basic elements of the medium—be they paint, brushes and canvass, or cameras, lenses and editors—to an ability to effectively use the medium to create an emotional experience in a viewer.

form) but still lack emotional impact and meaningful content. This situation leads us to the following adage: *content takes precedence over form.* In other words, the intended message in a production is more important than technical excellence or flashy embellishments. At the same time, significant technical problems—poor sound, a jittery camera, or a moving boom shadow in the background—will quickly divert attention away from the message or content.

The Best Work Is Invisible

All of the elements of production—lighting, music, sound, and editing—are best when they can solidly support and enhance content and, at the same time, remain unnoticed by the average viewer. When production elements call attention to themselves—either because they are poor or because they are ostentatious—attention is shifted away from content. In short, production work is generally best when it is, to the average person, invisible. (Of course, if it went by entirely unnoticed or unappreciated, we wouldn't have so many awards for film and television given out each year.)

A Director Directs Attention

Although we generally assume that the term *director* refers to the person's role in directing (steering) the work of production personnel, the term actually has a more important meaning: *one who directs the attention of viewers.* In this role the director moves from form into content and concentrates on skillfully and creatively using the tools of the medium to regularly direct the audience's attention to critical aspects of the message. Generally, the basic "message" has already been set down by the writer and producer. The director's role becomes one of directing the viewer's attention to a sequence of elements that will impart the intended meaning or message to the viewer.

In a sense the director is a tour guide for viewers. But instead of saying "if you will look out the window on the left of the bus, you will see. . . ," a good director cuts to a close-up of whatever is important for the audience to see at that moment. This could be considered an **insert shot,** or a close-up of something significant in the overall scene. The use of an insert shot is simply a way of directing attention to that significant element. The insert forces the audience to look at an aspect of the overall scene; at the same time, it brings out details that may not be readily apparent.

Good tour guides also help the audience understand things by adding significant information along the way. Good directors do the same. This could be considered a **cutaway**—cutting away from the central scene to bring in related material. In an interview with animal rights activists, the director might cut away to footage of animals being kept in distressing conditions.

One of the major roles of production tools is also to enhance the basic message. Music is a production tool when it enhances the atmosphere, tips us off to danger, or sets the mood for romance. Lighting can likewise suggest a cheerful atmosphere, or a dark, dim and seedy environment. Sets and props can do the same; plus, in a dramatic production, they can tell us a great deal about a character. A good example of this is an **atmosphere introduction,** a technique whereby a director tips us off to important things about characters by introducing us first to their environment or surroundings. Starting a dramatic production with a slow pan across a bright, immaculate, airy penthouse apartment garnished with ultramodern furniture and paintings can "speak volumes" about the person who lives there. Another example is shown in Figure 6.2.

Figure 6.2 An *atmosphere introduction* is a technique used to introduce a viewer to important information about characters by showing us their environment or surroundings. What would this dwelling say about the person who lives here?

All of the things we've been discussing can be included in the general term composition; some of them will be elaborated on in later chapters. For the remainder of this chapter we'll concentrate on a narrower and more traditional definition of the term.

Defining Composition

Composition can be defined as the orderly arrangement of elements in a scene which, when taken as a whole, conveys intent and meaning. The principles of both static composition and dynamic composition apply to television production. **Static composition** covers not only the inherent content of fixed images such as paintings or still photos, but also the basic elements that make up video scenes. **Dynamic composition** goes a step further and takes into consideration the effect of time: moment-to-moment change. This change can be within a single shot (primarily camera or talent moves), or it can apply to the overall effect of intrascene elements and editing.

By carefully studying the most enduring and aesthetically pleasing paintings over the centuries, as well as the most effective film and video scenes of the past 50 years, certain artistic principles emerge. These principles govern things we'll be discussing: the use of leading lines, framing, placement of the center of interest, and balance of mass and tone.

Rules vs. Guidelines

Even though these principles seem well established, they should nonetheless be considered guidelines and not rules. Composition is an art and not a science. If composition were a science, it could be dictated by a fixed set of rules and would end up being rigid and predictable, without room for creativity—and we could probably turn the whole process over to computers.

Since composition is part art, the guidelines can occasionally be broken. But, when they are, it is generally by someone who understands the principles and recognizes how, in the interest of greater impact, they can be successfully transcended in certain instances. When the vast majority of individuals break the guidelines, it is because they are not aware of them. The results speak loud and clear: weak, confusing and amateurish-looking work.

We will introduce 15 guidelines for composition. Loosely organized around these will be a number of related subtopics.

GUIDELINES FOR COMPOSITION

Guideline 1: Clearly Delineate Your Objectives

First, *clearly delineate your objectives and hold to them throughout the production.* The objectives or central intent of a production can be anything from an exercise in plain escapism to a treatise on spiritual enlightenment.

This guideline applies to both the total production and to each shot within the production. Few people would start writing a sentence without any idea of what they wanted to say. Visual statements are no different. If you don't know the specific purpose of the shot in the total production, you cannot expect your audience to somehow come away with a clear message. In fact, whatever meaning the shot might intrinsically contain will probably be confused or even buried by irrelevant and distracting elements.

Good writers, producers, directors and editors know the purpose of each scene. In a dramatic scene they might say, "Here we need to suggest a spark of affection between John and Sabrina." In a scene in a documentary a director might tell the videotape editor, "We need to make it clear here that this is a tedious and dangerous process."

So, before you roll tape on any shot, two things should be clearly established in your mind: the specific reason for the shot and the purpose of the shot within the overall production. "I couldn't resist it; it was such a pretty shot," is not a legitimate reason for including an extraneous scene in a production, no matter how pretty or interesting it is.

Bit Rate and Boredom   In electronics the term *bit rate* refers to the amount of data (or bits of information) transmitted per unit of time. By twisting this term slightly we can apply it to television production. The "data" in the case of production content, however, is quite diverse; it consists of such things as ideas per second, concepts per second, thrills per second, laughs per second and surprises per second.

The speed at which this information (data) is presented is directly related to the ability of a production to hold viewer interest. If information is presented either too slowly or at a level that is beneath an audience, the production is perceived as being boring. If it is presented too quickly or in too abstract a fashion, an audience can become lost and frustrated. In either case the audience will probably quickly consider other media options.

The speed at which ideas are presented has increased dramatically in recent years. We can clearly see this in long-running TV series. Compare specific soap operas of five years ago to the same productions as they are being done today. In order to stay competitive—hold an audience—these programs now feature exotic locations, faster cutting, greater and more frequent emotional swings, faster-moving and richer story lines, and those two ingredients relied on to increase the flow of adrenaline: regular dips into violence, or the threat of violence, and into sex, or the possibility of sex.

In novels, authors used to spend many pages elaborately setting scenes. Now readers are apt to say, "Enough! Get to the point!" Television writers used to be content following a single dramatic idea or plot for an entire show. To hold an audience today, dramatic television typically consists of numerous plots and sub-plots intricately woven together. In terms of assimilated ideas per unit of time, viewers have simply become more demanding.

"But," the question is often asked, "isn't good production always good production, no matter how much time passes?" Unfortunately, from a commercial perspective, the answer is "no." For example, to the uninitiated, most of yesterday's classic films are rather boring; most simply move too slowly to hold the attention of today's audiences. *Citizen Kane,* considered by many film historians to be this country's greatest film, is now difficult to get a group of average people to sit through. The film is also in black and white. Electronically as well as psychologically, color represents more "bits per second" of information.

Nice, but Not Essential   Including non-essential material in a production slows down the communication of information; and *slow* is almost the same as *boring* in today's fast-paced film and television fare. This brings us to an important maxim: *if in doubt, leave it out.* Once you know the purpose (thesis) of a production or a sequence within a production, include only what's relevant to support that idea.

Depicting Emotional States   In depicting emotions we often find the greatest difficulty in determining what's relevant. Seemingly unrelated scenes of people running through stalled city traffic, lines of people pushing through turnstiles and jamming escalators wouldn't be irrelevant to establishing a frenzied state of mind in a character trying to cope with life in the city. But a shot of "a darling little girl with a red ribbon in her hair" standing alone not only would leave the audience wondering what her role was, but would probably mislead them into believing that there is a relationship between her and the central character.

Finally, a good director and editor know when a point has been made and when to move on. As we will see in the chapters on editing, there are important implications here for how long scenes should be. For now we can summarize this aspect of composition by saying, *a scene, or series of scenes, should never be continued for one second longer than it takes to convey the essential information.* It is better to leave your audience wishing for a little more than a little less. When they want to see less, your production is in trouble.

In the case of our frenzied central character, a rush-hour montage of a few scenes will quickly establish the pressures surrounding him or her. Having then made that point, we will want to move on; in this case possibly to show the lack of success our frenzied character is having in coping with it all.

Guideline 2: Strive for Scenic Unity

Strive for a feeling of unity. If a good film or prize-winning photo is studied, it is generally evident that the elements in the shot have been selected or arranged so they "pull together" to support the basic idea. That idea may be just an abstract feeling. When the elements of a shot combine to support a basic visual statement the shot is said to have *unity.*

This concept also applies to such things as lighting, color, wardrobes, sets and settings. You might, for example, decide to use muted colors throughout a production. Or you may want to create a certain atmosphere with low-key lighting and settings with "earthy colors" and a lot of texture. By deciding on certain appropriate themes such as these, you can create an overall feeling or "look," that will give your production unity (Figure 6.3).

Guideline 3: Compose Around a Single Center of Interest

Compose and design individual scenes around a single center of interest. Before rolling tape on a scene, ask yourself what major element in the shot communicates your basic idea? Starting with the most obvious, it may be the person speaking. Or it may be something quite subtle and symbolic. Whatever it is, the secondary elements within the scene should support and not draw attention away from it.

Multiple centers of interest may work in three-ring circuses where viewers are able to fully shift their interest from one event to another. But competing centers of interest within a single visual frame weaken, divide and confuse meaning. Think of each shot as a statement. An effective written statement should be cast around a central idea and swept clean of anything that does not support, explain or in some way add to that idea. Consider this "sentence": "Woman speaking, strange painting on the wall, coat rack behind her head, interesting brass figurines on desk, sound of airplane flying by, man moving in background. . . ." Although we would laugh at such a "sentence," some videographers are prone to create visual statements that include such unrelated and confusing elements.

Figure 6.3   When the elements of a shot combine to support a basic visual statement, the shot is said to have *unity.* This concept also applies to such things as lighting, color, wardrobes, sets and settings. By deciding on certain appropriate themes such as these, you can create an overall feeling or "look" that will give a production a distinctive character.

Develop an Objective Eye   We are not suggesting that you eliminate everything except the center of interest, just whatever does not in some way support or, at the least, does not detract from the central idea being presented. A scene may, in fact, be cluttered with objects and people, such as an establishing shot of a person working in a busy television newsroom. But each of the things should fit in and belong; nothing should "upstage" the intended center of interest. A master (wide) shot of an authentic interior of an 18th-century farmhouse may include dozens of objects. But each of the objects should add to the overall statement: "18th-century farmhouse." An interview with a scientist may take place in an office full of scientific apparatus. But the apparatus belong there and represents the "natural habitat" of the scientist. Assuming that you are focusing on the scientist, just make sure you can put these supporting elements in a visually secondary position.

   Remember that the viewer has a limited time—generally only a few seconds—to understand the content and meaning of a shot. If some basic meaning doesn't come though before the shot is changed, the viewer will miss the point of the scene.

The Eye Sees Selectively   The eye sees selectively and in three dimensions; it thereby tends to exclude what is not relevant at the moment. It is easy for the eye to focus on a particular object and not be conscious of others. If you are talking to someone you will probably not be distracted by a coat rack directly behind the person's head. A TV camera does not see in the same way—just as the microphone is not able to hear selectively and screen out the sound of a passing airplane or a nearby conversation.

Use Selective Focus   If you were to videotape an interview with the woman in her office, described earlier, the coat rack might appear to be growing out of her head. Assuming for some reason that the coat rack can't be moved or the camera angle can't be shifted to exclude it, you might be able to throw it out of focus by using selective focus (refer to Figure 4.15). From Chapter 4 recall that shooting from a distance and using a zoom lens at an extended focal length (zoomed in) while shooting at a wide f-stop decreases depth of field and increases the selective focus effect. In order not to be distracting, competing objects need to be thrown far enough out of focus so that our eye will not be drawn to them.

A Basic Component of "The Film Look"   As we've previously noted, part of "the film look" that many people like centers on selective focus. Early films were not highly sensitive to light and lenses had to be used at relatively wide apertures (f-stops) to attain sufficient exposure. This was fortunate, in a way, because by focusing on the key element in each shot (and throwing those in front and behind that area out of focus) audiences were immediately led to the scene's center of interest and not distracted by anything else. Even with today's high-speed film emulsions, directors of photography in film strive to retain the selective focus effect by shooting under comparatively low light levels.

   The same principles that have worked so well in film can also be used in video. By throwing foreground and background objects out of focus, the videographer can reduce visual confusion, while directing attention to the center of interest (refer to Figure 4.15). This level of image control takes extra planning when you use today's highly sensitive CCD cameras. The auto-iris circuit generally adjusts the f-stop to an aperture that brings both the foreground and background into focus. To make use of the creative control inherent in selective focus, high shutter speeds, neutral density filters or controlled lighting must be used. The control of lighting is also important in another way.

Use Lighting to Focus Attention   The eye is drawn to the brighter areas of a scene. This means that the prudent use of lighting can be a composition tool, in this case to emphasize important scenic elements and to de-emphasize others. As discussed in the upcoming chapter on lighting, barn doors are commonly used with lights to downgrade the importance of elements in a scene by making them slightly darker.

Shift the Center of Interest   In static composition, scenes maintain a single center of interest; in dynamic composition, centers of interest can change over time. Although our eye may be dwelling on the scene's center of interest, it will readily

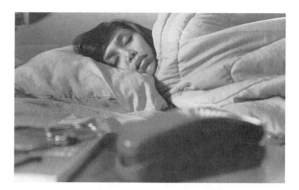

Figure 6.4   Through *rack focus* we have the ability to shift viewer attention within a scene. In the first of these three photos we see a woman sleeping. As the phone rings in the foreground we shift attention to the ringing phone by bringing it into focus. Finally, we shift focus again as the receiver is picked up and the woman starts talking.

be drawn to movement in a secondary area of the picture. Thus, movement can be used to shift attention. Someone entering the scene would be a good example.

We can also force the audience to shift their attention through the technique of **rack focus,** changing the focus of the lens from one object to another. Figure 6.4 illustrates how attention can be shifted with rack focus.

Shift Attention with Sound   In stereo and surround-sound we can shift attention from the center of interest to another area through sound placement. This is typically accompanied by movement, as, for example, when something that origi-

Figure 6.5 Except, possibly, for close-ups of people, a traditional guideline in composition is to place the center of interest near one of the crosspoints indicated by the *rule of thirds*. Although the rule of thirds is traditionally cited as a guideline in composition, other factors, such as balance, the placement of leading lines, etc., are often a stronger indicator of subject placement.

nally held a secondary role at one side of the frame suddenly "comes to life" and becomes the center of interest. There are many good examples of this technique in horror films.

Guideline 4: Observe Proper Subject Placement

In "gun sight fashion," most weekend snapshooters, armed with their disposable, point-and-shoot cameras, feel they have to place the center of interest—be it Uncle Henry, or the Eiffel Tower—squarely in the center of the frame. Quite often this weakens composition.

Rule of Thirds Except, possibly, for close-ups of people, it is often best to place the center of interest near one of the points indicated by the rule of thirds. In the **rule of thirds** the total image area is divided vertically and horizontally into three equal sections (Figure 6.5). Although it is often best to place the center of interest somewhere along the two horizontal and two vertical lines, generally, composition is even stronger if the center of interest falls near one of the four cross-points.

Handle Horizontal and Vertical Lines Weekend snapshooters also typically go to some effort to make sure that horizon lines are perfectly centered in the middle of the frame. This severely weakens composition by splitting the frame into two equal halves. According to the rule of thirds, horizon lines should be either in the upper third or the lower third of the frame. In the same way, vertical lines shouldn't divide the frame into two equal parts. From the rule of thirds, we can see that it's generally best to place a dominant vertical line either one-third or two-thirds of the way across the frame.

It is also a good idea to break up or intersect dominant, unbroken lines with some scenic element. Otherwise, the scene may seem divided. A horizon can be broken by an object in the foreground. Often this can be done by simply moving the camera slightly. A vertical line can be interrupted by something as simple as a tree branch. (Videographers have been known to have someone hold a tree branch so that it projects into the side of a shot in order to break up a line or make composition more interesting.)

Guideline 5: Observe Tonal Balance

The tone (brightness and darkness) of objects in a scene suggests weight. Against light backgrounds dark objects seem heavier than light objects. Once you realize that brightness influences mass, you can begin to "feel" the visual "weight" of objects within a scene—and strive for balance.

Guideline 6: Balance Mass

Just as a room would seem out of balance if all of the furniture were piled up on one side, the mass of a scene must be *balanced* to be aesthetically pleasing. Regardless of their actual physical weight, large objects in a scene seem heavier than small ones. By objectively viewing the elements in a scene, you will learn to see their "psychological weight" in composition. To do this it helps to imagine a fulcrum or balance point at the bottom center of each of your shots.

Several things can be done to try to balance a shot: the camera can be panned to the left or right, a new camera angle can be selected, or the lens can be zoomed in or out to include and exclude objects. Seldom will things actually have to be moved around.

Guideline 7: Create a Pattern of Meaning

Use a combination of scenic elements to create meaning. Most people are familiar with the ink blot tests used by psychiatrists. By presenting someone with a meaningless collection of shapes and forms an individual draws from his or her own background and thoughts and projects their own meaning into the abstract images. ("That looks like a mother scolding her son"; or "that looks like a school being crushed by a bulldozer.")

In the same way, if a variety of objects appear in a still photo or video scene, we try to make sense (possibly even unconsciously) out of why they are there and what they represent. We assume that things don't just come together by accident.

Good directors take advantage of this tendency and pay careful attention to the specific elements included in a scene. The most obvious example of this is the *atmosphere introduction,* where a director will open on a scene full of clues about the central characters, long before we see them. Early morning shots of a room littered with beer cans, overflowing ash trays, overturned chairs and shoes would not only suggest what happened the night before, but would tell us a lot about the kind of people who were there.

Elements in a shot may be bold and obvious, or they may be subtly designed to suggest almost subconscious meaning. Film critics have spent many hours discussing the symbolism and subconscious levels of meaning in films by directors such as Federico Fellini. Quite in contrast to the highly abstract meaning of many Fellini films is the concrete meaning required for news and documentary work.

While the director of a dramatic piece should, ideally, be a master at creating illusions and emotional responses, the job in ENG and documentary work is to clearly show things the way they are and let events and facts speak for themselves. This does not rule out striving for new and creative ways of presenting subject matter. Often, only by presenting the familiar in an entirely new way is an audience awakened, or possibly re-awakened, to its reality.

The Concrete and the Abstract   Whereas in news the object is to present images as completely and clearly as possible, a shot in a dramatic production should lead viewers toward intended meaning without being totally concrete. Most intelligent viewers want a bit of room to think and interpret on their own. The term "on the nose" is used in feature film writing to denote script dialogue or shots which have gone too far in "saying it all." In deciding just how far to go along the abstract-to-concrete continuum videographers must know their target audience. Intelligence and education are related to an ability to understand abstract ideas. This is why simplistic presentations are resented by adults and, at the same time, why the classics in music, art, literature, TV and film are not widely appreciated.

Considering the economic realities of the marketplace, videographers who wish to be successful do not have the luxury of blithely "doing their own thing" and not concerning themselves about whether their audience will understand their work. Good composition is primarily effective visual communication, and the most effective communication takes place when a videographer understands an audience and is able to steer the middle path between being totally concrete and "on the noise," and being so abstract that the audience misses the intended message.

Include Multiple Levels of Meaning   Is it possible to have it both ways? Yes, sometimes. Films and television programs can be designed to have multiple levels of meaning. Disney films such as *Aladdin* and *The Lion King* are examples. While children are being entertained by the animated characters and the simple story line, the grown-ups are picking up on the adult humor.

Figure 6.6   *Leading lines* are an effective way to lead a viewer's eyes through a scene, and especially to a scene's center of interest. Lines can also convey different feelings (Figure 6.7).

Although many illustrations could be given, let's consider just one more example—a scene from the highly successful motion picture, *The Graduate*. The closing scene can be interpreted in at least two ways. Some will say, and want to believe, that the film has a happy ending; others—equipped with clues that are integrated within scenes throughout the film—will say just the opposite. Possibly the real meaning of the ending doesn't matter, as long as it provides an efficacious experience for different people.

Suffice it to say, to be most successful, movies and television programs must strive for a broad-based appeal. If a writer, director and editor can "layer" a production with multiple levels of meaning and successfully provide "something for everyone" (which is, admittedly, not an easy task), the production will have a much greater chance of success.

Guideline 8: Use Leading Lines

The boundaries of objects in a shot normally consist of lines: straight, curved, vertical, horizontal and diagonal. Our eyes travel along these lines as they move from one part of the frame to another. Knowing this, it becomes the job of videographers to use these lines to lead the attention of viewers to the parts of the frame they wish to emphasize, especially toward the center of interest (Figure 6.6). When

Figure 6.7 Lines can be used in composition to suggest meaning. As shown here, strong vertical lines lend strength, power and dignity to a scene. Horizontal lines suggest stability and openness; curved lines suggest grace, beauty, elegance, movement, and sensuality; sharp, jagged lines connote violence or destruction; broken lines suggest discontinuity.

used in this way these lines are referred to as **leading lines** because they are selected or arranged to lead the viewer's eyes toward the center of interest.

In addition to moving our eyes around the frame, lines can suggest meaning in themselves. Straight, vertical lines suggest dignity, strength, power, formality, height and restriction (Figure 6.7). Horizontal lines suggest stability and openness. Diagonal lines can impart a dynamic and exciting look. Curved lines suggest grace, beauty, elegance, movement, and sensuality. Sharp, jagged lines connote violence or destruction, and broken lines suggest discontinuity.

Guideline 9: Frame the Central Subject Matter

By putting objects at one or more edges of the picture, a shot can be framed. *Framing* a scene holds attention within the shot and keeps viewers' attention from

Figure 6.8   By putting objects at the edges of the picture, a shot can be *framed.* Note here how the tree and shrubbery not only frame this photo but add depth and dimension. Recall that in Figure 6.3 the arch also adds an effective frame to the picture.

wandering or being distracted from the center of interest. To cite a common example, a leaning tree branch at the top of a scenic shot breaks up a bright sky and acts as a visual barrier or "stop point" for the top of the frame. Note in Figure 6.8 how framing a shot with foreground objects adds depth and dimension.

Guideline 10: Make Use of Visual Perspective

Use the effect of visual perspective to enhance or support the scene's basic idea. Although many people assume that "the camera never lies," the interpretation of scenes can be significantly altered through lighting, camera angles and lens focal length. As noted previously, camera positions and lens focal length alter the apparent perspective in a shot, as well as the apparent distance between objects. A minimal camera-to-subject distance coupled with a short focal length lens, or a zoom lens in its widest position, exaggerates perspective. Parallel lines will be wide apart in the foreground of the picture and rapidly and dramatically converge after a short distance (Figure 6.9). Note the different impression of the building in Figures 4.5 and 4.8. By creatively controlling such things as lens focal lengths and camera distance, quite different impressions about a subject can be conveyed.

Guideline 11: Convey Meaning Through Colors and Tones

Select colors and tones that convey meaning. A scene that is dark with many large shadow areas (a dark bedroom or a back alley at midnight) produces a far different feeling from a scene that is brightly lit (the stage of a variety show or a beach at noon). The predominance of bright or dark areas carries strong psychological

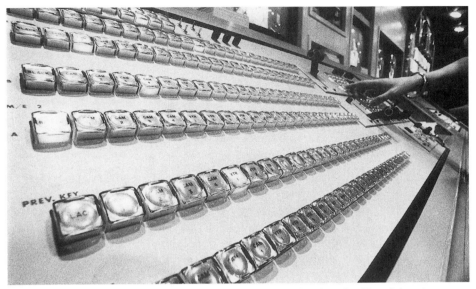

Figure 6.9 A minimal camera-to-subject distance coupled with a short focal length lens (or a zoom lens in its widest position) exaggerates perspective. Parallel lines will be wide apart in the foreground and rapidly and dramatically converge after a short distance.

meaning in itself regardless of what else is going on. Just as the selection of lighting and monochrome values in a scene suggests mood and meaning, so does the choice of color. In general, bright colors add energy to composition, while lighter hues impart a serene, harmonious and stable look.

There have been numerous studies on color preferences and the meaning ascribed to certain colors. We know, for example, that color preferences vary with age, sex and race. In general we also know that people prefer to see colors "in their place." Magenta-to-red colors may be popular until they are brought into a kitchen setting. A particular shade of green may be an attractive color until it becomes associated with the walls of a hospital room.

Surrounding colors also greatly affect color preference. When a color is used near its complement, its preference rating usually rises, as long as the complementary color is subdued and is not brighter or more intense than the original color.

Just as people prefer a balance between mass and tone in composition, they also prefer a color balance as seen on the color wheel (refer to Figure 3.11). In particular, they prefer a balance between calming and stimulating colors.

In balancing colors in a scene, be aware that it will take a larger area of cool colors to balance hot colors. Even though people prefer color balance, many times a videographer will want to intentionally skew this balance to achieve an intended psychological effect. For example, if a scene contains cool, pastel colors such as light green, the effect it creates on the viewer will be very different from the effect of a scene that contains fully saturated, hot colors, such as deep orange and burgundy.

Finally, keep in mind that our eyes initially tend to be drawn to the "warmer" areas of a picture. So, all things being equal, areas that are yellow, red and orange will be noticed before those that are blue, green or purple. By making your center of interest warm in color or light in tone (or both), you will immediately draw attention to it.

Guideline 12: Avoid Mergers

Avoid tonal mergers, dimensional mergers and border mergers.

Tonal Mergers   Important objects in a scene appear to blend together and lose their identity in what is called a **tonal merger.** This may be caused by a lack of lens sharpness or lighting problems or it may simply occur because the objects are of similar tonal or color values. Objects placed at different distances from a light will vary greatly in tonal value, depending on the level of illumination they receive. We've all seen flash pictures where someone in the foreground of the picture ends up being a washed out "white ghost" and someone in the background is completely black and without any trace of skin color.

Dimensional Mergers   We've noted that the eye sees selectively and in three dimensions. By closing one eye a videographer can often get a better idea of how a scene will appear when the third dimension is removed. At best, **dimensional mergers** can cause important scene elements to run together and lose meaning; at worst, they look ludicrous, such as when a fountain or tree is jutting out of an unsuspecting person's head. Although selective focus and the use of a backlight can alleviate this problem, the best solution, when possible, is to recompose the shot by either shifting the camera angle or rearranging the elements.

Border Mergers   Finally, **border mergers** occur when subject matter is cut off by the edge of the frame at an inappropriate point. A side view of a car showing all but the back wheels will probably give you an uncomfortable feeling that the back end of the car is just hanging in the air without visible back support. A shot of an individual cropped at the knees looks awkward. Cropping off feet or hands in a shot gives a similar result. A shot of a woman in a strapless dress cropped just above the top of the dress gives the illusion she is "topless." Tightening or loosening the shot would solve the problem in each case.

Guideline 13: Control the Number of Prime Objects

Control the number of prime objects in the scene. Generally, an odd number of primary objects provides stronger composition than an even number. In Figure 6.10 the composition seems somewhat divided. The addition of a third element seems to add unity. However, with the addition of a fourth element, the composition again seems divided. Beyond about five prime objects, the odd-even distinction gets lost in the overall complexity of the composition.

Figure 6.10 Generally, an odd number of primary objects provides stronger composition than an even number. With two objects composition seems divided. The addition of a third element adds unity. Note that when a fourth element is added, the composition again seems divided.

Guideline 14: Balance Complexity and Order

This aspect of static composition can be stated with the rule: *complexity without order produces confusion; order without complexity produces boredom.* A shot of a banana against a medium gray background will probably end up being a rather dull visual experience. Add a few apples, some grapes and an interesting fruit bowl, and you'll have a more engaging picture. But throw in 500 randomly arranged bananas on top of this and you'll end up with a visual muddle. Suffice it to say, the most interesting composition is a balance between order and complexity.

Guideline 15: Utilize the Meaning Inherent in Movement

Utilize the meaning inherent in the direction of movement. Where action comes from and moves to is significant. For example, movement from dark areas to light areas can symbolize liberation or emotional uplift. Upward motion—even something as simple as an individual getting out of a chair—catches attention because it suggests progress or advancement. Downward motion often connotes the opposite—a man collapsing into an overstuffed chair.

Action that progresses toward the camera is more powerful than action that moves away from the camera. The object itself may be moving, or the camera shot may change through a dolly or zoom. Often, televised speeches are worked out with camera operators so that the camera is zoomed in to add emphasis to a certain part of the speech. With this in mind, it is generally better (psychologically) during a speech to dolly in for emphasis and then cut (rather than zoom) back, as necessary, to a medium or wide shot.

Left-to-right movement is more engaging than right-to-left movement. The most engaging type of movement is diagonal, especially when it's from the lower left of the frame to the upper right. Related to this concept, a **canted camera** shot (a tilted camera angle, also called a Dutch angle), especially from a low angle, is often used to connote energy or power (Figure 6.11).

GRAPHICS

Television graphics range all the way from displaying the name of the person being interviewed in the lower one-third of a video frame to flashy computer-generated animated sequences that introduce "Monday Night At the Movies." Whereas all such visual material used to have to be limited to whatever could be directly reproduced by a video camera, today these images are entirely computer generated.

Titles

In much the same way as you can use a word-processor to create text on a computer screen, you can use a character generator (**CG**) to create text on a television screen. But with a CG you typically have a much wider variety of options and embellishments.

- You can readily switch to different type styles and sizes.
- You can add drop shadows, underlines, etc., to lettering.
- You can animate text sequences in various ways, such as making words grow, shrink, spin, tumble, or just move vertically and horizontally through the frame.
- You can create or scan in drawings or photos, and combine them in various ways to form a single image.
- You can add a full range of colors to graphics, or alter existing colors in graphics or photos.
- You can create three-dimensional figures that move through time and space and range all the way from abstract to lifelike.

As in the case of editing equipment there are two approaches: *software based* (which uses a desktop computer as a platform), and *dedicated* (equipment built to

Figure 6.11 A low camera angle often lends dominance or power to a subject.

perform one task, in this case, television graphics). Although dedicated equipment tends to have more specialized features and to be faster, the trend has been toward software based systems, at least for routine work. There are two reasons for this: the cost of software-based systems tends to be less, and software lends itself to quick and easy upgrades.[1]

With both approaches, graphics are normally created one screen at a time and stored as "pages." These pages can be recalled manually or automatically in any sequence. Simple graphics, such as lower-third names or titles, can be quickly retrieved by electronic page number and keyed in (superimposed)[2] over background material, such as a close-up of a guest. Pages can also be combined in layers

---

[1] Software versions are normally indicated by number. The first version (1.0) will be followed by a number of minor improvements (versions 1.1, 1.2, 1.3, etc.). Major upgrades will be indicated by version number changes such as 2.0, 3.0, or 4.0.

[2] Although the process isn't used much anymore, strictly speaking, the term *superimpose* refers to a process of combining two video sources in a kind of double-exposure effect where both images are present in the same place at the same time. In *keying* two images are also combined, but the material that is keyed in is electronically substituted for the background material. Because keys are opaque, they end up being much sharper and clearer than *supers* (superimposed images).

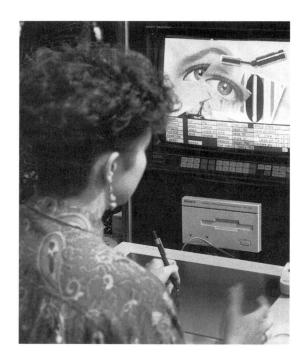

Figure 6.12   Normally, paint programs include two basic types of tools: geometric tools, which let you start with basic geometric forms and modify them as needed, and free-hand tools, which enable you to work like an artist on a piece of canvass.

or cells. This means that one or more images—general backgrounds, photos, product logos (symbols), etc.—can be combined as needed to build rich, "multilayered" graphics.

Image Editors

Image editors can be divided into two main categories: paint programs and image processors. Almost all are based on software designed and run on desktop computers.

Paint Programs   Paint programs are primarily designed for the creation of new art work. Although in some cases you might want to start with some scanned artwork and build on that, paint programs contain all of the tools necessary to completely create images. (*Scanned artwork* refers to pictures and graphics that have been copied by a camera or flatbed scanner—similar to a photocopy machine—digitized, and then stored on computer disks for use.) Normally, paint programs include two basic types of tools: geometric tools, which let you start with basic geometric forms and modify them as needed, and free-hand tools, which enable you to work like an artist on a piece of canvass (Figure 6.12). Freehand tools include a pencil, paintbrush, and airbrush, each of which can be varied in many ways. Paint programs have become so sophisticated that they can even simulate the brush

Figure 6.13 Computer drawing programs not only create scenes that rival reality, but also fully animate them. It is becoming difficult in television today to tell real-life scenes from computer simulations.

strokes of famous painters such as Monet and Van Gogh. In the hands of an artist, today's paint programs can be used to create anything from abstract art to illustrations with photographic realism (Figure 6.13).

Image Processors   Although the line between paint programs and image processors can be rather blurry, image processors are primarily designed to work with existing images, such as scanned photos and video grabs (images captured in still form from a video display and then saved to computer). They provide tools to select various areas of the captured image on the basis of color, luminance level, shape, and so on. Once these specific areas are isolated, they can be modified in numerous ways without affecting the rest of the image. Image processors can emulate all photographic darkroom effects, including lightening and darkening portions of the image, altering contrast, changing color balance, reversing polarity (the tonal scale), and combining images. In addition there are effects that go beyond basic darkroom capabilities: sharpening the image, airbrushing, and the application of various image manipulation filters, including all of the effects you normally see done to a video image by a special effects generator. Figure 6.14 illustrates some of the effects possible.

Figure 6.14   Video special effects programs can alter reality in spectacular ways. Here, two simple computer generated variations on an original scene are illustrated.

3-D Modeling and Animation Programs

Paint programs and image editors are primarily designed to manipulate still images. Today, however, we commonly see simulated three-dimensional images created by computers. These are animated-type video images that can be made to move in any desired way. Many such images rival photographic realism. Once the basic elements are created (modeled), both the "camera" (viewer perspective) position, and the "lights" (the apparent illumination on the scene) can be changed as desired. The effect of "lens" focal length can be selected to provide different visual perspectives on scenes. Simulated or hard and soft light (covered in Chapter 7) can be applied to objects and scenes. Unlike two-dimensional objects, which appear to have nothing behind them, three-dimensional objects consist of full forms (within computer memory) that can be made to rotate a full 360 degrees if desired. Typically, the various elements (objects) in a scene are constructed in independent *layers* in computer memory. Objects in each of the layers can be made to move or change in any way desired without affecting the other image layers. Among other things this allows the various layers to move at different speeds, as they naturally would if a camera were following a subject moving past foreground and background objects in a scene.

Typically, images are constructed in the manner illustrated in Figure 6.15. First, a "wire frame" outline is drawn. This frame can be automatically filled in and covered by the computer program. Surface textures, colors, camera (observer) angles, simulated lens focal length, "lighting" and a host of other variables can be programmed. In a process called **rendering,** the computer can "flesh out" these wire frames using the stipulated variables. When motion is involved, rendering also involves calculating what will take place during action.

Figure 6.15 Today's computer equipment can be used to design scenes with lifelike quality. As shown in panels (a) through (f), this is done in steps. In (a), the basic outline of the room and subject matter is created on the computer screen. Color is added to the lines in (b). In (c), shading and highlights are applied. In (d), the scene begins to take on a realistic quality. Texture mapping is added in (e). And, finally, the addition of shadows and reflections complete the scene (f). All photos © 1990 Pixar, rendered by Thomas Williams and H. B. Siegal using Pixar's PhotoRealistic Renderman™ software.

Since millions of **pixel points** (discrete image points) are involved in rendering, the process involves billions of computer calculations. Therefore, depending on the power of the computer and the complexity of the image and motion, rendering can take from a few seconds to many hours.

The effect of light on the appearance of real or computer-generated objects greatly affects how the subject matter will look. Lighting is the subject of the next chapter.

CHAPTER 7

LIGHTING

TELEVISION IS BASED on the medium of light. Just as sound must be skillfully controlled in audio production, light must be expertly controlled in television. Lighting can emphasize important details or completely hide them. It can flatter a subject by bringing out positive attributes while de-emphasizing or hiding less attractive attributes. As video—and especially HDTV—has begun to emulate the more artistic dimensions of film, there has been a greater emphasis on creative video lighting (Figure 7.1). But, before you can successfully control light, you need to understand its three basic characteristics: quality, color temperature and intensity.

LIGHT COHERENCE

Coherence, often called **quality,** is the hardness or softness of light. Light quality is probably the least understood and the most neglected of the three variables. In Figure 7.2 the objects are exactly the same, and so is the intensity and the color temperature of the lights. The only difference between the photos is the coherence of the light used.

Hard Light

Light that is transmitted directly from a small point source results in relatively coherent (parallel and congruous) rays. This gives the light a hard, crisp, sharply

Figure 7.1 One of the most effective creative tools in production is lighting. More than anything else, good lighting can establish the atmosphere and tone of a dramatic scene.

Figure 7.2 Shiny objects are particularly difficult for video. Fortunately, the knowledgeable use of lighting can solve the problem. When traditional lighting is used, the bright objects darken surrounding areas and cause major problems for video levels. Soft, diffused lighting solves the problem.

Figure 7.3 Several types of lighting instruments used in TV create hard light, including ellipsoidal spotlight shown here. When hard light is used to illuminate a face, the result is less than flattering. But in other applications, such as bringing out the texture in leather, or the engraving on a piece of jewelry, a hard light source can be quite useful.

defined appearance. The light from a clear, unfrosted light bulb, a focused spotlight, or the noonday sun in a clear sky all represent hard light sources.

Hard light casts a sharp, clearly defined shadow—the kind that would be desirable for creating a shadowgram of an animal on a wall with your hands, as well as the kind that, unfortunately, results in undesirable shadows of boom microphones on backgrounds. Several types of lighting instruments used in TV create hard light, including the beam-spot projector and the more commonly used ellipsoidal spotlight (Figure 7.3).

When hard light is used to illuminate a face, imperfections in the skin stand out. The result is less than flattering. But in other applications, such as bringing out the texture in leather, or the engraving on a piece of jewelry, this can be an advantage. In a dramatic scene a hard light source is sometimes used to simulate bright sunlight coming through a window.

Soft Light

Soft (diffused) light has the opposite effect of hard light—especially when lighting angles are also controlled. As shown in Figure 7.2, soft light hides surface irregularities and detail. Spun-glass or stainless-steel **diffusers** are used over the front of lights to soften and diffuse their beams (Figure 7.4). At the same time, diffusers also reduce the intensity of light.

Large **softlights** are used in production studios to create a broad, even area of light. However, because of their size, softlights are difficult to work with in the field, so videographers often rely on **umbrella reflectors** to create a soft lighting effect. As you can see in Figure 7.5, this is simply a light bounced off of the inside of a silver or white umbrella-like reflector. Since soft light tends to hide lines, wrinkles and blemishes, it is desirable in doing "glamour" work (Figure 7.6).

When placed close to the camera, a soft light source minimizes surface detail and the effect is commonly referred to as *flat lighting*. Although it has certain

Figure 7.4 Spun-glass or stainless steel diffusers are used over the front of lights to soften and diffuse their beams. Often videographers rely on umbrella reflectors (Figure 7.5) to create a soft lighting effect.

Figure 7.5 An umbrella reflector is easy to transport and provides soft, even lighting. Since soft light tends to hide lines, wrinkles and blemishes, it is desirable in doing "glamour" work (Figure 7.6).

applications, especially in extreme close-up work where shadows would obscure important details, flat lighting leaves subject matter somewhat "dimensionless." When used over a large area, it can impart an arid and sterile-looking appearance.

Most subject matter will look best when illuminated with a light source somewhere between hard light used at oblique angles (designed to bring out maximum surface detail) and ultrasoft light (designed to hide surface detail and minimize reflections).

Figure 7.6   Soft light is flattering, which makes it ideal for doing such things as cosmetic commercials. At the same time, the soft light minimizes form, detail and dimension in subject matter.

LIGHTING ANGLES

The angle at which light strikes a subject is extremely important in defining its appearance. Light angles establish the appearance of depth, form and texture in subject matter. A hard light source used at an oblique angle (65- to 85-degrees on either side of the camera) will bring out maximum surface detail (Figure 7.7). This effect occurs because, when surface shadows are created, texture (surface detail) is emphasized. Later in the chapter we'll cover the recommended angles for the various lights on a subject.

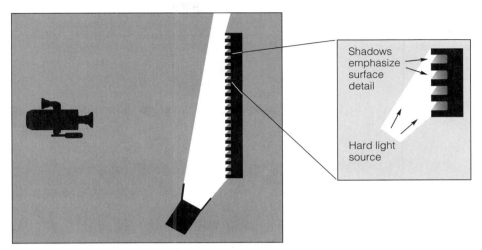

Figure 7.7   Note how a hard light source at an angle of about 70 degrees from the camera (Figure 7.11a) creates the shadow areas (Figure 7.11b) necessary to emphasize surface detail. The effect of this setup is illustrated in Figure 7.10.

COLOR TEMPERATURE

The second attribute of light, color temperature, was introduced in Chapter 3. By flipping to Color Plate 6 you can see the difference between the two basic color standards: 3,200° K for the incandescent lamps used in studios and 5,500° K for average daylight. At this point we need to elaborate a bit on several color temperature issues.

Sunlight's Varying Color Temperature

Although we've said that sunlight is about 5,500° K, the color of sunlight can actually vary rather greatly, depending on the time of day, the amount of haze or smog in the air, and geographic longitude and latitude of the area. Because of its angle to the earth in the early morning and late afternoon, sunlight must travel through more of the earth's atmosphere. The result is that more blue light is absorbed than red (shorter wavelengths of light are more readily absorbed) and the color temperature of the sun is shifted toward red (see Figure 7.8). At midday the temperature of direct sunlight rises to about 5,500° K. However, if the day is hazy or overcast, the temperature may go up to 8,500° K. Pure skylight, coming through a window, for example, can reach much higher color temperatures. Left uncorrected, skylight will impart a cold, blue look to skin tones, generally not a desirable effect.

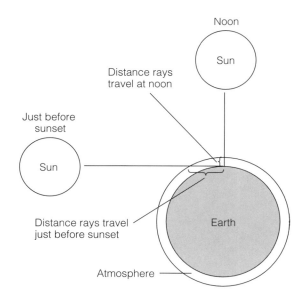

Figure 7.8   Because of its angle to the earth in the early morning and late afternoon, sunlight must travel through more of the earth's atmosphere. The result is that more blue light is absorbed than red (shorter wavelengths of light are more readily absorbed) and the color temperature of the sun is shifted toward red. During midday the temperature of direct sunlight rises to about 5,500° K.

Color Continuity Problems

Because of the significant variations in color temperature that can be encountered in doing on-location work, it is important to color balance video cameras whenever lighting conditions change. For about two hours after sunrise and two hours before sunset, color temperature changes rapidly. And, if the sun moves in or out of cloud cover, color temperatures (and light quality) will dramatically change. Although these changes may not be obvious to the eye, they can present major problems when you attempt to match successive scenes during editing. These color temperature and light quality examples represent two types of *technical continuity problems* (scene-to-scene technical inconsistencies) that you can encounter in video production.

LIGHT INTENSITY

The last characteristic of light that is essential to control is intensity. As we noted in Chapter 5, light intensity is measured in foot-candles (FC) or lux.

Typical Foot-Candle Intensities

To provide some points of reference, sunlight on an average day ranges from 3,000 to 10,000 FC; TV studios are lit at about 200 FC; a bright office has about 40 FC of illumination; moonlight represents about 0.01 FC; and starlight measures a mere 0.000005 FC. Although most TV cameras need at least 100 FC for good quality, many can produce acceptable pictures under one foot-candle of light.

Light Meters

Light meters are used to measure light intensity. As we will see, being able to establish rather exact foot-candle or lux intensities for the various lights is important. There are two types of meters: reflected and incident.

Reflected Light Meters   A **reflected light meter** measures the amount of light being reflected from the main subject matter in a scene. This is the type of built-in light measurement system used by most still cameras. Because this type of meter assumes that all subject matter reflects 18 percent of the light falling on it—a so-called average scene—it can be easily fooled by non-standard subject matter. The accuracy of reflected light readings can be improved by using a spot meter. **Spot meters** are a type of reflected light meter that can measure light within a three- to five-degree angle of acceptance. Whereas general reflected light meters are best used within a few feet or even a few inches from a subject, spot meters make possible light readings from a distance. A spot meter is often favored by lighting directors because they can simply stand next to a camera and compare the contrast and brightness values of subject matter throughout the scene. If there are five or more f-stops difference between important subject matter, the optimum contrast ratio has been exceeded.[1] This ratio can then be reduced either by throwing more light on the dark areas, or by reducing light intensity on bright areas.

Incident Light Meters   Whereas a reflected light meter is valuable in determining contrast ratios in a scene, an **incident light meter** can tell you how bright the various lights on a set are. Instead of measuring the amount of light reflected from subject matter, incident meters measure the amount of light falling on the subject. Therefore, to get an accurate reading with this type of meter you must point it directly at the light you are measuring (while standing at the exact spot the talent will assume). Some incident-type meters read directly in foot-candles or lux, others require a conversion scale to arrive at these values.

Significant unevenness in lighting around a scene causes variations in video and can result in dark or even washed out skin tones. It is possible to walk around a setting with an incident light meter and quickly find dark or "hot" areas where lighting needs to be adjusted.

There is another reason for being able to accurately measure light on a set. By subtly manipulating the brightness in the primary and secondary areas of a scene, you can achieve a sophisticated means of visual control. Because our eyes are drawn to light areas in a scene, light can be used to emphasize the scene's center of interest.

---

[1] Although we've noted that some CCD cameras can handle brightness ranges of 11 f-stops, the limiting factor, and the factor we must always keep in mind in production, is the home receiver.

Table 7.1	**Light Distance/Brightness Relationships**

1/2 the original distance	=	4 times the light
2 times the original distance	=	1/4 the light
3 times the original distance	=	1/9 the light
4 times the original distance	=	1/16 the light

Controlling Light Intensity

Of course, it does little good to know how to measure the brightness of lights if we can't control their brightness. There are several ways of doing this.

Intensity Control Through Varying Distance   First is light-to-subject distance. As the distance between a light source and the subject increases, the light is spread out over a larger area and the intensity decreases. Put more precisely, the intensity of light from an unfocused light source[2] decreases according to the inverse-square law. We'll leave precise FC calculations to the mathematicians[3] and illustrate this concept with a simple example. If you have 1,600 FC of light at a distance of 10 feet, and double the light-to-subject distance to 20 feet, you will end up with only about one-fourth of the original light, or 400 FC. If you triple the distance to 30 feet you will end up with about 178 FC. And, finally, if you increase the distance to 40 feet (four times the original distance) you end up with only about 74 FC. By keeping this general concept in mind you will quickly be able to vary the intensities of lights to conform to needed lighting ratios. Table 7.1 illustrates the relationship between distance and intensity.

Scrims   Another way to control the intensity of light is with **scrims,** which are similar in appearance to the diffuser shown in Figure 7.4. By using a single- or double-thickness scrim over a light, its intensity can be cut 30 to 60 percent.

---

[2] As the efficiency of lighting instruments is increased by using a focusing reflector and one or more lenses (which is not typical of lighting instruments used in video field production), this statement will cease to be completely accurate. When completely different types of lighting instruments are used together, a light meter must be used to judge exact intensities.

[3] Although you seldom need to calculate down to the FC, in case you are interested, here's how to do it. To find the change in illumination caused by a change in distance, take the factor by which the distance is increased, square it, and invert the result. Example: by moving a light from 12 to 24 feet, there is a distance change of 2×. If you square that you have 4; and 4 inverted is 1/4. If you started with 200 FC you would end up with 50 FC, which means you end up with one-fourth of the original illumination.

Focusing Lights Many lighting instruments can be focused, and this also influences intensity. By using a lever or a crank, the beam of these lights can be pinned down and concentrated over a narrow area, or flooded out to cover a larger area.

Dimmers Lastly, brightness can be reduced in incandescent lights by reducing the voltage to the lamps with **dimmers.** Unfortunately, this also affects color temperature. A rough rule of thumb is that for every one volt drop in the voltage to an incandescent light, the color temperature is reduced by 10° K. Since the human eye can detect a 200° K color shift, in the 2,000–4,000° K range, this means that a studio light can be dimmed only by about 20 percent (in relation to the other lights) without having a noticeable effect on color balance.

Incandescent Lights: Problems and Solutions

Thomas Edison found that by passing an electric current through thin filaments of carbonized threads in a glass-enclosed vacuum, a stable, bright glow could be created. He also discovered two other things: the amount of light rises with voltage and, beyond an optimum voltage, the life of the lamp quickly diminishes and it burns out.

Incandescent Light Problems

During the operation of a normal incandescent lamp (like the 75- or 100-watt lamp you may be using to read this book) atoms of the tungsten filament are slowly "boiled off." This results in three undesirable effects. First, these atoms are deposited on the inside of the glass envelope of the bulb. As the lamp gets older this darkens the bulb and reduces the light output up to 60 percent. Second, these tungsten deposits can drop color temperature 100- to 200-degrees over the life of the lamp. And finally, as the tungsten atoms are boiled off, the filament gets thinner, eventually burning in two.

Solutions These problems are solved by using **tungsten-halogen lamps**—also called quartz for quartz-iodine lamps; they are the most frequently used lamp in video production. Like standard incandescent lamps, they use a tungsten filament. However, the major shortcomings of incandescent lamps are virtually eliminated with quartz lights.

Normal glass can't be used at the high temperatures generated by tungsten-halogen filaments, so the lamp envelopes are made out of quartz. At the same time, the operating temperature of several hundred degrees Centigrade comes close to the melting point of some materials. Once the temperature goes up above 400° C, the lamp and its mount can melt. It is therefore important for lamp housings to have good ventilation and cooling.

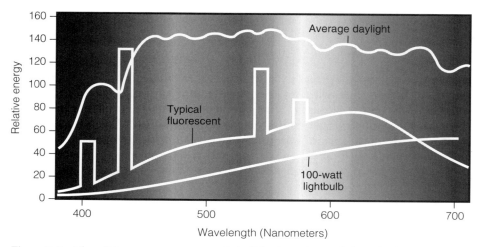

Figure 7.9   Three light sources are compared: daylight, incandescent light and a fluorescent lamp. Note that incandescent light (at the bottom of the illustration) contains a much higher percentage of reddish-yellow light than daylight (the wavy line at the top of the drawing). Although fluorescent lamps vary in overall color temperature, unless they are specially designed for TV work, they typically have "spikes" in the blue and green areas. Even though the eye does not normally notice this, the resulting pictures from film and some video cameras will have a pronounced blue-green cast.

There is one more important consideration in using quartz lamps. While the lamp is on, any foreign material clinging to the exterior surface of the enclosure, including fingerprints, will cause a localized heat build-up. This can rupture the quartz envelope. To avoid getting fingerprints on a lamp when it is changed, you should use a handkerchief or glove.

HMI LIGHTS

HMI lights were originally developed in Germany in the 1960s to aid television crews who needed a small, efficient, and intense on-location light source. The inventor of the HMI knew that battery powered, incandescent lights were a major problem in video field production. Because of their inefficiency, 80 percent of the energy for incandescent lights is converted into heat. (The figures are better for tungsten-halogen or quartz lights: 65 percent of the energy goes into heat and 35 percent is transformed into light.)

HMI, which stands for Hydrargyrum Medium Arc-length Iodide, emits an intense light that is the same color temperature as sunlight. But the normal high-energy bands of color inherent to discharge-type lights (see the section below on fluorescent lamps) was solved with the HMI light. These "color spikes" in the spectral response were smoothed out by the injection of mercury, argon and a few rare earth elements into the HMI tube.

HMI lights generate less heat than incandescent lights. This is an important consideration when shooting inside in a confined space. The less heat generated the more comfortable it will be for talent and crew. Makeup also holds up better.

Unlike incandescent or tungsten-halogen lamps, voltage drops associated with HMI lights produce an increase rather than a decrease in color temperature. But HMI lights have a voltage-correction feature built into their power supply. Minor changes in voltage—common at different times of the day in many cities—do not result in fluctuations in light output or color temperature. Since HMI lights consume fewer watts than incandescent lights (for the same light output), power requirements are also reduced. Although intensity cannot be controlled by dimming, scrims and mechanical shutters (similar to venetian blinds) can be used to reduce light levels.

The main disadvantage of the HMI light is the large, costly, high-voltage power supply that is needed. Even so, because of their color temperature, efficiency and high light output, HMI lights are an excellent choice for on-location production, especially for filling shadows caused by sunlight.

FLUORESCENT LAMPS

Fluorescent lamps belong to the group of lighting devices known collectively as *discharge lamps*—glass tubes filled with metal vapor, with electrodes at each end. Electric current passed between the electrode ionizes the vapor, which begins to glow, producing light. Unlike tungsten-type lights, standard fluorescent lamps have a broken spectrum (Figure 7.9). Instead of a relatively smooth mix of colors from infrared to ultraviolet, fluorescent light has sharp bands or spikes of color, primarily in the blue-green areas. Even though the eye will not notice these spikes, color shifts can result with video.

The Daylight Fluorescent

Using a popular fluorescent tube, the *daylight fluorescent*, for example, results in a color temperature of 6,300° K. This high color temperature, together with the bands of color, means that blue-green tones will be exaggerated and reds will be rendered slightly gray and dull. Although some video cameras have fluorescent filters included in their filter wheels, they can't completely or consistently solve these problems. For one thing, there are about 30 different tubes in use, each with slightly different color characteristics.[4]

---

[4] Between the *daylight* and the *warm white* fluorescent tubes is the widely used *cool white* with a color temperature of 4,500° K. If standard fluorescent lamps must be used, there are two basic approaches to solving the color balance problem: use color-correcting sleeves over the tubes, or an FLD (fluorescent-to-daylight), or an FLT or FLB (fluorescent-to-tungsten) filter on the camera.

Warm-White Fluorescent

The standard consumer-type fluorescent lamp that causes the least color temperature problems is the *warm-white* fluorescent at 3,200° K. Even though the tube also tends to make subject matter look slightly pale and greenish, the tube will produce satisfactory results, assuming the camera is color balanced on a white card and assuming perfect color fidelity isn't a major goal.

Color-Balanced Fluorescent

Thus far in this discussion we have used the term "standard fluorescent lights." In recent years at least two fluorescent tube manufacturers have started producing high-intensity fluorescent bulbs that use special internal compounds to smooth out the spikes found in standard fluorescent tubes.

Banks of color-balanced fluorescent lights produce a soft, virtually shadowless light over a wide area. This type of light has been gaining popularity in certain studio applications because it generates much less heat and consumes much less energy than incandescent lamps. However, since these fluorescent banks can't project light any great distance, their use is limited to subject matter that is relatively close to the lights. Often, color-balanced fluorescent banks are used to provide an overall even lighting and other, more coherent, lighting instruments are added as accent (key) lights.

OTHER TYPES OF DISCHARGE LIGHTS

Other types of discharge lamps can cause more severe color problems than standard fluorescent lamps. One type, the high-pressure sodium vapor lamp, used primarily for street lighting, produces a brilliant yellowish-orange light that will drastically skew color balance. Operating at even higher internal pressures are the mercury vapor lamps, sometimes used for large interior areas such as gymnasiums. These can result in a pronounced greenish-blue cast in video. Suffice it to say, to avoid unpleasant surprises with any standard discharge-type light it is wise to do a test using a good color monitor.

HANDLING MIXED LIGHT SITUATIONS

In on-location production situations, mixed sources will often be encountered. An example is a room that is illuminated partly by incandescent light and partly by sunlight coming through a window. If the camera is color balanced with the incandescent light, the areas lit by sunlight will appear blue and cold. Conversely, if the color balance is done in an area lit by sunlight, the remaining areas will appear yellow. (Refer to Color Plate 6 to see the effect of both daylight and incandescent light on one subject.)

Videographers who don't have time to completely control the problem by blocking out one of the light sources, should color balance on the dominant light source and hope the secondary (weaker) source will not be too distracting. (Obviously, what you can "get by with" will be much different in a news piece than in a cosmetic commercial.)

There are, of course, better solutions for handling mixed light sources. The simplest is to close the curtains or venetian blinds in the room and set up incandescent lights designed for on-location production. Another approach is used for more demanding single-camera film and HDTV dramatic productions: putting large sheets of straw-colored gel over the windows. (**Gels** are colored pieces of heat resistant transparent plastic, available in more than one-hundred colors.) The proper gel will bring the color of the exterior daylight to 3,200° K—the same color temperature as the incandescent lights. This daylight-to-incandescent gel also serves one other important function: it reduces the intensity of the exterior light by two f-stops.[5] This means that the intensity of an incandescent fill light within the room can be much lower.

You can also change the color of incandescent or quartz lights to 5,500° K (daylight). This is done by covering the lights with a CTB, daylight-blue gel. Unfortunately, gels also reduce the output of the lights from about 20 percent (for a half-blue gel) to more than 40 percent for maximum color correction. Even so, when the incandescent lights are used at rather short distances—as they normally would be in an interview, for example—the light loss typically is not a problem.

Using Colored Light as a Prop

Since the color of light suggests specific meanings and associations, sometimes having mixed light sources in a scene is desirable. For example, moonlight is typically simulated by slightly blue light. (Since it is reflected sunlight, when compared to incandescent light, this would be logical.) This color association could be used in lighting a dramatic night scene of a burglar looking through a window into an illuminated house. But since even a full moon has an intensity of only about 0.01 FC, it would be impossible with standard production equipment to produce a well-exposed video image by moonlight. But, dramatic television, like "Hollywood," frequently has to make things appear real through fabrication. In this case

---

[5] Depending on the manufacturer, this filtering material is referred to as 85N6, Lee 209, or RoscoSun 85N3. This material is available in large rolls that can be taped outside of windows.

an incandescent light with a blue gel placed behind and above the burglar would simulate moonlight. A second incandescent light inside the house (possibly with a light yellow or straw-colored gel to enhance the effect) would suggest normal night-time interior house light. To look realistic the interior light would also need to be somewhat stronger than the moonlight.

Keep in mind when using color as a prop that you must color balance your camera(s) with white light (and not the colored light). Otherwise, the special color effect you want will be lost when the camera "corrects" for it.

Color is also used to suggest other things: a flickering straw-colored light for fire, intense flashes of blue light for lightening, and a blue light that occasionally changes in intensity to simulate the light of a TV set. Colored lights can also be used to make backgrounds more interesting. For example, spotlights with colored gels can be focused on a gray cyclorama (cyc) to create (with a flip of a switch) an interesting background for a studio setting.

LIGHTING INSTRUMENTS

Lighting Kits

Today's producer of short, on-location segments needs lights that are light-weight, portable, and easy to set up. To meet this need there are lighting kits consisting of several 420- to 2,000-watt, open-faced tungsten-halogen lights with adjustable stands (Figure 7.10). Many of these portable lights can be focused; that is, their beams can be pinned-down or flooded. Most portable lights accommodate barn doors for masking off the sides of the beam and square frames for attaching gels, scrims and filters (to be discussed later). A lighting kit with four lights is considered adequate for single-camera, on-location interviews (although if you are willing to engage in some "creative compromises" you can get by with even fewer lights). For large interior settings you will probably want to combine the resources of several lighting kits.

Fresnel Lights

The light which for several decades has been the primary source of illumination in most film and TV-studio productions is the **Fresnel** (pronounced fra-*nell*) light. The Fresnel lens in the front of the light (named for the person who devised it) consists of concentric circles that both concentrate and slightly diffuse the light. The distance between the lamp and the Fresnel lens can be adjusted to either spread out (flood), or concentrate (spot or pin) the light's beam. This adjustment provides a convenient control over the intensity of the light. Although Fresnels are large and rather heavy for on-location video work, they provide an ideal mix between hard and soft light.

Figure 7.10 Today's producer of short, on-location segments needs lights that are light-weight, portable, and easy to set up. To meet this need there are lighting kits consisting of several 420- to 2,000-watt, open-faced tungsten-halogen lights with adjustable stands. A lighting kit with four lights is considered adequate for single-camera, on-location interviews. For large interior settings the resources of several lighting kits can be combined.

Ellipsoidal Spotlights

Rounding out the list of conventional lighting instruments are **ellipsoidal spotlights,** which produce a hard, focused beam of light (refer to Figure 7.3). Used with gels, they can project colored pools of light on a background. Some ellipsoidal spots have slots at their optical midpoint that accept a cookie (cucalorus)—a small metal pattern that can be used to project a pattern on a background.

Camera Lights

In ENG work where quality is often secondary to getting a story, camera-mounted, tungsten-halogen lights (often called sun-guns) are sometimes used as a sole source of illumination. These lights can be mounted on the top of the camera or held by an assistant. Although they can be plugged into a wall socket, for the sake of portability they are generally powered by the same 12-volt batteries that power the camera. Most have filters that can convert their color temperature to that of sunlight.

The quality from a camera-mounted light leaves much to be desired. As a result of the straight-on angle involved, picture detail and depth are sacrificed. Because of the relationship between distance and light intensity, the detail and color of foreground objects often becomes washed out and objects in the distance typically go completely dark. For this reason a camera light works best if important subject matter is all at about the same distance from the camera. This type of light provides the same questionable quality as the familiar single-flash-on-the-camera does in still photography.

There are two other disadvantages in using a camera-mounted light. First, it can be intrusive and even disruptive. This rather bright light mounted right above the camera lens tends to make subjects quite conscious of the presence of the camera. Consequently, the whole effect often becomes rather intimidating. Second, exposure can be a problem. As subjects move toward or away from the camera, or, in a fast-breaking news story, as people momentarily cross the camera's path, the camera's auto-iris may constantly readjust—at the expense of good exposure on the center of interest.

ATTACHMENTS TO LIGHTING INSTRUMENTS

Barn Doors

From the lighting instruments themselves, we now turn to attachments that are used with these lights. Adjustable black metal flaps called **barn doors** can be attached to some lights to mask off unwanted light and to keep it from spilling into areas where it's not needed (refer to Figure 7.10). While barn doors provide a soft cutoff (edge) to the parameters of the light, flags provide a sharper, more defined cutoff point.

Flags

Flags consist of any type of opaque material that can block and sharply define the edges of the light source. They are often created and shaped, as needed, from pieces of aluminum foil. Double or triple thicknesses of aluminum foil are often preferred for small flags because they are easy to shape and can stand the heat associated with lights. Flags are generally either clipped to stands or attached to the outer edges of barn doors. The further away they are used from the light source the more sharply defined the light cutoff will be.

Filter Frames

Filter frames are typically part of the barn door attachment that slides over the front of lighting instruments. They can hold

- One or more scrims, which will reduce light intensity
- One or more diffusers, to soften the light
- A colored gel, to alter the color of the light

All of these have been introduced earlier. Each attachment listed simply slides into a frame in front of the light.

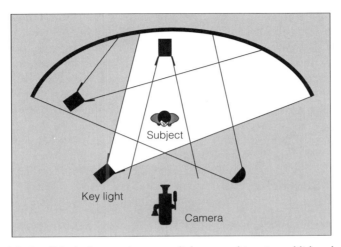

Figure 7.11 The key light is the most important light on a subject; it establishes shape, form and surface detail. But a key light alone can be harsh and create undesirable shadows. The addition of a fill light solves this problem (Figure 7.12).

Three-Point Formula Lighting

In typical lighting setups, lighting instruments serve four functions: as keys, fills, backs, and background lights. In describing the function of each of these we'll assume a standard, three-point (three-light) setup, the kind that can be used for all standard subject matter. We'll also concentrate on the "formula" or three-point approach to lighting, an approach that can be relied on to produce excellent results in most situations.

The Key Light

As the name implies, the **key light** (Figure 7.11) is the main light and the light that most affects the appearance of subject matter. In terms of coherence or quality, it should be in the middle of the hard-to-soft range.

In three-point (formula) lighting the key light is placed at an angle of between 30- and 45-degrees from either the left or the right of the camera. Forty-five degrees is best, because, among other things, it brings out more texture and form in the subject. For the sake of consistency, the 45-degree angle will be used throughout this discussion.

This brings us to the rule we'll need to keep in mind throughout this discussion, especially if multiple cameras and camera angles are involved in the production: *light for the close-up camera.* In most single-camera work this becomes simply a matter of establishing lighting angles on the basis of *the* camera. In multiple-camera shoots you may have to confer with the director during the camera-blocking phase of preproduction regarding which cameras will be taking most of the close-ups of each person. You will both have to work out which camera angles will be best in terms of the action and the lighting. One thing you don't want is to put lights *everywhere,* in a frantic effort to cover every conceivable camera angle.

The Rule of Simplicity

This brings us to the next rule of lighting: *the simpler the design, the better the effect.* Among other things, the key light creates the catch light in eyes—the (single) spectral reflection in each eye that gives the eyes their "sparkle." When you try to "put lights everywhere" it results not only in a multitude of catch lights, but generally in flat, lifeless lighting. Multiple key lights on talent areas not only violate the basic tenet of three-point lighting, but they create a confusing horde of shadows. Barn doors and flags can be a great help in keeping light out of unwanted areas.

To the Right or to the Left? We mentioned that the key light can be placed either to the left or right of the camera. Four considerations influence where the key should be placed:

- The subject's best side (flaws on one side of the face can be minimized by not highlighting them with a key light).
- The visible or assumed location of a source of light on the set (in a dramatic scene, the location of a window or table light, for example).
- Consistency (it is generally illogical for people sitting together to be keyed from different directions).
- Convenience (in EFP work there may be space limitations within a room that make it easier to put the key on one side or the other of the camera).

The Key's Vertical Angle

We have established the horizontal angle for the key light as being approximately 45 degrees to the left or right of the subject in relation to the camera. One other key light angle should be considered: elevation. This angle is also commonly 45 degrees.

Some lighting directors prefer to place the key right next to the camera, or at a vertical angle of less than 30 degrees. Sometimes in limited, on-location conditions this may be necessary. However, three problems result from reducing these angles:

the full illusion of depth and form will be sacrificed; there is a risk of having shadows from the key light appear on the background; the talent is forced to look almost directly into a bright key light while trying to look at the camera. The latter can make reading a camera prompter difficult. Ideally, when the talent face a close-up camera, he or she should see the key light 45 degrees off to one side of the camera, at an elevation of about 30 degrees.

Keys and Boom Microphones

Since the key light is the brightest light on the front of a subject, it's the one that will create the darkest shadows. Background shadows from boom microphones (Chapter 8) can be minimized by positioning the boom parallel to and directly under key lights. Later in this chapter, we'll see that by controlling subject-to-background distances and background lighting, boom shadows can be further reduced or eliminated.

The Sun as a Key

When shooting on location during the day the sun will normally be your key light. However, direct sunlight from a clear sky results in deep, black shadow areas with a major loss of detail. If the sun is directly overhead a "high-noon effect" will be created, producing dark eye shadows. (Put technically, you've grossly exceeded the brightness range of the video system in both instances.) Suffice it to say, direct sunlight, especially for close-ups, can look unflattering (not only to the person in front of the camera, but to your mastery of production skills, as well).

First of all, to get around the "high noon effect," it may be best to shoot sunlit, on-location productions in mid-morning or mid-afternoon when the sun is at an elevation of 30 to 45 degrees. (Of course, where the sun is at a particular time depends upon the season, and longitude and latitude of your location.) If subjects can also be oriented so that the sun (the key light) ends up being 30 to 45 degrees off to one side of the camera, lighting will be best—especially if a fill light (discussed in the next section) is used to slightly fill the shadows caused by the sun.

On an overcast day the diffused sunlight will provide a soft source of light. If the diffused sunlight is coming from behind the subject, it can provide good backlighting, while the ambient light from the overcast sky furnishes soft front lighting. With the proper level of cloud cover this can result in soft, flattering lighting. In camcorders with automatic exposure control, underexposure (with unnaturally dark skin tones) will result unless the *backlight control* is used in this situation. When switched on, these controls open the iris two or three f-stops to compensate for the effect that the bright background area has on automatic exposure. If the camera has a manual iris control, opening the iris while carefully observing the result in the viewfinder is probably a better option in backlit situations.

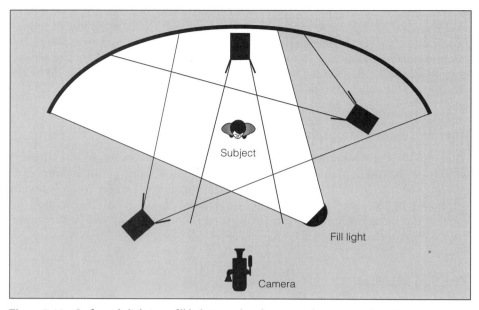

Figure 7.12   In formula lighting a fill light is used at about a 90-degree angle from the key. By being about half of the intensity of the key light (and slightly softer) it fills in shadows to an appropriate level.

The Fill Light

Whether in the field or in the studio, the key light establishes the dimension, form and surface detail of the subject. However, as we've noted, a key light by itself (be it the sun in a clear sky or a quartz light on a stand) produces heavy, distracting shadows. The purpose of the fill light is to partially (but not entirely) fill in the shadows created by the horizontal and vertical angles of the key light.

Positioning the Fill Light

The **fill light** should be on the opposite side of the camera as the key. It can be positioned at any point from right beside the camera to 45 degrees away. However, it's safest to place the fill 45 degrees from the camera. With the key and fill each 45 degrees from the camera position, an angle of 90 degrees is created between the two lights (Figure 7.12). By lighting a full 90-degree area, an important margin of safety is created, in case subjects unexpectedly move and camera angles have to be changed during the production. (Having to stop a production to change the position of lights can represent a time-consuming delay.) Although the vertical angle

Figure 7.13 Outside, when the sun is being used as a key, a reflector board can be positioned at about 90 degrees from the sun to reflect sunlight into the shadow areas. Reflector boards can be clipped to a stand, or held by an assistant.

for the key should be about 45 degrees, the vertical position of the fill is less critical. Generally, the fill is placed just above the camera, which means it ends up being slightly lower than the key. In this position it can easily do what it's intended to do: *partially* fill in the shadows created by the key light.

We've suggested that the fill light should be "softer" than the key light. A soft light source is able to subtly fill in some of the key's shadows without creating a second catchlight in the eyes.

Fill Light Options

Although a good choice for a studio fill light is a scoop, or a bank of color-balanced fluorescents, for on-location settings you will find these options a bit unwieldy. A portable quartz light—the same type you used for a key light—can be used with a diffuser. The diffuser not only softens the fill light, but it can appropriately reduce its intensity. For exterior scenes in sunlight either an HMI light or an appropriately filtered quartz light can be used as a fill.

An easier approach, especially for close-up work, is to use a white or silver reflector board. Outside, when the sun is being used as a key, the reflector board can be positioned at about 90 degrees from the sun to reflect sunlight into the shadow areas (Figure 7.13 and Figure 7.14). Large matte white Styrofoam boards are commonly used for exterior close-ups in ENG work. There are also folding,

Figure 7.14   The effect of a fill light in direct sunlight can be dramatic, especially for video that has a limited brightness range. These photos show the difference in using and not using a reflector fill (Figure 7.13).

silver reflectors that can reflect light much greater distances. Reflector boards can be clipped to a stand, or held by an assistant.

If a key light puts out a wide beam of light, part of the key light illumination can be reflected onto the subject to act as a fill (Figure 7.15).

THE BACK LIGHT

With the key and fill lights, two aspects of three-point lighting have been covered. The third aspect is represented by the back light. The function of the **back light** is to separate the subject from the background by creating a subtle rim of light around the subject (Figure 7.16). You will note from Figure 7.16b that the back light (sometimes called a hair light) should be placed directly behind the subject in relation to the close-up camera.

Compared to the key, a smaller, lower-wattage instrument can be used for a back light for two reasons. First, back lights are often placed closer to the subject than the key light, and second, with subjects confined to a limited area (like a chair) the beams of many lights can easily be "pinned down" (focused into a narrower beam) to intensify the beam.

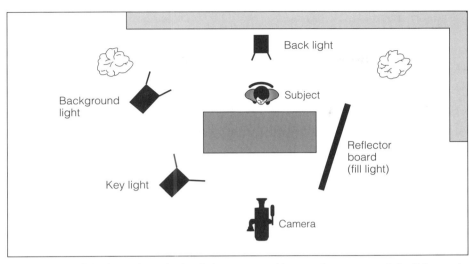

Figure 7.15 If the beam from the key light covers a wide enough area, part of the light can be redirected for fill. A silver or white reflector at close range will provide the needed 2-to-1 lighting ratio (with the key twice as bright as the fill).

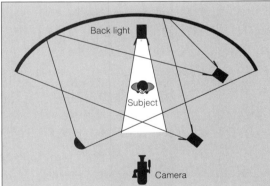

Figure 7.16 A back light provides separation between a subject and a background. In addition, it adds highlights to hair and clothing. By using only a back light (and no key or fill lights) a person's identity can be hidden.

Positioning the Back Light

In determining the position of the back light, remember that from an overhead perspective you should be able to draw a straight line from the lens of the close-up camera, through the subject, directly to the back light (Figure 7.16b). If a back light is placed too far off to one side, it will spill around one side of the subject and leave the other side dark.

Although the elevation of the back light is often dictated by conditions, a 45-degree angle is most desirable. If the back light is too low, it will be picked up by the camera; if it's too high it will spill over the top of the subject's head, lighting up the tip of the nose. (This has been called the "Rudolph effect" after a well-known reindeer.)

By using only back lights with no front lighting a silhouette effect can be created (refer to Figure 7.16a). This can be used for dramatic effect or to hide someone's identity. In trying to successfully eliminate all front lighting in the latter case, watch out for reflected light from the walls or floor. Occasionally, predominant back light alone can add drama to video, especially if clear details are less important than dramatic effect.

In addition to the main subject, there is also one other aspect of a scene that needs to be lit: the background.

BACKGROUND LIGHTS

Background lights are used to illuminate the background area and add depth and separation between scene elements. Once the background light is added, the lighting setup is complete.

Figure 7.17 shows the key, fill, back and background lights in position. Note that the three lights (key, fill and back light) form the points of a triangle. The formula lighting approach is also called "triangular lighting."

By studying Figures 7.17 and 7.18 you should be able to see the effect of each of the lights on the subject, as well as the effect of the background light. Any type of light can be used as a background light as long as it provides fairly even illumination across the background, does not hit the central subject matter, and is at the right overall intensity. This brings up the last major issue in formula lighting: the relative intensity of each of the lights.

LIGHTING RATIOS

Unless each of the four lights is at the proper intensity, the formula lighting approach will not work. Since the key light is the dominant light on the subject, it must be stronger than the fill light. In color production the fill should be one-half

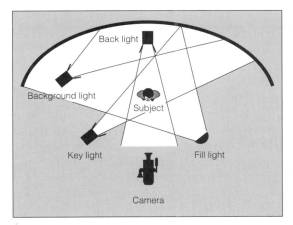

Figure 7.17 Background lights are used to illuminate the background area and add depth and separation between scene elements. Once the background and back lights are added to the effect of the key and fill lights, the lighting setup is complete (Figure 7.18).

Figure 7.18 In this photo all of the lights are in place: key, fill, back and background lights. Note how the subject is effectively separated from the background and how the difference between the key and fill light intensities provides dimension and form in the face.

the intensity of the key. This key-to-fill difference is expressed in terms of a **lighting ratio.** If the key light is twice as bright as the fill, the ratio will be 2:1. Using the 2:1 ratio, if the key light is 200 FC, the fill will be 100 FC. Although many lights may be used in a scene, the lighting ratio refers to the ratio between just two lights: the key and the fill.[6]

The purpose of controlling the key-to-fill ratio is to control the appearance of form, dimension and surface texture of subject matter. To achieve dramatic effects, and occasionally to meet the needs of special subject matter, other ratios can be used. More on that later.

---

[6] *Lighting ratio* is not the same as *contrast ratio*. The latter is the difference in brightness (reflectance value) between the brightest and darkest subject matter in a scene. Of course, since the amount of light an object reflects depends on the amount of light falling on it, the contrast ratio is directly influenced by the lighting ratio.

Table 7.2   **Lighting Ratios**

With f-Stop Differences between Key and Fill Lights

1:1	no difference	flat lighting
1:2	1 f-stop	general color photography
1:3	1-2/3 f-stops	general black and white photography
1:4	2 f-stops	low-key dramatic effect
1:8	3 f-stops	low-key dramatic effect

Table 7.3   **Lighting Ratios by Light Distance**

Multiply Key Light Distance by	To Decrease Light Intensity by
1.4	1 stop
2.0	2 stops
2.8	3 stops
4.0	4 stops
5.6	5 stops

If a foot-candle meter isn't available to establish the proper lighting ratios, a standard photographic light meter can be used. The f-stop differences between the intensity of lights can be translated into lighting ratios (Tables 7.2 and 7.3). For example, to achieve a standard 1:2 ratio, a light meter could be used to make the key light one f-stop less than the fill. The key light in this example could, when measured by itself, call for an exposure of f/16 and the fill light (by itself) an exposure of f/11. Occasionally, it is desirable to minimize or smooth out the surface detail of subject matter. If highly diffused key and fill lights are used close to the camera, there will be a flattening of the appearance of subject matter and a minimizing of surface detail and texture. Reducing the key-to-fill lighting ratio to 1:1 (with the key intensity equal to the fill intensity) adds to this effect (refer to Figure 7.2). Although form and dimension are sacrificed with flat lighting, it can be useful in minimizing wrinkles and skin problems and in creating a soft, flattering effect for the human face (refer to Figure 7.6). This might be important in a cosmetic commercial, for example.

In contrast, by increasing the key-to-fill ratio to 1:5 and beyond, surface detail and texture will be emphasized—especially if hard key light is used at an angle from 65 to 85 degrees. By manipulating these three areas of lighting—key-fill angles, lighting ratios and key-fill coherence—a striking level of control can be exercised over the appearance of subject matter.

Back-Light Intensity

To provide the subtle rim of light around subjects, the back light has to be slightly brighter than the key. In the case of an on-camera person, back-light intensity will depend on the hair color and what he or she is wearing. Subjects who have brown hair, and clothes in the mid-gray range, will require a back light one and one-half times the intensity of the key. Assuming a key light intensity of 150 FC, the back light would then be 225 FC. If you don't have a meter that reads in foot-candles, you can simply move the back light slightly closer to the subject than the key light, or until you see the desired subtle rim of light around the subject. An Afro hair style and a dull black coat will take considerably more back light than a blond wearing light clothing. Be careful to observe the effect on a monitor or in a well-adjusted camera viewfinder.

With subjects who have hair and clothing of similar reflectance, the intensity of the back light is not too difficult to determine. The problem comes in with dark hair and a light coat, or blond hair and dark clothing. In such cases the beam of the back light(s) can be partially masked off with barn doors so that the brightest part of the beam will hit the dark areas.

The color temperature of the back light is not nearly as critical as that of the key and fill lights. Within limits, dimmers can be used.

Background Light Intensity

Because the background is of secondary importance to the center of interest, it should receive a lower level of illumination. Generally, the intensity of background lights should be about two-thirds the intensity of key lights. This will ensure that the central subject matter stands out slightly from the background. In case you have forgotten Math 101, you can get two-thirds of any number by multiplying it by two and dividing the result by three. Therefore, if the key is 200 FC, the light falling on the background should measure about 130 FC. If you are using a photographic meter to set light intensities, the background light should read one-half to two-thirds of a stop less on the exposure meter than the key light.

Since backgrounds are typically one-dimensional (flat) and of secondary importance to the main subject matter, the placement of the lights and their angles is not critical. However, the light across the background should be even. By walking along the background with a light meter, any dark or bright areas can be quickly found.

Subject-to-Background Distance

Shadows on backgrounds from microphone booms, moving talent, and so forth, can be distracting and annoying. Background lights will lighten but normally not eliminate shadows. However, by moving subjects nine or more feet away from a background, you will find (if the key is at an elevation of 45 degrees) that shadows will end up on the floor instead of on the back wall. Remember also that if you position boom microphones parallel to keys you will minimize boom shadows on backgrounds.

Sometimes it is necessary for talent to move in close to a background. The use of a large softlight (Figure 7.5) will render shadows almost invisible, if you don't mind the soft, diffused look it will create in the video.

There is another reason that adequate subject-to-background distance should be maintained: you can make separate lighting adjustments on the background without affecting the main subject matter. This will provide the opportunity to control the tonal range and even the color brightness of the background. Unduly dark backgrounds can be "brightened up" by using a higher level of illumination, and bright, intrusive backgrounds can be "brought down" by lowering background illumination.

Once lighting is understood in terms of quality, angles, lighting ratios and the effect of keys, fills, back lights and background lights, a variety of effects can be created.

ON-LOCATION LIGHTING OPTIONS

Standard Three-Point Lighting

Three-point lighting is just as effective in the field as it is in the studio. However, field production typically presents many more problems (some might prefer the term "challenges") in placing lights. Figure 7.19 shows an on-location lighting setup in a small office for the two camera positions.

Because of time or space limitations, it is often not possible to set up a key, fill, back and background light, especially when doing fast-paced ENG work. It then becomes a matter of knowing what compromises can be safely made.

Filling with a Reflector

As we've noted, a reflector can be used as a fill light. This will save a bit of time by eliminating the need to set up a separate light (recall the setup in Figure 7.15). Sometimes, however, when time, space or lighting instruments are limited, you may have to eliminate the fill light altogether.

Using a Single Softlight

A single soft front light can replace both the key and fill. An umbrella reflector, or a light bounced off a large white card will work (Figure 7.20). Either light source can be placed 20 to 30 degrees off to either side of the camera. If the background

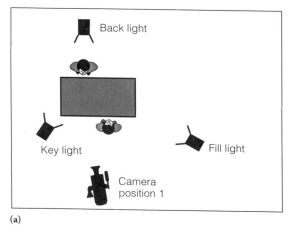

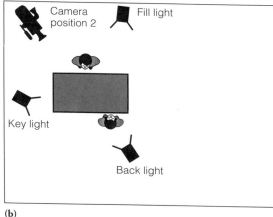

(a)   (b)

Figure 7.19 In doing single-camera interviews it is desirable to videotape the session in two segments. Two videotapes (an A-roll and a B-roll) are made. First the camera is focused on the person being interviewed (a). The interviewer asks the questions (off camera) and the answers are taped.

Then the camera and lights are moved and a second (B-roll) tape is made of interviewer (re)asking the questions (b). Various interviewer reaction shots that will be important to editing are also taped from this angle at the same time.

Note that because of the small size of the office, the fill and key lights provide the background light. In this example all of the lights are of the same type. A 2:1 lighting ratio is achieved by placing the fill light 25 percent farther from the subject than the key is. In this case it can be assumed that the key light is 4 feet away from the subject and the fill is 5-½ feet away. Since the back light needs to be slightly stronger than the key, its distance is slightly less than the key.

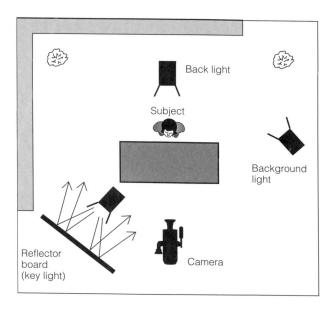

Figure 7.20 A light bounced off a white or silver reflector will provide a soft source of illumination for an interview.

is close behind a subject, this short distance may eliminate the need for a back-ground light. (Since you are using a diffused light source, shadows will be less noticeable.) A second light can be used as a back light to provide needed subject-background separation.

Bounced Light

The simplest and quickest lighting setup for doing a short interview is to use a single light bounced off the ceiling (Figure 7.21). The bounced-light approach works best with low, white, or light-gray ceilings. The white, acoustic tile commonly found in offices works well. Bounced light creates a soft even light throughout the room, an effect that is similar to what we see with overhead fluorescent lights.

A light mounted on top of a camcorder can be aimed at the ceiling for a bounced light effect. In this case the camera (and attached light) should be placed far enough back from the subject so that the light will come down at an acceptable angle. If the light is too close to the subject, dark eye shadows will result. If the walls of the room are a light, neutral color, they will reflect part of the bounced light and more fully fill in shadow areas.

To help compensate for the color that the ceiling and walls add to the light, remember to color balance the camera under the bounced (rather than the direct) light. Bounced light will not work, of course, if the ceiling is too high or too dark. While bounced light solves the problem of uneven lighting, its disadvantage is that the effect is often too soft; that is, it hides the texture, form and dimension of subject matter.

APPROACHES TO LIGHTING MULTIPLE SUBJECTS

Thus far, our discussion and illustrations have covered the lighting of one subject only. Unfortunately, things aren't always this simple. Figure 7.22 shows a lighting setup for multiple subjects. If you examine the figures carefully, you will note that the basic, three-point lighting approach has simply been duplicated for each talent position. This is the safe way of lighting several subjects in one setting, especially if you know which camera will be shooting the close-up of each subject. (Remember, you should establish your key and fill angles from the perspective of the close-up camera.) With each subject separately lit (as opposed to lighting several people with one set of lights) you can tailor the lighting to each individual subject. This can be important in accommodating blond hair, bald heads, and wide variations in clothing, skin tones, etc. Barn doors are commonly used to keep lights intended for one person from spilling over onto another person or area.

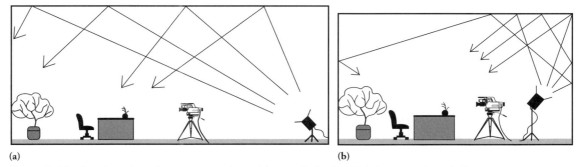

(a)   **(b)**

Figure 7.21   For short interview segments, the quickest and simplest lighting setup is a single bounce light. This technique works best in rooms with low, white or light-gray ceilings. Bounce light creates a soft, even light throughout the room, an effect that is similar to overhead fluorescent lights. In large rooms with light ceilings, the lighting setup shown in (a) can be used. For smaller rooms with light walls and ceilings, this can be modified as shown in (b).

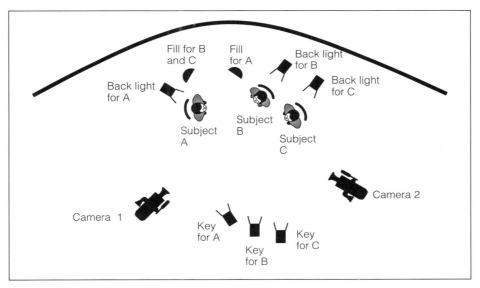

Figure 7.22   Lighting setups for multiple subjects. Note that the basic three-point lighting approach has simply been duplicated for each talent position. With each subject separately lit (as opposed to lighting several people with one set of lights) you can tailor the lighting to meet the needs of each individual.

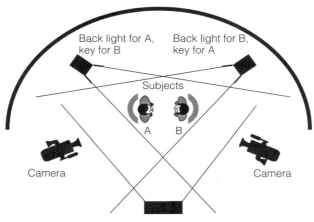

Figure 7.23 Sometimes lights can be used for multiple purposes. Here, the basic three-point lighting setup is achieved with only three lights. Note that the key light for A also serves as a back light for B; and the key for B serves as a back light for A. A single fill light serves both subjects.

Multiple Purpose Lights

Note in Figure 7.23 the key light for each subject is also serving as the back light for the other. If distances are carefully controlled, the lights will be 50 percent brighter as back lights than in their role as keys. This can work well under carefully controlled situations where you know in advance the color of each person's hair (or, in some cases the lack of hair), and the color of clothes that will be worn by each person. The position of the chairs in this case will be especially critical to lighting intensities. Once lighting is set up, neither chair can be moved without altering the lighting ratios.

Approaches to Area Lighting

So far we've covered subjects conveniently confined to one place. But what if one or more subjects must be free to roam around while on camera? There are four ways this can be handled.

■ First, the entire area can be flooded with a *base light,* which is an overall, even fill light. Scoops or color-balanced fluorescents would work here. Important close-up camera talent positions can then be keyed with lights at twice the intensity of the base light. A small piece of tape placed on the floor will provide marks for the talent to hit when moving from one major camera position to another. With this approach you will probably not want to barn off the lights any more than necessary, since illuminated areas should be kept large enough to give talent a margin of error in missing the marks.

■ Second, lighting for talent who must be free to roam involves keying, filling and backing the entire area. Here, the whole working range—assuming it's not too large—is treated as a single subject. This will require a powerful (high-wattage) key light positioned at a great enough distance to cover the entire set. If the key is placed in the center of the set, 90 degrees to the back wall, the angle will be appropriate for cameras positioned at each side of the set. One or more scrimmed Fresnels can serve as fills. (Scoops or banks of color-balanced fluorescent lights will not throw light far enough to cover a large area.) If more than one key has to be used to cover the area, they should be positioned as close together as possible to reduce the problem of multiple shadows and multiple catch lights in eyes. Multiple back lights will have to be used. They should be aimed so that they produce slightly overlapping pools of light over the whole talent area. The talent should be able to walk from one area to another without obvious variations in back light.

■ Third, lighting a large area requires dividing the set into individual areas and keying, filling and backing each area. Often, large interior settings are divided into four parts for keying, filling and backing. Typically, the lights at the edge of each of these areas will just begin to merge. With this approach it is important to make sure that close-ups will not be in the transition points between lighted areas. Keep in mind the sources of light that may be suggested by the setting, such as visible table lamps or windows. Place the key lights so they will be consistent with these suggested sources of illumination.

■ Fourth, lighting a large area would be appropriate to simulate an interior at night. This technique requires a lighting ratio from 3:1 to 6:1; the talent would move in and out of specifically defined set areas. Only important close-up areas would be lit, leaving the rest of the scene relatively dark. With this approach it is especially important to place keys so that they are consistent with the visible or suggested sources of light within the setting. If a person were sitting next to a reading lamp, the key would have to be angled so that the light would appear to be coming from the table light. This approach to keying, which is called *following source,* is widely used in dramatic productions. In some cases you may want to use a low-level base light over the entire set to keep "in-between areas" from going too dark.

Using a Stand-In

Whatever lighting approach you use, the lighting can be checked on camera by having a stand-in (a person of similar height, skin color and wearing similar clothing to the talent involved) slowly walk through the positions. During the show's dress rehearsal (with the actual talent) any remaining problems can be spotted and then fixed during the break between the dress rehearsal and the actual production.

High- and Low-Key Lighting

Contrary to what is sometimes written, low key and high key do not refer to the overall intensity of the key and fill lights, but to their ratios and angles. **Low-key lighting,** which produces a predominance of shadow areas, is created with a high key-to-fill ratio (1:6 and beyond) and oblique key angles. This technique would be used for dark, dramatic night scenes, etc. In contrast, **high-key lighting** is bright and upscale. It is represented by a low key-to-fill ratio with barely perceptible shadow areas. Daytime beach scenes and the interiors of offices under fluorescent lighting would be high key.

Single-Camera vs. Multiple-Camera Lighting

Compared to film, video productions (especially sitcoms, game shows, and so forth) sometimes look flat and dimensionless. The reason largely centers on lighting. Since film is almost always shot with a single camera (representing a single subject-to-camera angle), lighting can be optimized for every scene and take. In contrast, a typical television sitcom involves three or four cameras spanning almost 160 degrees. Since the director needs to be able to cut to any camera at any time, the lighting must be able to hold up throughout this range. To avoid the possibility of having any shadow areas, the safest way of lighting this type of production is to light relatively flat, using multiple key lights to cover every possible camera angle. As a result, dimension and form are lost—the things that make film scenes so much more interesting visually.

Fortunately, single-camera video production is able to take advantage of the same lighting strategies afforded to filmmakers. We've already introduced one of the strategies; it's called following source.

Following Source

In the late 1980s, television production moved to CCD cameras, which are similar to film in their ability to handle contrast ranges. Instead of a basically flat lighting approach, Hollywood lighting directors such as George Dibie[7] brought lighting

---

[7] George Dibie, a lighting director who received three Emmys for his innovative film and television work, was for many years president of the American Society of Lighting Directors.

techniques to television that were long associated with film. Dibie says, because of today's CCD cameras, I can now ". . . light for my video cameras exactly the way I light for film cameras." Whether you are simulating day or night, the most important thing is to follow source, according to Dibie: "Windows, doors, lamps . . . these are the sources of light in a scene. [For] . . . one camera or multiple cameras, you deal with the feel of the source." The technique of following source has now become a standard approach in many dramatic productions.

In following source, a lighting director must first determine where the obvious sources of illumination *are* (if they are visible), or *might be* (if they are not). If none is obvious, it becomes a matter of determining where a logical source of illumination might be. In a pool-room scene the light source might be a light above the pool table. It then becomes a matter of keying important camera close-up positions so that they are consistent with this suggested source of illumination.

Note in Figure 7.24 that the window is providing side light. The same effect can be achieved by using a **kicker light.** These lights can simulate such things as windows, table lamps and fireplaces. Kicker lights have an intensity that's greater than key lights, and they are normally placed slightly behind the subject, opposite the key.

CREATING A LIGHTING PLOT

In a large production a lighting director (after reading a script and consulting with the director and others) will draw a **lighting plot,** a scale drawing of the set with all lights indicated. Assistants will then use the plot to position lights. With the help of one or more stand-ins and lighting assistants, the lighting director will then check the final effect on a monitor.

USING EXISTING LIGHT

Considering the difficulty involved in setting up multiple lights, it is often best, when possible, to use existing light—the natural light present at a location. With today's sensitive CCD cameras, this is generally not a problem. For news and documentary work, existing light is actually more realistic since it represents actual conditions. Even so, existing light can present three problems:

■ The light may be of mixed color temperatures: a possible mixture of incandescent, fluorescent or even daylight from a window.

■ The overall light level might be too low. Although office areas are typically lit at 40 FC, which is well within the capability of CCD cameras, some stores must be taped in convention halls or meeting rooms where the light level can be much

Figure 7.24   A side light can add interest and realism to a scene. *Kicker lights* can simulate the effect of windows, table lamps and fireplaces. These special-purpose lights have an intensity that's greater than the key light, and they are normally placed slightly behind the subject opposite the key light.

lower. This means that cameras will have to use wide f-stops, often aided by the camera's built-in sensitivity boost.

■ Finally, the contrast ratio between areas of the scene may be too high. This is the most common problem. For example, the source of light may be coming from the wrong direction, and creating dark shadows in critical areas; the light can consist of hard, overhead light that creates eye shadows; or the light may vary greatly throughout the scene. In the case of an interior scene, moving a table lamp, closing the blinds or curtains, or switching on or off selected lights in the room may solve the problem.

SETTING UP LIGHTS

Unlike the studio situation, where lights are hung from the lighting grid, lights on-location are normally mounted on light stands. Key and fill lights are generally easy to position; stands are just placed at 45 degrees on either side of the camera. Back lights are another issue. They can't be hung from a lighting grid as they can in a studio, and a light stand behind the subject would be seen on camera. There are two possible solutions.

First, a back light may be clipped to the top of a book case, an exposed rafter or any convenient, out-of-view anchoring point. If this option isn't available, you might consider a light stand resembling a microphone boom, which can suspend the back light behind the person just above the view of the camera. Another option is assembling a *lighting goal post* out of plastic (PVC) pipe and clipping the light to the center. One or more back lights can be hung from the middle and the wires can be taped to the pipe. You'll want to make sure that the top and sides of the goalpost are safely outside the range of your widest shot.

The next solution is to use cross back lights. The two back lights are put on floor stands behind and on either side of the subject, just out of camera range. Many lighting directors prefer this effect because the lights spill around the sides of the subject giving a better subject-background separation.

POWER PROBLEMS

In setting up on-location lighting it is often necessary to figure out how many lamps a fuse or circuit breaker can handle. Although the standard house-current voltage in the United States is between 110 and 120, in doing calculations it is common to assume a voltage of 100. This not only makes it easier to do calculations—you can easily do them in your head—it automatically provides a safety factor. By assuming a voltage of 100, the following formula can be used:

watts divided by 100 = amps

Therefore, a 500-watt lamp would draw 5 amps. A 20-amp fuse or breaker could handle up to 2,000 watts; a 30-amp fuse up to 3,000 watts, and so on.

When setting up multiple lights, the total wattage is simply added together. If a 1,000-watt key light, a 500-watt fill, a 500-watt back light and a 500-watt background light were all plugged into the same 20-amp circuit, the combined amperage would blow a fuse or breaker. (Actually, it might take a few minutes to heat up the breaker enough to trip it, just long enough to get a good start on taping a segment.)

Figure 7.25   Lighting for sophisticated dramatic productions requires the skills and artistic ability of an experienced lighting director. These skills go far beyond the basic principles of lighting to an ability to creatively compose a lighting scheme that represents an artistic interpretation of both the scene and its role within the entire script.

To keep from overloading a fuse or circuit breaker, it will often be necessary to run extension cords from separately fused circuits, possibly from an adjoining room. But, if they are not made of heavy gauge wire, long extension cords can lower voltage to lamps, resulting in drops in color temperature.

Since limited power on some locations, especially in older homes, is often a problem, on occasion you may have no choice but to bring in an electrician to run a temporary, high-amperage line from the main fuse box. In remote areas a movie generator truck may have to be rented. Although they use a gasoline- or diesel-powered engine, because of extensive sound-proofing, they are virtually silent (an important consideration when you are doing sound recording on location).

THE ART OF LIGHTING

In describing the basic techniques for lighting in this chapter we've covered approaches that will provide highly acceptable results for most EFP work. At the same time, no attempt has been made here to cover complex lighting needs. (Entire books have been written on that subject. See bibliography.) The lighting required for sophisticated, multiple-camera dramatic productions, requires the skills and artistic ability of an experienced lighting director (Figure 7.25). The skills of such a person go far beyond the basic principles of lighting to a creative ability to compose a lighting scheme that represents an artistic interpretation of both the scene and its role within the entire script. At this level of sophistication lighting becomes a true art form.

8 AUDIO

IN THIS CHAPTER we'll look at the nature and importance of sound in production, microphones and their use, monophonic, stereo and surround-sound recording techniques, and production related communications systems.

The importance of sound in television has been demonstrated in experiments in which subjects were allowed to either see or hear, but not see *and* hear, typical television shows. The subjects who could only hear the audio typically gleaned more information on show content than did those who could only see the video. Even so, historically, far more attention has been paid to video than to audio.

Before we discuss some of the basic audio production concepts used in video field production, sound itself must be understood. Sound has two basic characteristics that must be carefully controlled: loudness and frequency.

LOUDNESS AND FREQUENCY

Loudness

Although sound loudness is measured in **decibels (dBs),** the term actually has two different definitions. The first is *dBSPL,* for sound pressure loudness, which is a measure of acoustic power. This is the type of loudness we can directly hear with our ears. These decibels can go beyond 135, which is considered the threshold of pain and is also the point at which permanent ear damage can occur. Various sound pressure decibel levels are shown in Table 8.1.

The second use of the term decibel, *dBm,* for the milliwatt reference level, is a unit of electrical power. These decibels are displayed on loudness meters. In audio production we are primarily interested in dBm, which reflects levels of electrical power going through various pieces of audio equipment.

Two types of **VU meters** are illustrated in Figure 8.1: digital and analog. Contrary to what logic might dictate, 0 dBm (generally just designated dB on a VU meter) is not "zero sound" but, in a sense, the opposite: the maximum desirable sound level. This may seem confusing until you realize that the 0 dB point on the meter is just a reference point. Therefore, it is possible to have a sound level on the meter that registers in negative dBs, just as it is possible to have a temperature of −10° F (10 below zero).

The dBm level going through audio equipment must be carefully controlled so that it stays within a certain range. If the signal is allowed to pass through equipment at too low a level, noise can be introduced when the level is later increased to a normal **amplitude** (audio level). If the level is too high (appreciably above 0 dB on the VU meter), objectionable distortion will result, especially with digital audio. To ensure audio quality, you must pay constant attention to maintaining proper audio levels.

Frequency

The second aspect of sound, **frequency,** relates to the basic pitch—how high or low the sound is. Frequency is measured in **hertz** or cycles per second (CPS). A person with exceptionally good hearing will be able to perceive sounds from 20–20,000 hertz.

A frequency of 20 hertz would sound like an extremely low-pitched note on a pipe organ—almost a rumble. At the other end of the scale, 20,000 hertz would be somewhere near the highest pitched sound that can be imagined, even higher than the highest note on a violin or piccolo. Since both ends of the 20–20,000-hertz range represent rather extreme limits, the more common range used for broadcast production is from 50 to 15,000 hertz. Although it doesn't quite cover the full range that can be perceived by people with good hearing, this range does cover almost all naturally occurring sounds.

The Frequency-Loudness Relationship

Even though sounds of different frequencies may technically be equal in loudness, human hearing does not necessarily perceive them as being equal. Figure 8.2 shows the frequency response of the human ear to different frequencies. Because of the reduced sensitivity of the ear to both high and low frequencies, these sounds must

Table 8.1   Typical Sound Levels in Decibels

Sound	Average Decibels (dB/SPL)
Some contemporary music concerts	140
Jet aircraft taking off	125
Subway express train (close)	105
Niagara Falls, noisiest spot	95
Heavy traffic	85
Interior of car at 40 mph	75
Dept. store/noisy office	65
Normal conversation	60
Soft background music	30
Quiet whisper, 5 feet	20
Sound studio	15
Outdoor "silence"	10

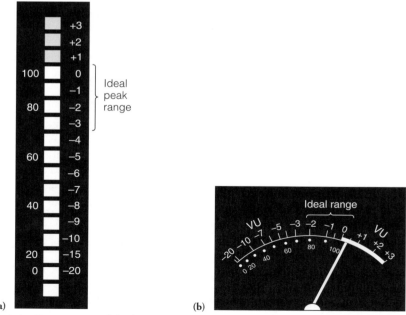

Figure 8.1 Two versions of the basic VU meter are illustrated in these figures. On most meters one scale represents volume units in dB (−20 to +3) and the other scale is the modulation percentage (percentage of a maximum signal: 0 to 100).

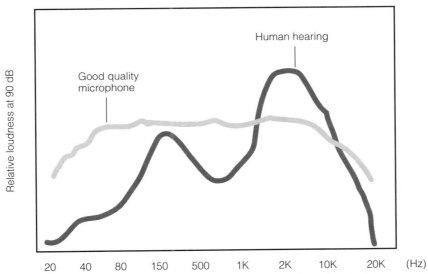

Figure 8.2 The frequency response of a good-quality microphone (top line) is compared with the frequency response of the human ear. Note that people perceive sounds as being much louder in the 2,000–8,000-hertz range.

be louder to be heard, or at least to be perceived as being equal to other frequencies. Note that to be heard a 25-hertz tone would have to be many times louder than a tone in the 1,000–10,000-hertz (1–10-kilohertz) range.[1]

Shaping Playback Response

Not only do we not hear all frequencies equally in terms of loudness, but equipment and listening conditions also greatly affect how different frequencies will be perceived. To compensate for some of these problems, we can adjust frequency-loudness characteristics of equipment. The primary purpose of the bass (low-frequency) and treble (high-frequency) controls on amplifiers, for example, is to shape the frequency-loudness characteristics. More sophisticated playback equipment will include a **graphic equalizer** (Figure 8.3), which goes a step further and allows specific frequency bands to be individually adjusted for loudness. These controls make it possible to adjust the frequency-loudness relationship at any point in the production and postproduction process. This may be necessary to compensate for equipment limitations, to try to match audio segments recorded under

---

[1] To reduce the number of zeros with large numbers, several prefixes are commonly used in audio and video: *kilo (K)*, meaning thousand, *mega (M)*, meaning million, and *giga (G)*, meaning billion.

Figure 8.3   A graphic equalizer allows control over specific frequency bands of the audio spectrum. Not only does this control make it possible to enhance audio playbacks by emphasizing and attenuating certain frequency ranges, but graphic equalizers can also be used during editing to help match the audio characteristics of segments.

different conditions, or simply to customize audio playback to the acoustics of a listening area.

Preserving the original relationship between the frequencies of sound and their loudness when they're reproduced is a major consideration in sound quality (fidelity). Any piece of audio equipment—microphone, amplifier, tape machine, or audio speaker—can adversely affect the fidelity of sound. However, the microphone (the device that initially transduces sound waves into electrical energy) and the audio speaker (the device that changes electrical energy back into sound waves) represent the weakest links in audio quality.

Only sounds that are totally electronically generated, such as those produced by a computer or audio synthesizer, do not need to go through a microphone to be reproduced. Everything else, the human voice, musical instruments, etc., must have their sound transduced into electrical energy before they can be recorded or broadcast.

Generally speaking, the "flatter" the frequency response of a microphone, the better it is, and the more expensive it is (refer to Figure 8.2). If you look at "the specs" (the printed technical specifications) of an inexpensive microphone you will generally find that its frequency response contains variations within the audible range—typically below 100 hertz and above 10,000 hertz. This indicates that the microphone will unnaturally emphasize or de-emphasize certain frequencies.

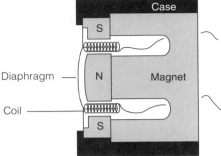

Side view

Figure 8.4 Hand-held microphones are often dynamic mics because they are better at handling the sound overloads associated with performers. When used at short distances it is best if the mic is tilted at about a 30-degree angle, rather than being perpendicular to the mouth. In a dynamic microphone, sound waves hit a diaphragm attached to a fine coil of wire. Since the coil is suspended in the magnetic field of a permanent magnet, any movement of the coil as a result of sound waves hitting the diaphragm generates a small electrical current.

To some degree it is possible to clean up the frequency response of a poor microphone in postproduction; however, even the most sophisticated audio postproduction work techniques can't work miracles.

Although there are almost a dozen different types of microphones (or mics, pronounced "mikes") in common use, two are most often used in video field production: the dynamic, and the condenser.[2]

Dynamic and Condenser Microphones

Dynamic Microphones

The **dynamic microphone** (also called a moving-coil mic) is considered to be the most rugged professional microphone (Figure 8.4a). In a dynamic microphone, sound waves hit a diaphragm attached to a fine coil of wire (Figure 8.4b). Since the coil is suspended in the magnetic field of a permanent magnet, any movement of the coil as a result of sound waves hitting the diaphragm generates a small electrical current.

---

[2] Although ribbon microphones are used in radio and in some TV studio applications, they are normally not used in video field production.

Many dynamic microphones are non-directional when it comes to the lower frequencies, but somewhat directional in their response to higher frequencies. Knowing this, problems created by a shrill or sibilant speaker can sometimes be reduced by putting the speaker slightly off to one side of the microphone.

The ability of a dynamic mic to withstand shock, major temperature fluctuations and high humidity has made it the first choice for television field production. The hand-held mics used by ENG reporters and stage performers are generally dynamic mics. Even so, when small size, and optimum sensitivity and quality are prime considerations, condenser microphones are often preferred.

Condenser Microphones

Condenser microphones (also called capacitor or electret condenser mics) are capable of delivering unparalleled audio quality (Figure 8.5a). At the same time, generally speaking, they are not as rugged as a dynamic mic, and problems can result from using some models under adverse weather conditions.

These microphones work on the principle of an electric condenser or capacitor. An ultrathin metal diaphragm is stretched tightly above a piece of flat metal or ceramic (Figure 8.5b). In most condenser mics a power source maintains an electrical charge between the elements. In one type, the electret mic, the capacitor is permanently charged at the factory.

With condenser or electret mics, sound waves hitting the diaphragm cause fluctuations in an electrical charge. Since this voltage fluctuation is extremely small, it must be greatly amplified by a pre-amplifier (pre-amp). The pre-amp can be located within the microphone housing or, in the case of a small, clip-on microphone, in an outboard electronic pack that can be put in a pocket or attached to a belt.

Because they require a pre-amp, this means that, unlike dynamic mics, most condenser mics require a source of power. This can either be from an AC power supply or from batteries. An AC power supply for condenser mics is often built into an audio mixer and is referred to as a **phantom power supply.** In this case the microphone cord serves two functions: it delivers the signal from the microphone to the mixer, and it carries power from the mixer to the condenser mic.

Although using batteries to power the microphone may be convenient (you don't have to find a source of AC power), they introduce a problem of their own. At the end of their life cycle which, depending on use, may be a year or more, the batteries usually go out without warning. For this reason, for important live or taped productions, two miniature condenser mics are often used together. If one mic goes out, the other can immediately be switched on. This double mic technique is called **dual redundancy** (a term that is itself redundant).

Although most condenser mics require a power supply, the use of a pre-amplifier means they deliver a higher-level signal, which generally translates into greater microphone sensitivity. Condenser mics also tend to be very responsive to high and low frequencies, giving them a full, clean, crisp sound. Because the transducer elements can be made very small, condenser mics can be easily hidden.

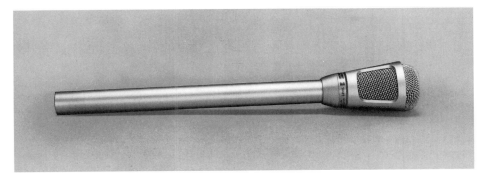

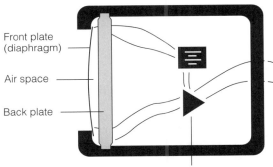

Front plate
(diaphragm)

Air space

Back plate

Battery-powered amplifier

Figure 8.5 Although condenser mics (also called capacitor or electret mics) can equal or exceed other types of microphones, they are not as rugged as a dynamic mic and problems can result from using some models under adverse weather conditions. Condenser mics have an ultrathin metal diaphragm that is stretched tightly above a piece of flat metal or ceramic. In most condenser mics a power source maintains an electrical charge between the elements. In the electret type, the capacitor is permanently charged at the factory.

DIRECTIONAL CHARACTERISTICS

A microphone is selected for specific purposes on the basis of its attributes. One of the most important of these consists of its directional characteristics. There are three basic directional categories: omnidirectional, bidirectional, and unidirectional.

Omnidirectional Microphones

Also called non-directional mics, **omnidirectional mics** are equally sensitive to sounds coming from all directions (Figure 8.6). Although this characteristic would have advantages in radio, where several people could stand or be seated around a single microphone, in video production it is almost always more desirable to use some form of directional mic. A directional mic reduces or eliminates unwanted sounds (such as behind-the-camera noise or ambient on-location noise) while maximizing sound coming from talent.

Figure 8.6 Microphones with non-directional, or omni-directional, patterns, are equally sensitive to sounds coming from all directions. Although this would have advantages in radio (where several people could be seated around a single microphone), in television it is almost always more desirable to use directional mics. Directional mics can reduce unwanted sounds (behind-the-camera noise, ambient on-location noise, etc.) while maximizing sound coming from talent.

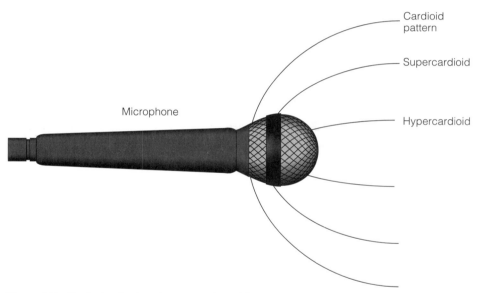

Figure 8.7 Professional microphones are selected for specific applications on the basis of a number of attributes—the most important of which are the mic's directional characteristics. In this (highly simplified) drawing the front side of three directional patterns is illustrated: cardioid, supercardioid and hypercardioid.

Bidirectional Microphones

As the name suggests, a **bidirectional mic** is primarily sensitive to sounds from two directions. Until the advent of stereo, bidirectional (also called "figure eight") sensitivity patterns had limited use in television, although they are commonly used in radio interviews. Later we will see that this figure-eight pattern has applications in stereo.

Figure 8.8 The most commonly used off-camera mic in electronic field production is the line mic, a type of highly directional shotgun mic surrounded by dark-gray foam rubber or a fur-like windscreen. Because line mics are quite directional, they require someone just outside of the camera's view to keep them carefully aimed at the sound source.

Unidirectional Microphones

The term **unidirectional** simply refers to a general classification of mics that are sensitive to sounds coming from primarily one direction. There are four subdivisions in this category: cardioid, supercardioid, hypercardioid and parabolic. Although these titles sound a bit formidable, they simply refer to how narrow the mic's pickup pattern is. Figure 8.7 represents a simplified comparison of the three most commonly used sensitivity patterns.

Cardioid   The cardioid (pronounced *car*-dee-oid) pickup pattern is named after a sensitivity pattern that vaguely resembles a heart shape. Microphones using a cardioid pattern are sensitive to sounds over a wide range in front of the mic, but relatively insensitive to sounds coming from behind it. Although this pattern might be useful for picking up a choir, the width of a cardioid pattern is too great for most TV applications. When placed 8 or more feet from a speaker, it tends to pick up unwanted surrounding sounds, including reverberations from walls.

Supercardioid   As the name suggests, the **supercardioid** is even more directional than the cardioid sensitivity pattern (refer to Figure 8.7). When this type of microphone is pointed toward a sound source, interfering (off-axis) sounds tend to be rejected. This polar pattern is similar to that of our ears as we turn our head toward a sound we want to hear and try to ignore interfering sounds.

Shotguns   A type of supercardioid mic widely used in on-location video production is the so-called **shotgun mic.** It is highly directional and provides good pickup when used off-camera at a distance of 8–15 feet from the talent. Figure 8.8 shows the protective housing for a shotgun mic. This elaborate housing muffles both the sound of wind and moving air, and noise associated with handling the mic during an on-location shoot.

Figure 8.9 Parabolic mics are the most highly directional type of microphone. They can pick up sounds at distances of 300 feet or more. Parabolic mics are not a practical choice of studio or general field production work, but they are often used in sports.

Hypercardioid and Ultradirectional   Even more directional are the hypercardioid and **ultradirectional** response patterns. Although their narrow angle of acceptance means that off-axis sounds will be largely rejected, this also means that they have to be accurately pointed toward sound sources. Regular adjustments have to be made if the talent moves. Some highly directional shotgun mics are included in the hypercardioid category.

Parabolic Microphones   **Parabolic mics** (Figure 8.9) represent the most highly directional type of microphone. Unlike the previous sensitivity patterns that are a characteristic of basic mic design, the parabolic reflector creates the polar pattern. In fact, only a basic unidirectional mic can be used in the focus of the parabola. Figure 8.10 illustrates how these mics work. The parabolic reflector can be from 18 inches to 3 feet in diameter. Because of the parabolic shape of the reflector, all the sounds along a very narrow angle of acceptance will be directed into the microphone from the surrounding reflector. Parabolic microphones can pick up sound at distances of 300 feet or more. Although these microphones are not a practical choice for general field production work, they are often used in covering sporting events.

Although all directional mics favor sounds coming from one direction, they still have some limited sensitivity to off-axis sounds. This means that ambient noise can still be a problem. For on-location work a good set of padded earphones is indispensable for an audio operator. When using hypercardioid and ultradirectional

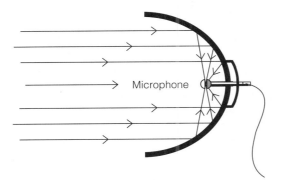

Figure 8.10 Parabolic mics work on the basis of a parabolic reflector, which directs all sounds along a very narrow angle of acceptance into the microphone at the center.

microphones, constant audio monitoring is especially important, to keep subjects in the center of their narrow pickup pattern.

Special Microphone Attributes

Proximity Effects

The use of highly directional microphones in general and parabolic microphones in particular results in a partial loss of some frequencies. This loss is not the result of a weakness in the microphone; rather, sound traveling over a distance loses low frequencies (bass) and, to a lesser extent, the higher frequencies (treble). Conversely, microphones used at a short distance normally create what is called a **proximity effect**—exaggerated low-frequency response. (Some mics also have "low cut" filters, which reduce unnatural low frequencies when the mics are used at short distances.)

When directional mics are used at different distances, the sound perspective or audio presence (balance of audio frequencies and other acoustical characteristics) will change with each change in microphone distance. If this problem is not recognized and controlled, the sound presence or perspective will annoyingly shift with each edit. This knowledge is important for postproduction editing.

Balanced and Unbalanced Lines

Most of the microphones used with audiocassette machines and consumer-type camcorders use unbalanced lines. The basic difference is one wire; **unbalanced lines** use two wires, **balanced lines** use three. (With stereo there is an additional wire in each case.) The monophonic miniconnectors used on cassette and camcorder mics have only two conductors (Figure 8.11). Professional mics normally use **XLR connectors,** which have three wires.

Figure 8.11 The most commonly used audio connectors include XLR (Canon) connectors on the left. Both the female and male versions are shown. Next are standard miniature (3.6mm) connectors and (on the right) an RCA phono connector. Note that the miniature connectors differ slightly. One (the second from the right) has a floating center contact separated by black insulating bands. This additional contact shows that it is a stereo connector.

Using unbalanced lines isn't a major problem with short cables. However, with long extension cables, and especially if mic lines are not in perfect condition, you will quickly encounter noise, hum and other undesirable audio problems. Suffice it to say, professional mics and camcorders rely on balanced lines.

Application Design

We have already discussed the basic microphone transducer types used in video field production, the dynamic and condenser. The application design of the mic configures the transducer and its housing to specific applications. We will discuss eleven applications: personal (including lavaliere and clip-ons), hand-held, wireless (RF), PZ, headset, contact, suspended, hidden, line, stereophonic, and quadraphonic.

Personal Microphones

Personal mics are either hung from a cord around the neck (a **lavaliere** or **lav** mic) or clipped to clothing (a **clip-on** mic). They can be either a condenser or a dynamic

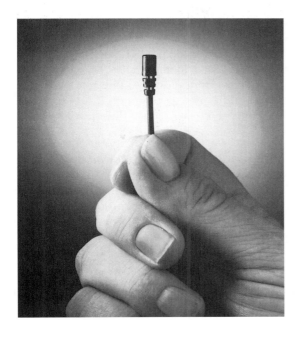

Figure 8.12 Condenser-type personal mics can be made quite small and unobtrusive—an important consideration whenever there is a need to conceal a microphone. This mic is only 0.2 by 0.3 inch.

mic. Condenser-type personal mics can be made quite small and unobtrusive (Figure 8.12)—an important consideration whenever there is a need to conceal a microphone.

Placement of Personal Mics   When attaching a personal mic, it should not be placed near jewelry or decorative pins. When the talent moves, the mic will often brush against the jewelry and create major, distracting noise. Beads, which have tendency to move around quite a bit, have ruined many audio pickups.

If a personal clip-on mic is attached to a coat lapel or to one side of a dress, you will need to anticipate which direction the talent's head will turn when speaking. Personal mics are designed to pick up sounds from only about 14 inches away. If an individual turns away from the mic, not only will the distance from mouth to mic be increased to about 2 feet, but the person will then be turned away from the microphone as well.

Hand-Held Microphones

Hand-held mics (refer to Figure 8.4a) are often dynamic, which are better at handling the sound overloads associated with some performers. Because these mics are often used at short distances, some special considerations should be mentioned. First, it is best if the mic is tilted at about a 30-degree angle, and not held perpendicular to the mouth. Speaking or singing directly into a microphone often creates unwanted *sibilance* (an exaggeration and distortion of high-frequency "*s*" sounds), *pops* from plosive sounds (words with an initial "*p*" or "*b*") and the undesirable *proximity effect* (the exaggeration of low frequencies).

Although most hand-held mics are designed to be used at a distance of 8- to 16-inches, this distance may have to be reduced in high-noise situations. **Pop filters,** which are designed to reduce the pops from plosive sounds, are built into many hand-held mics. However, when a mic is used at close range, it is also wise to slip a windscreen over the end of the mic to further reduce the effect of plosive speech sounds.

Microphone Windscreens   In addition to reducing the effect of plosives, **windscreens** (typically, a foam-rubber cap which goes over the top of the microphone) can eliminate a major on-location sound problem: the effect of wind moving across the grille of the microphone. Even a soft breeze can create a turbulence that can drown out a voice. During field productions, a properly fitted windscreen should be used on all microphones, including exposed personal mics. In an emergency a small square cube of soft, porous foam rubber cut to fit over the end of the microphone can be used.

Positioning Hand-Held Microphones   When a hand-held mic is shared between two people, audio level problems can be avoided by holding the mic closer to the person with the weaker voice. Inexperienced interviewers have a tendency to hold the microphone closer to themselves. The resulting problem is compounded when the announcer has a strong, confident voice and the person being interviewed is somewhat timidly replying to questions.

Headset Microphones

The **headset mic** was developed to serve the needs of sports commentators. It consists of a unidirectional dynamic mic with a built-in pop filter (similar to what is used by some popular singers on stage). In addition, padded double earphones carry two separate signals: the program audio and the director's cues. Having the mic built into the headset ensures a constant microphone-to-mouth distance, even when the announcer moves from place to place.

PZ Microphones

PZ (sometimes abbreviated **PZM**) stands for sound pressure microphone. This type relies entirely on reflected sound. In specific situations (such as when placed on a table top) a PZ mic will provide a pickup superior to that of other types of mics.

Contact Microphones

As the name suggests, **contact mics** pick up sound by being in direct physical contact with the sound source. They are generally mounted on musical instruments, such as the sounding board of a piano, the surface of an acoustic bass, or near the bridge of a violin. Contact mics have the advantage of being able to eliminate interfering external sounds and of not being influenced by sound reflections from nearby objects. Their flat sides distinguish them in appearance from small personal mics.

MICROPHONE CONNECTORS AND CORDS

Mic Connectors

To ensure reliability, audio connectors (refer to Figure 8.11) must always be kept clean, dry and well-aligned (without bent pins or loose pin connectors). Although the audio connectors themselves must be kept dry, in field production mic cables can be strung across wet grass, or even through water, without ill effects (assuming the rubber covering has not been damaged). In rain or snow in the field, moisture can be sealed out of audio connectors by tightly wrapping them with plastic electrical tape. It should be emphasized that this applies to microphone cables only. If AC power is used in the field for the camera, lights or recorder, these extension cables and connectors must always be kept dry.

Mic Cords

Care must be taken in using mics and mic cables around electrical equipment. Fluorescent lights can induce an annoying buzz in audio. Computers and certain types of medical equipment—especially if they are near audio cables or equipment—can also create noise. Running mic cables parallel to power cords often creates problems. The solution to hum or buzz in audio is often as simple as moving a mic cable a few feet.

Sometimes noise problems are the result of a break in a ground wire or the outer shield of a mic cable. To work properly mic cables require near-perfect conductivity through both their internal wires and the outer shield (ground) of the cable.

WIRELESS MICROPHONES

Wireless mics can be an ideal solution whenever the presence of microphone cables constitutes a problem. In a **wireless microphone,** a basic dynamic or condenser microphone is connected to a miniature FM (frequency modulation) radio transmitter. Because the audio signal from these microphones is converted into a frequency-modulated analog or digital radio frequency signal, they are commonly referred to as **RF mics.**

Figure 8.13 Wireless (RF) mics can be an ideal solution whenever microphone cables are a problem. In a wireless mic, a basic dynamic or condenser microphone is connected to a miniature FM (frequency modulation) radio transmitter. A receiver located within the production area picks up the signal.

Types of Wireless Microphones

There are two types of wireless mics: the self-contained (all-in-one) unit and the two-piece unit. Figure 8.13a shows a self-contained, hand-held unit where the mic, transmitter, battery and antenna are all within or part of the microphone housing. When small, unobtrusive clip-on mics are desirable, a two-piece unit is the best choice. Here the mic is connected to a separate transmitting unit that can be clipped to a belt, put in a pocket, or hidden underneath clothing.

Wireless Mic Applications

Since they solve many of the problems associated with using off-camera mics, wireless mics are now widely used in both studio and on-location productions. Today, camcorders even have built-in receivers for wireless mics, thus eliminating the troublesome cable that normally connects the reporter or interviewer to the camera.

Transmitting Range Considerations

As already noted, the audio detected by a wireless mic is converted to a low-power RF signal. This signal is transmitted either by an internal antenna within the microphone's case or by an external antenna (generally in the form of a short wire attached to the bottom of a separate transmitting unit). In the latter case the antenna should be kept straight and not folded over or coiled up, which can happen if the unit is shoved into a pocket. Some wireless personal mics make use of a loop of wire inconspicuously worn around the neck. Under optimum conditions wireless mics can reliably transmit over more than a 1,000-foot radius. This distance is reduced to 250 feet if obstructions are present.

Interference Problems

RF mics can have problems with dead spots, and distortion and fading caused by interference from nearby objects, especially if those objects are metal. The latter results in *multipath reception,* with the reflected signal interfering with the primary signal. This can be particularly bothersome if the talent is moving and the audio begins to rapidly fade in and out. As we will see, this problem can often be easily fixed.

In addition to multipath reception, RF mics can experience interference from other sources of RF energy. Because of FCC limitations, the FM mic signal must be of relatively low power. As a result, other radio transmitters can interfere with the signal (*RF interference*). Even though they are on different frequencies, nearby radio services emit harmonic signals that, if strong enough, can be picked up on the wireless mic frequency. In order for a wireless FM mic signal to be reliable, its RF signal must be at least twice as strong as an interfering RF signal.

RF interference can also take other forms. Most RF mics transmit on frequencies above the standard FM radio band in either the high VHF range, or in part of the UHF band. Since the UHF band is less crowded than the VHF band, it is preferred by audio engineers. Because many UHF frequencies are used by other services, many wireless mics allow the selection of different radio frequencies. On some professional equipment you will find ten frequency groups, each with seven channels to select from.

Wireless Mic Receiving Antennas

There are two types of wireless mic receivers. **Non-diversity receivers** use a single antenna mounted on the back of the receiver. This type of antenna is most prone to multi-path reception problems, especially if the talent moves from place to place. Two antennas are used in **diversity receivers.** Since the two antennas can be placed some distance apart, it is assumed that any time one antenna is not picking up a clear signal, the other one will. To keep the signals from interfering with each other within the receiver, electronic circuitry is used to automatically select the stronger and clearer of the two signals at any one moment.

With either diversity and non-diversity receivers, multiple wireless mics can be used at the same time by putting each on a different frequency. Assuming enough clear frequencies are available, it is possible to use more than a dozen wireless mics at one time.

Off-Camera Microphones

There are many instances in television production when it is desirable to place a microphone out of the range of the camera. For example,

- When a visible microphone would not be appropriate, as in the case of a dramatic production
- When a microphone cord would restrict the movement of talent
- When too many people are in the scene to use multiple personal, hand-held or RF mics.

Because of their non-directional nature, omnidirectional or simple cardioid-patterned microphones used at a distance of 10 or more feet will quickly start picking up extraneous sounds and, depending on the acoustics of the situation, cause the audio to sound hollow and "off-mic." Consequently, only a supercardioid or narrower pattern should be used as an off-camera mic. But even these mics will not solve the problem of excess reverberation or echo within a room.

Room Acoustics

Whenever a room has smooth, unbroken walls, or uncarpeted floors, *reverberation* (echoes from the walls) can be a problem. Even moderate reverberation is enough to reduce the intelligibility of speech and make audio sound hollow. Since the ear hears rather selectively, this problem may initially go unnoticed unless audio is monitored with high-quality earphones. Moving mics closer to the subjects is the simplest solution; but this is not always possible. Other solutions include using highly directional mics, adding sound absorbing materials to walls, or placing objects within a scene that will break up sound reflections.

Hanging Microphones

Hanging microphones are useful for covering sound from a large area, such as a choir or orchestra. Microphones can be suspended over a performance area by tying them to a grid or fixture just above the top of the widest camera shot. Suspended

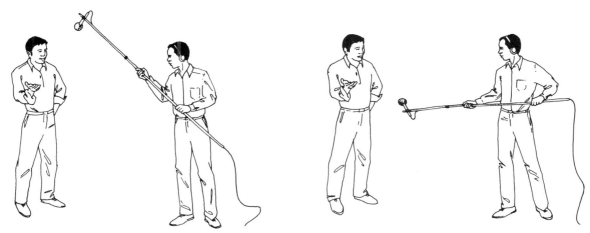

Figure 8.14   As the name suggests, fishpoles consist of a long pole with a mic attached to one end. An operator equipped with an audio headset can move the microphone to correspond with changes in camera shots and talent positions. Depending upon the camera shot, the fishpole can be either suspended above or below the speaker's head.

microphones should be checked with the lights turned on to see that they do not create shadows on backgrounds or sets. Since it is sometimes desirable to be able to follow the movements of talent, a fishpole or a boom mic is often a better choice.

Fishpoles

As the name suggests, **fishpoles** consist of a long pole with a mic attached to one end. Some have counterbalancing weight on the opposite end. An operator equipped with an audio headset can move the microphone to correspond with changes in camera shots and talent positions (Figure 8.14). Supercardioid and hypercardioid mics mounted in a rubber cradle suspension device called a *shock mount* are commonly used with a fishpole.

Microphone Booms

Microphone booms range from a small giraffe (basically a fishpole mounted on a tripod) to a large perambulator boom that takes two people to operate.

The **giraffe** or small-studio boom has an adjustable center column and a telescoping arm with a reach of 10–15 feet. The tripod legs are mounted on wheels; the microphone at the end of the boom can be swiveled to the left or right by the operator. The largest booms are reserved for studio use. They have a hydraulically controlled central platform where operators sit while controlling four things: the left or right movement of the boom arm, the reach of the arm, the left-to-right panning of the attached microphone, and the vertical tilt of the microphone.

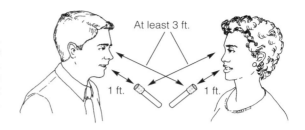

Figure 8.15 Unless precautions are taken, cancellation can be a problem in multiple-mic audio pickups. (The same problem can surface when people are sitting next to each other.) One solution, illustrated here, is to follow the "three-to-one" rule. This rule states that mics must be at least three times farther from each other than they are from a speaker.

Hidden Microphones

It is often possible to hide microphones close to where the on-camera talent will be sitting or standing and eliminate both the need for personal or hand-held mics and the problems that mic cords represent. Microphones are sometimes taped to the back of a prop or hidden in a table decoration.

When several mics are used on a set, each one not being used at a particular moment should be turned down or switched off until needed. This not only reduces total ambient sound, but also eliminates phase cancellation.

Phase Cancellation

Phase cancellation, which results in low-level and hollow-sounding audio, occurs when two or more mics pick up sound waves that are out of phase. When multiple mics are used on a set, there are four safeguards against phase cancellation:

- Place mics as close as possible to sound sources
- Use directional mics
- Turn down mics any time they are not needed
- Carefully check and vary distances between the sound sources and multiple mics to reduce or eliminate any cancellation effect.

As shown in Figure 8.15, a speaker's primary mic should be placed at one-third the distance (or less) of any other mic. If a good solution to phase cancellation is not impossible, in an emergency an engineer can electrically reverse the electrical phase of one microphone.

STEREO

Our ability to locate a particular sound is possible in part because we have learned, largely unconsciously, to understand the minute and complex time-difference relationship between sounds in our left and right ears. If a sound comes from our left side, the sound waves from that sound will reach our left ear a fraction of a second before they reach our right ear. This time difference is called a phase difference.

Depending on the location of a sound, we might also note a slight difference in loudness between sounds that occur on our left and sounds coming from our right. This also helps us to locate sounds.

The Stereo Effect

There are several approaches to creating the stereo effect in TV production.

First, there is *synthesized stereo,* where the stereo effect is simulated electronically. A slight bit of "reverb" (reverberation or echo) adds to the effect. Although this is not true stereo, when reproduced through stereo speakers the sound will be perceived as having more dimension than monaural sound.

True stereo, of course, is only achieved if the original sound is recorded with stereo equipment. At it's simplest level this consists of a stereo track of music or environmental sound added to a monophonic recording of narration. Although the approach is simple and widely used, it does not provide an overall stereo perspective.

A slightly more sophisticated approach, and one that is used in dramatic presentations, is the use of a stereo mic on the set, which is mixed with stereo music and effects during postproduction. Although important dialogue is still held to "center stage," the stereo pickup adds important dimension and stereo acoustics to the recording. Beyond this, we move to the creation of complex stereo tracks in postproduction through multi-track recording.

Multi-Track Stereo Recording

By recording the various sources of sound on separate audio tracks, the sources can later be placed in any left-to-right sound perspective. This provides maximum flexibility in postproduction. Recorders are available that will record from 8 to more than 40 separate audio tracks on a single piece of 1-inch or 2-inch audio tape. Even more audio tracks are available through synchronizing two or more, multi-track recorders together with SMPTE time code. (Time code will be discussed in Chapter 12). During the editing phase the audio from the numerous tracks is mixed together to provide the desired mix and left-to-right placement of each sound element. By keeping the original multi-track tapes—a procedure that should always be followed in sophisticated audio production work—changes can later be made simply by loading the original multi-track tape, rerecording an audio track, if necessary, and then redoing the mix.

In recording a sophisticated contemporary music session, the various instruments and vocal parts are often recorded at different times on separate audio tracks. Performers recording their specific parts rely on earphones to hear playbacks of previously recorded material. Later, the various tracks are creatively mixed together to achieve the best artistic effect. Keeping the various tracks separate not only provides maximum flexibility in doing a final stereo mix, but also allows an instrument or vocalist to be rerecorded, if needed, without having to redo the entire session.

By manipulating the sound-phase relationships between the individually recorded sources, and placing sounds on the left-to-right stereo perspective, an engineer can completely construct the physical orientation of a music group. Any instrument or vocalist can be placed at any point along the left-to-right perspective, even though this placement may bear little resemblance to the original location. This process of individually recording the separate sound elements not only makes it possible to control the placement and balance between each sound source, but each track can be separately enhanced with reverberation, filtering, etc.

The multiple-track recording method is preferred in contemporary music because it affords maximum postrecording flexibility. In contrast, recordings of classical music and orchestras are often done with only one strategically placed stereo mic. In this case, the sound mix and balance are the responsibility of the conductor. The job of the recording technician is simply to capture this carefully crafted result by placing a high-quality stereo mic in a central, acoustically desirable place in the auditorium.

Stereo Microphones

The simplest solution to stereo recording is to use an all-in-one stereo mic, which consists of two mics mounted in a single housing. The mic can be hand held, mounted on a camera, or suspended from a boom.

To give maximum control over directional characteristics, most stereo mics use two condenser elements placed about 1-½ inches apart. The upper element can be rotated over 180 degrees to provide a variety of offset angles. Numerous directional patterns can generally be selected.

Stereo mics can give an adequate stereo effect, especially in EFP applications where things need to be kept simple and audio can be successfully miced ("miked") from one location. However, this approach is limited in its ability to provide optimum **stereo separation**—a clear and distinct separation between the left and right stereo channels. For this reason in more sophisticated production, many audio technicians prefer to use two separate mics.

The M-S Micing Technique

In the M-S technique, bidirectional and unidirectional (supercardioid) mics are used together.[3] The bidirectional mic's polar pattern, which is shaped like a figure-8, is aligned so that its areas of maximum sensitivity are parallel to the scene (Figure 8.16). This means that the areas of minimum sensitivity are oriented toward the center of the scene and toward the camera. The dead spot that is directed toward the camera ends up being an advantage, because off-camera noise is re-

---

[3] M-S, which stands for *mid-side,* is the recording approach most used in video production. A second stereo micing technique, the X-Y technique, in which two mics or elements are aimed at subject matter in a "Y" or "V" pattern, is used in demanding audio applications such as creating soundtracks in conjunction with a DAT recorder.

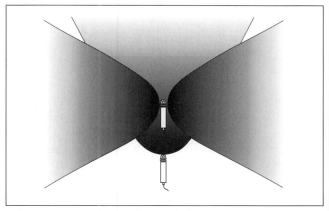

Figure 8.16 In the M-S stereo micing technique, bidirectional and unidirectional (supercardioid) mics are used together. The bidirectional mic's polar pattern is aligned so that its areas of maximum sensitivity are parallel to the scene. Areas of minimum sensitivity are toward the camera (which tends to reduce off-camera noise) and toward the center of the scene (the area covered by the directional mic). The M-S micing technique allows for maximum control over the stereo effect.

duced. The second dead spot, the one oriented toward the center of the scene, is covered by the directional mic.

The outputs of both mics are fed through a complex audio matrix circuit that uses the phasing differences of the two mics to produce the left and right channels. Adjustments to this circuit allow considerable latitude in varying the overall stereo effect, including altering the pickup pattern or stereo image from 1 to about 127 degrees.

Maintaining a Stereo Perspective

Stereo TV has an ongoing sound perspective problem because camera angles and distances shift with each new camera shot. It is almost impossible and, in fact, it would be rather disconcerting in most instances for the stereo perspective to shift with each change in camera angle. For example, in an on-location sequence if the sound of the ocean, nearby machinery or a playground flipped to the right and back again with each reverse-angle shot, these sounds would be rather disorienting to a listener/viewer.

Concessions in Stereo Perspectives

To solve this problem, inventive concessions in stereo sound perspectives are regularly made. In the case of an ocean sound effect, a sound mixer might place the ocean in a left-to-right perspective that matches a wide-angle establishing shot and then, especially if the subsequent dialogue close-ups are short and numerous, simply maintain the original stereo perspective throughout subsequent shots. Although, strictly speaking, the stereo perspective would not accurately conform to close-ups, this concession would be better than flipping the ocean back and forth with each cut.

Using Pan Pots

Another solution, especially if the close-up dialogue shots are long, is the use of a pan pot to subtly shift the ocean slightly with each shot so that a true left-to-right stereo perspective is simulated. A **pan pot** consists of two or more faders (volume controls) ganged together. They can be used to slowly move a source of sound from one stereo channel to the other.

Holding Dialogue to "Center Stage"

To ensure maximum intelligibility, especially for monophonic audio systems, the dialogue for the typical one and two shots of a dramatic production should be kept in the center of the stereo perspective. In most cases, this will conform to the visual perspective shown on the screen. A full stereo effect can then be added with background music and sound effects.

Stereo in Sports Coverage

In sporting events a general background stereo pickup of the crowd is typically mixed in with a monophonic feed from the play-by-play narration. If there are two announcers, pan pots can be used to place them slightly to the left and right of center. Having individual mics directed fully into either a left or right channel, as is sometimes done, makes the announcers sound unrealistically isolated from each other.

Sometimes a stereo mic mounted on a sideline camera will be mixed into existing program audio when that camera is switched up. This technique would be appropriate to pick up the sound of cheerleaders, or sideline activity.

Guidelines for Stereo Placement

The stereo placement of various audio sources within a setting often ends up being a creative decision. Although no set of rules can be established to cover every situation, there are two guidelines: First, try to simulate an authentic stereo reality when possible. Second (and even more important), avoid the use of any production technique, in either audio or video, that diverts viewer attention away from production content. It is better to hold back on authenticity rather than introduce an effect that will call attention to itself.

Stereo Playback

The final stereo signal should be reproduced through two, good-quality speakers, placed at equal distances from the TV set. The speakers are normally positioned

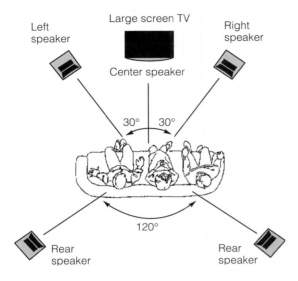

Figure 8.17 Whereas stereo covers about a 120-degree frontal perspective, surround-sound and quadraphonic techniques attempt to reproduce sounds in both the front and back of the listener—a full 360-degree sound perspective. Most systems require that listeners sit approximately in the middle of four or five speakers.

from 9- to 12-feet apart and aimed at about a 45-degree angle toward the viewer. The distance between the speakers depends on the distance of the listener; the farther back the listener is, the greater the distance between the speakers.

SURROUND-SOUND TECHNIQUES

Whereas stereo covers about a 120-degree frontal perspective, **surround-sound** and **quadraphonic-sound** systems attempt to reproduce sounds in both the front and back of the listener—a full 360-degree sound perspective. Today, many productions are done in surround-sound, even though the number of homes equipped with surround-sound decoders is still somewhat limited. In playing back true surround or quadraphonic sound, at least four speakers are needed (Figure 8.17).

Considering the relatively small size of TV screens, a 360-degree sound perspective is a bit unrealistic. Not only does it not match the limited visual area, but placing four or five speakers an equal distance from all listeners/viewers strains the decorative schemes of most rooms in which TVs are located. There is another way.

By analyzing the way we hear sounds, psychoacoustic researchers have come up with a surround-sound system that uses only two speakers. One version, introduced during the Super Bowl XXIV broadcast, expands the stereo sound perspective significantly, even adding the illusion of a vertical dimension. To achieve the expanded effect, multi-channel audio recordings are digitized and fed into a computer during postproduction. A special six-axis joystick is used to place audio sources in specific sound perspectives. (In addition to rotating 360 degrees, it also telescopes vertically to represent height.) Although the system has the advantage of needing only two speakers, the four- or five-speaker approach is capable of greater realism.

Quadraphonic Microphones

For surround-sound TV applications **quadraphonic mics** can be used that have four mic elements within a single housing. Typically, an upper capsule containing two elements picks up sound from the left-front and right-rear. Another capsule, mounted below this one, picks up sound from the right-front and left-rear. In postproduction the four audio tracks can be mixed with tracks of music and effects (M&E) to develop a full surround-sound effect.

SINGLE AND DOUBLE SYSTEM SOUND

Single System Recording

When all of the needed sound is recorded directly on the videotape as the tape is shot, the technique is referred to as **single system recording.** This approach is used in news and documentary work. Today's VCRs can record from two to eight channels of audio along with the video. Four channels are adequate for most professional needs. However, complex stereo techniques require more audio channels than are available on videotape machines. To meet these needs there is double system recording.

Double System Recording

In **double system recording** a multi-track audio recorder is synchronized with a VCR and used to record from eight to more than 40 separate audio tracks. As we've noted, recording each source of audio on a separate track provides maximum flexibility during the postproduction phase. Double system sound recording has been the standard for motion picture production since the earliest days of sound.

PRODUCTION COMMUNICATION SYSTEMS

PL Systems

Although not heard by an audience, effective behind-the-scenes audio links are crucial to the production process. Early in the history of television it became obvious that, when multiple cameras were used, the various tasks of production personnel had to be coordinated through one or more private channels of communication. The **PL** (private line) or **intercom** (intercommunication) link that evolved was based on the headset concept, which was borrowed from telephone operators.

With the attached microphone and at least one earphone, production personnel can talk to each other and receive instructions from a director. (One of the reasons directional mics are important in production is to reject behind-the-camera, PL-line conversations between crew members.) Most PL or intercom systems are wired together on a kind of party line. In this way each member of the production crew can hear and talk to everyone else. To handle complex productions involving personnel at different locations, specialized PL subsystems are often necessary where certain groups of crew members will be on their own communication system. Production equipment such as cameras, large mic booms, or switchers have provisions to plug in PL-line headsets. Wireless headsets with built-in radio receivers and transmitters are also available for production personnel who don't want the restriction of being hard-wired to a piece of equipment.

Headsets can be equipped with two features that help in high-noise situations. One is a *push-to-talk button.* Normally the headset microphones and earphones are always on, so that both hands can be kept free to operate equipment. But, by keeping the individual microphones off until needed, the overall noise level on the headset party line can be kept to a minimum in high-noise situations. The second feature, large padded earphones, helps to screen out competing sound. Both of these features are necessary in covering high-noise sporting events and during telecasts of popular music concerts.

IFB Systems

Thus far we have been talking about the communication link between behind-the-scenes production personnel. Often in ENG and EFP work it is necessary for a director to relay messages directly to on-air talent via a personal earphone, sometimes when they are actually on the air. For this, **IFB** (interrupted or interruptable feedback) communication systems have been devised. An IFB circuit normally carries the outgoing program audio, including the announcer's own voice when he or she is on the air. However, the program audio can be interrupted by either an important message from the director or by an audio feed from a remote program source. The latter could be an announcer, a reporter, or a person being interviewed at another location. For live news reporting, the field reporter's earphone is often hooked up to the station's broadcast audio. This allows the reporter to hear the on-air cue as well as to answer questions from on-air personnel in studio situations.

Audio Recording and Playback Devices

Thus far, we've discussed audio production in terms of live pick-ups with mics. But, of course, much audio comes from prerecorded sources: turntables, tape machines, CDs, DATs, and computer disk drives.

Turntables and Reel-to-Reel Tape Machines

Although records and reel-to-reel tape machines used to be the primary source of prerecorded material, they have now been largely replaced by audio carts (cartridges), CDs and DAT machines.

Cart Machines

Cart machines (cartridge machines) contain a continuous loop of 1/4-inch audio tape within a plastic cartridge (Figure 8.18). Although tape lengths vary from 15 seconds to 1 hour, most carts are 30 and 60 seconds, for commercials and public service announcements, and 3 minutes for musical selections. One of the advantages of cart machines is that they automatically cue themselves and start almost instantly—a feature that makes tight audio edits possible. The first cart machines were analog, but in the late 1980s, digital cart machines were introduced.

The functions of the basic controls on cart machines—start, stop, play and record—are self-evident, except possibly for one thing. In order to record on some cart machines the record button has to be held down as the play button is pressed.

Carts rely on inaudible tones recorded on the tape to automatically cue up the starting points of segments. To speed cueing, some machines accelerate tape transport between the point at which one segment ends and the start of the next segment. If there is only one "cut" (segment) on the cart, the "next segment" will be the beginning of the tape loop.

Until the advent of DAT machines (to be discussed), carts were widely used in postproduction for recording and playing back background sound and narration.

Compact Discs (CDs)

Because of their superior audio quality, ease of control and small size, CDs (compact discs) have become a preferred medium for prerecorded music and sound effects.

Like all digitized audio, the original analog signal, generally from a microphone, is first converted to digital information by an analog-to-digital converter. An image of the digital data is "stamped" into the surface of the CD in a process that is similar to the way LP records (with their analog signals) are produced. When a CD is played, a laser beam is used to illuminate the digital pattern encoded on the surface. The reflected light (modified by the digital pattern) is read by a photoelectric cell.

The overall diameter of a typical audio CD is a little less than 5 inches (12.7 centimeters) across. Although only one side is used (the other side is used only for the label), CDs are able to hold more information than a 12-inch LP ("long playing") phonograph record can on both sides. In addition, the frequency response and dynamic range are significantly better on a CD. For short selections, special "singles" are available, CDs that are only 3 inches (7.6 centimeters) across.

Figure 8.18   Cart machines (cartridge machines) contain a continuous loop of 1/4-inch audio tape within a plastic cartridge. The first cart machines were analog, but in the late 1980s, digital cart machines were introduced. In the mid-1990s digital audio workstations and media servers started replacing audio tape for postproduction work.

A standard CD contains a spiral track which, if "unwound" would come out to be 3.5 miles (5.7 km) long. The width of the track is 1/60 the size of the groove in an LP record, or 1/50 the size of a human hair. Because of the minuscule size of the track, imperfections in the mechanics or optics of CD player, or in the CD itself, will cause immediate problems.

CD Defects   Occasionally, surface stress occurs in the CD manufacturing process resulting in disc warp. If the surface of the CD is sufficiently warped, the automatic focusing device in the CD player will not be able to adjust to the variation. The result can be mistracking and loss of audio information.

CDs can also have other manufacturing problems, including pinholes, air bubbles and black spots. Some of these defects are an inevitable part of the CD manufacturing process. It is only when the areas involved become relatively large[4] that they cause audio problems. These defects can often be spotted when the CD is held so that light is reflected from its surface.

---

[4] Specifically, the size is 100 μm for bubbles, 200 μm for pin holes and 300 μm for black spots. (The unit μm, which stands for micron, or in this case micrometer, is equal to .000001 meter.)

By far the most common CD problems stem from things that happen to the CD after it is manufactured. Although CDs don't build up surface noise the way records do, scratches, fingerprints, dust and dirt on the CD surface will cause a loss of digital data.

Automatic Error Correction   CD players attempt to compensate for the loss of a signal in three ways: error correction, error concealment (interpolation) and muting.

For small problems, error-correcting circuitry within the CD player can detect lost data (drop outs) and, based on the existing data at the moment, accurately supply the missing data. If the loss of data is more substantial and the CD player can't automatically "figure out" what has been lost, error-correcting circuits can automatically build an "audio bridge" across the missing information by substituting data that conforms to (blends in with) existing audio. In most cases the substituted (interpolated) data will be so similar to the lost data, that the effect will not be detected. However, if error concealment circuitry has to be invoked repeatedly within a short time span, the result will become noticeable. In loud passages you may hear a series of clicks or a "ripping sound." Error concealment will generally not be noticed during quiet passages.

When a large, contiguous block of data is missing or corrupted, the CD player will simply mute (silence) the audio until good data again appears. A large scratch on the surface of a CD can cause audio to disappear for some time, giving the impression, when audio returns, that the player has skipped tracks.

Programming CD Playback   In addition to their high quality and compact size, one of the major advantages of CD players is their ability to be programmed for instant starts at precise points. This ability makes it possible for an audio operator or a video edit controller to trigger preset musical transitions and audio effects at preprogrammed points and to instantly recue them as needed.

Digital Audio Tapes (DAT, RDAT)

DATs (digital audio tapes) can record and play back with an audio quality that exceeds what is possible with CDs. The 2- by 2-7/8-inch DAT cassette contains audiotape 3.81mm wide and is about two-thirds the size of a standard analog audiocassette (Figure 8.19). The 2-hour capacity of a DAT cassette is 66 percent greater than a standard 80-minute CD.

DAT exists in two forms: one for general consumer (home) use and one, referred to as **RDAT** (recordable digital audiotape), for professional applications.[5] The difference is the incorporation of an electronic device in the consumer version that is designed to foil attempts at pirating (making illegal copies of commercial recordings).

---

[5] Both systems are commonly referred to simply as *DAT.*

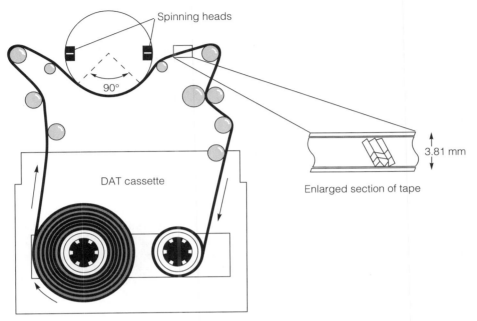

Figure 8.19   DAT systems use a headwheel that spins at 2,000 rpm and writes digital information on a tape less than 4mm wide.

Serial Copy Management System   Standard, consumer-type DATs incorporate a Serial Copy Management System. This system relies on a signal in the recordings that can be detected by an electronic component (chip) in the minidisk player. When the signal is present it is not possible to make a digital copy of the copy-righted material. (In some instances analog copies are possible, however.) RDAT players do not have the same copy limitations.

DAT systems use a headwheel that spins at 2,000 rpm—similar to a video cassette recorder. Encoded in the audio signal of a DAT recording is a control subcode that can be used for several types of data, including (in professional models) a time code reference. Many machines feature solid-state memory, which can retain from 5 to 15 seconds of audio. Retaining audio in memory makes it possible to do instant starts, cross-fades from a single machine, and numerous editing effects. Some four-head DAT machines have the capability of playing back audio a fraction of a second after it's recorded in order to reveal any recording problems. The four-head machines also can be used to read an existing audio track, add music or effects as needed, and then immediately rerecord the result within a fraction of a second.

DAT Time Code   In early 1992, a time-code system was introduced by several manufacturers, which makes it possible to automatically cue and control DATs with split-second accuracy. The time-code system, referred to as the IEC Sub-code

Format, also ensures that tapes recorded on one DAT machine can be played back without problems on any other machine using the time-code format. The DAT version of SMPTE time-code involves a sophisticated technique of translating hours, seconds, and video frames (1/30-second intervals) into a signal that can be recorded with the digital audio. Since the time-code format has been designed to be universal, it can be used with any of the world's video standards.

DAT time code is especially valuable in postproduction where time code can be used to accurately synchronize a wide range of audio sources with video. In audio and video workstations DAT machines can be programmed to automatically cue themselves, and start and stop as needed.

Audiocassettes

During the mid-to-late 1980s the medium of choice for prerecorded music at the consumer level was the analog cassette. After going through several generations of refinement, professional audiocassette machines were developed that can record and play back the full audio range (25 to 20 kilohertz with metal tape). Although they lack many of the advantages of DAT recording, professional cassette recorders represent a comparatively simple and inexpensive recording option.

Audio Control Devices

Audio Mixers

The sources of audio we've been discussing must be carefully blended and controlled in the production and postproduction processes. This procedure is normally done in a TV studio or production facility in an **audio console** (or audio board). For video field production smaller units, called **audio mixers,** do the same thing on a smaller scale. Both audio consoles and audio mixers can

- Amplify the level of incoming signals
- With the help of VU meters, allow for level (volume) adjustments for individual audio sources
- Allow for the smooth mixing (blending together) of multiple audio signals
- Allow for the aural monitoring of individual sources, as well as the total effect (mix) of audio
- Route the combined effect to a transmission or recording device

In addition, sophisticated audio mixers and audio boards allow the operator to manipulate specific characteristics of audio: alter the left-to-right "placement" of stereo sources, shape frequency characteristics, add reverberation to audio, and so on.

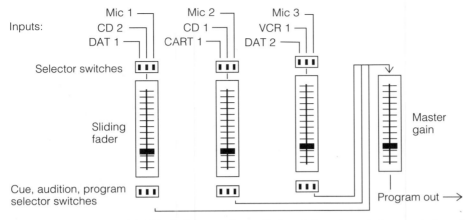

Figure 8.20   This simplified block diagram of an audio board shows how a selector switch can be used to assign one of three audio sources to each fader. Note that the output of each fader can be directed to a cue speaker, an audition speaker or to program out. The master gain fader simultaneously controls the output of all faders.

Figure 8.20 shows a simplified block diagram of an audio mixer. Even though audio mixers can control numerous audio sources, these sources break down into two categories: mic-level and line-level inputs. As the name suggests, mic-level inputs handle the extremely low voltages associated with microphones. Line-level inputs are associated with the outputs of amplified sources of audio, such as CD and tape players. Once inside the audio mixer, all audio sources are changed to line-level and handled in exactly the same way.

Multiple Microphone Setups in the Field

If only one mic is needed in the field, it can simply be plugged into one of the audio inputs of the camera. But when several microphones are needed, and when their levels must be individually controlled and mixed, a small portable audio mixer is the best solution (Figure 8.21). The use of an audio mixer requires a separate audio person to watch the VU meter and maintain the proper level on each input.

Portable, AC- or battery-powered audio mixers are available that will accept several mic or even line-level inputs. The output of the portable mixer is plugged into a high-level VTR audio input (as opposed to a low-level mic input). Most portable mixers have from three to six input channels. Since each pot (fader control) can be switched between at least two inputs, the total number of channels that can be addressed ends up being more than the number of faders. However, just as in the case of an audio console, the number of sources that can be on at the same time is limited to the number of pots on the mixer. In addition to the faders that control the inputs, a master gain control determines the levels of all inputs simultaneously and a pot controls headset volume.

Figure 8.21 Portable AC- or battery-powered stereo audio mixers will accept several microphone or line-level inputs. Most mixers have from three to six stereo input channels.

Figure 8.22 Linear faders, also referred to as vertical faders or sliding faders, are widely used in professional audio consoles today. With the type of audio console shown, you can not only vary the amplitude of sounds but add filtering and reverberation, change the left-to-right stereo placement of sources, and alter the frequency characteristics of sounds.

Audio Mixer Controls

Audio mixers and consoles use two types of controls: faders and switches. **Faders** (volume controls) can be either linear or rotary in design. As noted, faders are also referred to as attenuates or gain controls. Rotary faders are commonly called pots (from *potentiometers*). Linear faders are also referred to as vertical faders and slide faders (Figure 8.22).

Normal audio sources should reach 0 dB on the VU or loudness meter when the vertical fader or pot is one-third to two-thirds of the way up (open). Having to turn a fader up fully in order to bring the sound up to 0 dB indicates that the original source of audio is coming into the console at too low a level. In this case the probability of background noise from the audio source increases. Conversely, if the source of audio is too high coming into the board, "opening" the fader very slightly will cause the audio to immediately hit 0 dB. The amount of fader control over the source will then be limited, making smooth fades difficult. This brings up an important attribute associated with some faders.

Since faders use a system of varying resistance, zero resistance means that the fader is turned up to its maximum point—that no resistance is being placed in the path of the audio signal. Maximum resistance means that the fader is totally blocking the audio—that the volume control is down all the way. To reflect the various states of attenuation (resistance) the numbers on some faders are the reverse of what you might think: the numbers get higher, to reflect more resistance, as the fader is turned down. Maximum resistance is designated with an infinity (∞) symbol. When the fader is turned up all the way, the number on the pot or linear fader may indicate 0, for zero resistance.

Level Control and Mixing

Maintaining optimum audio levels is important, especially in digital audio. Normal audio levels should be maintained so that the loudest sounds regularly peak at 0 dB. (With a set of stereo VU meters, you will want to hold the loudest channel at any one time to about 0 dB.)

The skillful mixing of audio goes far beyond watching a VU meter. Audio operators must monitor and control the total subjective effect as heard through the speakers or earphones being used to monitor the final audio output. For example, when an announcer is talking over CD music, and we try to run both the music and announcer's voice at 0 dB, the music will drown out the announcer's words. Letting the music peak at about −10 dB, and letting the voice peak at 0 dB will probably provide the needed effect: dominant narration with supporting but non-interfering background music. The level of the music will probably be increased somewhat during long pauses in narration, and then brought back down just before narration resumes. The exact music level will depend on the nature of the music itself: whether it is inherently bright and intrusive or soft and mellow.

Instrumental music is preferred as a background to narration. However, if the music has lyrics sung by a vocalist (definitely *not* recommended as background to narration), their volume will have to be much lower so as not to compete with the narrator's words. As long as the final mix from the audio mixer or audio board is maintained at about 0 dB for maximum levels (you will not want to bring up intentionally soft musical passages to 0 dB) the proper mix and blending of audio sources should be left up to "the ear." Some issues related to mixing stereo sources will be discussed later in the chapter.

Using Audio from PA Systems

In covering musical concerts or stage productions, it is possible to use an appropriate line-level output of a public address (PA) amplifier and feed it directly into the high-level input of a mixer. (The regular speaker outputs from the PA amplifier cannot be used; they can severely damage the mixer.) A direct line from a professionally mixed PA system will result in decidedly better audio than using a mic to pick up sound from a PA speaker.

AUDIO QUALITY CONSIDERATIONS

Audio quality can be no better than the weakest link in the audio chain: mic, amplifiers, recorder, recording tape, playback mechanics and electronics, and audio speakers. When properly used, today's high-quality audio amplifiers almost never represent a limitation on quality. One critical point, however, is the audio head on the recorder. Dirty, maladjusted, or magnetized audio recording and playback heads will quickly affect high frequency response and playback level.

Recording Head Problems

If the level or quality of the audio as played on one tape machine is noticeably different from another machine, there may be three possible explanations: head clog, a magnetized head, or loss of head alignment.

Head Clog

Although some of today's audio and video recorders are equipped with self-cleaning heads, problems can still occur if the microscopic gap in audio (or video)[6] heads is clogged with dirt or the oxide coating of the recording tape. This problem is referred to as **head clog.** With analog machines moderate head clog can result in a loss of high frequencies. With digital machines there will typically be a complete loss of audio.

Head clog requires cleaning the audio heads, either with a cotton swab dipped in an appropriate cleaning agent or with a special cleaning tape. There are both "wet" and "dry" types of head-cleaning tapes. A dry cleaning tape is simply put in the recorder/player and played for a specified length of time. Since most cleaning tapes are somewhat abrasive, care should be taken not to exceed the recommended time. A "wet" cleaning tape (actually, it's only slightly damp) uses a solvent-cleaner

---

[6] With many videotape machines the highest quality audio tracks are recorded with the video heads. Consequently, problems with video heads will also affect audio quality.

that must be applied to the cleaning tape before it's used. Although possibly less convenient to use, wet cleaning tapes more readily dissolve residue clogging the microscopic gap in tape heads.

With machines using spinning heads (DATs, VCRs) the machine may have to be opened up to take care of a severe case of head clog. The heads in these machines are easily damaged. If you are not totally confident in your ability to take the top off your DAT or VCR to clean the heads, leave this servicing to a technician; these heads are expensive to replace. The heads of analog audio recorders are sturdier, more accessible, and much easier to clean.

Magnetized and Misaligned Audio Heads

Audio playback heads depend on their ability to respond to the minute magnetic patterns recorded on an audiotape. If the heads themselves become slightly magnetized, audio quality will be degraded. Demagnetizing tools are available that can demagnetize record/playback heads.

Through continued use the audio heads in analog recorders and players can become misaligned. Correcting this involves monitoring a special audio test tape while physically repositioning the heads with set screws. Aligning audio heads, which shouldn't have to be done very often, is best left to a technician.

AUDIO LEVEL CONTROL DEVICES

Four types of devices are commonly used in audio production to maintain or modify loudness (amplitude): compressors, limiters, AGC circuits and audio expanders.

Compressors

An **audio compressor** brings up low amplitude sounds and pulls down the amplitude of loud sounds (Figure 8.23). As a result, the **dynamic range** (the range in loudness that equipment can reproduce) is held much closer to 0 dB, the point of maximum loudness. Program audio that has been compressed seems louder to the ear than does non-compressed audio.

Limiters

An **audio limiter,** which is not as sophisticated as a compressor, is widely used on video production equipment (Figure 8.24). Unlike compressors, which are designed to affect both ends of the loudness range at the same time, a limiter simply keeps the audio level from exceeding 0 dB.

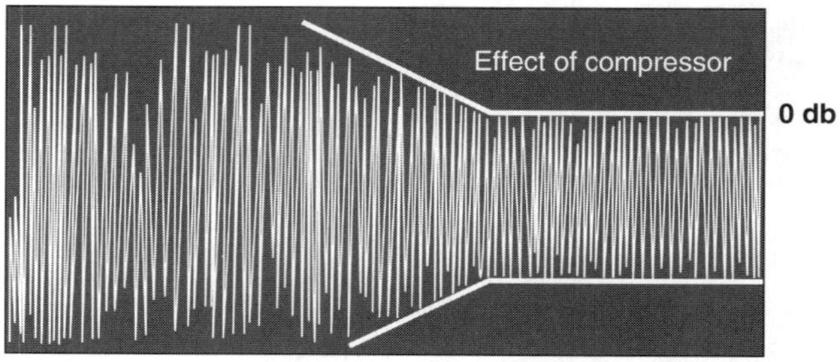

Figure 8.23 Audio compressors bring up low amplitude sounds and pull down the amplitude of loud sounds. As a result, the average loudness is held much closer to zero dB. Audio that has been compressed seems louder than non-compressed audio.

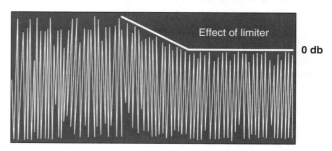

Figure 8.24 Audio limiters are a kind of safety device that keep audio levels from exceeding 0 dB. They are not as sophisticated as compressors or AGC circuits.

AGC Circuits

Most consumer-type and some prosumer-type camcorders have an automatic audio level control circuit called **AGC,** for automatic gain control. Whereas in professional camcorders audio levels can be manually controlled, in many non-professional camcorders the AGC circuit cannot be switched off. Although the presence of AGC circuits has undoubtedly saved many productions from silent disaster, they can also create some problems.

These AGC circuits go a step beyond limiters. If the average level of the audio is low, these circuits will raise it; if it is high, they will bring it down (Figure 8.25). Although AGC circuits free the video operator from having to worry about manually controlling audio levels, they cannot intelligently respond to the needs of differing audio situations.

Problems with AGC Circuits   Since AGC circuits are simply designed to always maintain maximum audio levels, they will make annoying background sounds louder whenever no other sound is present. This means that during pauses in dialogue, the loudness of background noise may suddenly increase. If subsequent audio processing circuits in VTRs used during editing also have AGC circuits, the problem will quickly be compounded.[7]

---

[7] Although the AGC circuits in non-professional camcorders can't be turned off, limiters and AGC circuits in editing equipment generally can.

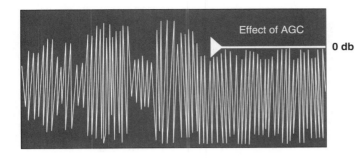

Figure 8.25 Automatic gain control (AGC) circuits are widely used in portable videocassette recorders. If the average level of the audio is low, these circuits will raise it; if it is high, they will bring it down. AGC circuits can create problems in specific recording situations.

In addition to bringing up objectionable background sound during quiet moments, AGC circuits can also introduce a reverse problem. Since they respond to loud noises by quickly pulling down audio levels for several seconds, this means that words can be lost during a conversation when an AGC circuit reacts to a loud sound, such as someone bumping the microphone.

Because of the effect of the AGC circuit in bringing up sound levels during a period of silence, the first few seconds of audio may be badly distorted, until the AGC sets the proper level. To get around this problem, many videographers who are stuck with an AGC circuit they can't switch to manual control have the on-camera talent say a few words just before the actual start of the segment. This can be simply a countdown, "5, 4, 3, 2, 1," or anything to allow the AGC to adjust proper audio level. Later, during editing, this "false start" can be edited out.

The last problem area for AGC circuits is in recording music. Although most of the AM rock radio stations of the 1960s and 1970s preferred the maximum-loud sound that audio compressors and AGC circuits could deliver, the artists often complained that their carefully balanced audio levels were destroyed. Everything in the recording, whether intended to be loud or soft, came out sounding about the same. Even though AGC circuits don't have the magnitude of control over dynamic range that sophisticated compressors do, they can still compress the natural and intended dynamic range of music. In recording long musical passages, the natural dynamic range of the music can be preserved by switching off AGC circuits if possible and manually riding gain.

Audio Expanders

To complete the discussion of amplitude control devices, we should mention the **audio expander** (Figure 8.26). Audio transmitted over telephone lines or satellites often ends up being overly processed and suffering from a restricted dynamic range. An expander can restore the audio to its normal range. In the process it can also reduce noticeable background (ambient) noise and audio hiss and hum.

Figure 8.26   Audio transmitted over telephone lines or by satellites often ends up being overly processed and suffering from a restricted dynamic (loudness) range. As shown here, an audio expander can restore audio to its normal dynamic range. In the process it can reduce background noise.

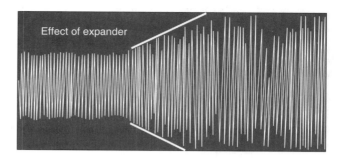

Music Synthesizers and MIDI Interfaces

Synthesized Music

Whereas mainstream TV dramatic productions used to require a full orchestra to create background music, the majority of the music we hear in today's network productions is synthesized. Synthesized music is electronically created, sometimes by only one musician. Working with electronic keyboards and an array of electronic equipment, these electronic musicians can realistically simulate anything from a harmonica to a full symphony orchestra.

MIDI

In the early 1980s a complete set of system hardware and software standards were adopted for electronic music and sound effects. This standard is referred to as **MIDI** for Musical Instrument Digital Interface. The MIDI system is credited with starting a technological revolution in music. Using MIDI, musicians can interconnect a full range of keyboards, computers and music synthesizing devices to produce an unrestricted range of musical sounds and effects. Normally, a computer is used as a central controlling device (Figure 8.27).

A central feature of composing with MIDI is the building of layers of musical sounds from sampled segments. Sampling in this context involves digitally recording sounds or musical segments from live or prerecorded sources. Once a sound is sampled, it can be endlessly modified. Musical segments can be cut and pasted in the same way a writer uses a word processor to move and copy words, sentences and paragraphs.

Starting with a simple beat an electronic composer can add electronic instruments, one by one, until a complete musical "group" is realistically created. It is possible to alter the tempo of music without changing its pitch. Also possible is tempo mapping, in which time-code numbers are assigned to specific points in video and automatically shrink or expand the music to fit the designated intervals.

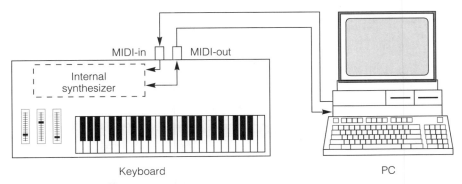

Figure 8.27 For sophisticated audio editing—especially for conforming audio to video and working with MIDI—there are computer audio editing programs and editing workstations. Since both audio and video sequences can be visually represented on the computer screen, music, narration and sound effects can be slowly "shuttled" back and forth to synchronize them with specific points in an edited video production.

Since MIDI composing and editing is non-destructive to original sampled sounds, you are free to try a variety of effects. In video and audio postproduction, MIDI devices can be synchronized with SMPTE time code and music, and sound effects can be precisely keyed to specific scenes and transitions. Whenever you don't like something you have done, you can readily "undo" your last edit decision—or even your last few decisions—and instantly be back where you started so you can try something else.

COMPUTER-BASED AUDIO EDITING SYSTEMS

Desktop Editing Systems

Today, audio editing is commonly done with the help of a desktop computer and special software. This type of editing is referred to as **desktop editing** or **PC-based editing.** These systems, as well as the dedicated audio workstations to be discussed,

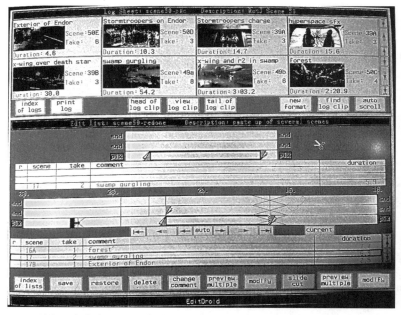

Figure 8.28   Although desktop sound editing software varies, most use a time line that shows time progression in conjunction with the various layers of sound. Note here that numerous sounds can be heard at the moment represented by the vertical line on the computer screen.

make use of computer storage devices that allow an operator to digitally record sounds and then play them back instantly, in any order. Computer hard disks and solid-state memory chips are used as recording media. The computer hard disk is considered **non-volatile memory,** because information is retained on the disk even without power. In contrast, the random-access memory (RAM) chips in the computer represent **volatile memory** because memory is lost when power is turned off. During the audio editing process information is held in volatile memory whenever there is a need for instant access or the manipulation of sounds in real time. More lengthy segments, and segments which are to be saved, are transferred to the computer's hard disk. Once editing is completed, the results can be fed ("printed") to an external recording medium, such as DAT, for subsequent use in productions.

Typically, the software for this type of editing system graphically represents the audio segments along a **time line** on the computer screen. Time lines are used in both audio and video editing systems to visually represent in a linear fashion what's going on at any point (Figure 8.28).

Once needed audio segments are brought into the system, it becomes an easy task to call up segments, make modifications and mix multiple audio tracks together into a stereo or mono track. Audio can be time-compressed, expanded, filtered, echoed, raised and lowered in pitch, and even played backwards—whatever is needed. With enough hard-disk storage, an entire digitized sound-effects library can also be put on the hard disk for instant recall during the editing process. As editing demands expand beyond a basic desktop computer, dedicated audio editing equipment, referred to as editing workstations, are used.

EDITING WORKSTATIONS

For sophisticated audio editing, and especially for conforming audio to lengthy video productions, there are dedicated **editing workstations,** or tapeless workstations. Since both audio and video sequences are visually represented on a computer screen, music, narration and sound effects can be slowly "shuttled" back and forth to synchronize them with specific points in an edited video production.

Workstations allow maximum flexibility in conforming audio to video. They can handle the full range of audio sweetening requirements, including the creation of an unlimited number of special audio effects.

With all of the "basics" now covered in the audio and video process, we can turn our attention to the actual production process—starting with news and documentary productions.

CHAPTER 9   VIDEO RECORDING

IN THIS CHAPTER we'll look at the various approaches to recording video, including the strengths and weaknesses of each.

With the exception of prime-time dramatic productions, most of today's television programming is produced on videotape. In contrast to the blurry *kinescope recording*[1] process of yesteryear, today's videotape recorders routinely reproduce television programming that is technically indistinguishable from a live show. Even when made-for-TV productions are produced on film, they are almost always transferred to a recording medium such as videotape or hard disk before editing and broadcast.

Recording a production has many advantages:

- Mistakes can be corrected during postproduction.

- Program segments can be re-organized and re-arranged for optimum pacing and effect.

- Program content can be improved by using an array of editing and post-production techniques.

- The length of a program or segment can be shortened or lengthened to fit programming needs.

---

[1] Before the advent of videotape recording in 1956, the only way to preserve a video production was to use a motion picture camera to film it from a TV monitor. The quality of the resulting *kinescope recording* left much to be desired.

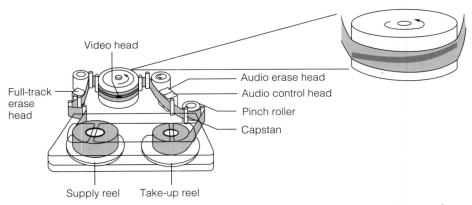

Figure 9.1 Videocassette recorders (VCRs) all work in basically the same way. The tape from a cassette is automatically threaded into the VCR so that it is wrapped around the video heads and pulled past the audio heads by the capstan roller. Since the video heads are spinning at the same time the tape is moving, the combined speed makes it possible to record the high frequencies associated with video.

- Production costs can be saved by scheduling production talent, crew and production facilities for optimum efficiency.
- Once recorded, programming can be time-shifted to meet the needs of U.S. time zones and the programming preferences of local stations.

THE VIDEO RECORDING PROCESS

Videotape consists of a strip of plastic backing coated with a permanent layer of microscopic metal particles imbedded in a resin base. These particles are made of materials such as iron or cobalt which are capable of holding a magnetic charge.

The video heads are made from a highly permeable material that can be quickly magnetized by an electric current—in this case a current responding to changes in a video signal. A microscopically small opening between the heads focuses the varying magnetic fluctuations within the gap. As the heads rapidly move across the tape, the varying magnetic fields affect the alignment of the magnetic particles in the tape's magnetic coating.

When a videotape is played back, the process is reversed; the magnetic fluctuations in the tape induce magnetic changes in the video heads which are, in turn, converted into minute voltages. After being amplified millions of times, these voltages can be brought back to the level of a normal video signal. Figure 9.1 shows how a typical videocassette machine works.

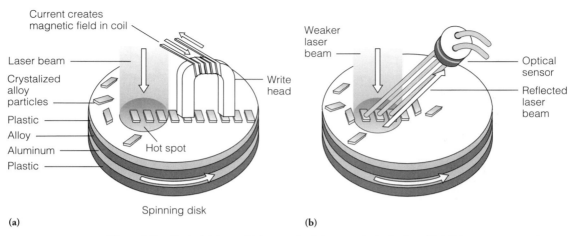

Current creates
magnetic field in coil

Laser beam

Crystalized
alloy
particles

Plastic

Alloy

Aluminum

Plastic

Hot spot

Write
head

Spinning disk

(a)

Weaker
laser
beam

Optical
sensor

Reflected
laser
beam

(b)

Figure 9.2   Optical drives, which started gaining popularity in the mid-1990s, can store much more data than hard drives. Instead of a metal disk covered with a magnetic film, optical drives use a plastic- and alloy-covered aluminum disk. In the "write" mode a laser beam preheats the alloy so that the magnetic head can readily alter the pattern of the crystallized particles within the alloy. In the "read" mode a much weaker laser beam illuminates the same area again, but this time an optical sensor detects the previously altered alloy particles and translates these changing patterns back into a digital signal.

Disc-Based Recording

Videodiscs

Although there have been several videodisc systems over the years, one of the more popular designs works on the same general principle as the audio CD (Chapter 8). Unlike a phonograph record, which is played back by a needle (stylus) following the patterns in a groove, the information on videodisc is read by a laser beam. Since nothing actually comes in contact with the surface of the disc—other than light— videodiscs don't wear out with repeated use. Like phonograph records the data is recorded along grooves in a spiral pattern. But the grooves in a videodisc are much more closely spaced; in fact only a single micron (.000001 meter) separates them. Data is encoded on the disc in the form of *pits* (microscopic indentations). As the disc spins, light from the laser is reflected from the surface of the disk. The presence and absence of pits correspond to ones and zeros, the basic binary code of digital information.

Like audio CDs, videodiscs were initially "read only"; that is, the information (generally in the form of feature-length films) could be "read off" of the disks with home videodisc players, but not recorded. It was some time until a practical "read-write," or *rewritable* videodisc system was developed (Figure 9.2). A typical videodisc can hold up to 1 gigabyte (one-billion bytes) of digital information. With a billion bytes of data on a disc it would seem like a hopeless task to be able to locate a specific bit of information. Not really: by using two playback heads the machine can find any precise point on the disk in a fraction of a second.

Disk-Based Camcorders

The concept of disk recording was expanded in late 1995 when **disk-based camcorders** were introduced. Although computer-type hard disk cartridges are considerably more expensive then videotape, they offer a major advantage in post-production speed. Instead of having to transfer the original camera footage to a video server before editing (to be discussed below), the computer type hard drive can be removed from the camera and plugged directly into an editor for random-access editing. When time is limited, as it often is in ENG work, it is possible to broadcast the original footage directly from the camcorder's disk drive.

VIDEO SERVERS

During the mid-1990s production facilities started to move to computer-based disk recording for postproduction work. Instead of videotape or a large videodisc, **video servers** (also called **media servers** or **file servers**) store audio and video information on high-capacity computer disks. In this form, the access time is virtually instantaneous (in most cases less then one ten-millionth of a second).

The normal procedure is to use videotape to initially tape the footage in the field and then transfer the raw footage directly to the video server for editing. Typically, a production facility will have a large, high-capacity video server, which can be simultaneously accessed by numerous **workstations**—computer based editing, special effects and general audio and video postproduction desktop work areas located throughout the production facility (Figure 9.3). The video server, therefore, becomes a kind of depository of audio and video segments that are in some phase of postproduction. Once editing is complete, some broadcast stations transfer the result to videotape for later broadcast; others hold the final result in the video server and directly access it as needed for broadcast. The latter is commonly done with short news segments in newscasts.

Although video servers represent a much more expensive storage medium than videotape, some stations elect to broadcast entire 60-minute programs directly from the video server. This can be an advantage when postproduction time is limited, as, for example, in quickly putting together a *backgrounder* (a background piece) on a major world event, or when developments in a late-breaking news event may make last-minute production changes necessary. Once aired, the production can be "printed" from the server to videotape for economical, long-term storage.

Now that we've looked briefly at the various recording methods, we need to look at some critical components of the recording process.

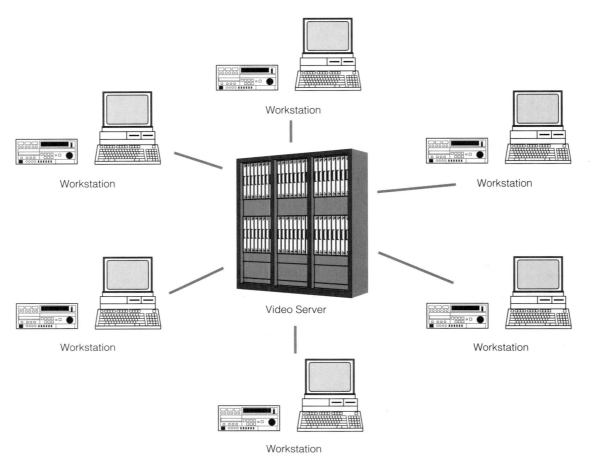

Figure 9.3   A video (or media) server is actually only a high-capacity computer disk storage device that can service numerous workstations (audio and video editing stations) throughout a production facility. After footage is taped in the field, the videotape can be transferred to the server and thereafter randomly accessed and edited at any of the workstations. Because of the digital non-linear nature of servers, there have been exceptional instances when a broadcast would start from a server on a 60-minute news report while editing was still in progress on the last part of the same program.

THE TIME-BASE CORRECTOR

As we saw in Chapter 3, the video picture consists of hundreds of lines of video information scanned 30 times a second. This means that every second a television system must be able to precisely scan more than 15,000 lines for standard NTSC television, and more than 35,000 lines for HDTV. To keep video chaos from breaking out between various pieces of equipment that are processing this high-speed information, there must be precise timing (synchronizing) pulses present to control the starting and stopping point for scanning each of these lines, as well as the intervals when the scanning beam must be blanked out between lines and fields. Even slight fluctuations in these timing pulses can result in unstable (jumpy) video, a serrated (jagged) edge to vertical lines, or, even a complete loss of a discernible picture. Although timing precision is relatively easy to maintain within purely electronic circuitry, once mechanical devices are introduced as part of the recording and playback of these precisely timed signals, fluctuations invariably arise. Left uncollected, these variations create picture instability, which gets worse each time the recording-playback process is repeated. As part of its responsibility to ensure broadcast quality, the Federal Communications Commission (FCC) has set guidelines for the broadcast signal. Among these guidelines are some that cover the tolerances for the stability of the timing pulses, so-called *time-base stability.*

Until the development of a "little black box" called a **time-base corrector (TBC),** only large, expensive tape machines using 2-inch wide tape could meet FCC requirements for time base stability. It was the invention of the TBC in 1973 that made it possible for the timing errors in the signals from small cameras and VCRs to be corrected. In a short time the TBC revolutionized television news. Videotape machines, which previously could be transported only in a medium-sized truck, suddenly could be carried from place to place by one person. Small video cameras and recorders could then be used for on-location, broadcast-quality production, just the way film cameras had for decades.

Today, TBCs are routinely used in TV production, especially when tapes must be copied or edited. Although TBCs can be separate, stand-alone units, professional videotape equipment commonly has TBC circuitry built-in.

VIDEO RECORDER CLASSIFICATIONS

For the price of one of the original broadcast-quality videotape recorders sold in the mid-1950s you could buy more than 100 camcorders today—even without adjusting for inflation! Suffice it to say, for some time there was a huge gulf between broadcast-quality video recorders and equipment intended for institutional and personal use. Thanks to major innovations in technology, this gap has now greatly diminished. Even so, during the evolution of video equipment several general classifications of video recorders emerged: **broadcast quality** (the highest quality), **industrial** (for corporate, educational and institutional applications), and **consumer** (for use by the general public). More recently, the term **prosumer** has been coined, which combines the terms professional and consumer. This high-end consumer equipment is used by serious videographers, many of whom use video in their work or avocation.

Today, as the gap between broadcast-quality equipment and consumer equipment continues to shrink, it is not unusual for broadcast stations to use S-VHS and Hi8 (high-end consumer) videotape formats in their broadcast news operations. This brings up the next topic.

VIDEOTAPE FORMATS

Unlike film which has retained the same basic gauges or formats for decades, videotape has progressed through some 20 different, incompatible formats. Many were introduced with considerable fanfare, only to be quietly dropped a few months or years later when interest was found lacking or something better came along. In the discussion to follow we'll skip over most of these formats and concentrate on only the most recent and widely used ones.

One-Inch, Reel-to-Reel

The last of the open reel[2] videotape formats to be widely used was the **one-inch, type-C** format (Figure 9.4). Type-C was the first videotape system to offer good still frame, and slow and accelerated motion playback capability. When high-definition VCRs were introduced in the late-1980s, modified type-C machines were used to record the HDTV signal. Although one-inch machines dominated professional production for many years, by the mid-1990s these machines were being rapidly replaced by cassette formats.

In the mid-1980s Sony, RCA and Panasonic introduced new, broadcast-quality recording techniques based on formats that had already gained wide acceptance in the home video market: the half-inch videocassette. These two broadcast-quality (and incompatible) half-inch formats were called Betacam and M-format. Not only was the mass-produced half-inch tape used by both of these new formats at a fraction of the cost of earlier formats, but the reduced size of the cassettes meant that for the first time, at least in the professional arena, it was possible to combine a broadcast-quality camera and recorder into one unit.

Betacam

Sony, which pioneered development of the half-inch Betamax videocassette for home use, introduced **Betacam** in 1981, their professional version of Beta. In 1986, they improved this with Betacam SP, for superior performance. Because the

---

[2] As opposed to today's cassettes, in which the supply and take-up reels are both housed within a single plastic container (cassette), reel-to-reel formats require the handling of two separate videotape reels.

Figure 9.4 Type-C was the first videotape system to offer good still-frame and slow and accelerated motion playback capabilities. In the mid-1990s the dominance of the one-inch, type-C format started to fade in favor of digital formats.

Figure 9.5 Sony, which pioneered development of the 1/2-inch Betamax videocassette for home use, introduced the Betacam professional analog format in 1981. Digital Betacam was introduced in late 1994.

improved version rivaled or exceeded the quality of one-inch, type-C recording, some facilities started relying on Betacam for both studio and non-studio production (Figure 9.5). Betacam went through several upgrades, which added numerous new features, along with improved audio and video quality. In late 1994, **Digital Betacam** was introduced which brought the advantages of digital quality to the widely used Betacam line.

The M-Formats

At about the same time that Betacam was introduced, a half-inch, broadcast-quality cassette format was introduced by Matsushita (Panasonic) and RCA. The format used a cassette that appeared identical to the VHS format which had been widely accepted for home use, although the tape inside was significantly different. The new format was referred to as the **M-format** because of the way the tape wrapped around the video head assembly.

A few years after its initial release the M-format was significantly improved with the introduction of the **M-II** format. With the change to M-II, the original two M-format audio tracks were increased to four. These two new tracks are recorded with the high-speed video heads using a high-quality FM-type signal. The audio signal is switched into a part of the video track as the video is being recorded. Unlike the limited quality audio tracks that are recorded longitudinally along the top and bottom of the videotape, the quality of these additional audio tracks is equal to what can be achieved with the best audio recorders. Like Betacam, M-II video quality equals or exceeds what was possible with the one-inch, type-C, reel-to-reel VTRs. Panasonic[3] went on to pioneer in the development of a series of digital videotape formats.

The D-1, D-2, D-3 and D-5 Formats

The "D" in the D-series of formats stands for *digital.* Digital video recording has a number of important advantages over analog.

- A digital videotape can be copied more than 50 times without quality being affected, an important consideration in postproduction sessions that require numerous layers of video effects.

- Because of the error-correction circuitry the effects of problems such as dropouts and abrupt or severe VCR movements are not apparent.

- Digital videotapes have a much better "shelf life" than analog tapes, which means they are better suited for storage and archival use.

- The audio and video quality of digital recordings exceeds the best analog recordings.

As of this writing there are five digital videotape formats in general use. The aforementioned Digital Betacam, plus D-1, D-2, D-3 and D-5.[4]

The D-1 Format   The D-1 format is a digital component format that retains two digitized chrominance (color) signals and a luminance (black and white) signal

---

[3] By this time the original RCA, formerly a world leader in broadcast equipment, and a company that had helped develop the original M-format, had almost completely dropped out of the professional audio and video equipment manufacturing business.

[4] Reportedly, there was never a *D-4* format because the number *4* is unlucky in the minds of Japanese manufacturers.

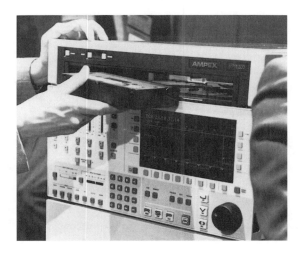

Figure 9.6 In appearance, D-2 machines resemble a 3/4-inch analog VCR. However, these digital machines use special cassettes and have four digital audio channels.

throughout most of the production and postproduction process. By keeping these signals separate, D-1 makes possible elaborate and multiple layers of chroma-keying and *compositing* (bringing together numerous generations of video). However, because three discrete signals are involved, D-1 requires more extensive (and expensive) circuitry. In addition to creating elaborate video effects, D-1 offers an important advantage in doing video animation and in building complex graphics. Until the D-5 format arrived on the scene in 1995, D-1 was unsurpassed for video quality and record-playback flexibility.

The D-2 Format   Although the D-2 format relies on a composite signal (a process of combining the color and luminance information)[5] for most production and postproduction work, the quality of D-2 is indistinguishable from D-1. Only in doing highly demanding and complex postproduction effects does the difference become significant. At the same time, D-2 is more practical because it does not require nearly as much signal processing circuitry. In appearance, D-2 machines, both table-top and portable, resemble the ¾-inch analog machines used for several decades in ENG and industrial television (Figure 9.6).

---

[5] In order to simplify the recording process, especially in consumer-type camcorders, luminance (Y) and color (C) information is typically combined to some degree into a single *composite* signal. Unfortunately, this results in some loss of video quality and the introduction of subtle picture aberrations (artifacts). These problems become increasingly noticeable and objectionable with each generation, that is, each time the original tape is copied. A superior, but more technically demanding recording technique, involves keeping the color and luminance information separate throughout the recording and playback process. This is referred to as *component* recording, since the basic components of the video are recorded as separate signals. To retain the quality advantage represented by component recording, many of today's cameras and recorders have separate inputs and outputs for the luminance and color (Y/C) signals.

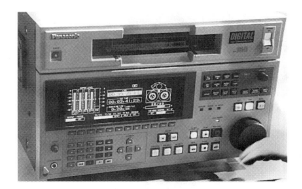

Figure 9.7 During the 1992 Olympics in Barcelona, Spain, 1/2-inch, D-3 digital recorders received widespread attention. Although there was not a D-4 format, a few years later the D-5 format was introduced by Panasonic.

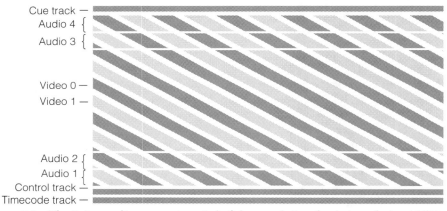

Cue track —
Audio 4 {
Audio 3 {

Video 0 —
Video 1 —

Audio 2 {
Audio 1 {
Control track —
Timecode track —

Figure 9.8 The D-3 recording system is typical of the complexity of today's professional VCRs. Note that a total of four digital (also called PCM for pulse-code modulation) audio tracks are recorded, two at the top and two at the bottom of the video tracks. Ten helical heads spinning at 5,400 rpm are necessary to record and play back audio and video. It takes six helical tracks to record a single video field. The speed of the video heads combines with the speed of the moving tape to create a total headwriting speed of 24.4 meters per second.

The D-3 Format During the 1992 Olympics in Barcelona, Spain, the D-3 format first received widespread attention (Figure 9.7). By using more than 250 cameras and recorders and taking advantage of a digitized signal through most of the recording, production and postproduction processes, the advantages of digital recording and postproduction became fully apparent. The D-3 cassettes can record up to 125 minutes on metal evaporated tape.

Since the D-3 recording system is typical of the complexity of today's professional digital VCRs, it can be used as an example of how these digital formats are configured. Note in Figure 9.8 that four high-quality digital audio tracks are recorded at the top and bottom of the video tracks. Ten video heads spinning at 5,400 rpm are necessary to record and play back the audio and video. Four of the heads record video, four are *confidence heads* that can immediately play back the audio and video signals as they are being recorded, and two are erase heads, which can erase previously recorded material. It takes six helical tracks to record a single video field. Since the speed of the video heads combines with the speed of the moving tape, the combined movement creates a head-writing speed of 24.4 meters per second, or somewhere between 5,000 and 6,000 miles per hour!

The D-5 Format   The D-5 format combines many of the features of previous digital formats, while avoiding the quality problems inherent in compressing and combining video information. D-5 cassettes will record up to 2 hours of program material on a single metal evaporated videotape cassette. Because of its ability to record much more data per unit of time, the D-5 format can be readily adapted to HDTV production.

The Evolution of Industrial and Consumer Formats

Because several of the consumer formats have set patterns of change in broadcast-quality equipment, and since several of these formats are being accepted in industrial and broadcast applications, it is useful to study their evolution and present status.

The *Betamax* format, which was introduced by Sony Corporation in 1976, was the first consumer format to be widely accepted. Hundreds of thousands of Beta-type machines have been sold throughout the world. The original Beta format went through several revisions, mostly to extend playing time. Nevertheless, by the early 1990s Betamax had virtually disappeared from the scene, having lost the competitive battle to its rival, VHS. However, as we've seen, this loss was more than offset when the basic Betamax concept was later reincarnated as the highly successful Betacam professional format.

VHS

Although the **VHS** (Video Home System) format was introduced a full year after Betamax, it attracted immediate attention because of its two-hour playing time, a feature that the early Betamax machines didn't share. This not only made it possible to record feature films and football games off the air, but it later ushered in what was to become a major attraction for VCR sales: movie rentals.

As time went on the original two-hour VHS capacity was increased to four hours, then to six hours. A special cassette was even introduced that could record eight hours of programming. It should be kept in mind, however, that to extend VHS recording time, tape speed must be slowed down. This, in turn, has a negative impact on both audio and video quality. For this reason, the "standard play" (highest speed) mode of VHS machines is preferred when quality is a major consideration.

In 1983, a compact version of the VHS cassette was introduced: **VHS-C.** Since the new cassette was about half the size of the standard VHS cassette, it became possible to significantly reduce the size of camcorders. VHS-C cassettes can be played in VHS machines with the use of an adapter shell.

When production started in the 16:9 format **W-VHS** was introduced. W-VHS is an analog format that uses a special metal powder-coated tape capable of recording the extra data associated with the wide-screen format.

Since all of the basic VHS formats are composite (see footnote 5), they suffer from quality limitations, especially after being copied one or more times. As the basic VHS format was used in more and more applications and limitations became more evident, pressure mounted to improve its quality. The need was answered when **S-VHS** (super VHS) was introduced. By increasing the bandwidth of the luminance (detail carrying) component of the VHS signal and adding the option of component signal processing, the sharpness of the standard VHS picture was significantly increased. In fact, under optimum conditions an original S-VHS videotape can exceed the quality possible with the standard NTSC broadcast process. The problem, of course, is that few tapes are broadcast in their original form; they normally must be edited. In the process they suffer a significant loss in quality.

This loss can be reduced by copying the original material to a broadcast-quality tape format, or video server before editing. Once transferred to a higher-quality medium, generational loss is reduced during postproduction. Using this technique, S-VHS and the Hi8 format (to be discussed) become *acquisition formats*—tape formats used simply to acquire the footage in the field.

8mm Video

Although Sony lost the battle for home video to VHS, they didn't abandon the market. Instead, Sony took over a format pioneered in part by Eastman Kodak: **8mm** (a size then linked to the great popularity of 8mm home movie film). With the introduction of small 8mm videocassette, the size and weight of the basic camcorder dropped more than 50 percent. The tape cartridges, which are 3.7 by 2.5 by 0.6 inches, are about the size of a standard, analog audiocassette (Figure 9.9). Since the 8mm cassette is much smaller than even a VHS-C cassette (and it records considerably more program material), 8mm video became the choice of those needing the smallest and lightest-weight camcorder equipment.

To obtain a high-quality video signal with the small format, videotapes were developed that had pure metal and metal-evaporated coatings, a significant improvement over the original oxide coatings. Since this new tape technology made it possible to record and play back at much higher signal levels, these tape formulations were quickly adopted by other video formats.

Sony also developed a high quality version of 8mm called **Hi8,** just as Panasonic had done by introducing S-VHS. Although there are technical differences between S-VHS and Hi8, the same basic quality-enhancing techniques were used in each case.

Figure 9.9 Although 8mm videotape is much smaller than the VHS or VHS-C cassettes, it offers the same high, first-generation quality. It also has a time-code address track to facilitate editing. The Hi-8 version is comparable to S-VHS.

Like S-VHS, Hi8 immediately attracted the attention of news and documentary producers looking for a small, light-weight and inexpensive alternative to traditional broadcast-quality equipment. In covering high-risk, foreign news assignments, S-VHS and Hi8 equipment is considered expendable. Since these units are a fraction of the cost of professional camcorders, if one is confiscated, badly damaged, or has to be left behind, there is no great financial loss.

VCR OPERATIONS

Regardless of the format, VTRs and VCRs have a number of common features. The five basic functions on any videotape machine are *play, record, stop, rewind, fast-forward* and *pause.* Although VCR functions are basically self-explanatory, two things should be mentioned. In order to put some machines into the record mode, the *record* button has to be held down and then the *play* button pressed. A small red light indicates when the machine is recording. Since the recording process erases previously recorded material, the tape should be checked to make sure there is nothing on it that might later be needed. If in doubt, the tape can generally be fast-forwarded past the material in question.

Unlike the *stop* mode, which disengages the tape from the head, the *pause* button allows the tape to stay in contact with the spinning video heads—ready for an instant start in either the record or playback modes. If left too long in pause, however, the heads will wear away the recording surface of the tape. This will not only damage the tape and result in **dropouts** (momentary glitches in the picture), but it can cause **head clog.** Once the microscopic gap in the video heads are clogged with any kind of matter, recording and playback are impossible. At best, a slightly snowy picture will result; at worst the picture will roll, break up, and rival a Nebraska snow storm.

Some tape machines have **confidence heads,** which are able to play back the recorded signal a fraction of a second after it has been recorded. Without confidence heads the operator can only monitor the video from the camera, which provides no indication of possible recording problems.

Spot Checking a Tape

Unfortunately, many machines do not have confidence heads and the effects of dropouts or head clog are not realized until the tape is later played back in the camera viewfinder or on a TV monitor. For this reason tapes should be *spot checked* (checked at various spots) after recording. Many VCR operators only look at the last few seconds of the tape, assuming that if anything went wrong, the problem carried through until the end of the tape. Although this is a safe assumption in many cases, for important productions lasting ten minutes or more an even safer approach is to do end, middle and beginning checks. (Occasionally problems such as head clog develop early in the recording process and later clear up.) Full spot checks are done by stopping the tape at the end of the recording, rewinding it a few feet and checking the last 5 or 10 seconds of the tape; then rewinding the tape to about the midpoint and checking again; and, finally, rewinding the tape to the beginning and checking the first 5 or 10 seconds of the recording. During spot checks, operators should

■ Check for absolute image stability (no horizontal jitter or vertical flutter or roll).

■ Check for the presence of dropouts or video noise. Assuming the material can't be easily rerecorded and the dropouts aren't too bad, there are electronic dropout compensators that can unobtrusively fill in missing data as the tape is edited or copied. Video noise is normally the result of low video levels (reflecting low light levels) or dirty video heads. In the latter case, "playing" a head cleaning tape for about 5 seconds will often solve the problem.

■ Check for general sharpness and picture quality. If the video is being played back in the field through the camera viewfinder, keep in mind that the small image represents a limited indication of how the final picture will look. Even so, it can reveal problems. When you are miles from a repair facility, as you often are in video field production, remember that even though a segment may have a technical problem, it is often wise not to record over it. When a major technical problem is emerging, the second attempt sometimes produces even worse results. Today's sophisticated signal-processing equipment will sometimes solve instability problems and salvage the original recording.

■ Check for good audio quality, including an acceptable balance between audio sources. The presence of most kinds of noise can't be completely eliminated in postproduction. Moderate variations in audio levels, however, are easy to fix.

■ Finally, check on difficult or questionable camera moves, including pans, zooms, dollies and trucks. (Whenever possible, remember to shoot two or more takes of important scenes, especially scenes involving complex camera moves.)

Basic VCR Adjustments

The Skew Control

The **skew** control found on some VCRs determines videotape tension, which in turn affects the length of the video tracks recorded or "read" from the videotape. This tension is adjusted by tape guides, which hold the moving videotape around the video heads. Improper skew adjustment is typically indicated by flagging, or a bending and wavering of vertical lines at the top of the frame. Although the skew adjustment is disabled when a VCR is in the record mode, this adjustment may need to be made when tapes are played back, especially on a machine other than that on which it was recorded. Most skew controls have a center "indent" position, which indicates a normal setting. As VCRs get older, the needed tension may go beyond the range that can be adjusted by the skew control. When this happens, an engineer or person familiar with the operation of the VCR can adjust the internal tape guides so that the skew adjustment once again falls within the normal range of control.

Tapes that have been played many times, stretched, or subjected to high temperatures often require a skew adjustment before they can be played. Because different TV set and video monitor electronics react differently to video problems, you will probably find that skew problems show up differently depending on the equipment.

The Tracking Control

Tracking refers to the ability of a VCR to precisely (and generally automatically) align itself with the narrow video tracks recorded on the tape. As with skew, the tracking control is only used to correct problems during tape playback. On most videotape formats tracking errors show up either in the form of a horizontal band of video noise or, in severe cases, in a total breakup of the picture. When tracking errors show up it is generally because the playback machine and record machine do not agree on the precise location of the video tracks. Some VCRs have tracking level meters. This is simply a readout of the overall amplitude of the recorded video signal. If automatic tracking fails and tracking falls below the optimum level indicated on the meter, the tracking control should be adjusted for maximum signal.

Occasionally, poorly recorded tapes have tracking levels too low to enable a tape to be reliably locked in for a stable playback. Trying the tape on a different machine will sometimes help, but other times it will make the situation worse.

VCR Meters and Status Indicators

In addition to the meter for tracking, most VCRs will have a number of other status indicators. There should be one or more meters for monitoring audio levels. Professional machines, especially those used for editing, often incorporate video level meters as well. These meters indicate only the maximum video level and tell nothing about the quality of the video signal. (The video could conceivably consist of nothing but a blank screen.)

The eight-digit SMPTE time code reading is also displayed on many professional VCRs. (Time-code will be discussed in detail in Chapter 12.) Machines that do not display time-code generally have a tape index or tape counter readout. This is often a digital readout similar to the mileage indicator in an automobile. Since many of these are based on an internal geared connection rather than an electronic signal from the tape, they cannot be relied upon for highly accurate cueing. In addition, there is no way to reliably convert these numbers into minutes or seconds. As we will see, SMPTE time code, which represents hours, minutes, seconds and video frames, is accurate to within 1/30 and, in some cases, 1/60 of a second.

Maintaining Videotape

In the early days of videotape recording, both videotape and record-playback heads had a rather short life. Although both have been greatly improved, there are still some problems that should be understood.

Most types of videotape shed microscopic particles during use. These particles can gradually fill in the gap in record-playback heads, resulting in both increased head and tape wear, and in a microscopic separation between the tape and the tape heads. This separation can both create video noise and dropouts. A momentary

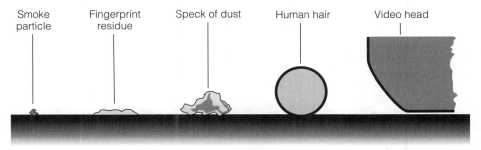

| Smoke particle | Fingerprint residue | Speck of dust | Human hair | Video head |

Videotape surface

Figure 9.10 A momentary head-to-tape separation of only 4 microns (one-twentieth the size of a human hair) can cause video dropout. Videotape also sheds microscopic particles during use. These particles can gradually fill in the gap in record-playback heads, resulting in both dropouts and increased head and tape wear.

head-to-tape separation of only four microns, which is 1/20 the size of a human hair, will cause a tape dropout (Figure 9.10).

A process called *packing the tape* is recommended when a new tape is used for the first time. This process, which involves fast-forwarding the tape to the end and then rewinding the tape again to the beginning, accomplishes two things. First, variations in tape position and tension that can cause recording problems will be minimized. Second, any loose oxide on the tape that has been shed will have a chance to drop away from the tape before getting lodged in the record-playback heads.

Videotape should not be stored in temperatures that exceed 80° F. Some types of tape stored at 90° F will only last about a year. It has been shown that videotapes can be destroyed in less than one hour when stored at 150° F. A cassette sitting in the sun in a closed car will quickly reach that temperature. In the summertime, automobile glove compartments and trunks can also exceed 150° F. Temperature problems will especially affect material that has already been recorded on the tape.

Now that we've covered the basic production tools and concepts, we can turn our attention to the actual process of creating television programming. We'll start with the type of production most commonly done in the field: news and documentary production.

CHAPTER 10 NEWS AND DOCUMENTARY PRODUCTION

TODAY, ELECTRONIC NEWS gathering or ENG technology routinely takes us directly to where news events are happening, often *as* they are happening. During a typical newscast in many cities it is not unusual to see the sports anchor doing a live pregame or postgame report from a baseball stadium, the entertainment editor getting reactions from people as they emerge from a theater or concert hall, and the weather person reporting in the rain (Figure 10.1).

THE DIFFERENCE BETWEEN ENG AND EFP

Electronic News Gathering (ENG): Although the same equipment is generally used in ENG and EFP work, the primary intent in news is to "get the story." In 90 percent of news work there will be time to ensure audio and video quality, which is what the news director and producer will expect. But if ENG compromises must be made on important stories, they are made in audio and video quality, not in story content. The most-watched and celebrated television news story in history was shot by one low-resolution black-and-white video camera. It was humankind's first steps on the moon. Although the quality of the footage was poor, no TV news editor said to NASA, "you've got some interesting footage there, but we'll have to pass; the quality just doesn't come up to our usual standards."

Figure 10.1 Minutes after events happen, camera-equipped helicopters are able to transmit live pictures back to the TV studio. Gyrostabilized camera mounts eliminate helicopter vibration.

Sometimes ENG stories will have to be shot with a camera-mounted sun gun while running backwards in front of a moving subject. Although picture, sound and camera stability may be sadly lacking, poor video and sound on an important story are better than no video or sound.

Electronic Field Production (EFP) goes beyond just news and encompasses many types of field productions, including commercials, music videos, on-location dramatic productions and various types of sports coverage. EFP work generally provides the opportunity to ensure maximum audio and video quality. As equipment gets smaller and easier to transport, and as field-to-studio links become easier to establish and more reliable, we're seeing more and more EFP production. And given the average viewer's preference for the authenticity of on-location settings, this trend will undoubtedly continue.

Differences Between News and Documentary Production

Because of time constraints news is often accused of presenting facts without context, information without interpretation. Since news in most markets is highly competitive, there is pressure on reporters to pull a story together and get it on the air before the competition does. In contrast, in documentary work there is typically much more time to think through an approach, to research the topic, and to develop the various angles.

Because documentaries are longer than normal news pieces—from 10-minute "minidocs," to 60-minute productions—the subject matter can be explored in much more depth than in a typical news story. Some documentaries take an issue, develop the various viewpoints and let members of the audience draw their own conclusions. More often, the documentary producer will develop one side of an issue and simply let opposing views be heard. For example, if the documentary is on unsanitary conditions uncovered in the meat-packing industry, "opposing views" may take the form of emphatic assertions that government standards are being met. At this point one or two government employees in charge of inspections might be interviewed. When confronted with evidence that's been uncovered, they admit to being so understaffed they can't keep up with inspections.

Handling Controversial Subject Matter

What you don't want to do with any issue is take a side and not seek out opposing views—no matter how strongly you feel about the issue. In speaking to potential spokespersons, especially qualified people representing opposing viewpoints—you need to explain the subject matter of the documentary, including a description of the thrust of the documentary's content. You should also carefully document your attempts at finding opposing views. Many producers send these people registered letters, just so they can't later say they did not understand what was going on, or that they were denied the opportunity to present their side. If potential spokespersons refuse to respond to your registered letter, and are constantly unavailable for comment, these events should be carefully documented. The fact that they turned down an opportunity to reply should be mentioned in the documentary along with any reasons they might have given. People who feel they were not given an opportunity to present their side can initiate a costly law suit and a demand for equal air time. (At the same time, keep in mind that when an issue is being litigated, their attorney might restrain them from being interviewed, a fact that should also be mentioned in the documentary.)

Providing an opportunity for all sides of an issue to be heard in news and documentary work not only reduces the chances of finding yourself in a lawsuit, but also adds credence to your work, and adds the element of conflict. We'll take up some of these issues from the legal perspective in Chapter 14.

ENG PERSONNEL

Although the number and type of positions involved in producing a daily newscast will vary from two or three people in a very small station to more than 100 in New York, Los Angeles, and Chicago, several key positions should be mentioned.

The **news producer** is the person who is most directly in charge of the newscast. This person makes the major minute-by-minute decisions on both the technical and content aspects of the newscast, both prior to and during the broadcast. Larger stations may have **segment producers** who are in charge of specific stories or newscast segments. Some stations will have an **executive producer** who supervises the other producers.

Two types of directors are involved in putting the newscast on the air. The first, the **news director,** is the top person in the news department. This person controls the budget, hires and fires personnel, and has ultimate responsibility for the station's newscasts. Much further down the ladder of responsibility is the **on-air director** for the newscast. This person's responsibility is to take the plans of the producer and "call the shots" in the on-air phase of the broadcast. Unlike the situation in film and in many TV programs where the director has major control of the production and its content, in news the director's responsibility is basically to coordinate the technical elements of the broadcast.

As the title suggests, the **ENG coordinator** starts with the story assignments made by the **assignment editor** and works with reporters, ENG crews, editors, technicians and the producer to see that the stories make it all the way through the technical, tactical and news editorial labyrinths to "air." ENG coordinators must not only thoroughly know their studio and location equipment, but also understand news.

SOURCES OF BROADCAST NEWS

Broadcast news comes from four basic sources: from news services such as the Associated Press; from media outlets such as newspapers, radio and TV stations; from press releases provided by a wide variety of corporations, agencies and special interest groups; and directly from a local reporter's primary sources. The Associated

Press (AP) operates bureaus in 120 U.S. cities and in more than 130 foreign countries.

Until recently, the news from these wire services was all printed out on large rolls of paper in teletype fashion. Today, stations have computerized newsrooms and the steady stream of news is electronically written onto a computer hard disk. Using a computer terminal, the news editor can quickly scroll through an index of stories that have been electronically stored. Key words and phrases are used to find stories relating to specific topics. After the stories are selected, they can be called up in complete form and rearranged and edited as needed. Once edited and organized, the stories can be printed out on hard copy (paper) and, in the case of soft-copy prompters, fed directly to a studio prompter for on-camera reading.

Television stations affiliated with a network receive daily afternoon and evening satellite feeds of scores of news stories provided by network news reporters and affiliated TV stations. Since most of these stories are not used on the network's nightly news, they make good regional, national and international segments for local newscasts. *Independent stations* (those not affiliated with a network) have scores of television news services to which they can subscribe, including the world-wide resources of the Cable News Network (CNN).

Whatever the source, the news feeds are videotaped and reviewed by the local news producer. Stories selected for broadcast are normally saved to a video server, or assembled on one or two videotapes, and then "rolled into" the local news as needed. Regional, national or even international stories can often be developed from a local perspective. A major event taking place in a foreign country can elicit reactions from local people of the same nationality; a shake-up in a New York company may affect employees or related businesses in the station's area; or a crime wave in an adjoining county may cause local people to react.

News personnel also constantly scan other media for stories. If the morning newspaper has a story of interest, the assignment editor may have a reporter contact the appropriate people to update the story and arrange for videotape. A well-established TV news department also gets tips from viewers on possible stories.

Finally, the daily mail inevitably brings in a flood of press releases, public relations stories and other information that the senders hope will be used on the air. Even videotapes highlighting achievements and new products and information are regularly sent in by corporations, government agencies and universities. Al-though there may be slow news days, there are never "no news days." It becomes the job of the assignment editor or news director to cull through the various sources of news and select the stories that seem most significant. In so doing, several areas of balance must be maintained.

Depending on the orientation of the newscast and the relative importance of the stories on a particular day, some balance between local, regional, national and international news must be considered in the selection of stories. There must also be visual variety. In particular, this involves a balance between ENG segments and stories simply read on-camera with supporting graphics. Finally, there may be an attempt to balance the proportion of "hard" and "soft" news stories, that is, straight, factual stories and human interest feature stories.

What Determines Newsworthiness?

No attempt will be made here to go into detail on the elements involved in covering and writing news. For those considering a career in television news reporting, there are excellent books that deal exclusively with this subject. (See the Bibliography at the end of this text.)

Twelve Factors in Newsworthiness

Those involved in ENG work must understand the 12 factors that constitute news value, or newsworthiness:

- timeliness
- proximity
- exceptional quality
- possible future impact
- prominence
- conflict
- the number of people involved or affected
- consequence
- human interest
- pathos
- shock value
- titillation component

Timeliness   News is what's new. An afternoon raid on a rock cocaine house may warrant a live ENG report during the 6-PM news. However, tomorrow, unless there are major new developments, the same story will probably not be important enough to mention.

Proximity   If 15 people are killed in your hometown, your local TV station will undoubtedly consider it news. But if 15 people are killed in Manzanillo, Montserrat, Moyobambaor, or some other distant place you've never heard of, it will probably pass unnoted. But there are exceptions.

Exceptional Quality   One exception centers on how the people died. If the people in Manzanillo were killed because of a bus accident, this would not be nearly so newsworthy as if they died because of stings from "killer bees," feared insects that have invaded the United States. Exceptional quality refers to how uncommon an event is. A man getting a job as a music conductor is not news—unless that man is blind.

Possible Future Impact   The killer bee example illustrates another news element: possible future impact. The fact that the killer bees are now in the United States and eventually may be a threat to people watching the news, or to their relatives living in another state, makes the story much more newsworthy. A mundane burglary of an office in the Watergate Hotel in Washington, D.C., was hardly news until two reporters named Woodward and Bernstein saw the implications and the possible future impact. Eventually, the story behind this seemingly common burglary brought down a presidency.

Prominence   The 15 deaths in Manzanillo might also go by unnoted by the local media unless someone prominent was on the bus, possibly a movie star or a well-known politician. If a U.S. Supreme Court Justice or your local mayor gets married, it's news; if John Smith, your next-door neighbor, gets married, it probably isn't.

Conflict   Conflict in its many forms has long held the interest of observers. The conflict may be physical or emotional. It can be open, overt conflict, such as a civil uprising against police authority, or it may be ideological conflict between political candidates. The conflict could be as simple as a person standing on his or her principles and spending a year "fighting city hall" over a parking citation. In addition to "people against people" conflict, there can be conflict with wild animals, nature, the environment or even the frontier of space.

The Number of People Involved or Affected   The more people involved in a news event—be it a demonstration or a tragic accident—the more newsworthy the story is. Likewise, the number of people affected by the event—be it a new health threat or a new ruling by the IRS—the more newsworthy the story is.

Consequence   The fact that a car hit a utility pole isn't news, unless, as a consequence, power is lost throughout a city for several hours. The fact that a computer virus found its way into a computer system may not become major news until it bankrupts a business, shuts down a telephone system, or destroys important medical data at a major hospital.

Human Interest   Human interest stories are generally soft news. Examples include a baby beauty contest, a person whose pet happens to be a 9-foot boa constrictor, or a man who makes a cart so that his two-legged dog can move around again. On a slow news day even a story of fire fighters getting a cat out of a tree might make a suitable story. Human interest angles can be found in most hard news stories. A flood in Tennessee will undoubtedly have many human interest angles: a child reunited with its parents after two days; a boy who lost his dog; or families returning to their mud-filled homes.

Pathos   The fact that people like to hear about the misfortunes of others can't be denied. Seeing or hearing about such things commonly elicits feelings of pity, sorrow, sympathy and compassion. Some would call such stories "tear jerkers." Examples are the child who is now alone after his parents were killed in a fire, the elderly woman who just lost her life savings to a con artist, the blind man whose seeing-eye dog was poisoned.

This category isn't limited just to people. How about the kittens who lost their mother when it was hit by a car, the horses that were found neglected and starving, or the dog who sits at the curb expectantly waiting for its master to return from work each day—even though the man was killed in an accident weeks ago.

Shock Value An explosion in a factory has less shock value if was caused by gas leak than if it was caused by a terrorist. The story of a 6-year-old boy who shot his mother with a revolver found in a bedside drawer has more shock and, therefore, news value than if the same woman died in an automobile accident. Both shock value and the titillation factor are well known to the tabloid press. The lure of these two factors is also related to some stories getting inordinate attention—such as the sordid details of a politician's or evangelist's affair—which brings us to the final point.

Titillation Component This factor primarily involves sex and is commonly featured—some would say exploited—during rating periods. This category includes everything from the new fashions in men's and women's swim wear to an in-depth series on legal prostitution in Nevada.

PACKAGING THE NEWS

With the exception of features and special in-depth reports, the newscasts in most TV markets will feature many, if not most, of the same stories. What makes one station favored over another is how the news is presented. (It's not so much what you say as how you say it!) This not only includes how professional and well-liked the on-air personalities are, but also how well stories are illustrated with video footage and graphics.

Videographers working in news commonly receive their basic instructions from reporters or assignment editors. However, depending on the station and the reputation a particular videographer has for creativity and an understanding of news, considerable latitude may be given in selecting shots and even in pursuing specific angles of a story. First of all, since stories tend to break when they are least expected, this means that, day or night, videographers must always be prepared (Figure 10.2). Not to be prepared may mean missing the story. But, even as important as that may be, there is much more to covering the news than just getting to the scene with both yourself and your equipment intact. Reporters must find creative ways to effectively communicate the essential ideas of the story. Those who thoroughly understand news and the full range of audio and video techniques available will be able go beyond simply getting technically acceptable video. Talented videographers not only are in demand by the best reporters but they also get the most challenging and interesting assignments.

Figure 10.2   Packing cases for cameras and equipment make it possible to transport equipment safely. A complete ENG unit, including camcorder, tapes, microphones, AC power supply and a small camera light can be packed into a single foam-padded case.

Typical Interview Setups

Although it is impossible to discuss the wide range of news situations videographers will face in covering news, one situation will be repeatedly confronted: the basic one-on-one interview. Using only one camera position for a two-person interview represents a production compromise (primarily weak camera angles); but with one-camera, live ENG reports there is generally no choice.

However, when an interview is being videotaped, another approach is commonly practiced using two camera positions (Figure 10.3). Note that the camera angles provide strong, over-the-shoulder angles, rather than the much weaker profile shots typically associated with only one camera position.

In the first setup position (Figure 10.3a), the camera is focused on the person being interviewed. From this angle two shots are possible: a close-up looking almost directly into the line of vision of the person being interviewed, and a shot over the shoulder of the interviewer that can even be used momentarily while the interviewer is speaking. When the camera position is reversed (Figure 10.2b), the same two shots are possible on the interviewer. Interview production techniques will be covered in much more detail in Chapter 12.

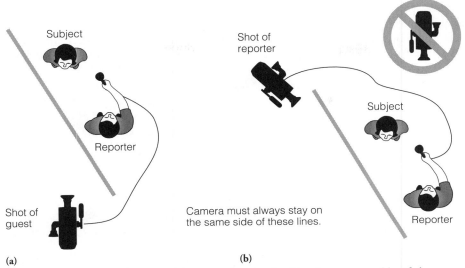

Subject

Shot of
reporter

Reporter

Subject

Shot of
guest

Camera must always stay on
the same side of these lines.

Reporter

(a) **(b)**

Figure 10.3 From positions a and b strong over-the-shoulder shots are possible. If the camera wanders past the line shown, however, a disorienting reversal of screen direction will occur. This occurrence is discussed further in Chapter 11.

THE FIELD-TO-STUDIO LINK

A major part of ENG, especially live ENG, is the field-to-studio link. Personnel in the control room must have the ability to coordinate the work of numerous field crews and, during a fast-breaking news story, to rearrange the elements in the news show as it is broadcast. Although there may be constant pressure at stations to be "first with the news," the legal and public relations consequences of airing a story with a major factual error or distortion of the truth can be quite damaging. Repeating an erroneous and damaging rumor to your friend will probably have no consequences; *broadcasting* the same rumor can result in multimillion-dollar lawsuits and even put an end to a promising career. One of the more important sayings in news is: *if in doubt, check it out.* We'll cover more on this issue in Chapter 14.

POINT-TO-POINT SIGNAL TRANSMISSION

It does little good to have cameras on the scene of a major news story if you can't get your signals back to a TV station or production facility. Programming can't be broadcast directly from a remote location; it has to be sent to a broadcast facility first. There is, of course, videotape. But videotape involves delay; in fact, in major metropolitan cities with typical traffic problems, a delay of at least an hour. In that time your competition can have the story on the air and, if it's a major story, have stolen your audience.

Today, of course, we routinely broadcast major stories live. Since the approach to getting a major story back to the station is critical to getting it on the air, we need to examine how this process works. There are four basic ways of transmitting a video and audio signal from one point to another: coaxial cable, fiber optics, microwave and satellite links.

Coaxial Cable

The first method devised for conducting video signals from one point to another was coaxial cable. Coaxial cable, or coax, still represents the basic medium for interconnecting video equipment. Unlike fiber optics, microwave or satellite links (to be discussed below), coax does not require transduction (a fundamental alteration of the basic video signal form) before the video can be transmitted. The flexible braided shield surrounding the single central wire serves both as a shield and an electrical ground.

Coaxial Cable Problems   Coaxial cable is the ideal choice for carrying normal video signals over distances of up to a few hundred feet. Beyond this, the loss in signal strength will adversely affect quality unless the signal is re-amplified. Although it is possible to repeatedly re-amplify the signal for transmission over long distances, with analog signals problems develop during this process. For one thing, every time a standard analog signal is amplified, at least some small amount of signal degradation takes place. And the problem becomes cumulative. Each stage of amplification adds, however slightly, to the overall degradation. Therefore, for longer distances a better transmission medium is needed. The answer is fiber optic cables.

Fiber Optics

Unlike coaxial cables, which rely on electrical energy to carry signals, the medium for conducting signals in fiber optic cables (also called optical fiber or OF cables) is light. Light waves have an extremely high frequency (about 10^{-6} of a meter) and travel at a speed of about 186,000 miles or 2,910 cm per second. The extremely high frequencies mean that a single OF cable can theoretically carry trillions of bits of information per second.

Although it would seem that a conductor with this capacity would have be to very large, in fact, the thickness of an optical fiber is only slightly larger than a human hair. The tiny, flexible, glass or plastic fiber is coated, both for protection and to enhance its characteristics as a reflective wave guide for the light it carries. Fiber optic cables normally carry numerous OF strands within a single enclosure.

Advantages of Fiber Optics   Compared to a coaxial cable an optical fiber has the following ten advantages:

- *Much greater capacity*   The information carrying capacity of OF is more than 100 times that of a normal copper wire.

- *Low and very uniform attenuation over a wide frequency range*   The loss of signal strength in coaxial cables varies with video frequencies, which greatly complicates uniform amplification of multiple signals.

- *Virtual immunity to interference*   Radio frequency interference of various types can interfere with coaxial cable signals.

- *No problems with leakage*   When coaxial cables are used to conduct video at radio frequencies, the signal can create interference by being induced into nearby electronic components.

- *Insensitivity to temperature variations*   Unlike OF transmissions, electrical resistance and attenuation in coaxial cables vary with temperature.

- *Extremely small size*

- *Will not "short out" in bad weather or even in water*

- *Low cost*   The basic ingredient in the glass fiber is sand, a raw material considerably cheaper than copper, the central conductor used in coaxial cable. (Some optical fibers are made out of a special plastic, which costs even less.)

- *High reliability*   The fibers do not corrode or break down in moisture or salt air.

- *Light weight*   Since they are not based on metal conductors, OF cables are lighter and much easier to transport and install.

Optical Cable Applications   The long video cables required in doing some remotes can be extremely heavy and bulky. A good example would be a major golf tournament, which requires many thousands of feet of camera cable. By using a single, high capacity OF cable instead of multiple coax-based cables, both number and weight of required cables are reduced.

As telephone companies continue to move toward optical fiber as the basic medium for communications, video transmissions are becoming as simple as hooking up video equipment to a telephone circuit and dialing the right number. Once this technique becomes commonplace, some of the need for microwave and satellite links will be all but eliminated.

Microwave Links

In much the same way that a light beam can be focused and projected from one point to another, microwave signals can be transmitted in a straight, unobstructed line from a transmitter to a receiver. In broadcasting, microwave was originally used primarily to provide coast-to-coast links for the television networks and for studio-to-transmitter links. As remote broadcasting became more popular, TV stations

Figure 10.4 Small, tripod-mounted microwave transmitters are commonly used in ENG work to send video signals over short distances. Since microwave signals can be blocked by many types of obstructions, several "short-hop" microwave units sometimes have to be used to get a signal around obstructions to a major receiving point.

invested in large field production trucks equipped with microwave dishes. Athletic events, parades, major civic meetings and other multicamera productions are among the special events covered.

Short-Hop Transmitters Today, small, "short hop," solid-state microwave transmitters and receivers can be mounted on lightweight tripods (Figure 10.4). These small, highly portable transmitters, sometimes referred to as "window-ledge transmitters," make it possible to set up a link from an office building, for example, and relay the signal to a central production van. At this point a more powerful microwave transmitter can be used to send the signal to one of the city's primary relay points (generally on top of a tall building). From there the signal is relayed back to the studio or production center, either by a microwave or fiber optic link.

The most important thing to remember about microwave links is that you must have a straight, line-of-sight path between each transmitter and receiver. Obstructions including heavy rain, sleet, or snow can degrade, divert, or completely eliminate the signal.

Vans, Boats and Airplanes   The news vans used by many TV stations are often equipped with antennas on telescoping poles which can, assuming there are no obstructions, beam a microwave signal back to the station from almost anywhere in the station's coverage area.

Although normal microwave signals go in a straight line, occasionally it is necessary to modify the originating signal so that it can be received over a relatively large area. For example, if a television signal were coming from a moving car, motorcycle, boat, or helicopter, it would be virtually impossible to keep the transmitter and receiver in perfect alignment with traditional microwave equipment. For these applications special omnidirectional transmitters and microwave "horns" (modified dishes) can send signals over wider areas. The latest generation of mobile microwave transmitters and receivers can continually align themselves to maximize their point-to-point signals.

Satellite Links

Geosynchronous satellites rotate at the same speed as the earth and are, therefore, stationary in relation to the earth's surface. Each satellite or "bird" is composed of a number of **transponders:** independent receive-transmit units.

Two classifications of satellites are used: those that use C-band frequencies (between 3.7 and 4.2 gigahertz, and from 5.9 and 6.4 gigahertz) and those that operate on the much higher Ku-band frequencies (between 11 and 12 gigahertz). (Recall that a gigahertz is one billion cycles per second.)

C-Band Satellites   C-band was the first satellite frequency range to be widely used in broadcasting. Compared to Ku-band, this range is more reliable under adverse conditions, such as heavy rain and sleet. At the same time, the frequencies used are more congested and vulnerable to terrestrial interference. Because C-band frequencies are also used in standard (ground-based) microwave transmissions, problems develop between C-band satellite receivers and nearby microwave transmitters that are being used for other services. The C-band also requires large receiver and transmitting dishes—up to 30 feet for a full-size ground station. Although dish size may not be a major problem in permanently mounted installations, even the scaled-down 3- to 4-meter, C-band dishes impose limitations on satellite newsgathering (SNG) trucks (to be discussed). For one thing, these vehicles encounter problems getting to remote areas.

Ku-Band Satellites   Ku-band dishes are about one-third the size those used for C-band. For SNG vehicles this greatly simplifies transportation and setup. Because Ku-band also has fewer technical restrictions, it means that users can set up satellite links and immediately start transmitting without waiting for FCC clearance. This "spontaneity factor" is an important advantage for Ku-band, especially in electronic newsgathering.

Satellite Distribution of Network Programming   SNG is just one use of C-Band and Ku-Band satellite services. Cable (CATV) companies receive much of their programming from satellites. Networks and production facilities routinely distribute their programming via satellite. This is typically how productions originating in the Los Angeles-Hollywood area are sent to the East Coast for network distribution. Once they arrive on the East Coast, they are recorded, scheduled into the network agenda, and then beamed back to satellites at intervals appropriate to the time zones of affiliated stations across North America. Each network affiliate has a permanently mounted satellite receiving dish. The down-linked program can be broadcast directly from the satellite feed or recorded for later use. When the network-to-affiliate link is not being used to relay regular programming, it is used to send news stories, *promos* (program promotion segments), and other useful segments. Although some satellite programming, such as HBO, is scrambled, which means it is only available by paid subscription, hundreds of satellite channels can be viewed by anyone with a satellite receiver. For those interested in news, watching unedited "raw feeds" from the field—intended only as a field-to-studio transmission—provides interesting insights into how stories are shot. (What doesn't get on the air is sometimes more interesting than what does!)

Flyaway Satellite Links   Not all satellite dishes are mounted on vehicles. In the late 1980s portable, free-standing satellite uplinks—commonly referred to as **flyaway units**—were introduced (Figure 10.5). These units can be disassembled and transported in packing cases to the scene of a news story. Flyaway units are used in areas not accessible to SNG vehicles, including remote regions, off-shore areas and third-world countries. During the 1991 Persian Gulf war the flyaway satellite uplink, with its ability to be set up anywhere within 30 minutes, permanently changed the nature of international electronic newsgathering.

Covering SNG Assignments   Today, satellite transmissions have become routine and, for the most part, quite reliable. However, there are still occasional problems. At times it is safer to transmit a videotape from a field location than to do a live feed. The videotape can be done a short time before the scheduled satellite time without sacrificing timeliness.

Even satellite segments that are broadcast live typically rely on videotaped segments. Often, a reporter will do a live introduction and then previously recorded footage transmitted a little earlier from the scene via satellite will be rolled in from the production facility while the field reporter narrates from the field. This allows the production facility to edit the raw footage to a desired length prior to the "live" report, and establish a time for the total field report.

The Hazards of News and Documentary Work

A final word. Part of the excitement of news and documentary work is being on the "front line" of news events. If there is a major airline crash, ENG reporters are

Figure 10.5   Flyaway satellite uplinks are used in areas not accessible to SNG vehicles, including remote regions, off-shore areas and third-world countries. The satellite uplink shown will fold up and fit into a suitcase.

on the scene reporting; if a major civil disturbance breaks out in a large city, ENG reporters may find themselves reporting the story while dodging bricks and exploding canisters of tear gas. There is no doubt that by comparison other professions seem rather dull.

Although most local assignments are routine, during major accidents, emergencies and disasters news and documentary personnel may face definite hazards. Although celebrated heroes sometimes emerge in these situations, people not accustomed to extreme stress often react irrationally, irresponsibly and dangerously. Physiologists might attribute this to adrenaline interfering with the normal reasoning processes. Whatever the reason, reporters quickly learn that people often go into a kind of "shock fog" and cannot be counted on to respond rationally during, or for some time after, extreme stress. Add to this the fact that a crew will be working under its own broadcast-related pressures, and it becomes obvious that special precautions must be observed when major accidents and life-threatening assignments are covered. Suffice it to say, appropriate personal precautions and safeguards are a critical part of both news and documentary work.

Once reporters leave the arena of local news, risks can become even greater. During 1994, 75 newspeople were killed or "disappeared" around the world. Most were killed in countries who fear a free flow of information would threaten political control. However, even in Western countries like the United States, investigative reporters working on sensitive stories have been killed before they could broadcast their findings. The fact that some news and documentary work can be considered "high risk" occupations, even in peacetime, attests to the media's power in exposing impropriety and corruption. As we've repeatedly seen, once such activities are exposed to public view, corrective action often follows. This is one of the things that can make news and documentary work highly rewarding, both personally and professionally.

Yet to be covered is the crucial editing phase of video field production. In news and documentary work it is in editing that the essential structure, direction and meaning of the production is created. This postproduction phase is the subject of the next two chapters.

CHAPTER 11 PRINCIPLES OF EDITING

THE POWER AND control that a good editor can have over the success or failure of the final production can hardly be overestimated. In the hands of an expert or, more accurately, an artist, editing can establish the structure of the production and control its overall mood, intensity and tempo. This phenomenon was realized more than 75 years ago when the esteemed Russian director V.I. Pudovkin said: "Editing is the creative force of filmic reality . . . and the foundation of film art." Since then editing has become even more important.

During the early days of motion pictures, film production consisted of planting the camera in one spot and having the action take place continuously in front of the lens until the reel of film ran out. If major problems were encountered during the shooting, the whole reel was reshot from beginning to end. The final result was somewhat like watching a stage play from the 20th row of a theater, without the benefit of color or synchronized sound. The film editors of the day were simply technicians given the routine task of cutting out dead footage at the beginning and end of reels. It apparently didn't occur to anyone for some time that the camera could be stopped and moved in the middle of the reel, that retakes of short segments could be done, or that scenes on a reel could be routinely cut apart and spliced together in a different order.

Gradually, this approach to "editing" changed, mostly out of necessity. Someone, probably trying to rush a film to completion, wondered: "Why should I do this whole scene over again from the beginning when I can just redo the bad part and splice it into the reel?" So what started out being a way to patch up a mistake ended up, with some refinements, introducing a major new dimension to the art of film making (Figure 11.1).

(a)

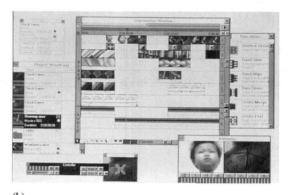

(b)

Figure 11.1   Quickly rearranging scenes to test various effects became much easier when random access editing for desktop computers was introduced. Media servers, which started being widely used in 1996, added even greater flexibility and speed to the editing process. Both of these concepts will be discussed later in the chapter. With the editing system shown, various screens of information related to the editing process can be selected by the user.

Continuity Editing

Once editing began, it was soon discovered that audiences didn't have to see all of an event in real time in order to understand what was going on. In particular, it was found that routine and uninteresting elements could be left out of a scene and the audience would just assume they had taken place. It was at this point that **continuity editing** (or cutting to continuity) to preserve the sequential essence of an event, without showing all of it, was born.

As editors began to experiment with shortening, rearranging and intercutting scenes, it soon became obvious that the film editor had great power in shaping the meaning of a story. As an example of how rearranging scenes can shape meaning, let's look at what we can do with only two shots:

1. A man glancing up
2. Another man pulling a gun and firing toward the camera

In this order it appears that the first man was shot. However, if you reverse the order of these two scenes, an entirely different meaning emerges: the first man is watching a shooting.

Let's look at what we can do with three shots.

1. People jumping from a boat
2. A burning boat
3. An explosion

Let's look at the possibilities with just these three shots.

■ In the 1-2-3 sequence shown the shots suggest that people are jumping from a boat seconds before it catches fire and explodes.

■ A 3-2-1 order suggests that there is an explosion on the boat and then it bursts into flames; as a result, the people have to jump overboard.

■ In a 2-3-1 sequence people flee from the boat after a fire causes an explosion.

■ If the sequence is changed to 2-1-3, it appears that, as a result of a fire, passengers jump overboard just in time to escape a devastating explosion.

And all this is only with three scenes. When scores of takes of scenes are available to editors—which is normally the case in dramatic productions—they have considerable power in shaping both the basic continuity and message of the production.

Continuity Editing in an ENG Story

From dramatic interpretation we now move to a sequence designed to accurately represent events in a news story. Consider the following list of 13 shots of an ENG news story of what appears to be a murder.

1. An extreme close-up of a knife on a street
2. A close-up of a policewoman using a handkerchief to pick up the knife
3. A victim being loaded onto a stretcher
4. A man being handcuffed
5. Handcuffed man being put into a police car
6. An ambulance driving off
7. A police officer questioning a bystander
8. A wide shot of the crime scene
9. The police car driving off
10. A pool of blood on the pavement
11. A wide shot of onlookers
12. A stretcher being loaded into an ambulance
13. A close-up of several bereaved onlookers

There are three content areas for the videotape editor to consider: logical sequence, creative sequence, and legal and ethical suitability.

Often, ENG footage can't be shot in logical sequence. If the ENG cameraperson in the above example arrived just as the man was being handcuffed, this scene would have to be shot first; and it would have to be gotten quickly, or be missed. The next shots on the tape might be of the victim being loaded onto a stretcher, the stretcher being put in an ambulance, and the ambulance being driven away. Possibly it would be only after these scenes were shot that the cameraperson would have time to get shots of the crime scene, crowd shots, etc. One way that the videotape editor could arrange the 13 shots is as follows:

8. A wide shot of the crime scene
3. The victim being loaded onto a stretcher
10. A pool of blood on the pavement
1. An extreme close-up of a knife on the street
4. A man being handcuffed
2. A close-up of a policewoman using a handkerchief to pick up the knife
11. A wide shot of onlookers
5. The handcuffed man being put into a police car
12. A stretcher being loaded into the ambulance
13. A close-up of several bereaved onlookers
6. The ambulance being driven off
7. A police officer questioning a bystander
9. The police car driving off

Based on documented experience with TV audiences, if not personal ethics, an editor or news producer may decide the close-up shot of blood on the pavement to be inappropriate for a dinnertime newscast. If the shots of the man being handcuffed clearly show his identity, a legal issue is raised. What if later facts reveal that the man was an innocent bystander who in the confusion was mistakenly identified as a murderer? Could he sue the station and its personnel for putting him in a false light? To be on the safe side, and depending on station policy, some camerapersons will include shots of the suspect that do not reveal his identity: scenes from the back, a mosaic pattern obscuring the face, or a close-up of hand-cuffed hands. Some stations might stand on the simple fact that "this man was arrested." These would be some of the legal and ethical considerations in editing this piece. Now, what about the logical and creative aspects?

The rearranged sequence listed above was done in what is probably a logical, time-based (continuity) sequence. Note that there are actually three concurrent stories in this ENG report:

■ The sequence of events involving the arrest of a suspect, including the assumed weapon

■ The events involving picking up and removing the body of the victim

■ The ongoing reactions of bystanders to what has taken place and to what is going on

So the first job of the editor is to accurately intercut these three concurrent events both to preserve the logical sequence of each, and to show their interrelationship. In our example, 13 original shots are listed. In an actual news story of this type there will probably be several times that number of shots to choose from. This situation brings up a related point.

The footage taken vs. the footage used is referred to as the **shooting ratio.** Compared to film, videotape is relatively cheap, so shooting ratios are not a major concern. Editors often advise videographers to *get it all on tape, and figure out later if we can use it.* Editors routinely complain about not having enough shots to choose from; but they seldom complain about having too many. Sometimes that "extra shot" taken "almost without reason" ends up being an essential editing transition between two shots that otherwise couldn't be used.

Altering Expected Continuity

Cutting to continuity (continuity editing) largely involves making edits based on what is expected. Good editors in dramatic television, like good directors, are masters at manipulating audience emotions. To do so they must sometimes break from the expected.

For example, unfulfilled expectations are often used to create audience tension. Let's take this simple shot sequence as an example: Someone is working at a desk late at night. There is a knock at the door. The person sitting at the desk routinely calls out, "Come in." But a moment later the calm expression on that person's face dramatically changes. Why? We don't know. Where is the shot of who or what just came in? What happens if we don't cut to that expected shot? The audience is then just left hanging with curiosity and apprehension or, depending on how it's handled, with frustration and resentment.

Here's an example of the latter. In a story about the introduction of design changes in U.S. paper currency a reporter holds a newly designed $100 bill as a treasury spokesperson talks about the specific changes that were necessary to foil counterfeiting. Let's assume that the whole time all we see is a two-shot of the two men and at no time do we ever see a close-up of the newly designed $100 bill.

Obviously, we would want to see a close-up of the bill so we could see the changes being discussed. Unless you want to leave your audience hanging for momentary dramatic effect, always keep in mind what you think the audience expects to see at any given moment. If you always keep this in mind while editing, your **edit decision list** (sequence of edits) will largely "write itself."

Causality

In a dramatic production it would generally be inappropriate to cut to a shot of someone answering the phone unless we had initially heard the phone ring. A ringing phone brings about a response: the phone is picked up.

A good script, enhanced by good editing, reveals causality, both in deed and story line. For example, we may see a female corpse on the living room floor during the first five minutes of a dramatic film but not find out for sure that her husband killed her (the cause) until 90 minutes later.

Note that here effect precedes cause. In fact, many directors in dramatic film and television feel it is more interesting to regularly show effect before cause. But, regardless of whether cause or effect comes first, we expect to see these relationships tied together, or at least suggested.

Occasionally, we can safely assume cause. For example, if we are shown a shot of someone with all the signs of inebriation (effect), we can safely assume he has been drinking (cause); if we see a shot of someone leaving for a skiing trip followed by a shot of her arriving back home on crutches, we will assume she had a skiing accident. In these cases the "cause" can be safely assumed.

In our example of the murder, just knowing that the husband did it is not enough (maybe for the police it would be, but not for most viewers). In causality there is also the question of *why*. This brings up *motivation*. Possibly the murder resulted from revenge, hatred, or any of the other age-old motives. But even knowing that the motive was revenge is not enough for a well thought-out, satisfying production. Since we assume that revenge doesn't occur without a cause, we may want to know the origin of the husband's need for revenge. Answering this question may necessitate taking the viewer back to an incident in the past. We may be led to discover that the woman had a string of lovers. As a consequence we would also expect to see the suspicion, jealousy, resentment and anger building in her husband's behavior. Finally, we see that these negative emotions can be contained no more. Now we understand. Editors must perceive the dynamics of these cause-and-effect relationships to skillfully handle them.

It might seem that what we've been talking about is relevant only to dramatic productions. But cause-effect relationships are present in all types of productions, even documentary and ENG pieces. An ideal documentary or ENG piece on a tornado for example, would show the approaching storm, the effect of this knowledge on the people in its path, including their preparations, the tornado hitting and then subsiding and, finally, the results of the storm. In most news stories, however, we see only the results of causes. Even so, the more logically ENG stories can be assembled, the better an audience will understand them.

ACCELERATION EDITING

At the beginning of the chapter we noted that early films were shot in real time. Today, a film audience would become restless indeed and, in television, would quickly turn to another channel if events in a production were all shown in real time. Let's say you want to tell the story of a girl preparing for an important date. The process of picking out clothes, taking a shower, drying her hair, putting on her clothes and makeup, checking the whole effect, making necessary adjustments, and then driving to some prearranged place, might take 90 minutes. That's the total time devoted to most feature films. (And the really interesting part hasn't even started yet.) If productions were confined to "real time," telling someone's life story would also present a bit of a problem.

In film and video production, time is routinely condensed and expanded. The 90 minutes it may take to go get ready for the date can be shown in 10–15 seconds. In the case of the woman getting ready for a date this could consist of the following:

1. A shot of the woman concluding a conversation on the phone

2. A quick shot of her pulling clothes out of her closet

3. Her silhouette through a shower door while taking a shower

4. A shot of her blow-drying her hair

5. The woman heading for the door

6. A driving shot

7. The woman pulling up in front of the prearranged meeting place

If you really want to collapse time and not make any real points about the woman's preparation for the date, you could just get the tail end of a telephone conversation setting up the date and then cut directly to the woman arriving at the agreed upon place. Although the latter might seem like a jump-cut, the audience has become conditioned to jumping across hours, days and even years in a single cut.

In video editing, action is generally compressed but, occasionally, an editor or director will want to drag out a happening beyond the actual time represented. To illustrate the power of slowing down events, the noted director Alfred Hitchcock (*Psycho, North By Northwest,* etc.) used the example of a scene where a group of people sitting around a dinner table were blown up by a time bomb. In a real-time version of the scene, the people sit down at the table and the bomb goes off. End of people; end of scene. In the second version the people gather, talk, and casually sit down at the dinner table. A shot of the bomb ticking away under the table is shown, revealing to the audience what is about to happen. The guests at the table, unaware of the bomb, continue their banal conversations. Closer shots of the bomb are then intercut with the guests laughing and enjoying dinner. The intercutting continues until the bomb finally blows the dinner party to bits. The latter version understandably succeeds in creating far more of an emotional impact. A similar approach of dragging out events is often used in horror films during a particularly frightening or gruesome scene. And, if for some reason the director and editor don't think this approach will create enough audience reaction, the film or tape can be shown in slow motion, just so we don't miss any of the gore.

INSERT SHOTS

While holding to the basic continuity of a story, an editor can greatly enhance the look of a production with the prudent use of insert shots and cutaways. An **insert shot** is a close-up of something that exists *within* the basic scene, as shown by the establishing (wide) shot. This insert shot adds needed information that wouldn't otherwise be immediately visible or clear. In our earlier example of the new $100 bill, a close-up of the bill would be an insert shot. In the example of the street murder scene, a close-up of the knife on the ground would be an insert shot. (Someone in a medium or wide shot glancing at the object would provide perfect motivation for the cut to the insert shot. Once the person glanced at the object, we would, in fact, expect the insert shot to follow.)

CUTAWAYS

Unlike insert shots, which show significant aspects of the overall scene in close-up, recall that cutaways cut away from the main scene or action to add related material. During a parade we might cut away from the parade to a shot of people watching from a nearby rooftop, or a child sleeping through the commotion on the sidelines.

RELATIONAL EDITING

In relational editing scenes, which by themselves seem not to be related, take on an interrelated significance when spliced together. Relational editing techniques cash in on the human tendency to try to make meaning out of events, even if there isn't any. Many years ago the Russian film makers Pudovkin and Kuleshov established this principle in an experiment. They alternated film segments from a long take of a man sitting motionless and expressionless in a chair with several scenes. Included were a close-up of a bowl of soup, a shot of a coffin containing a female corpse, and a shot of a little girl playing. To an audience viewing the edited film, the expressionless man suddenly became involved in the emotional scenes, to the point of representing a cause or an effect. Although the shot of the actor's face was without expression, when it was preceded by the shot of the coffin, the audience thought that the actor showed deep sorrow. When the same shot followed the close-up of the food, the audience perceived hunger in his face; and when it was associated with the shot of the little girl, the audience saw the actor as experiencing parental pride. Thus, one of the most important tenets of editing was experimentally established: the human tendency to try to establish a relationship between a series of events. In the case of the wife who was shot, what if we proceeded the shooting with one of the these shots:

- The woman covertly taking a large sum of money out of a safe
- The woman buying an international airline ticket
- The woman caught in bed with a lover
- The woman loading a gun and putting it in her purse

If the murder scene described earlier was preceded by one or more of these four shots, the circumstances surrounding the murder could be interpreted differently.

THEMATIC EDITING

In **thematic editing** (also called **montage editing**) images are edited together that are related in theme only. Although the term *montage* as used in early film work had a different meaning, today montage or thematic editing refers to a rapid, impressionistic sequence of disconnected scenes designed to communicate feelings or experiences. This type of editing is often used in music videos, commercials and film trailers (promotional clips). In contrast to most types of editing, thematic editing is not designed to tell a story by developing an idea in a logical sequence. The trailer for the original *Alien* film (one of the first trailers to use the thematic technique) was produced even before shooting on the actual film was completed. Footage was more or less randomly cut together to conform to the rhythm of the theme music. The intent was simply to communicate action, excitement and danger, and not to suggest a story line. Through thematic editing, commercials often highlight good times, romance, or adventure. Rather than telling a product's "success story," the commercials are designed to create a feeling or mood. The sponsor hopes that these good feelings will be both transferred to and associated with their product.

PARALLEL CUTTING

Daytime soap operas typically have several stories taking place simultaneously, as do most sitcoms and general dramatic productions. This simultaneous activity is referred to as parallel action; when the segments are cut together to follow the multiple story lines it's referred to as **parallel cutting,** which is also used in documentaries.

By cutting back and forth between the ministories taking place within the overall story, production pace can be varied and overall interest heightened. The action can be as simple as intercutting between the story of three bank robbers as they try to elude police, and the simultaneous work of the police as they try to catch them.

JUMP-CUTS

When we discussed acceleration and thematic editing, we were referring to intentional discontinuities in action. Audiences have learned to appreciate the technique of cutting out extraneous footage to keep a story moving. But all discontinuities in action are not effective. When they aren't, it's called a *jump-cut*—a confusing, unsettling, or aesthetically rough jump in content. Many weekly television series—those that are shot single-camera, film-style—provide good examples of discontinuity in action.

- A two-shot of a couple talking on a boat will show their hair blowing gently in the breeze; but in an immediate close-up of one of them, the wind has inexplicably changed its intensity.

- A close-up of an actress may show her laughing, but in an immediate cut to a master shot we see that she is not even smiling.

- A man is walking with his arm around the waist of his girlfriend; but a cut to another angle suddenly shows that his arm is around her shoulder.

Bridging Jumps in Action

Various editing techniques can be used to solve these problems. We'll start with how a jump-cut in a major dramatic production might be handled. In the getting-ready-for-a-date example, we might see the girl hang up the phone in the kitchen and quickly walk out a door on the right of the frame. After exiting the kitchen (moving left-to-right), let's assume we then immediately cut to a shot of her entering the bedroom from the right (now moving right-to-left) to get her clothes from the closet. The audience is left with a question: Why did she instantly seem to turn a full 180 degrees and start walking in the opposite direction to get to the bedroom?

When successive scenes are shot hours or sometimes even weeks apart, which they commonly are in single-camera, film-style video production, it is easy to overlook continuity problems such as this. In documentary and news segments these jump-cuts could be the result of mismatches in action between camera takes, or segments that must be removed from long-winded answers to questions.

The solution to most of these problems is the use of cutaways and insert shots. In the case of the continuity problem above we could even add an extra element to the scenario: a quick shot through a steamy glass enclosure of her taking a shower. Not only is relevant information added and visual variety introduced, but by the time you come back to the basic scene, an alteration in the time sequence or in the position of the actors is to some degree expected. In most EFP and ENG productions the cameraperson will usually take a variety of B-roll shots, which can be used as insert shots and cutaways.

Bridging Interview Edits

Interviews must be routinely cut down to conform to time limitations. Cutting a section out of dialogue will normally result in an abrupt and noticeable jump in the video of the person speaking. The resulting jump-cut can be covered by inserting a three- or four-second B-roll cutaway shot over the jump, while maintaining the edited A-roll audio track. These cutaways are often reaction shots ("noddies") of interviewers just listening to someone speak, and possibly nodding their head as they listen. Since video editors depend greatly on this supplementary B-roll footage to bridge a wide range of editing problems, the director or videographer should always take the time to tape a variety of (B-roll) shots.

The 1-2-3 Formula

Jump-cuts not only relate to unacceptable jumps in action, but also can result from major, abrupt changes in subject size. As we've noted, going from the establishing (long) shot directly to a close-up of an individual is rather abrupt. An intermediate medium shot is needed to smooth out the transition. There is a well-established 1-2-3 shot formula that covers this. It starts with (1) a momentary long (master or establishing) shot, (2) a cut to a medium shot, and then (3) cuts to various over-the-shoulder and close-up shots. At some point the shot order is reversed. This may be required when it's necessary to "back out of a scene," or to accommodate major changes in actor or talent positions. If a scene is long, it may be necessary to occasionally remind viewers where everyone and everything is. When you cut back to a shot in this way it is referred to as cutting to a *re-establishing shot.*

Although this long-shot-to-medium-shot-to-close-up formula is traditional, there will be many times when an editor will opt for another approach. By starting a scene with an extreme close-up, especially of a crucial object, and then backing out, the editor can immediately focus attention on the scene's center of interest. In a drama the starting close-up could be a snapshot of a child, smashed eyeglasses, a gun, or other key subject matter. From here the camera could dolly or zoom back to reveal the surrounding scene.

Shooting-Angle Considerations

Another type of jump-cut results from cutting to a shot that is almost the same as the one that preceded it. An example would be cutting from one three-shot to another three-shot from a similar angle. Not only is it hard to justify a transition when the new shot is not significantly different, but a cut of this type simply looks like a mistake. As a result, some videographers adhere to the "30-degree rule." According to this rule a new shot of the same subject matter can be justified only if a change of angle of at least 30 degrees in the shooting angle is involved. Of course, in cutting to a different shot—for example, from a two-shot to a one-shot—this rule would not apply, since the two shots would be significantly different to start with.

CROSSING THE LINE

Another example of an undesirable angle change occurs when screen direction is reversed by crossing the line, or the *action axis* of a scene. Any time a new camera angle exceeds 180 degrees you will have crossed the line and action will be reversed (refer to Figure 10.2). Occasionally, a director will intentionally violate the 180-degree rule for dramatic effect. For example, during a riot scene a director may choose to intentionally cross the line on many shots in order to communicate confusion and disorientation. Assuming that confusion is not the objective, an editor must always remember to maintain the audience's perspective as edits are made.

TECHNICAL CONTINUITY PROBLEMS

A technical continuity problem is an abrupt and undesirable change in audio or video characteristics.

Audio Continuity Problems

In the area of audio, technical continuity problems include shot-to-shot variations in sound ambiance, frequency response, or audio level caused by cutting together scenes that were shot under different conditions. In highly demanding applications many of these problems can be helped, if not made imperceptible, by technicians skilled in using graphic equalizers, reverberation units and a wide range of sound-shaping equipment. For day-to-day video field production, it becomes a matter of maintaining absolute consistency between scenes. Switching microphones, moving to rooms with different acoustics, and varying the distance between the subject and the microphone all result in audio continuity problems.

Normally, the easiest sound problems to fix, those that are well within the control of the most basic editing equipment, are related to minor level variations. It's just a matter of adjusting levels during postproduction. This technique assumes, however, that there is no significant background sound present. If there is—on-location sounds are quite common in field productions—the level of the background sound may annoyingly jump or drop with each level adjustment.

A related problem is the discontinuity of background sounds. For example, the sound of a passing car or airplane may abruptly disappear when you cut from one shot to another. Keeping these possible problems in mind during production can help avoid major problems during postproduction.

Video Continuity Problems

In video there can be continuity problems related to color balance, light levels, camera optics and, in analog recording, tape generation loss. Intercutting scenes from cameras with noticeably different color balance will immediately be apparent to most viewers. Within limits, knowledgeable engineers with the proper equipment can match at least the skin tones from two unmatched video sources. Color shifts in backgrounds, especially in isolated scenes, will often go unnoticed, since the audience has no way of knowing the original color or brightness of the background. (But they do know what skin tones are supposed to look like.) Minor postproduction corrections can also be made for differences in video levels. But, once again "the best defense is no offense"; that is, you won't have to worry about spending considerable time fixing problems if you can learn to avoid them in the first place.

MUSIC CONTINUITY CONSIDERATIONS

Another continuity problem relates to background music. When skillfully used, music can smooth the transition between segments and create overall production unity. Except in music-centered productions, music should add to the overall mood and effect without calling attention to itself. Vocals should be avoided, especially when the production contains normal (competing) dialogue. Music should match the mood, pace and time period of the production. Ideally, the beginning of the music should coincide with the start of a video segment and end as the segment ends. Of course, this rarely happens, unless the video is specifically edited to match the music or the audio is edited to the length of the video.

Conforming Music to Video

If the music runs long, which is generally the case, check to see if a segment can be cut out of the music. This can often be done, especially when a piece contains repetitive sections separated by momentary pauses. The best way to customize a music section to video is to use a digital editing workstation or PC editing program. In addition to electronically cutting out musical segments to shorten selections, and repeating sections to lengthen music, segments can be, within limits, digitally compressed or stretched without noticeably affecting the audio frequency range.

Backtiming Music

If adding or subtracting, or digitally altering music segments does not work, the music can be *back-timed* so that it will conclude with the scene. If the music is longer than the video segment, the music can be started an exact interval before the beginning of the video segment. At the appropriate point the video can be started, and the music subtly faded in. Here's an example. If a video segment were one minute, 43 seconds long, and a music selection three minutes, 13 seconds long, the music would be started one minute, 30 seconds before the video. Both would then end at exactly the same time. (As you will note in the next chapter, time code greatly facilitates the timing of audio and video segments.) The least desirable solution to music timing is to fade the music out in midstream at the end of a scene. This will be especially noticeable if the music is almost finished or if it has just gotten under way.

Tapping into Music Libraries

Libraries of background music can be purchased on CDs that suggest themes such as "Manhattan Rush Hour," "Serenity" and "Heavy Machinery." Since music and effects (M&E) generally go together, sound libraries also include just about every possible sound effect. Most sound-effect libraries contain several variations of each category of sound, which eases the problem of making a particular effect blend naturally and realistically into a sound track. When audio workstations or computer-based audio editing is used, sound-effect libraries are routinely transferred onto computer disks. They can then be selected from a screen menu, programmed into an editing sequence, and recalled instantly as needed.

Six Editing Guidelines

Production techniques are best when they go unnoticed by the average listener and viewer. Editing, in particular, should be invisible. In the interest of making editing as smooth and unobtrusive as possible, six guidelines should be considered. As with the guidelines for good composition, we are avoiding the term "rules." The following guidelines also introduce some important editing concepts.

Guideline 1: Make Motivated Cuts

Edits should be "motivated." Transitions should be suggested by on-camera action, dialogue or music. In making any transition there is a risk of breaking the concentration of the audience and subtly pulling attention away from the production's central focus. When cuts are motivated by production content, they are most apt to go unnoticed. When someone glances to one side during a dramatic scene, it is best to immediately cut to whatever has caught the actor's attention. When we hear a door open, we expect to see a shot of the person entering the room.

Guideline 2: Cut on Subject Movement

Whenever possible, cut on subject movement. When you cut on subject movement, some of the action will be included in both shots. If a woman is getting out of a chair, cut at the midpoint. If cuts are motivated by action, the action will divert attention from the cut, making the transition more fluid. In addition, subtle jump-cuts are less noticeable, because the viewers tend to be caught up in the action itself.

In cutting to various shots, keep in mind the 30-degree angle rule already discussed. Not only does it look better, and avoids a possible jump-cut, but minor mismatches in action are concealed when the new shot represents a significant change in subject perspective.

Cutting with the action calls for a good eye for detail. To avoid a jump-cut in single-camera production, you need to be sure the subject is doing the same thing in exactly the same way in each shot.

Matching Action   In matching action not only should the relative position of feet or hands, etc., in both shots be the same, but also the rate of movement. In single-camera production where the various camera angles are shot at different times, it is important that actors and directors duplicate the exact action in each take. This duplication also applies to the general energy level exhibited by actors in their voice and gestures. Part of the art of acting includes maintaining consistency in the various takes. To facilitate editing, directors will generally give the editor several takes of each scene.

Often it is necessary to cut to a scene as a person leaves the frame and cut to the next scene as the person enters, such as when a person walks out of one room and enters another. In this case it is best to cut the first scene as the person's eyes pass the edge of the frame, and then cut to the second scene about six frames before the person's eyes enter the frame of the next scene. The timing here is significant. It takes about a fifth of a second for viewers' eyes to switch from one side of the frame to the other. (A person exiting the first scene on the right enters the next scene on the left.) During this time the viewers' eyes are unfocused, and whatever is taking place on the screen becomes a bit scrambled. Because of this "lost interval," some editors prefer to overlap visible action in successive scenes by four to six frames. When this technique is used, not only does the viewer not miss anything, but a kind of "subjective jump-cut" is avoided.

Cutting after Subtle Action   Although we've talked about cutting on (within) action, when the movement is subtle and is used to motivate an edit, you need to cut just after the action ends. An example would be a reaction that amounts only to a shift of the eyes: you hear a door open, a person glances to one side, and you immediately cut to a person entering the room. In this case you use the action to provide motivation for the cut and then make the cut at the precise second the action (the eye movement) ends.

Editor as Magician   When someone in a scene is talking, attention is generally focused on the person's mouth or eyes. Like a good magician, an editor can use this to cover a slight mismatch in action in another area of the frame. Suffice it to say, in order to know what can and cannot be done, an editor must be aware at every moment of where the audience's attention is likely to be directed.

Sudden, loud sounds are even used by editors to cover jump-cuts. An unexpected loud sound will cause viewers to blink. In the one-fifth of a second it takes to blink, a subtle jump-cut will go undetected. Any on-screen diversion can be used in this way.

Guideline 3: Edit to Accommodate the Medium

Edit to conform to the strengths and limitations of the medium. This guideline primarily addresses the fact that significant picture detail is lost in the 525- and 625-line systems of broadcast television. The only way to really show needed details is through close-ups. Therefore, it is up to the editor to keep in mind the precept: *television is a close-up medium.* Except for establishing shots designed to momentarily orient the audience to subject placement, the director and the editor should emphasize medium shots and close-ups.

In addition to showing detail, close-ups convey intimacy. They are appropriate for interviews, dramas and love stories, but generally not appropriate for light comedy. In comedy the use of medium shots makes it much easier to follow characters around the set. At the same time, medium shots do not seriously and deeply "pull the audience into" the show's subject matter or the actors' thoughts and emotions. Many comedy directors feel that the use of loose one-shots or even two-shots helps keep the mood light.

In contrast, in interviews and documentary work it is generally desirable to try to "zero in on" a subject's reactions to provide clues to the person's general character. Close-ups help do this.

Guideline 4: Determine the Length of Shots

Cut away from a scene the moment the visual statement is complete. Interest quickly wanes in a scene once the essential visual information is conveyed. "Slow moving" suggests that an audience has grown impatient with the pace of a production. A large part of the responsibility for keeping a production moving rests with editing. Shots with new information stimulate viewer interest, as long as they are presented at the right time.

There are several considerations in determining shot length. First is the amount of information you wish to convey. In the 13-shot, ENG murder scenario outlined earlier, the shot of the knife on the pavement should take only about two seconds, since only two elements need to be communicated at that moment: "knife" resting on "pavement." Because we are probably not interested in what kind of knife it is or the condition of the pavement, two seconds are enough to make this statement and enough to associate the object later picked up by a policeman as being the knife we saw.

Accommodating Visual Complexity   Shot length is also dictated by visual complexity. Often, travelogue shots can be relatively short, since it may take only a few seconds for the viewer to grasp or be reminded of essential information. Examples would be of a shot of a beach, a mountain stream, or a winding road. If some sort of action is included, the shot will require more time: children playing on the beach, people fishing in the mountain stream, or a native family making its way along the winding road with all their belongings. In the case of the native family, you will also want to consider how much information viewers need to know. If the production is about the family, you will want to hold the scene long enough for viewers to recognize the individual family members and even start learning things about them. By holding the scene of the family and even cutting to various angles, you are, in fact, tipping the audience off that this particular family is in some way important to the story. After "becoming involved with" this family by dwelling on them for a period of time, members of the audience will naturally develop some expectations. They will assume that the production will either follow this family's story or that the production will at least periodically "check on their progress."

In contrast, montage editing shots may be only a fraction of a second (10–15 video frames) long. Obviously, this is not enough time even to begin to see all of the elements in the scene. But the idea in this case is simply to communicate general impressions, not details.

The next major consideration under this guideline, subject familiarity, is illustrated by two brief examples. Since most people have seen many shots of the Statue of Liberty, a scene showing it would need to be only in the form of a "brief, symbolic reminder"—probably just three seconds, or so. On the other hand, the audience wouldn't appreciate only three seconds of a strange little green man who just landed his flying saucer on the White House lawn.

Next, cutting rate depends on the inherent or implied tempo of production content. Tranquil pastoral scenes imply longer shots than scenes of downtown New York at rush hour. Although you can enhance and increase production tempo by cutting rapidly during rapid action, this technique can do little to speed up slow action.

Varying Tempo   A well-written script should have periodic swings in tempo. A constant fast pace will tire an audience; a constant slow pace in both production content and editing can quickly put an audience to sleep or, in television, induce them to look for something more engaging on another channel. If the visual or audio content of the production does not naturally vary, the editor, possibly with help from music, will want to try to cut segments in a way that provides changes in pace. This is one of the reasons that editors like parallel stories; pace can be varied by cutting back and forth between stories.

It is often helpful to plot editing pace to see variations over time. This can easily be done by plotting time against the number of edits. If an average 22-minute production (30 minutes minus commercials) has 275 edits, the average scene will be six seconds long.

Editing to Hold Audience Interest   In editing segments, guard against peaking interest too soon and letting the remainder of the piece go downhill. Try to lead the segment with something fairly strong (a "hook") that will immediately engage audience interest. Given the many TV channels vying for viewer attention, the first few seconds of a show are crucial to holding an audience. It is during these opening seconds that viewers are most tempted to "channel hop" and see what else is on. Because of this, TV programs often show the most dramatic highlights of the night's program at the beginning, and nightly newscasts regularly "tease" upcoming stories just before commercial breaks.

In editing news and documentary stories it is best to open with a strong audio or video statement and then, when an audience is interested in knowing the details, fill in needed information. But in the process of filling in information, try to gradually build interest until it peaks at the end. This will leave the audience feeling good about the program or video segment.

Guideline 5: Make Use of B-Roll Footage

The real story is in the B-roll. Recall that the so-called B-roll contains scenes that supply supplementary information to the main (A-roll) story. In a single-camera ENG interview the "backbone" information—the interview subject answering the questions—is on one videotape (the A-roll) and supplementary information is contained on a second tape (the B-roll). The B-roll will largely consist of insert shots and cutaways.

In an interview the A-roll footage typically consists of a rather static looking "talking head." We can almost always make the piece stronger by cutting in supplementary footage. One valuable type of cutaway, especially in dramatic productions, is the **reaction shot:** telling reactions from others to what is going on or being said at the moment.

Reaction Shots   Reaction shots are desirable because they

- Make edits possible in the audio track of the speaker
- Provide important clues to how others are responding to what is being said
- Stimulate the pace of the show
- Introduce visual variety
- Can cover "bad moments" in A-roll footage (such as jerky camera movement, someone walking in front of the camera, or the speaker momentarily moving out of the frame)

In a news piece the B-roll consists of scenes that support, accentuate or in some way visually elaborate on what is being said. By using strong supplementary footage, the amount of information conveyed in a given interval increases. More information in a shorter time results in an apparent increase in production tempo, which tends to hold viewer interest.

Insert Shots   Insert shots are also considered B-roll footage. Howard Hawks, an eminent American film maker, said: "A great movie is made with cutaways and inserts." As we've noted, insert shots are close-ups and extreme close-ups of important objects within the basic scene. A news segment that shows a treasury agent holding and talking about counterfeit $100 bills may call for a number of extreme close-ups to show details of engraving problems. A segment on the work of a diamond cutter will need extreme close-up inserts of the diamond as it is marked and cut.

Cutaway Shots   As we also noted earlier, cutaway shots move away from the main scene to add related visual information. A cutaway during a parade may show a child asleep in the midst of all the noise and confusion. In this case we have cut away from the main event (the parade) to show something related to it and going on at the same time. During interviews, cutaways are generally needed to reinforce or illustrate what the speaker is talking about. If an inventor who has just perfected a perpetual-motion machine is being interviewed on his accomplishment, we would fully expect to see his creation. In fact, we would be a bit perturbed if we didn't. If a narcotics agent is being interviewed on finding a major illegal drug lab in your home town, you would expect to see footage of the lab, including where it was located and what was in it.

Guideline 6: Employ the Principle of Parsimony

The final editing guideline is, *if in doubt, leave it out.* This phrase should be hung in every editing bay. If you don't think that a scene adds significantly to what is being said at the moment, including it will (at best) slow down story development, and (at worst) blur the focus of the production and sidetrack the central message. Let's look at an example of each.

Some novelists used to spend many pages describing settings, right down to the last detail. Today, regardless of how eloquent a writer is, readers quickly grow impatient with such verbosity. In a novel you can skip over such loquaciousness; in television you can't, with the possible exception of fast-forwarding a VCR recording. Television and film viewers who have become accustomed to rapidly moving plots and energetic editing, quickly grow restless when a production seems to drag. This is one of the reasons it is so difficult to get an audience to watch classic films. Although they have many praiseworthy qualities, they just seem to move too slowly for today's audiences.

Although we've talked about the importance of cutaways, there are times when they aren't advisable because they will detract from the central focus of the production. For example, a TV evangelist paid hundreds of thousands of dollars to buy time on national television. His message was engrossing, dramatic and inspiring, or it should have been if the director hadn't chosen to regularly do cutaways to cute, fidgety kids, couples holding hands, and other interesting things going on in the audience. Although the director undoubtedly thought these cutaways added interest and visual variety, they only succeeded in breaking the mood in which the preacher had invested considerable time, money and effort to develop. Instead of continuing to follow the message, members of the TV audience were commenting on, or at least thinking about, "that darling little girl with the red ribbons in her hair," among other things. People watching TV generally have plenty of distractions right in the room where the TV is located; we don't need to add any more.

Before we turn our attention to the actual editing process, we need to look briefly at some concepts related to editing hardware.

Dedicated and Software-Based Edit Controllers

A **software-based editor** uses a modified desktop computer as a base. Depending on the software loaded, videotape editing is just one of the tasks it can perform. A **dedicated editor,** on the other hand, is especially designed to do only video editing. Dedicated editing equipment was the norm until desktop computer editors started to become available in the late 1980s. However, it was not until the mid-1990s that sophisticated video editing hardware and software became widely available for desktop computers. As previously noted, it was the Video Toaster system for the Amiga computer that represented the first, widely used desktop editing system. After this, things changed rapidly. Many manufacturers started making editing hardware and software, not only for the Amiga, but for the Apple and IBM computer standards.

Linear and Random-Access Editing

Linear Editing

The first approach to editing, **linear editing,** requires that edits be made in their proper sequence during the editing process. In a typical ENG segment this would mean starting with the countdown leader, followed by scene one, followed by scene two, all the way to the last scene. This is a little like writing a term paper with a typewriter. You need to have things well outlined and organized before you start, because once committed to paper, changes are difficult to make.

Random-Access Editing

Because segments can be inserted, deleted and moved around at any point in the editing process, **random-access editing** is more like working with a word processor. This approach is impossible with linear editing because of the need to find and record segments in a 1-2-3 sequence. To get around this limitation, in random-access editing the original segments are digitized and transferred to computer disks before editing starts. Once in this form the computer editing system can access them in any order, almost instantly. Segments are not permanently recorded anywhere; the edit decisions exist in computer memory only as a series of internal time code markers.

The final output can be handled in two ways. It can be "printed" in final, linear form to a videotape, or it can remain on computer disk and be recalled as needed. The latter approach, which is often used for segments in newscasts, requires a high-capacity storage device such as a video server (refer to Figure 9.3).

Using Video Servers   As we noted in Chapter 9, once video footage is brought in from the field, it can be immediately transferred to the server and then be recalled as needed for editing and broadcast. One of the main advantages of using a video server for newscasts is that news segments can be quickly re-edited, which is commonly done at stations that have multiple newscasts during the day. However, transferring raw footage to a server does represent an extra step. If time is limited and only a few edits are needed, you can save time by reverting to linear editing and using the edited master tape for broadcast.

With this background to editing, we can now turn our attention to the actual editing process.

CHAPTER 12 EDITING TECHNIQUES

THE CONCEPT BEHIND linear editing is simple: the tape containing the original footage is transferred segment by segment onto a tape in another recorder. In so doing, the original segments can be shortened and rearranged, bad shots can be removed, and audio and video effects can be added. Although the concept is simple, the actual editing process, as it starts to reflect a wide variety of artistic and technical possibilities, can become quite complex.

CONTROL-TRACK EDITING

The first automated videotape editing machines kept track of pre-roll and edit points on the tape by electronically counting control track pulses recorded along the edge of the videotape. These pulses are recorded at a rate of 30 per second to correspond to the 30-per-second frame rate of NTSC video. Except for the 8mm format, this series of pulses, which is referred to as a **control track,** is recorded on an audio-type, linear track as the tape is being recorded. The method of editing that locates segments based on a count of control-track pulses is referred to as **control-track editing.**

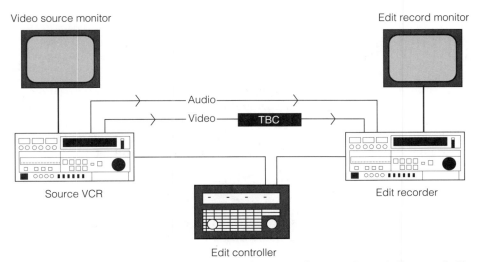

Figure 12.1 In basic control track editing, two videotape machines are electronically controlled by an edit controller. The linear editing process involves locating segments one by one, on the tape in the source machine and sequentially recording them on the tape in the edit recorder.

In basic, linear, control-track editing, two videotape machines, a **source machine** and an **edit recorder,** are electronically controlled by an **edit controller** (see Figure 12.1). The person doing the editing uses the edit controller to find each segment, mark the beginning and ending edit points, and then to perform the actual edit.

Although control-track editing is satisfactory for non-demanding applications, it has two major shortcomings. First, it relies on the ability of the equipment to maintain an accurate count of thousands of control-track pulses as the tapes go forward and backward at varying speeds. Because of a number of technical limitations, absolute accuracy is difficult to maintain; edit points can end up being off by many video frames.

Because errors generally center on videotape problems that interfere with an accurate count of the control-track pulses, operators have learned to keep an eye on the editor's digital tape counter as tapes are shuttled back and forth. If the counter momentarily freezes as the tape is moving, it indicates that the equipment has lost an accurate count of control pulses.

There's another weakness in control-track editing. Since the control track count is valid only during the editing session, once the machine is shut off, there is no way to replicate the edit decisions. As we will see, time-code solves this and a number of other problems.

SMPTE/EBU TIME-CODE

Time-code—more accurately called **SMPTE/EBU time-code**[1]—is an eight-digit numerical code that can electronically and visually identify each frame in a video production (Figure 12.2). Using these eight numbers, points on a tape can be specified to an accuracy of 1/30 second. Some equipment even allows for "field-rate accuracy," which means that edit points can be indexed to 1/60 second.

The Advantage of Replication

One advantage of time-code lies in its ability to record editing decisions and then to replicate them, with modifications, if desired, at another time. A designated time-code point cannot vary from one editing session to another, from one machine to another, or even from one country to another. Editing instructions like "cut the scene when Janice picks up the book," leaves room for interpretation. (At exactly what point in the action do we cut the scene?) Even more importantly, there is the very real possibility that different takes of the same scene will become confused. But even though a tape may be four hours long, "02:13:54:10" refers to one very precise point within that total time. Time-code data on hundreds of edits involving complex video and audio switch points and effects can be electronically stored in a computer-based edit controller (Figure 12.3). Once time-code information is entered in a sophisticated editing system, the operator can sit back and watch previews of complex edit decisions and make adjustments as needed.

Breaking the Code

Although an eight-digit number like *03:16:51:22* might seem imposing, its meaning is very simple: "3 hours, 16 minutes, 51 seconds and 22 frames":

03	:	16	:	51	:	22
hours	:	minutes	:	seconds	:	frames

Since time-code numbers move from right to left when they are entered into an edit controller, you must enter hours, minutes, seconds and frames, in that

---

[1] Initially, several incompatible systems of time-code were introduced. In 1969, the SMPTE (Society of Motion Picture and Television Engineers) acted to establish a uniform system. The resulting standard, which was also adopted by the European Broadcasting Union, was thereafter referred to as the SMPTE/EBU time-code. Since all these initials are hard to say (and audio and video people are notorious for creating quick designations for complex terms) the system is now simply referred to as "SIM-tee time-code."

Figure 12.2 This slate visually marks the beginning of a video segment and also includes a time-code marking, which is read: 2 hours, 26 minutes, 20 seconds and 17 frames. These eight numbers can electronically and visually identify each frame in a video production.

Figure 12.3 Computer-based desktop editing systems now make video editing possible for any computer user with the appropriate hardware and software.

order. By entering only six numbers instead of eight, the machine assumes "00 hours," since the combination of numbers entered, as they move from right to left, would reach only to the minutes designation. The hours designation can go from 00 to 23, the minutes and seconds from 00 to 59, and the frames from 00 to 29. Thirty frames, like 5/5 of a mile, is impossible because 30 frames equals one second. Likewise, 60 minutes in time-code is impossible. The next frame after 03 hours, 59 minutes, 59 seconds and 29 frames would change the counter to: 04:00:00:00.

Some examples of adding and subtracting time-code segments should help in understanding how it works. If one segment were 8 seconds, 20 frames long, and the second segment were 6 seconds, 17 frames long, the total time would be 15:07.

08:20	first segment
+06:17	second segment
14:37,	or 15:07 total time

Note in this example that since 37 frames is over one second, before we can do our final math we must subtract one second (30 frames) and add it to the total number of seconds. We end up with 7 frames left over (37 − 30 = 07 frames).

Let's look at another question. If the time-code point for entering a video segment is 01:23:38:16 and the out-point is 01:23:45:08, what is the total time of the segment? The answer is just a matter of subtracting the smaller code numbers from the larger numbers:

out-point	01:23:45:08, or	01:23:44:38
in-point		−01:23:38:16
total time		= 00:00:06:22

Note that since we can't subtract 16 frames from 08 frames, we have to reverse the procedure followed in the first example; we have to change the 08 to 38 by borrowing a second from the 45. For people who regularly do time-code calculations, computer programs and small hand-held calculators are available.

User Bits

Before we turn to other aspects of time-code, we need to mention that the digitized SMPTE/EBU signal has room for some additional information beyond the basic hours, minutes, seconds and frames. First, there are error-correcting signals that can detect technical time-code errors and be used by the equipment to make necessary corrections. Second, there are user bits that can record information about the production, such as reel number, day and scene number. Because of the limited digital space left over for user bits, they can accommodate a total of only four alphabetical characters or eight numerical digits, or a limited combination of both. Here is an example of a user bit designation:

R7:S2:T12 for Reel 7, Scene 2, Take 12

Some automated videotape systems utilize the user-bit data area to record start and stop cues for triggering various pieces of audio and video equipment during a production or postproduction sequence. User bit information must be recorded on the videotape along with the original time-code.

Drop-Frame Time-Code

Before moving on, we need to understand one more thing about time-code: the difference between drop-frame and non-drop-frame. Basic SMPTE/EBU time-code assumes a frame-rate of 30 per second, which actually is valid only for black and white television. For technical reasons, when NTSC color television was introduced, the frame-rate was dropped to 29.97 frames per second. Although the difference may seem insignificant, in some applications it can result in significant timing problems. If you assume a rate of 30 frames per second instead of 29.97, as many basic editing systems do, you end up with a 3.6-second error every 60 minutes. Specifically, if you record a program in the non-drop-frame mode until the time-code reads 01.00.00.00 (one hour), the actual time of the program will be one hour and 3.6 seconds. Since broadcasting is a to-the-second business, a way had to be devised to correct this error; for obvious reasons, just lopping off 3.6 seconds at the end of every hour was not the way to do it.

The Drop-Frame Solution   The error of 3.6 seconds equals an extra 108 frames per hour (3.6 times 30 frames per second). So, to maintain accuracy, 108 frames must be dropped each hour, and done in such a way as to result in the least amount of confusion. Although the solution devised to solve this problem isn't exactly elegant, it works.

First, it was logically decided that the 108-frame correction had to be equally distributed throughout the hour. (It's better to be cheated a few frames here and there than suddenly to have 108 frames disappear in the middle of a scene.) A little math will tell you that if you dropped one frame per minute it would result in a total of only 60 frames per hour. Sixty from 108 leaves 48. So, that method won't work. If you dropped 2 frames per minute, you would end up with 120 dropped frames per hour instead of 108. That's 12 too many. But, technically, since you can't drop half frames, this is as close as you can get by making a consistent correction every minute. So the problem then becomes one of what to do with the 12 extra frames. The solution is every 10th minute not to drop 2 frames. In an hour that totals 12 frames, since there are six 10-minute intervals in an hour. Many edit controllers have a drop-frame/non-drop-frame switch. When you use the drop-frame mode a signal is added to the SMPTE/EBU time-code that automatically lets you and the machine know that drop-frame is being used. Since the frame-dropping occurs right at the changeover point from one minute to the next, you will see the time-code counter on an editor suddenly jump over the dropped frames every time the correction is made.

Error of 3.6 seconds	= 108 frame-per-hour error
Dropping 2 frames per minute	= 120 frames (12 too many)
Dropping 1 frame per minute	= 60 frames (48 too few)
Solution: drop 2 frames per minute except every 10th minute	
Total	= 108 frames per hour

For non-critical applications, such as editing news and industrial television segments, drop-frame isn't needed; in fact, due to its consistent nature the non-drop-frame mode makes precise, predictable, frame-accurate edits easier (it doesn't skip frames every minute). However, if you are involved with producing 15-minute or longer programs for broadcast, you should either use an editor with a drop-frame mode or in some way compensate for the error.

Adding Time-Code

Time-code is not an inherent part of videotape in the same way that edge numbers are permanently imprinted on motion picture film. With the help of a time-code generator, the SMPTE/EBU time must be recorded on the videotape as the production is being shot or, later, when the tape is being reviewed. Since the time-code numbers represent "the address" of needed segments on a videotape, these codes must be logged (written down) so that the segments can later be located. Although reviewing a tape and logging scenes by time-code and scene descriptions may seem like a chore, it can save much time during the editing phase of most productions, and it may save you, or someone doing editing for you, from using the wrong take of a scene.

Before we move further into this topic, we need to distinguish between three basic approaches to recording time-code:

- Longitudinal time-code
- VITC (vertical-interval time-code), commonly pronounced "VIT-see"
- RC time-code

Approaches to Recording Time-Code

Time-code can be recorded on videotape in two ways: on one of the audio tracks or as part of the video signal.

Longitudinal Time-Code   Time-code is digital information, but it still can be recorded on one of the analog audio tracks on a videotape. Although the longitudinal system of time-code is the easiest to record and it is often more accessible in desktop editing systems, it has a number of weaknesses. With the NTSC system of television, the complete SMPTE/EBU time-code signal consists of 2,400 bits of digital information per second. Although this signal is recorded like an analog audio signal, there is an important difference. When the digital numbers are translated into an audio signal (much like a modem does on a computer), signal degradation will quickly set in when the tape is copied. To solve this problem a **jam sync** process is used to regenerate the longitudinal time-code as a new copy of the tape is being dubbed. If this isn't done, after several generations a longitudinal signal will be unreliable, especially when the machine is played back at slower or faster than normal speeds. (Remember, whenever the time-code display freezes on a set of numbers for a moment while the tape is moving, you know that a time-code error has occurred.)

Vertical Interval Time-Code (VITC)   VITC time-code overcomes most of the problems inherent in the longitudinal system. As the name suggests, with **VITC** the time-code information is recorded with the video in the vertical interval of the picture. (This area is normally hidden from view, but is revealed as the black bar that separates frames when a picture on a TV set loses vertical sync and rolls.) Because VITC is recorded by the video heads of a recorder, this means that whenever a picture is visible (including when the tape is stopped on a freeze-frame), the time-code can be read. Because standard VITC is recorded by the VCR's video heads, it can't be erased the way standard longitudinal time-code can, at least without having to re-record the video in the process. In addition to solving problems associated with generational loss and varying tape speeds, there are three other advantages to VITC time-code.

- VITC provides indexing down to the individual video fields (1/60-second intervals). This level of accuracy is sometimes needed in doing precise audio and video editing.
- Since the VITC signal doesn't take up an audio track, the track can be used for other audio needs in production or editing. (Although some videotape formats have a special longitudinal track reserved for time-code, others use one of the audio tracks for time-code recording.)
- Finally, because of error-checking components of the VITC signal, it is highly immune to reading errors caused by tape dropouts.

RC Time-Code   The 8mm and Hi8 videotape formats include space in the video section of the recording format to record eight-digit time-code. Unlike the VITC approach, it is possible to record or re-record time-code in the RC approach without affecting the video signal. (The video heads can quickly switch from recording or playing back video to recording or playing back time code as they swipe across the tape.) This is a major advantage when you want to add time code to video you've already shot, without having to dub the tape and lose a generation of quality.

Recording Time-Code

Unfortunately, time-code doesn't initially come on videotape the way edge numbers do on film: you have to put them there. With the help of either a time-code generator built into a VCR or a separate (stand-alone) time-code generator, longitudinal time-code can be recorded on the tape either as it is shot, or later when the tape is reviewed. With VITC you must record the time-code as the tape is shot in the camera, unless you want to dub the tape and lose a generation of quality in the process.

Time-code numbers can be set to start at any set of numbers. If user bits are not implemented, you may want to use the hours column of the time-code to identify the reel numbers. (You'll want to avoid having the same time-code numbers on more than one reel used in an editing session.) Hour 01 becomes reel one, etc. (This assumes, of course, that the material on the tapes is less than one hour in length.) Both numeric key pads and small thumb-wheel dials are used for setting the numbers.

How Time-Code is Displayed

There are three ways of displaying time-code.

- First, small numerical displays are used by some simple time-code editors. Although these normally consist of illuminated red or green numbers, occasionally LCD displays are used.
- The second method displays the time-code numbers over the video itself.

- Third, some edit controllers use a high-resolution color monitor to display both the time-codes and actual video frames of the in-points and out-points of video.

There are two approaches to displaying time-code numbers over the video. With **keyed-in time-code** a character generator is coupled with a time-code reader and the eight-digit code is keyed over the video. In contrast to keyed-in code, which is only temporarily superimposed over the video picture, there is **burned-in time-code.** Instead of two signals being combined as they are displayed, in burned-in time-code the video and the numbers are permanently merged into one signal. This is done as a copy of the original footage is made. The resulting **window dub** has a major advantage; it can be played back on any VCR and viewed on a standard TV set. Since only special tape machines are equipped to read and reproduce keyed-in time-code, **window burns** (tapes with burned-in time-code) represent a major advantage. When it's necessary to review footage away from a production facility, especially on a distant location, special equipment doesn't have to be shipped; any tape machine can be used.

With both keyed-in and burned-in time-code you are given many options for displaying the code: large numbers, small numbers, white numbers, black numbers, colored numbers, numbers with drop shadows, numbers against a solid background, etc. Probably the most legible display is simply white numbers with black borders, where the numbers are just large enough to be seen from the distance you will be viewing the display, and small enough so as not to obscure important background picture video information.

Logging Time-Codes

Searching for points on tapes without the aid of time-code can be time-consuming and frustrating as you repeatedly go forward and backward looking for various segments. It can be particularly confusing if multiple takes of scenes are on a tape. Since the time-code numbers associated with various scenes are more or less permanent, it is possible to describe needed segments by simply logging the time-codes of starting and ending points. Later, you will be able to find a segment either by looking for the time-code address or by entering the eight-digit codes into the edit controller and letting the machine find the needed segment for you. With all this as a background, we can now move to on-line and off-line editing.

On-Line and Off-Line Editing

On-Line Editing

In **on-line editing** the original footage is used to create the final edited master. In **off-line editing** a copy of the original footage is used to assemble a work print that is used as a guide for later creating the final on-line version. Why divide editing into two, seemingly redundant, phases?

Any creative process is time-consuming. Hours are often spent on just a few minutes, or sometimes just a few seconds, of a production. An important part of the editing process is trying out music and effects in a variety of ways to see what works best. Even after a production is seemingly finished, further input from a producer, sponsor or director may necessitate adding, tightening or eliminating segments. This time-consuming process of trial and error can be extremely expensive if full-time engineers and costly, high-quality equipment are involved throughout the process. On a per-hour basis the on-line editing of dramatic productions typically costs more than five times as much per hour as off-line editing. Early in the history of video editing it was found that a great amount of money could be saved if editing was divided into off-line and on-line phases.

Off-Line Editing

The purpose of off-line editing is to create a preliminary version (a rough cut) of a production from a copy of the original videotape(s). This rough cut is then used as a visual representation of the final on-line production (possibly to show a producer, client or sponsor) and then, when there is agreement, as a blueprint for creating the final, on-line production. More importantly, time-codes determined during the off-line phase are compiled into an edit decision list (EDL) that can be used to program the automatic sequencing of on-line editing equipment.

In brief, off-line editing has the following advantages:

- It can save a producer a considerable amount of money.
- Since a copy of the original footage is used, there is no worry about damaging the original.
- A variety of personal computers can be used to do off-line editing.
- Since some off-line systems can print storyboards showing the beginning and ending frames of edits, including notes on accompanying dialogue and effects, a client or advertiser can have "hard copy" illustrations indicating how the final product will look.
- By using an off-line window burn of a production, footage can be evaluated and pencil-and-paper EDLs can be created using only a simple consumer VCR.
- Once an off-line EDL is created, it can be loaded into an on-line or off-line editor at a later date and used as a basis for revisions, without the need to re-enter all of the previous editing decisions.

The first step in the off-line process is to make a copy of the original footage, complete with the original time-code. Typically this off-line copy is made on a VHS, S-VHS, Hi8, or 3/4-inch machine. The original footage is then put safely away to await the on-line phase of editing.

ORDER	REEL #	START CODE	END CODE	SCENE DESCRIPTION/COMMENT

VIDEOTAPE LOG

Production _____ **Operator** _____ **Date** _____ **Page** __ **of** __

Figure 12.4   Videotape Log Form

Logging Scenes

Once the off-line copies are made, they can be labeled and a time-code list of the scenes logged. Figure 12.4 shows a form for logging scenes. In the original footage, any scenes that have major problems don't need to be logged. At the same time, all acceptable scenes that can conceivably be used should be listed on the log. This will provide the editor with a full range of editing options. Although many tape logs are filled in by hand, computer programs are also available. Most people who learn to use lap-top computers for logging feel they are able to log tapes faster, and the results don't suffer from legibility problems associated with hastily scribbled notes.

The Paper-and-Pencil Edit

Once scenes are logged, a paper-and-pencil edit can be done. This involves reviewing the log and numbering the scenes (in the left-hand column) in the most logical order. If a computer logging system is being used, the scenes can be moved around on the screen and assembled in the desired sequence. Pop-up time-code calculators, which reside in computer memory until you need them, will simplify time calculations as you make your decisions.

Later, the editor may elect to make changes in the order suggested by this so-called paper-and-pencil edit (based on time or script restraints, etc.). Even so, this phase is important. It suggests the basic story outline intended and it provides initial structure to get the off-line process underway.

If you can go directly to a random-access editor, you can skip the paper-and-pencil edit. Once the scenes are logged and loaded into the system, you can juggle them around on the screen and immediately see the results.

Figure 12.5 shows the newstape log generated by the homicide scenario covered in the last chapter. After the tape was shot and brought back to the studio, the reporter wrote down the codes and scene descriptions as she reviewed the tape.

Once the scenes are logged, the reporter or editor can do a rough paper-and-pencil edit by writing in the most logical order of the scenes. Note the numbers shown in the left-hand column of Figure 12.5 indicate the desired sequence for the scenes during editing. (You might also have noticed that the total number of scenes has been expanded somewhat from the sample shown in Chapter 11 and that the edit decisions have changed.) Once the scenes are logged and the paper-and-pencil edit is done, the off-line or on-line process can begin.

Creating EDLs and News Scripts with Notebook Computers

For people in news production who must prepare EDLs and scripts in a hurry, the current generation of light-weight notebook-sized (or lap-top) computers is ideal. The time-codes and scene descriptions can be typed in while viewing the videotape on a monitor. Then the computer can be moved to another (possibly quieter) area while the script is written. If a split screen is used, one half of the computer screen can be devoted to the word processor for writing the script. The other half can

Story: ELM STREET HOMICIDE

Reporter: WEST

Camera: MYERS

Date: 06/23/95

Tape: N159

Page: 1 OF 1

ORDER	START CODE	END CODE	SCENE DESCRIPTION
4	00:04:12:22	00:04:20:02	ECU knife
5	00:04:20:02	00:04:30:00	CU, police picking up knife
2	00:04:30:00	00:04:45:07	loading victim in stretcher
3	00:04:45:07	00:04:56:02	suspect being handcuffed
-	00:04:56:02	00:05:01:27	CU suspect
6	00:05:01:27	00:05:46:12	loading victim in ambulance
8	00:05:46:12	00:06:02:22	policeman questioning man
1	00:06:02:22	00:06:12:28	WS crime scene
-	00:06:12:28	00:06:15:28	pool of blood
7	00:06:15:28	00:06:21:25	WS onlookers
10	00:06:21:25	00:06:32:02	ambulance driving off
9	00:06:32:02	00:06:44:27	three bereaved onlookers
12	00:06:44:27	00:06:54:29	police car driving off
10	00:06:54:29	00:07:01:13	police photographer working
11	00:07:01:13	00:07:19:24	WS onlookers
-	00:07:19:24	00:07:29:01	CU woman watching
-	00:07:29:01	00:07:39:02	policemen examining knife

Figure 12.5 Newstape Log

contain the log of the scene descriptions and associated time-codes. Once the script is finished, you can print out both the time-code log for the person doing the videotape editing and a copy of the script. After you view the edited version of the tape, you can bring up the script again on your computer, make adjustments as needed, and then feed the final script from your computer directly into the newsroom computer.

EDIT DECISION LIST

Event	Roll	AV	Play In	Play Out	Record In	Record Out
1	1	AV	01:03:33:10	01:03:46:01	01:04:00:07	01:04:12:23
2	1	AV	01:06:20:01	01:06:56:24	01:04:12:23	01:04:39:17
3	1	V	01:06:47:01	01:06:56:11	01:04:39:17	01:04:48:28
4	1	V	01:07:36:03	01:07:55:24	01:04:48:28	01:05:08:20
5	2	A	04:08:04:10	04:08:09:23	01:05:08:20	01:05:14:04
6	2	A	04:04:53:07	04:05:06:05	01:05:14:04	01:05:57:27
7	1	AV	01:05:11:11	01:05:21:19	01:05:37:27	01:06:08:06
8	1	AV	01:06:45:01	01:06:53:03	01:06:08:06	01:06:16:09
9	1	AV	01:07:06:26	01:07:16:11	01:06:16:09	01:06:26:04

Figure 12.6   Edit Decision List

THE OFF-LINE PHASE

Except in news and some documentary work, where the need to save time is of prime importance, most professional productions will incorporate an off-line editing phase.[2] Recall that in off-line editing the edits are made using copies of the original footage. Using these copies you simply develop a fully edited version of your production. Within the limits of equipment, the off-line version of a production should be as close as possible to the desired final result.

With most off-line systems, editing decisions are recorded on a computer-type disk. If desired, an edit-by-edit printout can also be recorded on paper. Figure 12.6 shows an EDL generated by a desktop editing system. Note that in addition to the time-code listing of all the scenes, a visual reference is available, at the bottom of the screen, that shows the opening and closing frames of selected scenes.

The EDL information stored on the computer disk can be fed to any compatible editing machine and all of the edit decisions automatically duplicated. Considering that a one-hour documentary can contain 600 or so edits (each with a reel

---

[2] As technology improves to the point we can store and edit all of our footage in high resolution digital form, and the full range of sophisticated on-line postproduction tools are available in a desktop editor or workstation, the need for an off-line phase will probably be eliminated.

number, in-point, out-point, etc.), having this information in a form that can be read into an editor in a few seconds can save hours of time in rekeying (re-entering) all the time-code information.

The Editing Process

When only straight cuts and fades to black are required, only two VTRs are needed—a source machine for raw footage and an edit recorder where the edited master will be built. A simple two-machine setup, the kind that can be used for basic news and documentary work, is shown in Figure 12.1. Simple, two-machine editing setups do not require time-code. In fact, with allowances for some loss of accuracy, control track (non-time-code) editing will prove faster for doing simple segments.

When only two machines are used, dissolves, wipes and many special video effects are not possible. For these techniques, you need to tie in a video switcher or special-effects unit and have the ability to use multiple sources of video at the same time. It is also at this point that the use of time-code becomes essential. In addition to controlling multiple video sources, sophisticated editing units can also be used to control an audio mixer and a variety of audio playback machines.

From this overview, we'll now examine the actual editing process. There are two general types of linear editing: assemble and insert.

Assemble Editing

In **assemble editing** the edited master is built sequentially, like links on a chain, complete with audio, video and control tracks. This "all at once" feature represents both an advantage and a disadvantage. The advantage is that the process is much faster than insert editing. The disadvantage is that since the all-important control track is transferred along with the audio and video, problems will quickly arise from any disruption that takes place when these control pulses are transferred from one tape to another. During playback any control track disturbance can cause the edited master to suddenly lose color or synchronization (sync), or cause the picture to roll or break up. Control-track problems will also cause speed variations as the playback machine tries to regain synchronization. If music is recorded on the tape, these variations can be quite noticeable.

Because of the possibility of these instability problems under less-than-perfect technical conditions, assemble editing is generally used only when a limited number of edits is required as, for example, in splicing together a few major program segments. If an assemble edit is done during a fade to black, the chance of problems being visible (or audible) is minimized. The general success of using assemble editing will depend on how good the editing equipment is and the quality and stability of the control track in the original video footage.

INSERT EDITING

The danger of the control problems is minimized with the more widely used technique of **insert editing.** Here, a continuous, uninterrupted control track is first laid down (recorded) on the edited master even before editing starts. This is done by first recording black or color bars on a segment of the final tape—enough to cover the length (duration) of the piece being created. This process is called **blanking a tape** (or *blacking a tape*). In recording black or color bars a stable signal source such as a direct feed from a sync generator must be used. On most machines this process cannot be speeded up (it takes 60 minutes to blank a 60-minute tape), so tapes are often blanked during lunch breaks. Of course, blanking erases whatever was previously on the tape. During editing, video from the source machine(s) is then inserted, edit by edit, onto the tape, replacing the black or color bars. The control track is left undisturbed.

Edit controllers have *insert* and *assemble* buttons to let the operator select the needed editing mode. It is important not to confuse the two. If you accidentally hit assemble during a normal insert editing session, the original control track on the blanked tape will be erased.

THE PRE-ROLL PHASE

Since multiple videotape machines cannot instantly come up to speed and synchronize, a pre-roll phase is needed. This means that about a five-second head start is required before each edit. The pre-roll phase has definite implications for how productions are shot. If action or dialogue start immediately after the original tape is rolled, it may make a pre-roll during editing impossible. Therefore, forgetting the five-second roll cue when a segment is originally taped may make the segment impossible to use.

Once the editing machines start from their pre-roll point, the control track pulses or the SMPTE/EBU time-code numbers are used by each machine to automatically vary its speed (from about 50 percent above and below normal playback speed) until it gets in sync. The pre-roll phase is not necessary with disk-based editing or video servers.

Defining an Edit

In editing a simple production with a linear editor, you typically are working with two reels, the reel containing the material you've shot and the (edited master) reel, which will eventually become your finished project. Although to many people the basic editing process seems complicated, in essence it is as easy as finding and entering

- The starting point on the playback reel for the material you want to add
- The starting point for the new material on the edited master
- The stopping point on the edited master (or, on many machines, you can just stop the edit when you are safely past the new material)

When using a control-track (non-time-code) editor, these edit points are entered by pushing a button at the desired points. Although editing equipment varies in its operation, often these points are entered with buttons labeled MARK IN and MARK OUT. With time-code machines the desired edit points can either be noted by entering the eight-digit codes, or the controller will automatically enter the appropriate time-codes when the desired position on the tape is noted. There are four types of edits:

- Audio only
- Video only
- Audio follow video (when both are kept together at an edit point)
- Split edit (sometimes called an "L-cut") where the audio of a new scene leads (comes before) the corresponding video. For example, you might hear a telephone ring at the end of one scene and then see a cut to the next scene where the phone is being answered.

Although audio and video are normally transferred together, there will be many occasions where you will want to record the video separately from the audio. This is commonly done, for example, when you want to continue with the audio from an interview while substituting B-roll video segments. The "Mr. Muscles" ENG piece, which follows, illustrates this situation.

Preparing a Typical News Package

A news **package** is a preproduced, ready-to-run recorded news segment, typically introduced on camera by a news anchorperson. ENG pieces sometimes start with a *stand-up,* in which a field reporter, generally standing in front of the news scene, "intros" (introduces) and "extros" the segment (a word coined by the profession referring to the on-camera wrap-up). Although news has gotten away from the standard 1-2-3 sequence of (1) a stand-up intro, (2) an interview, and (3) a stand-up extro, this (rather timeworn) approach is still valuable in illustrating how a simple news package can be shot and assembled.

In the example to follow, let's assume that after an opening stand-up there is a short sound-on-tape (SOT) interview; at the end of the interview there is the extro where the field reporter signs off with the standard tag: "This is Mary Mirthful reporting for TV-3."

Let's assume that you were sent to do a 60-second ENG report on Mr. Sam Sinew, who has just won the title of Mr. Muscles. The crowning took place in a nearby city and the news cooperative has provided satellite footage of the ceremonies. You will be the on-camera reporter for the local story. Mr. Sinew has agreed to grant you an afternoon interview, in just enough time to edit the piece and get it on the 6 PM newscast.

You decide to start the report with a stand-up outside the Mind & Muscles Academy where Mr. Sinew is a student. First, you write out both an opening and a closing to the piece on 3-by-5 cards. The stand-ups, you decide, will be more interesting with some between-class activity in the background; so while you wait for classes to change, you can memorize the stand-up opening and closing.

Shooting the A-Roll Footage

Once classes start to change, you will have about eight minutes to get good takes of both the intro and extro. The camcorder has been color-balanced and the shot is framed with the Administration Building in the background. Suddenly, students emerge from doors and you have the camera operator roll tape. You wait about seven seconds and tag the piece with an identifying audio slate: "Mr. Muscles intro, take one."

You then wait for a few seconds, and start your introduction. If you fluff some words, someone walks in front of the camera, or a motorcycle roars by, obliterating the sound, you can start the whole thing over with the preface: "Mr. Muscles intro, take two." It will save time if you just keep the tape rolling between takes.

When the intro is finished, you go directly to the extro. In most circumstances you would find it preferable to record the opening and closing after doing the interview; but, since the interview is in the afternoon and the piece needs to be edited before news time, this approach will save time. Before starting the closing segment, you look over your notes as the camera operator changes the camera angle slightly, reframes, refocuses and rolls tape. Both the intro and extro are recorded on the camcorder's A-roll. If something surprising does come out of the interview, you might possibly have time to redo either the intro or the extro before leaving the campus. But you've done your research and at this point this seems like a pretty mundane and predictable story.

After doing the intro and extro on the A-roll, you and your camera operator move the equipment inside to one corner of the weight training room where

Mr. Sinew has agreed to do the interview. After Mr. Sinew arrives, a lav mike is clipped to his Mind & Muscles Academy tanktop and an audio check is made.

After the tape is rolled, you wait for about five seconds, and start asking Mr. Sinew the questions you've prepared. You lead off with a question about his family, which you will probably not use; it's simply designed to get Mr. Sinew to relax a bit in front of the camera. All of Mr. Sinew's responses are recorded on the A-roll. As the interview progresses you make a note of two things that can be illustrated with B-roll cutaways: he regularly plays basketball to maintain agility and as part of his scholarship he works in the weight room as an assistant trainer.

Shooting the B-Roll Footage

Once your questions are answered, the B-roll cassette is inserted into the camcorder and it is moved about 150 degrees to get reverse-angle shots of you (re)asking each question.[3] This time, of course, the lav mike is on you, rather than Mr. Sinew. Your subject consents to stay in the same place, providing reverse-angle, over-the-shoulder shots. Since most guests are not familiar with the single-camera technique of re-asking each of the interview questions for the B-roll, you caution Mr. Sinew to refrain from answering your questions as they are re-asked. If your guest didn't have the time to stay through the recording of the B-roll questions, the camera operator could just hold a close-up on you as you asked the questions. (To match up the camera shots and angles in the latter case, it would be important that the interviewer address questions to the exact space previously occupied by the guest.)

For editing purposes, it is important to leave about a seven-second pause between each question. Ideally, when the piece is edited, Mr. Sinew's answers can be assembled in such a way that the questions will be obvious and, therefore, unnecessary. To include them will simply slow down the interview. Just the same, you'll want to tape them. Once you start editing the piece you may find that one or more of the questions ends up being essential to make sense out of Mr. Sinew's answers.

Although the interview is seemingly over at this point, there are still three things left to shoot on the B-roll. First, 15 or so seconds of "noddies." This is footage of you, the interviewer, just looking at Mr. Sinew or, if he has to leave, looking at the place where he was sitting. Depending on the interview, you can register subtle expressions appropriate to the content, such as interest, concern, or humorous reactions. These reverse-angle cutaways will be important in covering edits. Next, you may elect to shoot 10- or 15-seconds of two-shot silent footage over the shoulder of Mr. Sinew as you look on and he talks about anything at all that will result in general head movements. The latter, which does not show Mr. Sinew's face, can also be used to cover an edit as he speaks. (Since this is a short interview, you probably won't need both of these segments.) Finally, your camera

---

[3] Although the B-roll and A-roll approach to doing the questions and answers is common for short interviews, it is possible to use two (or more) cameras locked together with a common time-code. In doing lengthy interviews this procedure offers more flexibility in editing.

operator should record 10–15 seconds of room tone (ambient, background sound that exists when no one is speaking). We'll discuss the function of room tone later. Although you will probably use only a small portion of this "after-the-interview" footage during editing, there seems to be a Murphy's law that governs this phase: you'll always seem to find an indispensable need for whatever footage you fail to get!

At this point you'll need to move on to the B-roll cutaway shots. First will be a short sequence of Mr. Sinew assisting a coach in the weight room. Your camera operator should get at least two camera angles on this. To cover the basketball angle you get Mr. Sinew to find one of his friends for a brief one-on-one session in the gym. On both of these segments the camera operator should use a stereo mic to get general background sound. (In this case, a stereo mic on the camera should suffice.)

This finishes the taping at the school. Once you're back at the station, you can dig through the news cooperative footage from the night before and find the story on Mr. Sinew's coronation as Mr. Muscles. At this point you have all the elements for your ENG package. On the A-roll you have

A-1. The stand-up intro to the piece

A-2. The stand-up extro to the piece

A-3. Mr. Sinew's answers to your questions

On the B-roll you have

B-1. All of your questions to Mr. Sinew

B-2. Your silent reaction shots

B-3. An over-the-shoulder shot of Mr. Sinew

B-4. Room tone

B-5. Footage of Mr. Sinew assisting a coach

B-6. Shots in the gym of the one-on-one basketball session

On a C-roll you have

C-1. Shots of the coronation

C-2. Shots of Mr. Sinew walking down the ramp after the ceremony.

Armed with these three tapes, you find a playback machine with a SMPTE/EBU time-code recorder. If your facility had a video server, you would then transfer all of the footage to the server for a random-access editing session. But first, we'll discuss a non-linear editing approach.

Your first step is to watch the A-roll footage of your intro and extro and Mr. Sinew's answers to your questions. As you view the tapes you fill out a paper-and-pencil EDL listing a description and the starting and ending time-codes of the best segments. (If time-code wasn't recorded on the tape as it was made, you'll probably need to put time-code on as you review it.) Once you check the segments you initially would like to use, you then do a bit of math, and discover you have almost two minutes of footage. Since you've only been given one minute for the whole package, you draw a line through the interview segments that seem less important. Although it's still too long, you'll be able to condense some of Mr. Sinew's comments during editing. During this pruning process you are careful to keep references to your cutaway footage: the coronation, being a training aid, and playing basketball.

After logging that you load the B-roll and note the time-codes of your questions, the footage of Mr. Sinew helping a coach in the weight room, and the shots in the gym. Finally, you put in the C-roll and review the footage of the coronation. You log the codes on two short segments: the moment of the actual coronation and a few seconds of Mr. Sinew walking down the ramp with his crown.

At this point you gather up your tapes, notes and your paper-and-pencil EDL and move to an editing station to wait your turn. (Just before news time, the videotape editor may be busy finishing other segments.) This scenario, of course, assumes that your facility has a regular videotape editor. In small production facilities you will have to do your own editing.

In outline form, here is the complete (but tentative) sequence for the ENG package:

1. Your stand-up introduction in front of the school
2. Mr. Sinew's first interview response: talking about his coronation (your question for this response is not needed), over which you will insert
   a. video footage (with low background audio) of the coronation
   b. video footage (with low background audio) of his walk down the runway
3. Your question on extra-curricular activities
4. Mr. Sinew's answer to the extra-curricular activity question, over which you will insert
   a. two shots of Mr. Sinew helping a coach
   b. three quick shots of the one-on-one basketball session
5. Your closing extro

In the interest of making smooth transitions, or to add visual variety to the piece, the videotape editor may decide to change some things. The amount of "sprucing up" that can be done will depend on how much time the editor has. Since soft news and feature pieces can normally be done during slack hours (well ahead of the news deadlines), more editing time can be devoted to them. For this reason, these pieces often display more editing refinement and creativity. Since Mr. Muscles was crowned the night before, and the news producer wants to get the package on the evening's news, it's treated like any other news piece right before the deadline: it's done as quickly as possible.

Linear Editing Procedures

Using the Mr. Muscles piece as an example, at this point we can look at the step-by-step procedures involved in linear editing. Starting with a blanked tape containing SMPTE/EBU time-code, the videotape editor first cues in the tape about 10 seconds. Tapes need to be cued in a few feet before being used because over time the beginning of tapes undergo severe wear and tear as they are repeatedly threaded into machines. Within a short time this area will exhibit dropouts and other problems.

The first "segment" on the tape will be countdown leader. This is similar to Academy Leader in film, which flashes numbers in one-second intervals from 10 to 3. After the 3 disappears,[4] the screen blanks out for two seconds, after which the first scene of the ENG piece should appear.

Starting Procedures for Longer Segments

If the on-line editing session is designed to create a full-length program and not just a short ENG piece, two additional things will be recorded on the edited master before the countdown leader. First, it is standard practice to record 60 seconds of bars and tone ETP (electronic test pattern) along with a 1,000-hertz audio tone, at 0 dB. This allows those playing back the tape to adjust their equipment for the audio and video levels and color balance represented by the tape.

After the ETP, the tape goes to black and silence for a few seconds, and the second item, an audio and video slate, is recorded. The slate will visually and aurally identify the program with several types of information: the title of the program or series, the number of the program (if it has one), the director, the date of recording, and the planned air date, if there is one. For short news pieces, however, a slate and ETP are seldom recorded.

Continuing with our Mr. Muscles news package, after the last number on the countdown leader appears on the screen, the operator shuttles the tape forward in black for exactly two seconds and then enters the starting point of the first insert edit. In our example this will be the start of the stand-up intro to the Mr. Muscles piece.

Using your paper-and-pencil EDL as a guide, the editor can quickly switch back and forth between your A-roll, B-roll and C-roll tapes to find and cue needed segments. After each segment is found and checked, its in-point (starting point) and out-point are entered into the edit controller. The in-point for each new segment on the recorded (final-edited) master tape must also be entered in the edit controller. The out-point on the edited master is generally not necessary, since you can just stop the machine when you see that the full segment has been recorded.

A preview button on the edit controller will allow you to take a look (and adjust) each proposed edit prior to actually recording it on the edited master. Trim controls make it possible to automatically add or subtract frames from these tentative edit decisions without having to enter a new start or stop point. (At 30 frames per second, dropping 15 frames from a scene will reduce its length by one-half second; adding seven frames will add a quarter second, etc.) It is best to allow each

---

4 Some countdown leaders will show a very brief number 2.

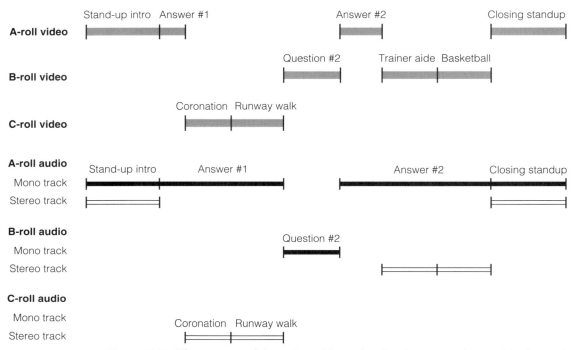

Figure 12.7   The sequence of the various video and audio elements in the Mr. Muscles ENG package is illustrated here. Note that the video and the audio (including both the mono and the stereo tracks) are from three videotapes: an A-roll, B-roll and C-roll.

segment on the edited master to run a bit long; it can be trimmed to the exact length needed when the start point for the next edit is entered.

Let's assume that at this point you now have the countdown leader, two seconds of black and the stand-up introduction recorded on our master tape. (Figure 12.7 should be used as a guide in this discussion.) The next step is to record the first segment of the interview. We want to start with Mr. Sinew talking on camera from the A-roll footage about the crowning the night before. Since you know that the two segments from C-roll footage run eight seconds total, you need to hold Sinew's references to that time. But, unfortunately, the answer to your question, in which he talks about both the crowning and his walk down the ramp, runs 39 seconds. Although that obviously presents a problem, it is only a temporary one. It will be necessary to cut out several parts of Sinew's dialogue to bring the references to the crowning and the walk down the ramp closer together so they will later coincide with the eight seconds of C-roll footage. You and the editor find that you can cut out numerous peripheral comments and bring the total segment time to eight seconds. Obviously, making these edits results in some jump-cuts in his on-camera video, but that's not a problem since these will be later covered with the C-roll coronation footage. Right now you are interested only in smoothly assembling A-roll audio. In making the deletions, you must be careful not only to retain the essence of Sinew's comments, but in no way to distort what he said.

After doing this A-roll segment, you can move on to comments about Sinew's plans for the year. This brings up his work at the academy. For this you find the appropriate A-roll audio in which he talks about being a training aid. Since there is no natural audio transition into this, the editor cues up your audio and video B-roll question to introduce it. (This is "Question #2" in Figure 12.7.) After that, about 10 seconds of A-roll footage of Sinew's response about his work as an aid can be used. (This is "Answer #2" in Figure 12.7.) The video portion of this will later be covered by B-roll footage of him working as an aid. Again, Sinew's comments must be condensed. And, again, the resulting jump-cuts will later be covered by B-roll footage.

Adding Room Tone

Sometimes, it is necessary to create a pause in narration. This might be appropriate to signal a major transition, or to simply allow the B-roll video to continue without commentary (generally, when the video runs a little longer than the corresponding audio). Although it would seem that pauses in narration would mean total silence, this is seldom the case. On most locations (including many "silent" TV studios) there is general, low-level background sound called **room tone,** which becomes obvious only when it suddenly disappears. Room tone is especially important in stereo and when the general level of ambient sound on the location is high. Rather than suddenly cutting to absolute silence during the interview audio, editors edit in room tone. Such refinements are even more important now that many TV sets have high-quality sound systems. (Incidentally, the use of room tone applies just as much to outside locations as to "rooms.")

Let's assume that at this point in editing the Mr. Muscles piece, the editor decides to depart from the initial paper-and-pencil edit, cut away from the interview narration at an appropriate point, and to go directly to the basketball session, complete with background sound. After holding the background basketball audio from the B-roll for a few seconds, the editor fades it under and brings in Mr. Sinew's voice and later his picture from the A-roll as he explains that he tries to keep agile by playing basketball.

Now all that's left is your stand-up extro (wrap-up) to the story. That runs 10 seconds. A running check of the edited segments to this point shows about 50 seconds; so, with the 10 second extro, things should work out just about right.

If the piece runs long, you have two choices: request more time for the piece, or cut it down. If it's a heavy news day or you are close to the deadline (and everything has been tightly scheduled), it will probably be safer to just look for a segment in the package to drop. Assuming that the piece was 15 or so seconds over, you could package it in two versions: with the coach's aide section for the early newscast and a second version with the basketball segment for the late-night newscast. (In the latter case you would want to make some changes anyway to give viewers of the later newscast a fresh perspective.)

Assuming you now have the segment at about 50 seconds, you can edit in the stand-up extro. After this there should be about ten seconds of black. (Otherwise, if the tape is not immediately cut during the broadcast, you run the risk of getting some inappropriate video or audio on the air.)

Adding Cutaway and Insert Shots

At this point all of the A-roll footage has been recorded (including a short question from the B-roll). Now the cutaway shots from the B- and C-rolls can be added. These will primarily be video-only insert edits that will leave the existing audio narration undisturbed. (Refer to Figure 12.7 to see where these come in.) However, for the sake of added realism, it will be desirable if two of the insert edits (the training room and basketball footage) carry low background audio. This will be recorded on a second audio track of the edited master.

Handling the Audio Mix

The audio mix can be handled in two ways. First, you can use three audio tracks on the edited master tape. One track will contain a monophonic recording of questions, answers and commentary. The second track (actually two tracks) is stereo and will consist of all background sound in the piece: the general sound behind the opening and closing narration, the background sound from the C-roll crowning footage, and sound in the weight room and gym. When the videotape is broadcast, an audio engineer (using a well-marked script for a guide) can mix the audio from mono (voice) and stereo (background sound) tracks together.

In the pressure of a live broadcast, however, instructions can get garbled, concentration can lapse, or technical problems can suddenly emerge. At this point pessimists (some would say realists) are quick to quote Murphy's first law of live television: if anything can go wrong it will go wrong. (Some authorities add: and at the worst possible moment.) These people prefer to remove some of the element of risk by mixing down all audio tracks onto a basic stereo track before broadcast. If the three audio tracks (the narration and the two tracks of stereo from the B- and C-rolls) are mixed during editing, an audio engineer does not have to worry about bringing in the various sources of audio at the right time (during the pressure and confusion of a live broadcast).

Adding Narration

In producing many ENG packages, voice-over narration by a reporter will be appropriate. With the help of a video monitor, this narration is sometimes read live by the reporters as the piece is aired. An audio engineer can then mix the live narration with the appropriate audio on the videotape. Doing narration live assumes nothing will go wrong and that timing will be perfect which, as we've noted, is never a safe assumption in live television. It is much better to have the announcer record the narration on a DAT machine or audio cart prior to the start of the editing session. During editing, audio segments recorded on a DAT machine can be automatically rolled into the piece as needed. Time-code numbers on the video-tape can be used to trigger the prerecorded audio at precise points, or the audio segments can be rolled in manually.

Random-Access (Non-Linear) Editing

If you were using random-access editing, you would prepare for the session by transferring all the time-coded segments you think might be needed onto the editing system's hard disk or recordable optical disk. In the process the various scenes are "tagged": "Muscles question 1," "Muscles ball 3," "Muscles room tone," etc. In facilities using a video server this transfer can be done from playback machines outside the (generally rather busy) editing area.

Once all the scenes have been transferred into the editing system, they can be called up on the screen. Although editing systems differ, often with the help of mouse or track ball, the next step will be to "tag" several of the beginning video and audio segments so they can be displayed on the screen. Many systems use a relatively low-resolution freeze-frame of the opening (and sometimes closing frames) of each tagged segment. The fewer the scenes displayed on the screen the larger they can be—and the easier it will be to see details. (Without the ability to see needed detail, it is possible to inadvertently cut to a person whose eyes are closed, for example.)

Once the segments are visible on the screen, you will need to go through the sequence of steps required by the software to assemble the audio and video elements in the desired order. On many systems this is as simple as clicking on the needed audio and video segments with a mouse and dragging them down to the appropriate place on a **time line,** a linear representation of the sequence of various audio and video elements along a line (Figure 12.8). Most time lines can accommodate many audio and video elements at any one point, which allows you to combine numerous elements at the same point on the time line. The system remembers not only each of the elements along the time line, but also information related to audio and video levels, filtering, color balance, etc., for each segment. Transitions between elements such as dissolves and wipes can also be indicated and previewed. Changes in sequence are as simple as "grabbing" an audio or video segment on the time line with the mouse or pointing device and dragging it to a different point along the line. Segments can be taken out of the middle of audio and video sequences simply by marking the beginning and ending points of the sections to be deleted, and then immediately playing back the result to make sure it's what you want. If it's not, there is no harm done; you can either restore the deleted segment and re-adjust the beginning points or, if necessary, trim away more of the original segment.

Figure 12.8 Most desktop editing software uses a time line to indicate the sequence of the various audio and video segments. These systems remember not only each of the elements along the time line, but information related to audio and video levels, filtering, color balance, etc. Changes in sequence are as simple as "grabbing" an audio or video segment on the time line with the mouse or pointing device and dragging it to a different point along the line.

Unlike linear editing, all editing decisions with these random-access (non-linear) systems reside entirely in the electronic memory. All of the original footage remains in the system and editing decisions generate only internal electronic markers. This means that decisions can be changed at any time. With random-access editing there is also no need to go back later and do the insert edits or cutaways, as done earlier in the Mr. Muscles piece; they all can be programmed into the sequence as you go.

On-Line Considerations

In the Mr. Muscles piece you needed to get things done as quickly as possible; therefore, you skipped off-line and went directly to on-line editing. This is standard practice in news production. However, in critical editing applications an off-line step offers many advantages. You will recall that the goal of the off-line session is to create three things:

- An EDL (generally on a 3½-inch computer disk) in a format that can be read into the on-line system
- A hard-copy printout of the EDL (just in case)
- A videocassette of the completed off-line production, which will serve as an aural and video blueprint for the final on-line edit

As suggested earlier, it is a good idea, if time allows, to put the off-line version of the production aside for at least a few days and then come back and look at it again. During lengthy off-line sessions editors can become "too close" to a production. Time provides an important fresh perspective, closer to what members of the audience will have when they see the production for the first time. This new perspective will generally suggest a number of editing changes that should be made before the production goes on to the final on-line session.

Taking the Off-Line EDL to the On-Line Phase

Let's assume at this point that you

- Are completely satisfied with all of your off-line editing decisions
- Have built an off-line version of your show that will act as an on-line reference
- Have made a record (floppy disc) of the EDL in the format required by the on-line facility
- Have accurate time-code notes on all video and audio effects that will have to be added during the on-line session
- Have notes on corrections that will have to be made: color balancing, audio sweetening, and significant audio or video level changes that need to be fixed
- Have any video or audio that must be mixed together on separate reels (not required in some facilities)
- Have all of the original tapes and audio sources necessary for the final edited master of the show

With all this taken care of, it's time for the on-line session.

Since on-line time is expensive, you will want to resist making changes at this point. Many on-line production facilities will provide suggestions to improve your production; you will want to at least seriously consider them. Even so, the major creative phase of your work should be done before you turn your tapes and EDL over to the on-line facility. At this point you just may be called on to make decisions on problems you didn't foresee. As on-line editing progresses, you will want to carefully follow audio sweetening, video corrections and effects, and other on-line elements to make sure they end up the way you envisioned them. If you have done your job in the off-line phase, the final on-line phase should go smoothly.

We should also note in concluding this discussion of on-line editing that this phase may well become obsolete in a few years. As the storage capacity of random-access editing systems increases and the costs of computer-based memory come down, the many advantages of random-access systems will undoubtedly reduce mention of on-line and off-line editing phases to a footnote in future broadcasting texts.

EDITORS VS. TECHNICIANS

Many technicians can efficiently operate editing equipment, but there are few truly skilled and creative editors—men and women who, over time, have developed an almost intuitive understanding of the audio and video communication process. The sought-after video editors—the ones who win Emmy awards for their work— learn the operation and capabilities of their equipment so well that they are able to totally concentrate on the creative potential of the editing process. It is only by spending many hours doing editing that a person is able to move beyond the technology of editing to the art of editing.

13 DIRECTING AND MULTIPLE-CAMERA FIELD PRODUCTION

THE SUPER BOWL, the Academy Awards, the Rose Parade, government hearings, the Olympics: in many ways these multicamera field productions are similar to studio productions. But unlike the studio, which is tailor-made for production, field productions must be adapted to existing conditions. Unpredictable weather, changing sunlight, the intrusion of bystanders and a whole raft of capricious elements can interfere with the best-laid plans.

When you move from a single camera to multiple-camera production, things become much more technically complex. The signals from cameras and various pieces of video equipment have to be locked together with a common synchronizing signal; the activities of the various crew members must be coordinated through one or more PL communications systems; and a central switching and control point must be in place (Figure 13.1).

In this chapter we will look at some of these elements, along with the complete on-location multiple-camera production process. In particular, we'll focus on five major areas: preproduction planning, site surveys, facilities requests, directing, and setups for specific events.

THE IMPORTANCE OF PREPRODUCTION PLANNING

Although preproduction planning may not be the most glamorous aspect of production, it is the most important, especially for on-location multiple-camera

Figure 13.1   The control center for multiple-camera remote productions is typically a truck or van. This mobile production unit includes facilities equal to those found in some of the best studio control rooms.

production. (Recall the production maxim: *the most important phase of production is preproduction.*) More than one production has come to an untimely conclusion when it was discovered that a specific permit hadn't been obtained, or that someone had forgotten to do a preproduction check on power. Even if something as extreme as losing the entire production doesn't happen, a lack of planning can result in compromised quality and weakened production values.

Since multicamera remote productions involve a wide range of production personnel, a lack of preproduction planning can also waste the most costly aspect of production: the time of talent and crew. Directors who go into a production saying, "Well I'm not exactly sure how we're going to handle that, but I'm sure we'll figure something out once things get underway," are living dangerously and foolishly. One experienced field director was quoted as saying, "There's enough that'll go wrong during the production that you couldn't have possibly foreseen, without, at the same time, having to solve problems you already knew about."

With this in mind let's turn to the steps involved in doing a major multiple-camera field production. These steps, of course, will need to be scaled down to meet the needs of smaller productions.

The On-Location Survey

The most important step is the first one: the on-location survey. Although situations vary, an initial survey for a major, multiple-camera field production should include the following eleven points:

1. A check of available power. What will your total power needs be on the location in terms of watts or amps? Does the remote van that will house your production equipment take 120- or 220-volt power? Are there close fuse boxes or breakers, or will long power lines have to be installed? Is a portable generator the only solution?

2. Assuming the production is not going to be recorded, does the location provide for a clear satellite uplink or microwave path?

3. Will there be sound problems? Is there a street or playground nearby that is noisy during certain hours of the day? Depending on changing wind conditions, is it possible that an exterior location may end up being in the flight path of an airport? If the production will be done inside, will the existing acoustics present special problems?

4. What are the existing lighting conditions? If it's an interior shoot, will a large assortment of extra lights have to be set up? Will the facility's air conditioning be able to handle the heat resulting from extra lights? If the shoot is exterior, where will the sun be during the hours of the shoot? Will deep shadows caused by the position of the sun add to lighting requirements?

5. What changes will be necessary at the location to accommodate the script, talent and production equipment? For exterior locations this might include covering or changing existing signs, or altering structures to accommodate cameras and equipment. For interior locations there may be a need for renovations, repainting, or redecorating. All this becomes especially important in *period pieces* that are set in specific historic eras. (Would a room with a shag rug and stucco walls be appropriate in a period piece about Henry Ford?)

6. Will all of the needed facilities be available during all of the hours of the anticipated production time? In many situations a contract will be drawn up detailing (a) the time in days or hours when the facility will be needed, (b) the compensation that will be paid to the owner, (c) any changes that will be made to the property, including the interior or exterior of buildings (repainting, remodeling, redecorating, etc.), (d) the user's responsibility for restoring the location to its original condition, if that's deemed desirable, and (e) necessary insurance and bonds, and a statement on financial responsibility for taking care of property damage or related liability.

7. What are the total costs and conditions for using the location? Included are property rental, parking, and needed modifications and renovations. Are there local ordinances affecting production? Some communities, especially in Southern California and New York City, have strict ordinances covering production. Often

production hours and conditions are limited. Frequently, special permits, insurance and security bonds are required.

8. In the case of a scripted production, does the location meet the needs of the script? Is the setting fully consistent with the atmosphere suggested?

9. Does the location offer adequate toilet facilities for cast and crew? Are they readily available (as would normally be the case in a large athletic facility) or will portable facilities have to be rented?

10. Will adequate security, police and first-aid requirements be available? If equipment is to be left overnight, one or more security guards may have to be hired. If the production is in a densely populated area, off-duty police may have to be hired to keep onlookers from interfering with the production.

11. Are there nearby restaurants, or will food from a catering service have to be brought in? Even a nearby restaurant may not be able to handle a large crew within a short time, which can add unexpected delays to a production schedule.

On-Location Survey Factors

Although production needs will vary widely, we'll show two types of general production forms. One (Figure 13.2) is an initial survey, designed to aid early preproduction planning. Some items may need explanation. The *location contacts* are the people responsible for the property or facilities for the event. This would include head security personnel, or public relations, press, or event coordinators. *Maximum amps* refers to the maximum amperage that will be available in a designated area, above and beyond that which may be normally required at the location. Most circuits allow for 20 or 30 amps, which conservatively translates into 2,000 or 3,000 watts. (To provide a safety factor, 100 volts are used instead of 115–120 volts in the formula Amps = Watts divided by 100.) Although two or three 20–30-amp circuits will generally be adequate for basic video and audio equipment, lighting instruments can quickly exceed these limitations. Completely equipped mobile production vans sometimes require more than 100 amps of power.

The term *contractual limitations* refers to written stipulations governing the use of the property. These provisions can include a limitation on the number of vehicles that can be parked at the site, hours when taping will not be allowed, areas that will be off limits to production personnel, etc. Often, to reduce overall costs, even with overtime expenses included, production crews put in 10-hour days. However, in deference to local residents, a site contract may specify that no production work take place before 8 AM. Limitations may also be placed on the use of pyrotechnics (special effects involving fire, explosions, etc.). *Inherent site limitations* include possible noise or ventilation problems, a lack of restroom facilities and possible crowd-control problems. *Probable alterations* required refers to any obvious changes that will have to be made to conform to story, script or production needs. Possibly there

---

REMOTE SURVEY INFORMATION

PRODUCTION: _____   PRODUCTION DATE: _____

PRODUCER: _____   DIRECTOR: _____

LOCATION ADDRESS: _____

LOCATION CONTACT: _____   PHONE: (_____) _____

CONTACT: _____   PHONE: (_____) _____

CONTACT: _____   PHONE: (_____) _____

POWER: ____ 120 V.   ____ 220 V.   MAXIMUM AMPS WITHIN 700 FT. _____

MAIN POWER BOX LOCATION: _____

MICROWAVE/SATELLITE PATH NOTES:

_____

_____

_____

CONTRACTUAL OR INHERENT SITE LIMITATIONS:

_____

_____

_____

PROBABLE ALTERATIONS REQUIRED:

_____

_____

_____

Figure 13.2   Remote Survey Form

will need to be cleaning, painting, or remodeling done; or, to accommodate equipment, cameras, or microwave dishes, scaffolding or platforms may have to be built.

Once the information in the initial survey is obtained, reviewed and approved, the director and all related production personnel will visit the site to draw up a list of specific personnel and equipment needs.

The Fax Sheet

Most television stations and production facilities have their own Fax Sheet (facilities/equipment request form). The form illustrated in Figure 13.3 is typical. Generally, the fax form will be supplemented with drawings of camera and microphone positions, information on permits, parking, sketches of special construction

REMOTE FACILITIES / EQUIPMENT REQUEST

PRODUCTION: _____ PRODUCTION DATE: _____
LOCATION: _____
SETUP TIME: _____ REHEARSAL TIME: _____
PRODUCTION TIME: _____ DIRECTOR: _____

_____ VTR
      MASTER TAPES: _____
      _____ OFF-LINE FORMAT: _____
      _____ COMMON SMPTE TIME CODE   START: _____ :00:00:00

_____ LIVE
      _____ MICROWAVE   LINKS REQUIRED _____
      _____ SATELLITE   TRANSMISSION START _____ STOP _____
      _____ AUTHORIZATION _____ CONFIRMATION DATE: _____
      _____ SETUP NOTES: _____

CAMERAS	LOCATION	MOUNT	LENS	CABLE RUN
CAM #1				
CAM #2				
CAM #3				
CAM #4				
CAM #5				

MIC TYPE	LOCATION	CABLE RUN		MIC TYPE	LOCATION	CABLE
#1			#9			
#2			#10			
#3			#11			
#4			#12			
#5			#13			
#6			#14			
#7			#15			
#8			#16			

PRIMARY LIGHTING: _____ AVAILABLE   BASE LIGHT LEVEL _____ FC.
ANTICIPATED LIGHTING INSTRUMENTS: _____
_____

MAXIMUM LIGHTING WATTS: _____ SITE ELECTRICIAN: _____
AVAILABLE WATTS, LOCATIONS: _____
_____

      _____ SPECIAL PL DROPS: _____
COMMUNICATION _____ CEL PHONES: _____
    TWO-WAYS: _____   _____
    IFB: _____   _____

Figure 13.3 Remote Facilities/Equipment Request

needed, etc. Once the initial concerns outlined in Figure 13.3 are taken care of, more specific facility and equipment needs can be assessed and requested. If the production is to be recorded on location (as opposed to being done live or sent back to a production facility for recording), it will require special taping considerations, which will be discussed in upcoming paragraphs.

Even when done live, productions are not transmitted to viewers directly from the field; instead, they must first be sent to a TV station or a production facility and then to a transmitter or "head end" distribution point. A signal can be sent from the field in three ways:

- By fiber optics (optical fiber)
- By one or more microwave links
- By satellite uplink

Each of these requires specific preproduction planning. The placement of cameras, microphones and lights must also be carefully thought out.

Setup time refers to the time when arrangements have been made for the mobile van and equipment to be installed at the site. This must be far enough in advance of the rehearsal time to keep the on-camera talent from having to wait around for the setup to be finished. And the *rehearsal time* must be far enough in advance of actual production to ensure that any problems during the rehearsal—a totally inevitable occurrence—can be adequately dealt with before the actual production.

If the production is to be taped, the number and type of master tapes should be specified. Two things should be noted here. Multiple-camera productions should be double recorded. Although tape machines are highly reliable, making two master recordings ends up being cheap insurance against head clog, tape problems, or an electronic or mechanical failure. If the length of the production goes beyond the duration of a single recording tape, one or more additional tape machines will have to be started before the first tapes run out.

The blank for the SMPTE time-code information is for setting the time-code generator to a specific starting point in hours. As previously noted, when multiple reels are used in editing, a unique hour number can be selected to represent a VTR cassette or reel number. (If multiple tapes are used in editing and each starts with the "00" hour number, there is a good chance that a segment on one or more reels or cassettes will have the same time-code number.)

SELECTING CAMERA POSITIONS

Next on the form comes *camera positions.* A supplementary sketch is generally attached to the facilities request form to show the camera positions decided upon by the director. Camera mounts could include field tripods, rolling dollies, cranes, **camera jibs,** and cherry pickers. (Cherry pickers are tall, industrial crane devices normally used for changing street lamps. They can be rented from heavy equipment companies and make good camera cranes for high-angle shots.)

Several things should be kept in mind when deciding on camera locations. In addition to the obvious factors, such as not shooting against the sun and not placing a camera in a position that would result in a reversal of action ("crossing the line"), there are some special considerations for stationary cameras. If people suddenly jump up in front of your camera during the most exciting play in a game and block your shot, there may be little you can do. Members of the press or ENG camerapersons may also find the camera angle you've selected to be ideal. (They probably will, if it's a good one.) If they don't stand directly in front of your camera, they may simply block your shot from one or more angles. And there is another problem. If the crowd attending an event start jumping up and down in their excitement and shaking the camera platform, the resulting video may be unusable. Suffice it to say, in selecting camera positions you need to run through a number of "what if" scenarios.

Another aspect of the camera placement issue also must be considered. In order to hold public relations problems to a minimum, you will need to check to see if the location of cameras, lights or other equipment you will be using will block the view of individuals who have paid to attend the event.

On-Location Audio Concerns

The second page of the fax sheet starts with audio needs. Here the type of mic, its location and the amount of cable required should be noted. Because of the ambient noise common to remote locations, directional microphones are almost always required. If it is not possible to wire talent with personal mics, wireless ones will be the logical choice. In the latter case, an assistant must test each of the RF mics by slowly walking through the areas where they will be used. RF reflections (multipath reception) and dead spots are unpredictable. Since microphone problems are common, backup mics that can be put into service at a moment's notice should be provided for each area. When mounting "crowd" mics, which will pick up audience or crowd reaction, make sure they cover a wide area rather than favoring a few people closest to the mic. (More than one misplaced crowd mic has ended up getting the colorful comments of just a few close people rather than more generalized crowd reactions.) In determining where microphone cables will be run, plan for the shortest distance and avoid running the cables parallel to AC cords or power lines. In wet weather or when rain is possible, seal up cable connectors with black plastic tape. When installing either microphone or camera cables across hallways, run the cables over the top of doorways. This not only keeps people from walking over the cables, which can break wires, but it can eliminate injury or possibly even a lawsuit if someone trips over a cable.

Determining Lighting Needs

For exterior productions the director will want to make certain that the sun is behind the cameras. Although it is possible to use high-powered lights to fill in the shadows caused by shooting against the sun, this technique will not be effective for subject matter at any great distance. Even when shooting with the sun, some fill light in the form of a reflector board or 5,500° K lights will be desirable for close-ups.

For interior shoots the fax sheet calls for an estimate of the normal light level. Although this estimate is primarily intended for productions such as athletic events that will be done under existing light, it is also helpful in situations where lights will be added and some indication of base light level is needed. Once a lighting director visits the location, a list of needed lighting instruments and accessories can be drawn up. In order to handle any problems with power, it is important to have the name and telephone number of an electrician with knowledge of the location.

Production Communication

Finally, there is the important matter of production communication. For live productions or productions that are relayed back to a station or production facility, there should be at least two communication links: technical and production. Engineers at both ends of the remote link must be in contact to make video and audio level adjustments and to keep microwave or satellite signals in optimum adjustment. Production personnel at both ends of the link must be able to plan for commercial and station-identification breaks, which generally originate from video servers or tape at the station, and for updates on program and segment times. Except for some microwave and satellite feeds, which have their own PL audio channels, engineering and production links to the station or production facility are generally handled by telephone.

As discussed in Chapter 8, interruptable feedback (IFB) lines are used to communicate with on-camera talent. During a sports telecast, for example, a director may need to notify an announcer to go to a commercial, or tell a color commentator that an instant replay of a specific play is being cued for playback. During live sports broadcasts a *spotter* can use IFB to update sports announcers on statistics and general information appropriate to their commentary. Unlike live ENG reporters, who wear only a small, single IFB ear piece, announcers for sports events prefer padded, noise-canceling earphones that cover both ears. Although the earphones can be wired in several ways, in their normal mode both earphones carry program audio. This makes it possible for commentators to hear each other over the noise of the crowd. When a brief message needs to be relayed to an announcer (preferably when he or she is not talking) the audio on just one of the earphones is interrupted.

Although some field cameras allow for plugging in more than one PL headset, extra PL line "drops" (added outlets) generally have to be installed in field locations to accommodate production personnel who are not working close to a camera. And, of course, maximum mobility is possible if these crew members use wireless PL systems.

Whatever the system, a reliable two-way communication link to all production personnel is essential. If communication is lost, members of the crew will not know what is going on or what is expected of them. At best, confusion will result; at worst the entire production will become paralyzed. Because of the importance of PL communication, it is highly desirable—some would say absolutely essential—to have a fully functional standby PL line, which everyone can instantly switch to if problems develop in the primary system.

In high noise situations where the sound of a cheering crowd or loud music can quickly drown out the best PL communication system, special considerations must be taken. If tightly fitting, padded double earphones are used, much of the exterior noise will be eliminated. But if the noise is being picked up in each of the PL headset microphones, this approach will allow crew members only to more clearly hear the interfering noise! Normally, the microphones on PL headsets are on all the time, but to reduce accumulated interference under high noise conditions push-to-talk switches are used. This means that PL microphones will all be off except when a specific crew member relays information or responds to a question.

The last area of production communication mentioned on the fax sheet is *two-ways.* These are small transceivers similar to what police or security guards carry. They make it possible for production personnel to move around a remote site while still being in constant contact with key coordinating personnel.

Permits, Clearances, Bonds and Insurance

In small towns local officials probably will not have established procedures for handling on-location productions. However, some large cities require not only production permits, but also security bonds, insurance and specially assigned police. Most of the larger cities have film commissions that can provide a wide range of help to on-location film and video production personnel.

Remember, in covering paid events, things can radically change between the camera rehearsal and the actual production. For example, before the event, crew members may be able to move freely throughout a facility. But during a performance ushers or gatekeepers may have instructions to bar people from entering certain areas unless passes have been issued. Complicating this issue are the increased security measures now common with most public events.

The Equipment Inventory

Since space for production equipment is generally at a premium inside mobile trucks and vans, and since it is desirable to hold transportation costs to a minimum, only equipment that will be used should be transported to the scene of the remote. This does not mean that such items as extra lamps for lights, extra mics, or mic cables should be excluded. It is a rare remote in which some piece of equipment doesn't fail. The remote survey form and the fax sheet should be used as a guide in deciding on the list of production equipment. This list should be carefully drawn up and then double-checked as the equipment is packed. Arriving at the scene of a remote without a major connecting cable or piece of equipment may mean that everyone will have to sit around until someone can get the needed item.

Directing the Remote Production

Studio directors don't automatically make good field directors. Although directing a multicamera remote production is similar to directing a studio production, the remote director must be much more innovative in handling a wide range of unexpected problems. In a regular studio, production crew members typically get to know the basic routines associated with programs and often don't even have to be prompted by the director. But, during a field production, all crew members will depend heavily, if not completely, on the director for second-by-second cues. For one thing, multiple-camera field productions often involve material that can't be scripted. Although the director will typically have an outline of what will happen during a parade, an athletic event, or an awards program, much of the content will unfold virtually on a second-by-second basis.

We've already discussed the importance of a reliable PL system, but even the best system will be useless without clear and effective communication from the director. Because production involves the activities of a number of crew members (the number can range from six to 60) and conditions at many on-location sites is far from ideal, the director's instructions must be phrased clearly and succinctly.

The Director as a Psychologist

The director, especially in a complex, multiple-camera field production can never do everything alone. So, first and foremost, the director's job is to get crew and talent to function as a team and, in the process, to bring out the best work in each person. This means that the director sometimes ends up working more in the realm of psychology than television. In large-scale productions everyone is normally working under pressure, especially if the productions are done live or live-on-tape. Therefore, directors must be able to control their own tension and anxiety (not an easy task when all important production decisions rest on their shoulders) while being sensitive to the concerns, pressures, strengths and weaknesses of the talent and crew. The personalities and temperaments of the talent and crew typically range from the eminently artistic to the preeminently logical. A heavy-handed, threatening approach with the wrong person can temporarily destroy the person's effectiveness and turn a bad situation into a disaster.

Any director worth the title can stay on top of things when the crew, talent and equipment perform exactly as they are supposed to. But much of the value and respect that people place on directors rest on their ability to stay in control when, despite all the best-laid plans, things begin to fall apart. A camera may go out, a mic may fail, a crew member or on-camera person may suddenly get sick, or a key person may refuse to continue unless some special accommodation is made. When such things happen, the director will suddenly become the sole decision maker and may have to instantly devise a new "game plan."

The perspective of unclouded, 20-20 hindsight may show that a decision that had to be made quickly under pressure wasn't the best one. The only consolation is that even an imperfect decision is generally better than no decision at all. Vacillation, mixed signals, or indecisiveness at a crucial time can result in production paralysis.

Directing Strategies

For every visible or audible change that takes place during a production, several behind-the-scenes production steps are typically required. These steps normally involve coordinating the activities of a number of production personnel. Because production involves the activities of various crew members, the director's instructions must be phrased clearly and succinctly. To facilitate this process some relatively standard and somewhat abbreviated commands have been devised. Even the sequence of words in a director's sentence is important. For example, if the director says, "Will you pan to the right and down a little when you 'lose [your tally] light' on camera one?" all camera operators must wait until the end of the sentence before they know who the director is talking to, and then they must remember what the instructions were. However, if the director says, "Camera one, when you lose light, pan right and down a little," the first two words tell who, the next four words tell when, and the last six words tell what. After the first two words crew members know that only camera one is being addressed. This will get the attention of the camera one operator, and the rest of the crew members can concentrate on their tasks. The "when" tells camera one not to immediately pan and tilt, but to prepare for a quick move once the camera tally light is off. Preparation might involve loosening the pan and tilt controls on the camera's pan head and being ready to make the adjustment requested, possibly within the brief interval allowed in cutting to a reaction shot. Delays—even the one- or two-second delay involved in phrasing commands—can make the difference between a tight show and one where the production changes lag conspicuously behind the action.

Although the specific jargon varies somewhat between production facilities, directors tend to use some of the same basic terminology. To illustrate this, the director's PL line conversation for the opening of a simple interview show is traced in Table 13.1 on pages 326–327.

As you can see from Figure 13.4, this simple production uses two cameras, one of which moves from position A to position B. In position A the camera gets the establishing (wide) shot. In position B it gets close-ups and over-the-shoulder shots. Since the guests are different each week and will require different opening and closing announcements, only the show's theme music is prerecorded on the videotape. The opening and closing announcements (and the slate) are read off-camera, live. Excluding the commercial, all of what takes place in Table 13.1 covers only about a minute of production time.

Note that at the end of the show the opening wide shot on camera one will again be used. During the 30 seconds or so that the interviewer uses to wrap up the show, camera one will again truck right to the mid-position and zoom back.

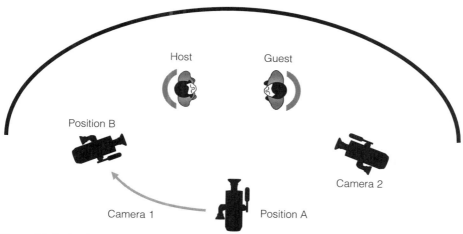

Figure 13.4   In this typical two-camera approach to doing an interview, position A for camera 1 provides a centered, wide shot of the set. Not only does this position provide the mandatory establishing shot, but the shot can also be used as a background for the opening titles and closing credits. When this camera moves to position B it can provide both an over-the-shoulder shot and, by zooming in, a close-up of the guest.

This shot will be used, possibly with dimmed studio lights, as a background for the closing credits and announce copy.

Note in the director's dialogue the constant use of the terms, "ready" and "stand by." Although this may seem unnecessarily repetitious, these cues are important. For one thing, crew members are generally attending to several things at once, including listening to two sources of audio: the PL line and the program audio. "Stand bys" warn them of upcoming actions. They also protect the director. If the director says "take one" when the cameraperson is not ready, the audience may see a picture being focused (complete with a quick zoom in and out) or a sudden, ungracious pan or tilt. In this case the director can't blame the cameraperson. No warning was given. However, if a "stand by" was given in reasonable time, the director has every right to expect the crew member involved to be prepared for the requested action, or to quickly tell the director about a problem.

In doing any production, you want to strive for the strongest possible camera shots at all times. During interviews the eyes and facial expressions can communicate a great deal, often even more than what the person is saying. Profile shots, even in close-up are not only weak from a composition standpoint, but much in the way of revealing facial expressions can be missed. This would be equivalent to shooting the close-ups from the center camera position in Figure 13.4. You can vary your shots by zooming back to an over-the-shoulder shot. The latter can also be used as a reaction shot while covering comments by the person whose back is toward the camera.

Table 13.1   Director and Production Comments for Interview Show

Director Comments	Explanation
Stand by on the set.	This essentially means "attention" and "quiet." The command is given about 30 seconds before rolling tape.
Stand by to roll tape.	Get ready to start the videotape that will record the show.
Roll tape.	The tape is rolled, and when it stabilizes after 5 to 10 seconds, a tape operator calls, "Speed." This means the tape is ready for recording.
Ready to take bars and tone.	This is the electronic test pattern (ETP) and audio tone that are recorded at an even zero dB. It will be used when the tape is played back to correctly set up playback equipment for proper video and audio.
Take bars and tone.	This will last from 15 to 60 seconds, depending on technical requirements of the station or production facility.
Stand by camera one on slate; stand by to announce slate.	Camera one's first shot is the countdown slate. This type of slate has visible, flashing numbers and preempts the use of countdown leader.
Take one. Read slate.	The announcer reads the basic program-identifying information; program name and number, date of recording, date of air, director, etc.
Ready black. Go black.	The technical director cuts to black for about three seconds.
Ready two with your close-up of Smith; ready mic; ready cue.	The show opens "cold" (without an introduction of any kind) with a close-up of Smith. This tease is intended to grab attention and introduce the show's guest and topic.
Take two, mic, cue! *Stand by one on the guest.*	Cut to camera two with its close-up of Smith, turn his mic on and cue him to start. Smith introduces subject and makes a quick reference to the guest.
Take one! *Take two!* *Ready black.* *Ready VTR 4.*	When Smith mentions the guest, the director makes a two- to three-second cut to the close-up camera and then back to Smith on camera two.
Roll VTR 4. Go black. *Take it.*	The commercial is rolled. While it is stabilizing, the TD cuts to black. The commercial is taken as soon as it comes up. The audio person brings up the sound on the commercial without being cued. During the commercial, camera one will reposition for the opening wide shot.
Camera one, truck right for a wide shot.	During the commercial, camera one repositions by trucking right to the middle of the set to get the wide shot. The camera zooms back to a wide shot.

The Need to Anticipate

One of the talents essential for a director is the ability to react instantly to changes in action. But reaction, no matter how quick, implies delay. This delay might not be too noticeable if a response were possible the instant the director saw the need for a specific action. But the total response time is equal to the accumulated time

Table 13.1   *Continued*

Production Comments	Explanation
Fifteen seconds; stand by in studio. Stand by opening announce and theme; ready one on your wide shot; ready two on a close-up of Smith. Stand by to key in title.	
Take one; hit music; key title.	The wide shot is taken on camera one, the theme music is established, and the title of the show is keyed over the screen.
Fade [music] and read.	The music is faded under and the opening announce for the show is read by an announcer.
Ready two with a close-up on Smith. Stand-by mics and cue.	The opening announce includes the show title, the topic and the show's host.
Take two, mics, cue.	This is a close-up of the show's interviewer, who now fully introduces the day's guest. The host starts the show.
Camera one, arc around for your close-up on the guest.	Camera one moves back to the opening position for the close-up of the guest. Smith covers the interval of the camera move by fully introducing the guest.
Ready on one.	When the camera is ready, he throws the first question to the guest.
Take one.	Guest answers first question.
	(Show continues alternating between close-ups of host and guest. Occasionally cameras will zoom out to get over-the-shoulder shots.)

involved in recognizing the need for a specific action, communicating that action to crew members and having them perform the action requested.

The solution is for the director to anticipate what is going to happen. At first it might seem that this implies precognitive abilities, but it is actually not as difficult as it might seem. During an interview an alert director should be able to sense when the interviewer's question is about to end or when a interviewee's answer is winding up. By saying "stand by" early and calling for a camera cut a moment before it's needed, a director will be able to cut from one camera to the other almost on the concluding period or question mark of the person's final sentence. By keeping an eye on the appropriate off-line camera monitor in the control room, as opposed to the line-out monitor showing the person talking, the director will often be able to see when the off-camera person is about to interrupt or visually react to what is being said.

Even the best of directors will miscalculate and occasionally cut to a camera at the wrong time. Possibly the guest suddenly decides to add another thought to a seemingly final sentence, or the interviewer starts to interrupt, but the guest just keeps on talking. In these cases it is sometimes more graceful for the director to stay with the new shot for a few seconds, rather than to quickly cut back to the original camera. The latter rather clearly signals that a mistake was made. Even so, such things could be considered rather minor, considering the consequences of the mistakes to be discussed in the next chapter.

14 LEGAL AND ETHICAL GUIDELINES

MORE AND MORE often, legal concerns are influencing production decisions. Litigation can range all the way from a slander suit resulting from malicious words uttered by reporters who didn't realize they were on the air at the time, to a threatened legal action if a clearly valid story on illegal activity is broadcast.[1] This chapter will point out some of the legal and ethical hazards in production and suggest some guidelines. At the same time, it can't be stressed too strongly that the law in these areas has varied with time, place and circumstances. Among other topics, these six areas will be covered:

- Invasion of privacy
- Access restrictions and rights
- Defamation (libel and slander)
- Staging
- Copyright
- Releases

In addition, this chapter will introduce some concerns that fall under the heading of ethical and professional issues. While these issues are not defined by law, they have definite implications for an individual's personal and professional credibility.

---

[1] In recent years, as the cost of litigation has increased, we have seen more and more frequent attempts at censorship through the threat of litigation. Even a broadcast station confident that a story on wrongdoing is valid, and that they would eventually prevail in a court of law, may back off when faced with the threat of costly, extended litigation.

INVASION OF PRIVACY

Private and Public Individuals

The law in many areas makes a distinction between private and public individuals. Once individuals enter the "public spotlight," either intentionally or through accidental circumstances, they are afforded much less legal protection with regard to their privacy.

Legal action can be taken against camerapersons if they wrongfully intrude on the solitude or seclusion of another person. Legally, this is a form of trespassing, and it is variously referred to as intrusion on seclusion, invasion of privacy, or just privacy. The intrusion may be direct and physical, such as entering a person's home or place of business to get pictures without permission, or it may be figurative, such as the use of an extremely long lens or a night viewing device to videotape private scenes. The latter area could also include shooting through a skylight from a rooftop, using secret two-way mirrors, or using a hidden recorder or wireless microphone. Most cases of intrusion stem from the inherent conflict between the desire of many individuals to keep certain aspects of their lives from being publicized or exposed and the curiosity of viewers and, therefore, news people to find out as much as possible about these individuals. Movie stars and popular singers are a favorite target of camerapersons, as are alleged criminals.

Conflicts in Legal Rights

The issue of invasion of privacy includes two legal areas that can come into conflict: the constitutional right of the media to be free to report the news and the right of individuals to maintain personal privacy. The principles of freedom of speech and freedom of the press can also conflict with the right of an individual to have an impartial jury trial, free from the influence of pretrial media publicity.

Unlike freedom of the press, protection against invasion of privacy is not specifically guaranteed by the U.S. Constitution. Nevertheless, over the years the right of individuals to their privacy has become an accepted part of tort and U.S. constitutional law.

The Public's Right to Know

There is also another important side to the privacy issue, a side that sometimes outweighs these personal rights. Some individuals wish to keep certain acts private because the acts are illegal, unethical, or at least morally questionable. The issue then becomes one of the public's right to know, which gets into the area of the disclosure of private facts. For example, does the public have a right to know that a person being considered for public office is guilty of significant illegal acts? Does the public have a right to know that a popular religious leader (whom many may try to emulate) widely proclaims certain moral values while personally disregarding these values in his personal life? Most news editors would say *yes* in both cases.

Our system of government and our way of life depend on an informed public. The degree to which the voting public is denied information is the degree to which it is vulnerable to the duplicity of self-serving individuals. Recognizing this fact, our courts have been quick to protect the news media's rights to gather and disseminate information. But the degree to which the media has a right to intrude on the private lives of people in the pursuit of this information is an issue that often must be settled in court.

Beyond this, however, there is a professional risk for members of the media when they are perceived as stepping over that often blurry line between their responsibility to inform the public and simply catering to voyeuristic appetites. The dilemma is, of course, that the latter is related to ratings; ratings are related to income; and income is related to personal and corporate success. This conflict between information and privacy brings up the following point.

Can "Truth" Be an Invasion of Privacy?

It has surprised many journalists to find that disclosing verifiable facts about someone can be actionable under invasion-of-privacy legal precedents. To be so, the information must

- Be published, broadcast or in some way disseminated to an audience
- Consist of information of a private nature
- Consist of information that would be highly offensive to a reasonable person
- Consist of information that is not deemed newsworthy or of legitimate concern to the public

Disclosing that an individual—especially a private individual—has AIDS, is a lesbian or male homosexual, or has served time in prison may fall into this category, *if* such facts are not deemed relevant to any present newsworthy story. There are two exceptions here: first, if the information could easily be obtained from public records and, second, if there is *consent;* that is, if the person knows you are a reporter and willingly discloses the information to you.

INTRUSION

One type of invasion of privacy, **intrusion,** is sometimes referred to as intrusion on seclusion, or intrusion on solitude. Some years back a TV station was sued for intrusion after a cameraperson had videotaped an employee of a pharmacy through its front window. A druggist working inside had been charged with cheating the state out of Medicaid funds. When the employee refused to talk with reporters, the camera operator set up the camera outside of the front window of the store and photographed the man through the window as he talked on the telephone. Since the taping was done from the exterior of the building and from a place that was deemed public, the court ruled that intrusion had not taken place because the cameraperson was showing something that the general public was free to view.

Privately owned restaurants and establishments are not considered public property, however. In one case a network news crew was sent to do an ENG story on restaurants cited for health-code violations. The crew entered an expensive French restaurant in New York City, with "cameras rolling." Although the proprietor asked them to leave, the crew continued to tape until they were finally escorted from the restaurant. During the commotion some customers ducked under tables and some even fled without paying their bills. Dismissing a First Amendment defense, the court ruled against the network saying that the First Amendment is not ". . . a shibboleth before which all other rights must succumb." In addition to the restaurant being private property, an important issue in the case was undoubtedly the disruptive nature of the intrusion.

Free and Restricted Access

These issues lead into one of the most troublesome areas for producers and ENG crews: access. It is important to note that access is rooted in state laws regarding trespassing and therefore differs somewhat in every state.

Legally, access implies a number of things, but here we'll look at the area where news personnel and public safety officials (primarily police) are most likely to clash. One of the grayest areas of access law—one that, unfortunately, is most often encountered by working photojournalists—is access to public locations that are under the control of public safety officials (Figure 14.1). Crime scenes, public demonstrations, and the disasters fall in this category. ENG crews covering breaking news stories seldom have time to consult lawyers; therefore, the crew's understanding of legal precedents in this area can help them avoid trouble.

Although the press and ENG crews are frequently, even routinely, given special access privileges to cover news, when "push comes to shove" (and barring state laws to the contrary) court decisions have generally held that the press has no privileges beyond those granted to the general public. With this in mind, it then becomes a matter of knowing state trespass laws. In general, trespass law restricts access to areas posted as private, or to property where the owner or the owner's agent has refused you permission. (In the latter case, however, you will generally be allowed to broadcast any footage taken before you were asked to leave.)

Guidelines for Intrusion

In deciding on the merit of an invasion of privacy suit, several questions should be asked. (We'll discuss them in more detail later.)

Figure 14.1   Sometimes access is restricted for safety reasons. While trying to cover a fire at a distillery, the author was refused permission to enter the premises. He subsequently shot this picture of the ensuing explosion which killed six people and injured 38.

1. If what you intend to photograph is visible to the average person standing on public property, intrusion on seclusion would be difficult to prove.

2. Was consent given to enter the property? Could the reporter have gotten the information from another source?

3. Is the information obtained newsworthy and of legitimate concern to the public?

4. Is there proof of prying on the part of the cameraperson or reporter?

5. Does the intrusion relate to something generally agreed to be of a private nature?

6. Would the intrusion be deemed objectionable to a reasonable person?

Although such terms as, "public," "legitimate concern," "consent," "prying," "private," and "objectionable," are all subject to interpretation, often by a court, some past interpretations may help.

Public property includes streets and sidewalks; therefore, photographing activities that take place in these areas, as well as things that can be seen from these vantage points, is generally safe. "Off-limit" areas would include the backs and sides of private dwellings that are not visible from public property and the interiors of buildings that would not normally be exposed to the general public.

Consent means being given permission to enter an area by a property owner or renter. If permission is granted, intrusion would be difficult to prove. At the same time it doesn't include an absence of objection. In one court case when a camera crew entered a bedroom along with paramedics and there was no objection, the court ruled that a lack of verbal objection did not constitute consent and that invasion of privacy had occurred.

You may also be given permission to enter an area by an authorized public safety officer. In *Florida Publishing Co. vs. Fletcher* a newspaper photographer was invited into a badly burned house by the Fire Marshall and asked to photograph a silhouette left on the floor by the body of a seventeen-year-old girl, who died in the fire. The girl's mother, who first learned the facts of her daughter's death from the newspaper article and its accompanying photographs, sued for invasion of privacy. Since the owner of the property was not present at the time and the photographer was invited to enter by officials present, the trial judge ruled in favor of the newspaper. Not only was there no objection to the entry, but there was an invitation to enter by the officers investigating the fire.[2]

The phrase, *legitimate concern to the public,* touches on an important point and a significant area of defense in intrusion cases. Videographers and still photographers who cross the line on intrusion often use the defense that the information they are able to photographically obtain is in the public's interest. In other words, the public has a right and possibly even a need to know the information. This "ends justify the means" defense has been used successfully in defending many charges of intrusion. Although the public interest can constitute a valid defense, the burden of proof in these cases is on the defendant. Clear evidence must be presented that the information gathered was of legitimate concern to the public and that no other way of obtaining the information was available. At the same time it should be emphasized that courts have rather consistently recognized the obligation of reporters and photographers to show respect for the "dignity, privacy and well-being" of subjects.

Prying connotes something beyond basic curiosity and moves into the area of offensive and inappropriate snooping. The disclosure of private facts is generally interpreted as relating to information about a person's private life that is not a

---

[2] Just when you think you can count on a principle—in this case being invited to come onto private property by a law official—a court makes an exception. In late 1994, a federal appeals court in New York ruled against CBS after a "Street Stories" camera crew was invited into a private apartment by a Secret Service agent. In a strongly worded opinion, which may reveal something of the court's interpretation of the circumstances, the court said, "a private home is not a sound stage for law-enforcement theatrics." The resident of the apartment, who was suspected of credit card fraud, had sued both the Secret Service agent and CBS for invasion of privacy.

legitimate concern to the public, and the disclosure of which would be highly offensive to a reasonable person.

False Light

Although ENG personnel are generally free to photograph people in public places without worry, when some sort of perceived distortion of facts occurs, there can be problems. In *Holmes vs. Curtis Publishing Co.*, Curtis Publishing ran a photo captioned "High Rollers at the Monte Carlo Club" as part of a story about Mafia involvement in gambling. A tourist, James Holmes, just happened to be sitting at a table near the Mafia men. A photographer used a long focal length lens to photograph the scene and as a consequence compressed the distance between the people in the picture. This distortion made it appear as if Holmes was with the Mafia men. Holmes sued, charging the picture, accompanying caption, and article put him in a false light. The court agreed and Curtis Publishing lost the case. Interestingly, if a normal or wide-angle lens had been used—probably not an option, considering the circumstances—Holmes would have been clearly set apart from the Mafia subjects and there would have been no confusion.

Here's another example of false light. Let's assume you are doing a documentary on prostitution. During the course of the documentary you tape night scenes in the area of 101 Park Street, which the announcer states is where most of the prostitutes in the city solicit. Let's also assume that by chance Mrs. Smith (who has been visiting her aunt at the time of your taping) is clearly visible in one of your scenes. Although you did not identify Mrs. Smith as a prostitute, in the context of the documentary the audience might make that inference. The result of this inference on the part of the audience could constitute a case of false light, and could precipitate a law suit.

Another example of false light happened a number of years ago when a cameraman and a reporter did an ENG piece on a New York ghetto. Slum residents welcomed them after the crew informed them that they were doing a series that might help clean up the ghetto. Footage of rat-infested alleys and overflowing garbage cans was included and several residents eagerly provided a vivid description of the undesirable conditions. After the story was broadcast, residents from a single housing unit brought the reporter and cameraman to court. They said that the coverage sensationalized the living conditions, thus putting them in a false light, and violated their right of privacy.

Regardless of the outcome of such cases, the broadcaster or producer must invest considerable time, effort and money in a legal defense.

Legal Pitfalls in Doing Docudramas

With the popularity of *docudramas* (dramas based on true stories) has come another problem in false light: fictionalization. In writing a script for a docudrama, time is condensed, the chronology of events is often altered, and "dramatic license" is commonly used to make the production more dramatic and interesting. In the process many authors and producers have been sued for putting people or even institutions in a false light. Although some courts have stated that actual malice must be proven in these cases, the docudrama remains a highly controversial type of production and, therefore, requires expert legal advice.

Offensiveness and Harassment

A second exception to the guideline on photographing in public places emerges when harassment or offensiveness is at issue. In *Galella vs. Onassis*—admittedly, a rather exceptional case—the court ruled that photographers, even in public places, can't be so offensive as to seriously interfere with the subject's right to be left alone. Galella, a still photographer, had for some time been pursuing Jackie Onassis (President John F. Kennedy's widow) and her children in order to get candid pictures. In its decision the court ordered Galella not to block Ms. Onassis' movements, which could place her safety in jeopardy, and to stay at least 25 feet away from her and even farther away from her children.

Press Passes

The issuance of official press IDs acknowledges that to some degree the media has some special privileges, even though courts have been reluctant to recognize this fact. Most law-enforcement officials try to work with the media by recognizing that press cards and press passes identify working members of the media and, as a result, special access privileges are given.

Even so, there are two sides to the access issue. Over-zealous reporters have often impeded the work of officials, disturbed evidence, and added to the confusion already present at a news scene. (There is no shortage of dramatic films and TV programs that make use of this hackneyed theme.) At the same time, officials have been known to bar, remove and even arrest reporters when the story was either embarrassing to the officials' superiors, or would have documented improper police conduct. Although arrests sometimes ensue, officials seldom let subsequent interference and disorderly conduct charges go to trial. The cases are usually dropped. Even so, the arrest or removal of ENG crews may accomplish their intended purpose—to keep news-gathering people from getting the story. In at least one case it was determined that members of an ENG crew were fully within their rights in covering an event; at the same time, they were found guilty of illegally disregarding an officer's requests to leave. For reporters this is one definition of a quandary!

Commercial Appropriation

Another aspect of invasion of privacy, **commercial appropriation** involves unauthorized use of an individual's or organization's prominence in order to influence a listening or viewing audience. A suggestion of endorsement of a product or establishment by a known personality, without the consent of that person, is seen as exploiting his or her prominence. The courts have recognized that well-known people acquire an identity that is of value and these people deserve to be protected from someone "cashing in" on that value without their consent.

The Boundaries of Commercial Appropriation   Let's look at an example. If you were televising a public event and wanted to show general shots of the audience in attendance, there would be no problem, even if one or more of the members of the audience were well-known. Individuals in this case are considered "background," much the same as a rock or a tree would be in another type of production. But if one of the people in the audience was a well-known, easily recognizable person and, by your choice of camera shots, you appeared to go out of your way to bring this fact to the attention of the audience, you could be guilty of trying to "cash in on" the person's prominence. As in many areas of law the distinction could end up being rather subjective. But in the first case the notable person is "just one of many" in the audience; in the second case the choice of the camera shot or shots deliberately brings the person's presence to the attention of the viewing audience.

There is an exception. If the public figure is actively taking part in an event being covered, he or she can be considered a part of the event. In such cases, the camera shots may dwell on the person as much as they wish.

CIVIL DISOBEDIENCE

Some photojournalists have been prepared to break the law to get an important story. However, as with any type of civil disobedience, the reporter must be prepared to pay the penalty. In most cases, reporters have little chance against armed police officers bent on stopping them. Even so, five guidelines have been suggested for the legitimacy of civil disobedience:

- Exhaustion of all legal avenues
- True belief that the restraining action is unjust
- Nonviolence
- Belief that the importance of the story to the public outweighs legal obligations
- Willingness to face the consequences

SHIELD LAWS

Another area in which reporters must face the legal consequences of their actions occurs when they try to protect the confidentiality of their sources of information. Although about half the 50 states have **shield laws** designed to keep courts from forcing newspeople to reveal their sources, these laws vary all the way from being essentially meaningless, to fully protecting news-source confidentiality. Without the assurance that newspeople will protect their confidentiality, few people are willing to risk their own welfare and "name names" in revealing inside information about crime and corruption. Some reporters have chosen to serve time in jail on contempt-of-court charges rather than break a promise to keep a source's name confidential. (One investigative reporter who has broken numerous stories about corruption and wrongdoing in high places wryly notes that without an ability to keep names confidential he would instantly lose all his inside sources and end up writing gardening articles or a "Dear Abby" column.)

Confidentiality and the My Lai Massacre

One of the more famous examples of information released only on the guarantee of confidentiality related to the infamous My Lai Massacre in South Vietnam where more than 100 civilians, mostly women and children, were killed, ostensibly because they were a threat to U.S. forces. The story of this massacre was leaked only after Army personnel who knew what had happened were promised confidentiality by the media. The U.S. Army Lieutenant responsible was eventually court-martialed.

The Two Sides of Shield Laws

Of course, there are two sides to the shield law issue. The Constitution says that citizens have a right to "face their accuser"—which is difficult if the identity of that person or persons is kept secret. At the same time, no responsible news medium would run a major accusatory story based on a single confidential source. Some news organizations, in fact, require that stories of this type be verified by three independent sources. The original source, therefore, only serves to launch an investigation.

MISREPRESENTATION

TV stations and production agencies have guidelines that forbid using any kind of deceit or misrepresentation in doing a production or getting a news story. In one famous case, reporters for a national magazine went to the home of a plumber who was suspected of practicing medicine without a license. In order to gain admittance a reporter posed as someone in need of medical assistance. Photos were taken with a hidden camera and the reporter used a concealed microphone to tape the conversation. The audio recordings, which were turned over to the government, were important to the subsequent case against the plumber. However, after the article was published, the plumber sued for invasion of privacy and was able to win damages. The court said, ". . . we have little difficulty in concluding that clandestine photography of the plaintiff in his den and recordation and transmission of his conversation without his consent resulting in his emotional distress warrants recovery for invasion of privacy. . . ." The clear misrepresentation that was involved undoubtedly influenced the court's decision.

Defamation

Ancient Roman law held that if any person slandered another "by words or defamatory verses" and thereby harmed his reputation that person should be beaten by a stick. Because judgments in defamation suits have in some cases can run into the tens of millions of dollars, some television people might prefer ancient Roman law to present U.S. laws.

Defamation is the communication to a third party of false and injurious ideas that tend to lower the community's estimation of the person, expose him to contempt or ridicule, or injure him in his personal or professional life. **Libel** is defamation by written or printed word and is generally considered more serious than **slander,** which is defamation by spoken words or gestures. As in all cases of defamation the injured person must be apparent to the audience (although not necessarily specifically named) and negligence on the part of the defendant (in this discussion, the journalist) must be established. In addition, the false statement must have been presented or interpreted by an average reader/viewer as fact.

Since the average cost of defending a libel or slander suit is more than $250,000, many stations and production agencies have insurance against libel and slander. But, insurance is expensive, and a poor substitute for a basic knowledge of the law.

Depending on the state, a false statement that is broadcast may be viewed as either libel or slander. The reasoning in some states is that when a statement is presented from a written script, it implies more forethought than an ad-lib comment and should be considered libel, just as a defamatory statement in a newspaper or magazine is considered libel. In some states courts have ruled that defamatory ad-lib statements are more spontaneous and "less considered" and should therefore be treated as slander. A few states have removed all distinctions between libel and slander. Ultimately, of course, the decision rests with the particular court.

Per Se and Per Quod Defamation

Defamation can be of two types: per se and per quod. When a statement is defamatory "on its face" without the need of additional information or knowledge, it is called **per se defamation.** Erroneously stating that a certain person is a "Communist" would be considered per se defamation. All the erroneous and damaging facts are conveyed by the statement. The "statement" could be either written or visual.

In the latter case it could be a picture of Sam Smith with the words "Member, Communist Party" keyed over the picture.

In **per quod** defamation additional facts are needed. To erroneously state that Sally Smith lives at 101 Park Street would not constitute defamation until the additional fact that this address is a known house of prostitution is taken into consideration. In this case the quite respectable Mrs. Sally Smith might be justified in initiating a per quod defamation case. In general, injury is presumed by the court in a per se offense and it is not necessary for the injured person to prove actual damage. However, in per quod cases the plaintiff typically must prove actual damage.

Trade Libel

Companies, corporations or groups can be damaged just as badly as individuals. Untrue statements that are broadcast about products—"all X-brand cars are 'lemons'"—can cost the manufacturers thousands of dollars in sales and result in trade libel suits. In addition to being almost impossible to prove, such statements carry connotations of actual malice. (Actual malice, which is an extremely important consideration in defamation cases, is seen as disregard for a statement's lack of truth and known falsity.) Instead of using a capricious word like "lemon," a carefully verified statement like "in Tazewell County 350 of the 400 X-brand cars sold in 1995 were returned to the dealer for transmission repairs within 10 days of purchase" could be used. Not only is the latter statement much more responsible, but it conveys essential information on the nature of the problem.

Legal Defenses against Defamation Suits

In a defamation suit there are three possible defenses: truth, fair comment and privilege.

Truth   A defense of **truth**—proving that the statement in question is, in fact, true—may not be as simple as it appears. Sometimes courts have required that the defense prove every detail of a statement, a task that can be difficult. There is one unusual case on record in which an Indiana man sued for libel because he was accused of stealing ten sheep. The defense of "truth" fell through and the plaintiff was awarded libel damages when it was proven that, in fact, fourteen sheep had been stolen. Generally, however, courts require that the defendant needs to establish only that the statement in question is true in substance.

Many people assume that if video producers or broadcasters accurately attribute a defamatory statement to the person who said it, they can escape legal action. Not so. A policeman at the scene of an accident in which three people were killed may say, "The accident was caused by John Smith, who was drunk." Even if it seems clear that John Smith was driving while intoxicated, the fact may not be able to be substantiated legally perhaps because of a technicality. Without substantiation, Smith may choose to sue a broadcaster who quoted the policeman.

Fair Comment   The courts have long held that the media are entitled to comment on people and issues, even when those comments are seen as being derogatory. The exception consists of comments that can be proven to be motivated by malice. A highly significant 1974 Supreme Court Case, *Gertz vs. Welch,* stated that "under the First Amendment there is no such thing as a false idea. However pernicious an opinion may seem, we depend for its correction not on the conscience of judges and juries but on the competition of other ideas." Although this sweeping language was narrowed somewhat by subsequent court decisions, Gertz is still commonly cited in issues of fair comment. (But remember, we're talking about ideas expressed as "comment," not ideas put forth as provable or unprovable "fact.")

Privilege   The last defense against libel is privilege. Privilege is generally limited to statements by public officials and statements made during legislative and judicial proceedings. For example, members of the U.S. Congress have a constitutional guarantee against libel or slander in statements made on the floor of either House, regardless of the question of malice. When a privileged proceeding is broadcast or videotaped, the broadcaster is protected against libel, assuming that the presentation is not edited or altered to reflect malice on the part of the broadcaster.

Under another form of privilege, producers and broadcasters can air opinions on matters of public interest. This was established early in libel law when a performing group sued a newspaper for publishing a highly derogatory review of their stage performance. The performers lost the case. The court decided that people who go on stage can be freely criticized, as long as no malice or "evil purposes" can be proven. It was at this point that an important legal distinction between public and private individuals was established. After finding themselves in the "public spotlight" (either by design or accident), people forfeit much of the legal protection they previously had against public criticism and invasion of privacy.

Honest Mistakes

To err may be human, but honest mistakes still cause damage, and the courts have held that false statements arising from accident, error, or carelessness may still be subject to settlement. However, once again, the severity of the offense is seen as being much greater if some type of malice can be proven and if the individual is not a public figure. In the previous example in which it was erroneously stated that Sally Smith lives at 101 Park Street (a known house of prostitution), the writer could say that it was "an honest mistake" caused by a typing error and that no actual malice was present. But Mrs. Smith (who lives at 9101 Park Street) might still be justified in launching a defamation suit if damage in the form of public ridicule and humiliation resulted from this "honest mistake."

Confronting Lawsuits

With this discussion as a background, it should be obvious that the best defense is no offense, and that producers must carefully check any questionable material before broadcast or distribution. At one TV station, the writer-producer subjects her work to a series of credibility checks. A questionable segment is viewed by the executive producer, by the news director and by the station's attorneys before broadcast. But, even after due care, what if you are still served a subpoena?

Handling Subpoenas

First of all, if the plaintiff's attorney asks you for background on the broadcast, be cautious. By agreeing you could weaken your rights under an existing shield law. Second, if a subpoena is issued, notify your lawyer and a superior at once. Any action to suppress a subpoena must be taken immediately to be most effective. Third, never agree to hand over a tape or transcript of the segment in question unless ordered to by the court.

Producers should also be aware that they should never make a comment regarding the truth of the challenged statement to anyone except their lawyers. If an error is broadcast and a producer says, "I'm really sorry, I was in a hurry and I just didn't check my facts," this could constitute an admission of guilt, even a "reckless disregard for the truth," which could constitute malice. Many cases have been lost after such admissions.

Issuing Corrective Statements

But if a definite error in fact is discovered after it has been telecast, you should immediately air a full corrective statement with an apology. This may not eliminate a lawsuit, but it frequently has served to reduce the damages awarded.

Staging

Staging applies to news and documentary work; in its negative sense it involves the alteration or misrepresentation of a situation. The motivation for such activity can range from a blatant effort to alter the truth to a subtle attempt to enhance the look of a scene. If staged footage is broadcast and it represents a conscious effort to alter the truth in a news story, the alteration can result in fines by the Federal Communications Commission. Simply "enhancing a scene," on the other hand, may be more a legal than an ethical issue. Let's look at two examples.

Unacceptable Staging

First, let's say you are taping an interview with a bereaved father of a boy who was shot by a policeman. During a shoot-out the unarmed boy was mistaken for a criminal. Let's also assume there has been a public outcry over the incident and that the family has gotten a number of letters of sympathy. You arrange to videotape a short interview of the father sitting at his desk, and you want to emphasize the public response to the incident. Since the few letters he has received seem "lost" on his big desk, you decide that it would make the picture much more dramatic if you borrowed a few dozen letters from your office and piled them on his desk.

Although the story becomes more dramatic as a result of your actions, you have changed the truth, and you are guilty of misrepresenting the facts. If the deceit becomes known, both you and your news department face a loss of credibility and possible disciplinary action. Furthermore, a pattern of misrepresentation of this type could threaten the station's broadcast license.

Questionable Staging

Second, let's assume that you are doing the same interview but, instead of misrepresenting the mail response, you simply ask the man to get a framed 8 × 10 photo of the dead boy from another room. You then place the photo on the desk so that it assumes a dominant position in the visual frame. This situation presents an ethical issue—one that some people would say constitutes an example of acceptable staging. Although the large photo sitting on the desk would, indeed, embellish the dramatic statement surrounding the father's loss, you have altered the reality of the situation by suggesting that the photo normally assumes a dominant position on the man's desk. Some videographers and reporters see nothing wrong with minor staging of this nature; others feel that tampering with the truth in any way violates their own code of professional and personal ethics.

To some degree altering a scene for the benefit of composition, lighting, sound or visual clarity is a normal and expected part of videography. For example, you might have to bring extra lights to the interview. Strictly speaking, in the process you are altering the reality of the situation. Or you might note before the interview that some polished brass bookends on a desk are highly distracting and ask if they can be removed during the interview. Again, you have altered the situation. On the other hand, a professional and ethical distinction can be made between removing distractions or optimizing technical quality, and altering or distorting the essential elements of a story.

Acceptable Staging

Let's say that you are doing an ENG story on the passing of the gavel from an outgoing president of a civic organization to the new president. You might find that the actual event was awkwardly done, the lighting was bad, or that your camera's view was blocked by a member of the audience. It would be reasonable (and probably even expected) for you and other members of the press to ask for a re-enactment of the event. In fact, since such occasions are often intended as "media events" anyway, the authenticity of such moments is almost never an issue.

When Authenticity Is an Issue

Sometimes the authenticity of an actual event is important. Trying to restage the moment when an athlete cleared the pole to set a world high-jump record would be an entirely different matter than the passing of the gavel to a new president of a civic organization. Another example of unacceptable staging would occur if you arranged an event for a news or documentary piece. Let's say you are doing a documentary on an inner-city gang, and as part of the program you want to show a controversial initiation procedure. Let's assume that you contact the leader of the gang who decides to cooperate, but you find that the initiation of the last gang member took place a month earlier and another initiation is not planned. At this point you suggest that the gang restage the last initiation ceremony for the benefit of your camera. After discussing your camera and sound needs and suggesting the gang members you would like in the segment, they agree.

Is there a problem with this situation? Most definitely, at least if you later represent the staged initiation as being the original. For one thing, you created this initiation ceremony solely for the sake of the documentary; otherwise it wouldn't have taken place. And, since the ceremony was staged solely to accommodate the needs of the documentary, there is the question of just how authentic it would end up being and how much it would be altered—both by you and by the gang members—in the interest of the documentary. If the ceremony were quite important to your documentary and you didn't mind a certain loss of authenticity, keying the word "re-enactment" over the staged scene might solve the problem.

Using "Comparable Footage"

Although it's not considered staging per se, a related issue that frequently comes up is the use of "comparable footage" in editing news and documentary pieces. As a videotape editor in a highly competitive news market you might be tempted to cover today's lack of good footage of a forest fire with some dramatic scenes from a similar fire that happened last year. Or you might be tempted to cut in some unused scenes from yesterday's fire in today's story on the same forest fire. All professional and ethical issues aside, you should be aware that the FCC has taken a very dim view of such substitutions, unless the substitution is made quite clear to the viewing audience. Simply keying the phrase "file footage" or an earlier date over the footage will suffice.

DRAMATIC LICENSE

In contrast to the guidelines covering news and documentary production is the use of *dramatic license* in dramatic production. For example, several well-known feature films on Vietnam have been shot in the Philippines because the landscape is similar and, at the time, it was safer and more economical. If the scene of the gang initiation were part of a dramatic feature film, staging would not only be acceptable but, given the nature of feature film production, essential. Suffice it to say that in dramatic productions, the audience does not expect to be told what is and is not authentic, but news and documentary production is an entirely different matter.

COPYRIGHTED MATERIALS

Music, illustrations and published passages are almost always copyrighted and cannot be used for profit or general distribution without *clearance* or permission from the copyright holder. Occasionally, this permission is granted without charge, and requires only on-screen credit. More often a fee must be paid to the copyright holder. Using a copyrighted work without permission can result in a $25,000 fine and one year in prison. (That's for a first offense; it gets even worse after that.) At the same time, you can feel reasonably safe using copyrighted material to create videos that will be viewed only by family members, or once by a video production class.[3] However, if you are producing the video for profit (for example, taping someone's wedding for pay), or you intend to enter the piece in a video contest (for which prizes are awarded), not only will you need permission to use copyrighted material, but you will also need a signed release from the principal talent. (Talent releases will be discussed later.)

There is one area of exception to all this. Footage and music from any and all (past and present) works by the federal government can be used without permis-

---

[3] The law states that the presentation "must be without any purpose of direct or indirect commercial advantage; and it must be without payment of any fee for the performance to any performers, promoters or organizers; and there must be no direct or indirect admission charge." There are exceptions in the law, however, for educational, religious or charitable purposes.

sion. This means, for example, that you can use some World War II footage done by the War Department. But watch out for productions done for the federal government by an outside production agency. Whatever non-government material they contributed will undoubtedly be copyrighted.

The Fair Use Act

An admittedly vague and, therefore, frequently debated part of copyright law is the fair use act. The **fair use act** allows copyrighted material to be used in limited ways for the purpose of criticism, teaching, scholarship, or research without the permission of the copyright holder. Also included in this act is the use of these materials in news. Although this area of copyright law is in dire need of clarification, many have assumed that, under the uses specified, portions of the copyrighted works can be used for a limited time, as long as such use does not appreciably affect the income that could be derived from the work by the copyright holder. Even under these conditions, however, more than one copyright holder has chosen to launch a copyright infringement case.

MUSIC

Works in Public Domain

Any work whose copyright has expired is considered in the **public domain,** which means it can be used without permission. But, in the case of music, watch out. Although the original version of a composition may be in public domain, recent arrangements, including works derived from the original, can be and probably are copyrighted.

ASCAP and BMI Music Licenses

It is important to note that the standard **ASCAP** (American Society of Composers, Authors and Publishers) and **BMI** (Broadcast Music Incorporated) performing rights license, which broadcast stations must have in order to play musical selections on the air, does not cover the use of music in commercials, public service announcements and productions. These licenses cover only the standard on-air broadcast of recordings, such as you would find featured on most music radio stations.

At the same time, ASCAP and BMI track the royalties due for musical use and can get you started in securing rights to the music (check the label of the recording to see which applies to the work in question).

Securing Rights to Use Music

Obtaining clearance is normally a three-step process.

- First, you need to request a synchronization license from the music copyright owner, which grants you permission to use the music for the interval needed.
- Second, you must negotiate with the record company for dubbing rights to obtain permission to use the recording produced by the specific record firm.
- Third, you must obtain permission from any vocal or instrumental artist featured in the recording.

Since this three-step process can be cumbersome and time-consuming, video producers commonly use the services of agencies that specialize in securing music clearance. These agencies can quickly find the owner of a copyright, negotiate a fee, and obtain written permission to use the music.

Music Libraries

Music production libraries, which exist in many cities to serve the needs of producers, contain cleared versions of all types of pop and classical music. In this case payment is made to the library only once, and the production may feature the music indefinitely, or for the time specified. If the terms of usage change (when the production is re-done or substantially changed, for example), this change must be reported to the library.

Many production facilities purchase CDs or DATs of a vast array of music and sound-effect recordings designed specifically for production use. Along with the purchase come the rights to use the collection as needed. The musical selections in these libraries are easier to cut and edit than most popular songs because they have been written with the needs of the video and film producer in mind. In the case of sound effects, complete libraries of recordings are routinely transferred onto a hard disk, to be instantly called up during the computerized editing process.

Advantages of Original Music

Many producers prefer to use original music. Not only does this solve clearance problems, but since the music is tailored to the production, it can meet the pace, mood and time requirements of the scenes. There is another important advantage of using original music. Many compositions, especially recent popular songs, have emotional baggage associated with them. The music may bring to mind a scene in a movie or a specific situation in a music video. Although this reminder might seem desirable, it can also be unpredictable; people react to films and videos in different ways. For this reason it is often better to start off with a "clean psychological slate" and use music that you know has no "baggage" associated with it.

If original music involves numerous musicians or an orchestra that must abide by the requirements of a union contract, producing original music can be costly. However, if the background music is relatively simple (for example, a guitar, flute or organ) and it is performed by the composer, original music can be done rather inexpensively.

Synthesized Music

Today, music synthesizers and MIDI samplers create music for the majority of dramatic TV productions. In the hands of an expert, a synthesizer and sampler can duplicate anything from a single instrument to a full orchestra. Since synthesizers and MIDI samplers can also be used to create almost any needed sound effect, this equipment is also being used with editing workstations to create and synchronize sound effects with video. The use of synthesizers has mitigated many of the cost and copyright problems previously associated with the use of music and effects.

OTHER TYPES OF COPYRIGHTED WORKS

Music, of course, is not the only medium that is copyrighted. Text from books, magazines and newspapers, as well as drawings, photos, videotapes and voice recordings are almost always copyrighted. Except in news, where, in most cases, a limited portion of a work may be used if it directly ties in with a story, copyrighted materials cannot be included in a production without the permission of the copyright holder. With most published materials, clearance is a two-step process: getting permission from the publisher or producer and getting permission from the author or talent involved. Sometimes permission will be given with only a request for a credit at the end of the production; other times the copyright holder will request a fee or royalty. In the latter case the producer will have to decide if the use of the copyrighted material warrants the fee requested.

Whatever the case, since verbal agreements are difficult to later substantiate, it is important to get the agreement in writing. Such agreements should clearly outline usage terms, including the fee paid, a description of the copyrighted material, the name of the production, and the broadcast or syndication time frame.

As we've noted, there are depositories of audio and video materials that exist solely to serve the needs of film and video producers. These libraries contain a range of films, videotapes, photos and drawings on almost every subject. Anything from drawings of World War I battles to video of the most recent *Playboy* playmate is available. The fee charged, which gives the user rights to use the material under agreed upon conditions, is based on such things as acquisition costs, talent fees, and duplication expenses.

Figure 14.2 Digitized video scanners have made it possible for video artists to use a copyrighted photo or drawing as the basis for their own electronically-embellished creations. Whether or not the final result bears much resemblance to the original, an artist will be in violation of copyright laws if usage permission is not secured for the source material. In these illustrations, an original photo and two electronically altered versions are shown.

Electronically Altered Materials

Digitized Images

Digitized video scanners have made it possible for video artists to use a copyrighted photo or drawing as the basis of their own electronically embellished creations. Although the final result (after it is resized, recolored, solarized, reversed, or otherwise altered) may bear little resemblance to the original material, there still is a copyright issue. If the original artist, photographer, or publisher recognizes her material, she may choose to pursue a case of copyright infringement (Figure 14.2).

Sampling Audio Recordings

The wide use of audio sampling to copy and then, to varying degrees, alter sections of copyrighted music in the electronic creation of new (and presumably original) compositions brings up another controversial area of copyright law. If electronically sampled music or effects used in the building of music or effects are recognizable by the original artists, a copyright infringement lawsuit can be launched. Recently, several cases have been launched after an artist recognized that a sampled section of his work was included in the composition of another artist.

RELEASES

Talent releases (also called *model releases* and *personal releases*) grant a videographer or producer permission to "publish" (broadcast or distribute) a "person's likeness" (picture), with or without compensation, under the conditions specified in the release. When it comes to the need for talent releases, news is treated differently from other types of production. In news and ENG work the courts have recognized that it is impractical to require subjects to sign releases prior to the broadcast of footage. However, in producing segments that do not come under the heading of "news," the rules change. Except for subjects in public places who are unrecognizable and appear as "background" to your scenes, it is wise to always have releases signed. This would be especially important if the person's appearance contributed to any type of "commercial compensation," or if the person appeared in scenes shot on private property.

Most producers make it a habit to have releases signed before taping starts. This procedure can help avoid problems when, after a production is shot (and production expenses incurred), the people involved decide to hold out for more favorable terms. Having a witness sign the release helps ensure that after the fact objections don't arise.

The sample talent release shown in Figure 14.3 is a brief and all-encompassing release. (Some legal authorities would say it is too brief and too all-encompassing to meet captious needs.) Whenever possible, a talent release should go beyond this and specify usage, including the specific production, broadcast or distribution conditions, specific fees paid (if any), and any other conditions and terms.

Having a signed talent release doesn't automatically protect you from all possible suits. (A lawyer may try to prove compulsion, misrepresentation, or that you exceeded the conditions of the release.) However, once signed, most subjects rightly feel that a suit will be on tenuous legal ground.

Location releases may be required in some instances, when permission is necessary for shooting images of certain locations. Facilities where admission is charged, including some popular theme parks, constitute an example. Figure 14.4 illustrates one type of location release. In this case you are not dealing with a need to simply photograph a location, but to bring in an entire production crew (and associated equipment, props and possibly set pieces) for the sake of shooting one or more scenes in a production. This sample release is quite general; the ones used by major production companies are far more complex.

TALENT RELEASE FORM

Talent Name _____

_____

I hereby consent for value received and without further consideration or compensation to the use (full or in part) of all videotapes taken of me and/or recordings made of my voice and/or written extraction, in whole or in part, of such recordings or musical performance

at _____   on _____ 19 _____
　　　　　　(Recording location)　　　　　　　　　(Month)　　(Day)　　(Year)

by _____   for _____
　　　　　　　(Producer)　　　　　　　　　　　　　(Producing organization)

for the purposes of illustration, broadcast, or distribution in any manner.

Talent's signature _____

Address _____   City _____

State _____   Zip code _____

Date ____/____/____

_____

If the subject is a minor under the laws of the state where modeling, acting, or performing is done:

Legal guardian _____   Guardian _____
　　　　　　　　　(Signature)　　　　　　　　　　　(Please Print)

Address _____   City _____

State _____   Zip code _____

Date ____/____/____

Figure 14.3   Talent Release Form

LOCATION RELEASE FORM

Having full authority to do so, I hereby grant _____
permission to use the property at _____ for the purposes of
photographing and recording scenes for the production _____ during
the hours of _____ on the following days: _____

_____

Permission includes, but is not limited to, the right to bring cast, crew, equipment, props
and temporary sets onto the premises for the time specified.

Total compensation for the specified time period will be: _____

If the property is available beyond the specified time period, compensation will be at the rate of
_____ per _____ .

I understand that all items brought onto the premises will be removed at the end of the
production period and that the location, including buildings, landscaping and all things associated with same will be fully returned to their original condition, except as mutually agreed
upon and indicated below.

_____

_____

It is further understood that any damage to the property will become the responsibility of
the production agency and any needed repair or restoration will be carried out within 14 days
of the last specified day of production.

Property Agent	**Production Agent**
Signature _____	Signature _____
Printed name _____	Printed name _____
Title _____	Title _____
Street address _____	Street address _____
_____	_____
Phone number _____	Phone number _____
Date _____	Date _____

Figure 14.4   Location Release Form

15 ALLIED FIELDS AND CAREERS

IN THE FIRST part of this chapter we'll look at the two major divisions of non-broadcast video: institutional video and *private video,* or the use of video equipment to meet personal and avocational needs. In the second part of the chapter we'll turn our attention to careers, job preparation and personal attributes associated with success.

When most people think of television they think of broadcasting. Although broadcast television is the most visible and prominent part of the television business, this visibility is deceptive. In terms of personnel and equipment, the largest segment of television is actually associated with non-broadcast production. Throughout this chapter we will refer to this set of activities as institutional video.

OVERVIEW

Included in the category of **institutional video** are corporate, religious, educational, medical and governmental applications. This general non-broadcast area is variously referred to as corporate video, non-broadcast television, institutional video, professional video, and private television.

Although the field of institutional video may not be as visible or glamorous as over-the-air broadcasting, for the aspiring television professional it holds a number of important advantages. In addition to being larger in terms of personnel and equipment, salaries are often higher, job security is better, working hours and conditions are much more predictable, and there are typically more "perks."

The primary goal of institutional video, of course, is to serve the needs of a specific institution or organization. These needs can lie in a wide variety of areas including education and training, management-employee relations, public relations, basic news and information, or marketing for new products and services. We'll look at many of these applications in more detail later.

For some time, the fastest-growing segment of video recording has been private video. As a result of this growth a large number of U.S. families own a camcorder today. As in the case of institutional video, there is no well-defined terminology in this area; however, in this discussion, we are including the range that extends from home videos to various types of personal avocational videography. The latter includes video work intended to directly or indirectly generate revenue.

To start our discussion of institutional and private video, we'll look at a type of video production that spans both broadcast television and institutional video: religious programming.

RELIGIOUS PRODUCTION AND PROGRAMMING

Religious production and programming represents a large component of television production today. Although some of this programming is broadcast through normal TV outlets, a great percentage is available only on satellite or cable channels.

Religious programming can have a wide range of goals, including

- Programming intended to inform an audience about an acute human need, such as hungry children in a third-world country.

- Programming intended to stir an audience to act on a social problem, such as homelessness, drug abuse or teen-age pregnancy.

- Programming designed for instructional and inspirational use, such as talks by a spiritual leader.

- Programming intended to provide basic information, such as a production documenting the work of a particular denomination's missionaries.

- Closed-circuit programming, from regular educational productions delivered by satellite (such as those used by Catholic schools across the country) to simply putting TV cameras in a sanctuary so that an overflow crowd can see the service on TV monitors.

Although religious television has different goals, it shares the same production techniques as institutional television.

Institutional Video

Applications

Institutional video has proven itself in many areas, including

■ *A management-employee link* Without an effective management-to-employee link, morale can suffer and rumors are likely to fill the information vacuum. Institutional video has been especially effective as a tool for supervisors or managers to reach employees with information on policies, progress, or problems; it can also be used to simply relay holiday greetings. Institutional video can be particularly valuable if the institution has branches in various locations.

■ *Instructional video* In an era of ever-accelerating change, the ability to keep employees informed on the latest techniques and developments is a major concern. Video, especially *interactive video,* which can vary a presentation according to user input, has become a powerful tool. Among its many advantages is its ability to use on-camera specialists to provide consistent training. More about this later.

■ *Public relations* A major part of institutional public relations is the dissemination of information both within an organization and to the general public. The information can range from general corporate announcements to crisis management. Television is a natural vehicle for effectively communicating such information. In addition, many institutions regularly create videos to announce new products, research developments, or major institutional changes. These tapes, which are considered a kind of high-tech press release, are sent to the news directors of area TV stations in hopes of getting them on the air. If the news director uses the piece, or even some portions of it—which often happens on a slow news day—the resulting publicity can be well worth the production expenses.

■ *Marketing* New products and services are of little value unless potential consumers know about them. "Point-of-sale" videos, which highlight a new product or service, are common in many retail stores. These are often seen in the home improvement, makeup and hardware departments.

Even more important for marketing are the many products and services designed for specialized audiences. While the mass media may be a cost-effective way of reaching a general audience, it is not a cost-effective way of informing a limited number of people about specialized products and services. For example, if a large manufacturer of farm equipment introduces a self-propelled combine with many new features, a way is needed to demonstrate and detail these features to the relatively small number of farmers across the country (and possibly around the world) who might be interested. By producing a videotape of this new combine and distributing it to dealers, not only will the dealers be informed about the new equipment, but interested farmers may also want to view the tape at their farm-equipment dealer.

Structure

Workers in the field of institutional video fall into two categories: those who work full-time for an institution that has a television production division, and those who work for the many independent production facilities that routinely take on institutional projects under contract. Even if productions are contracted out to an independent production facility, media personnel within an institution must have a knowledge of video production techniques and be able to effectively coordinate the work of these outside professionals.

Organization

Today, the organization of institutional production can typically take one of four approaches:

    1. *A fully staffed and equipped in-house department that produces all its own productions*

    2. *A fully staffed and equipped in-house department that not only produces videos for its own organization, but also brings in additional revenue from outside sources* This department can produce programming for other organizations or rent its facilities to other agencies whenever the staff is available.

    3. *The maintenance of a full-time staff to handle routine in-house work, while contracting out major productions that require more specialized facilities, equipment, and personnel* For example, by drawing on scores of free-lance producers, some of the large U.S. corporations are able to turn out more than 150 productions a year.

    4. *The maintenance of a partially staffed in-house facility that uses outside contractors (also called outside vendors) to do all basic production work* In these cases the in-house staff is used to initiate, guide and coordinate work that has been contracted to independent production facilities. This arrangement offers several advantages to the company. First, it reduces the pay and benefits associated with maintaining a large staff of full-time employees; second, it enables the organization to shop around for the best talent and prices for each project; third, it can readily be expanded or reduced, as needed, to keep pace with the varying (often seasonal) production needs of the organization.

    Whatever the approach, institutional production often requires the help of equipment rental houses that can supplement the in-house equipment. It is rarely cost-effective to purchase expensive equipment only for occasional in-house use.

The Field of Institutional Video

In the early 1990s, it was estimated that more than 35,000 non-broadcast businesses were producing regular television programming in the United States. Since many are not listed in production directories, the number may actually be much larger. The institutions represented include high schools and colleges that have simple facilities designed to develop instructional videos, as well as large corporations that have larger facilities. In the latter case the facilities are often more elaborate than those found in the larger commercial TV stations.

Several professional organizations are associated with institutional video. One of the best-known is the International Television Association (ITVA). Other organizations, such as the International Association of Business Communication, the International Teleproduction Society, and the Society of Motion Picture and Television Engineers (SMPTE) have strong institutional video components.

Areas of Proven Effectiveness

Institutional video has been found to be particularly effective in seven areas:

1. When graphic feedback is necessary
2. When close-ups are required to convey important information
3. When it is necessary to interrelate a wide variety of diverse elements
4. When subject matter can best be seen and understood by altering its speed
5. When special effects such as animation can best convey information
6. When it is difficult to transport specific personnel to needed locations
7. When basic information must be repeated to numerous audiences over time

These areas are discussed in detail in upcoming subsections.

The Power of Immediate Feedback   Sometimes video feedback can be much more effective than even personal feedback from a teacher. For example, the Equestrian Education program at Pepperdine University (Malibu, California) has been in existence for many years. Mr. Jim Wiley, who heads the program, has taught hundreds of students to ride, including Olympic contestants and some well-known Hollywood stars. Classes have intentionally been kept small, allowing Wiley to give students personal feedback on riding problems and techniques. Results of this personal instruction were always positive, but slow. Wiley often had to repeat the same information numerous times before a student would be sufficiently motivated to incorporate the suggestions into actual performances.

When camcorders came along, Wiley started individually videotaping the performance of students (Figure 15.1). Afterward, he would review the tapes—often in slow motion—and use one of the audio tracks on the videotape to record a personal critique for each student. By studying the tapes, the students could clearly see what they were doing while the specific problems were being pointed out. Since Wiley kept careful statistical records of student progress over the years, it was easy to chart the rate of improvement before and after the use of television. After he started using videotapes as an instructional tool, the average rate of student progress accelerated dramatically.

With the advent of high-speed shutters on CCD cameras, which can slice time into clear 1/10,000-second intervals, it has become much easier to study slow

Figure 15.1 After this instructor started using slow-motion studies of student performance as an instructional tool in an equestrian course, the average rate of student progress accelerated dramatically. By studying the tapes, the students can clearly see problems that need to be corrected.

motion playbacks of a wide range of athletic performances. A frame-by-frame study of a golf swing, a tennis return, or a triple somersault can reveal information on athletic performances that can be invaluable to both coaches and performers (Figure 15.2).

The Power of Close-ups   Video is also the best vehicle when information must be shown through close-ups, especially extreme close-ups (Figure 15.3). The video camera can also photograph objects or events that are humanly impossible to witness first-hand. With high-quality video cameras not much bigger than your thumb, it is also possible to get pictures in hazardous and hard-to-reach places. This has been especially important for medical applications, which are discussed later in this chapter.

Interrelating Diverse Elements   Video and film have the unique ability to interrelate elements. For example, if you want to instill an understanding of the artistic dimension of good video lighting, you can start by bringing together a collection of artistic masterpieces illustrating how form and texture have traditionally been emphasized by lighting. From here you can move to samples of well-lit scenes from classic films. After instilling an artistic perspective, you can then move to video and look at the effect of various lighting approaches in television. The resulting perspective will be much different than if you initially approach lighting from the perspective of typical lighting instruments and optimum light levels as revealed by a waveform monitor.

Figure 15.2   With the advent of high-speed shutters on CCD cameras, which can slice time into clear 1/10,000-second intervals, it has become much easier to study slow motion playbacks of a wide range of athletic performances. A frame-by-frame study of a golf swing, a tennis return or a track star clearing a hurdle can reveal information on athletic performances that can be an invaluable aid to both coaches and performers.

As we noted in Chapter 11, the interrelationship of visual elements in a production generates its own meaning and emotional response. With the video medium, meaning can be conveyed much more powerfully and convincingly than by words alone. A primary factor is television's ability to engage the viewer with sight, sound and motion—all at once. This combination of elements opens the door to affecting the emotions; once these feelings are tapped, messages can be much more compelling.

For example, you might be assigned to do an environmental piece demonstrating the effects of ocean pollution on sea life. Since a link between pollution and environmental destruction needs to be established (and the two phenomena can be separated by many miles), you might decide to intercut shots of blameworthy factories dumping pollutants into a river with the negative environmental effects on sea life. You would assume that seeing such things as devastated coral reefs and dead fish and birds would evoke a negative emotional response in viewers. It is only by visually linking the cause and the effect that this relationship could be established.

Here is another example, one that shows how corporate television can be used to the benefit of both the corporation and its employees. A study within a large corporation found a strong correlation between smoking and health-related job

Figure 15.3 Video can be highly effective in revealing information through close-ups. Here, the detail in a leaf is shown in a way that would be almost impossible to see with the unaided eye.

absenteeism. From a purely economic standpoint, it was decided that if a documentary could convince only 14 percent of employees to stop smoking, the total cost of the production could be recouped within three years.

Since most of the harmful effects of smoking aren't immediately apparent, you would need to bring cause and effect together. The point could be made rather dramatically by showing long-time smokers with severe emphysema, including some who are forced to use oxygen bottles in a cart in order to breathe. A cross section of a blackened lung from an autopsy of a four-pack-a-day smoker might also dramatically make a point. However, problems can result when highly dramatic approaches are used. (See "Problems with Overstatement" in this chapter.)

Altering Time   The next major advantage of video, especially in the institutional setting, lies in its ability to alter events in ways that make information more accessible and understandable. Although we may witness a key football play in real time, it may not be until we see the slow-motion playback that we are able to fully understand what took place.

A number of years ago a large Canadian paper mill put a high-speed, pulp-to-paper machine into operation, the kind that produces the huge rolls of newsprint used by newspapers. At low speeds the machine worked fine, but each time the machine reached full speed the paper would tear and the facility would be transformed into a confetti factory. At full speed the machine simply moved too fast to enable observers to see where the problem developed.

After repeated failures and many hours of cleaning up the resulting messes, the corporation called on a production company with high-speed photographic equipment. Bright lights were set up to illuminate every recess of the machine. The start-up process was repeated once more.

When the footage was played back, seconds were transformed into minutes. As the machine reached full speed, a slow tear started to appear in a span of paper between two high-speed rollers. As soon as the tear was complete (within a fraction of a second in real time) the supply of paper suddenly had nowhere to go. Instantly, it flew throughout the room, entered parts of the machine and was chewed up. It then became evident that some of the moving parts were out of balance, and at high speed the rollers shifted enough to tear the already taut paper. Once the problem was seen, it could be fixed.

At the other end of the scale are the **time-and-motion studies** intended to speed up actions. Most of us see a period of many hours represented in just a few seconds every night on our local television station. Satellite weather photos taken at regular intervals and displayed in succession create a time-lapse photographic record of cloud and storm movements over many hours.

In the corporate arena, an hour's work by a secretary sitting in an office, for example, can be compressed into ten or fifteen seconds. In this way the full pattern of actions over a period of time can be studied. Awkward, repeated movements become obvious. For example, it might become evident that although a telephone seems nicely positioned on the desk, a secretary, who spends much of her time at the computer keyboard, must regularly reposition herself to answer the phone. And, although having a filing cabinet on either side of the desk might be aesthetically pleasing, through a time-and-motion study it might become evident that considerable time and energy are wasted over the course of eight hours simply moving from one cabinet to another. Photographic studies of assembly-line workers have also revealed awkward motions that not only resulted in fatigue, but contributed to assembly-line errors.

Although film was originally the only medium that could be used to alter time, today special video equipment can both compress and expand time. With this powerful tool at their disposal, video personnel should be familiar with the basics of altering time. Here are two examples.

Let's assume that a company wants to study the effects of a new industrial solvent that takes 30 minutes to work. Let's further assume that the department involved would like to include a demonstration of the solvent in a production intended to introduce the new product to corporate executives and sales personnel. Watching a solvent slowly attack a surface for 30 minutes would not only take up all the production time (and set a new record for boring television), but the effects of the solvent would be lost to viewers over this lengthy time span. However, by compressing the 30 minutes into 20 seconds, the process would become clear. The question then becomes how to convert 30 minutes to 20 seconds.

Since the production is intended to be played back on standard VCRs (running at a standard NTSC frame-rate of 30 per second) the only practical solution is to alter the camera recording frame-rate. As a standard rule, if we shoot fewer than 30 frames per second, we will (on playback) speed up time; if we shoot more than 30 frames per second we'll slow down time. The trick is to know just how much to speed up or slow down the camera recording rate.

Our solvent example, in which we need to condense 30 minutes into 20 seconds, can be diagrammed as follows:

30 frames per second for 20 seconds	=	600 frames
600 frames divided by 30 minutes	=	20 frames per minute
20 frames per minute	=	one frame every 5 seconds

Thus, by recording (or editing) one frame every five seconds, 30 minutes can be shown in 20 seconds. The same basic approach of dividing the total number of frames needed by the actual time of an event will work for other time-compression problems as well. Here's another problem: if a rose takes 30 hours to bloom, how can the process be shown in one second? (Answer: by taking a frame every hour for 30 hours.) What if we want to show the same rose blooming, but this time show it in five seconds? (Rounded-off answer: by capturing one video frame every 10 minutes.)

Now let's reverse things and expand time. Let's say that the industrial solvent we talked about earlier was found to be too slow. Another department discovers that a high-powered laser beam will do the job in just one second. In order to make necessary adjustments in the laser the department needs to study the progressive effects of the high-powered beam over a period of at least six seconds. How many frames per second are necessary to slow down the action?

30 (frames-per-second) × 6 seconds = 180 frames-per-second

So by increasing the camera recording speed by a factor of six, an event that takes one second can be stretched out over a six-second period.

Animation   One of video's real strengths is in representing and explaining concepts through animation and visual effects. Even though the time-lapse photogra-

phy previously mentioned falls into this category, we're primarily talking about artificially generated illustrations designed to show complex ideas in a simplified fashion. Although computer-generated drawings can be effective in illustrating concepts, the real strength of video lies in adding illustrative movement—in animating sequences.

Animation can be defined as the presentation of a succession of still images in such a way as to give an illusion of continuous movement. The illustrations in Figure 15.4 show how a succession of still photos can be combined to create continuous movement. Note that each frame represents a discrete step in the movement sequence. Although creating the picture-by-picture and frame-by-frame animation process is quite time-consuming and, therefore, costly, the effectiveness of the results often justifies the expense.

In recent years computer-based technology has significantly reduced the cost of animation. Today, electronic paint (graphic) programs can simplify the animation process by using basic instructions to extrapolate an animated sequence. Using Figure 15.4 as an example, an electronic artist can program the beginning frame and the ending frame of the sequence and the computer can electronically create the intermediate steps (frames) of movement. As computing power has expanded and the costs have come down, animation has become a much more attractive production option.

Related to this is the process of **morphing,** whereby a computer is given a starting image and an ending image; the program calculates and displays the intermediate steps as a fluid transition between the two images.

Portable Expertise   The next major advantage for video in institutional settings is the ability to videotape recognized experts and make this expertise readily accessible over time to many people in many places. Although this advantage is taken for granted today, in the beginning of institutional video, being able to disseminate information in this form was a major step forward. Not only does a recognized expert carry a lot of weight, but the information is likely to be very timely and accurate. Such things often make up for deficiencies in presentation polish.

Replication Advantages   The last major advantage of institutional video production lies in the cost savings derived from being able to repeat presentations. Al-

Figure 15.4 In recent years computer-based technology has significantly reduced the cost of animation by using basic instructions to extrapolate an animated sequence. Using this simple sequence of still frames as an example, an electronic artist can program the beginning frame and the ending frame of the sequence and the computer can electronically create the intermediate frames.

though there may be a substantial cost involved in doing a production, once done, many videotapes can be used for months or possibly even years.

Let's assume that a corporation spends $10,000 on a simple, 60-minute production designed to indoctrinate new employees. (The content would typically include a basic explanation of benefits, insurance options, retirement, sick leave, vacation options, and explanation of the many forms that have to be periodically filled out.) Let's also assume that when the various branches of the corporation are considered, the company hires about 850 employees per year. Finally, let's assume that the basic subject matter of the production can last five years without a major revision. This means that the audience for the production will total about 3,000 persons. In terms of cost-per-viewing, the amount is only about $4.25 per person.

In determining the cost-effectiveness of this production, three factors should be considered: first, the session would take about an hour and the personnel representative and the new employees would both be making much more than $4.25 in hourly wages; second, the new-employee sessions would have to be scheduled around the responsibilities of everyone involved; third, having to repeat the same information over and over for each new employee would not be the most effective use of a personnel person's time. When all these things are taken into consideration, a video production may well be a cost-effective and desirable option.

A second example illustrates another aspect of this issue. A number of years ago the architectural department of a large university wanted to include the ideas of a well-known and highly creative architect in its curriculum. However, the man, who was semi-retired in Europe, had no interest in traveling to the United States. Arrangements were made to send a production crew to his home, where he had many photographs and models of his work. A highly informative interview was conducted and the many photos and models were used as B-roll to illustrate the discussion. Because of this production, the university had much more than a single "personal appearance"; it had a clearly illustrated and highly informative production that could be used for many years. By offering this interview to other universities for a standard rental fee, the university could also, over time, recoup a good percentage of its production expenses.

Today, education represents the largest segment of institutional video. There are hundreds of companies that specialize in producing informational, educational and instructional productions for schools. One of the best-known sources of daily informational programming for grade schools is the Channel One service. Although this news and information service was at first quite controversial because of its commercial content, soon more than 10,000 U.S. schools were using the programming on a regular basis.

Medical Applications

Cameras can now be incorporated into small fiber optic probes, which can examine the condition and functioning of living organisms. Prior to the development of these endoscopic techniques, problems could only be clearly seen during an autopsy—after it was too late to do anything about them.

A camera over an operating table can document noteworthy medical procedures either for a closed-circuit audience or, through videotape, for later review by physicians and medical students. Although remote-control video cameras are typically mounted above the operating table, cameras and lights strapped to the headbands of surgeons are also used. Such close-ups are far superior to what students, residents and interns can see from a traditional operating-room observation theater.

Today, most of the large medical facilities have production centers. Both standard NTSC and high-definition video systems are used. Many medical production facilities are now interconnected by video networks so that productions can be shared.

The pharmaceutical and medical supply companies comprise a major source of medical productions. These productions are designed not only for hospitals, clinics and educational facilities, but for viewing by the general public via special health-related cable and satellite channels. Many physicians also routinely use videotapes in their offices to explain surgical techniques to patients.

Problems with Overstatement

Admittedly, attempts to change behavior or beliefs are associated more frequently with institutional video than with standard broadcast productions. However, in attempting to persuade an audience, especially a well-educated one, you must be careful not to overstate points. To do so can result in a wholesale rejection of your ideas if your points are exaggerated or overly dramatized. In extreme circumstances a reversal of the intended effect can take place. Early drug films, for example, were so emotionally overstated that they ended up being ludicrous. This resulted in a wholesale rejection of all the arguments presented. It was assumed that everything said in the productions was fallacious, even when perfectly valid points were made. Today's audiences are rather wary of being manipulated, especially by those they perceive as having vested interests.

This issue is a particular problem in corporate video where the interests of companies and employees are sometimes perceived as not coinciding. While accurately representing the goals of an employer, the corporate television producer must approach productions from the perspective of the needs and interests of the target audience. The ability to satisfy these two factions often ends up being a producer's most difficult task.

Institutional Program Formats

Although most institutional productions incorporate more than one content format, it may be helpful to isolate the various formats for the sake of discussion.

First is the **lecture format.** In terms of holding audience interest over time, this format is by far the least effective. Without an array of attention-holding audio and video embellishments, the success of this format rests entirely on the skill of on-camera talent. Probably the worst version of the lecture format is the so-called "chalk talk," in which speakers stand at a podium and occasionally write notes on a chalkboard while turning their backs to the camera. The presentation can be slightly improved by using an overhead projector. But unless the light intensity on the screen is carefully balanced with the light on the speaker, major brightness problems develop. The advantage of the lecture format, of course, is that it's easy, fast and inexpensive.

In the **interview format,** a host interviews a guest (generally an expert or high-ranking official) on specific topics. The interview is the mainstay of documentary programming, although most producers wisely strive to reduce the "talking heads" component to a minimum by adding as much B-roll footage as possible. Unless this is done—and especially if a truly skillful interviewer can't be found—the interview ends up being only a small step above the lecture approach in its ability to hold an audience. Corporate executives will often suggest interviews to communicate basic information. Even though many executives are quite effective in their jobs, on camera they can come across as stilted and even somewhat inarticulate. Since these people are typically above—sometimes far above—video production personnel on the corporate ladder, working with them to produce the best possible on-camera presentation can require real diplomacy. Although suggestions can be made, production personnel can go only so far in dictating production elements and approaches.

The **documentary approach** uses broadcast news-gathering techniques to cover material centering around a single, cohesive theme. Although broadcast documentaries typically try to cover both sides of an issue, in institutional video a distinct point of view is more typical. Also, unlike broadcast television, institutional documentaries are typically shown to many audiences over time. Such documentaries are almost always done single-camera, film-style.

Finally, there are the **semi-dramatic** and **dramatic formats.** Although drama can be the most engaging way of presenting information, it is also the most demanding. Even though it is difficult for those working in institutional video to compete with the dramatic programming seen on broadcast television, institutional dramatic productions are regularly done—sometimes even rather effectively. Production centers located near large cities—primarily Los Angeles (Hollywood), New York, Chicago and Miami—can draw on the scores of struggling actors waiting for their chance to "be on the screen"—any screen. Many will work for no pay, just for the chance to gain professional credits by getting a speaking part in a production. Even more experienced actors who are "between jobs" will often work for scale, the minimum pay set by SAG, the Screen Actors' Guild. It then becomes a matter of effectively directing these dramatic scenes to create a believable result.

Holding the Audience's Attention

Many studies have considered the factors that result in effective television programming. One of the things that consistently emerges is the need for constant variation. There must be variety in sound, variety in visual information and variety in presentation style. Although these areas have been mentioned in earlier chapters, we need to note here that they are especially important in institutional video. Interestingly, in broadcast television, commercial breaks serve to add variety and give viewers a needed intermission from program content. It is estimated that, no matter how effectively presented, most viewers can't absorb more than 10 minutes of straight information at a time. After 10 minutes, unless there is a major change in pace, presentation style, or content, your audience may not be able to "stay with" the ideas being presented.

In a lecture or interview you can hold attention by interjecting a story, or cutting to a preproduced supplementary segment that explains or illustrates the matter being discussed. Short, prerecorded dramatic skits can be used to emphasize points in a humorous way. Bad acting is often easier to overlook when it isn't supposed to be taken seriously. Just varying the rate at which content is presented will provide some variety. Whatever method is used, make sure you break or at least momentarily alter the presentation at least every 10 minutes. Ideally, these variations should be done in a way that supplements (rather than diverts attention from) the central subject matter.

The Future of Institutional and Private Video

We are approaching a time when a broadcast quality video camcorder will be within the reach of most families and anyone with a personal computer will be able to do audio and video editing. Even now S-VHS and Hi8 camcorders exceed broadcast norms for picture resolution and sound quality. But good pictures and audio do not ensure good content. As audiences for broadcast television are exposed to ever-more-sophisticated production techniques, their expectations for corporate video also rise. Those who best understand the principles underlying these new electronic tools will be in a position to push the limits of technology into creative new areas.

Today, the personal and avocational use of video production is going far beyond recording birthday parties, trips to Disneyland and that new arrival in the family. Here are some examples:

- A citizen concerned about a dangerous intersection spends days videotaping "near misses." Afterward, he edits the tape and shows it to the city council. A traffic light is then installed.

- A woman in Los Angeles uses the video camera as a kind of personal therapist. By videotaping herself as if talking to a trusted friend, she is able to more fully articulate fears and yearnings. After a period of time, when the tape is played back, she is able to somewhat objectively view herself as "another person." (Are not most of us much better at recognizing and solving the problems of other people?)

- In an effort to preserve family history, a dying woman is videotaped while she discusses the life and times of family members who have passed on.

- An animal rights group uses videotape to record evidence of the inhumane treatment of cattle. The tape ends up in a network documentary.

- A family member coldly records the embarrassing antics of another family member who is regularly under the influence of alcohol. The resulting tape has a profoundly sobering effect.

- A psychiatrist uses a camcorder to treat anorexia. In an effort to break the physical illusion they hold about themselves, he tries to get patients to see themselves as others (the camera) see them.

- A young woman who could never get her grandmother to write down her prize-winning strudel recipe, makes a video documenting each step, including "the pinch of this and a handful of that."

- A dying man records a complete will on videotape, talking personally to each person named.

- For insurance purposes a homeowner carefully videotapes the contents of each room of his house.

- During the Persian Gulf war of 1991, 450 camcorders, 350 TV sets, 370 VCRs and 250,000 blank videocassettes are sent to soldiers in Saudi Arabia as part of the "Better Than a Letter" campaign to stay in touch with friends and relatives back home.

- In the same war, in an effort to get footage of conditions within the country during the Iraqi occupation, the networks hand out camcorders to citizens as they cross the boarder to Kuwait.

- A Tampa, Florida man focuses a video camera on a hot tub in his neighbor's back yard. The resulting footage reportedly documents "lewd and lascivious behavior" taking place between the neighbor and his girlfriend.

As many people become adept at handling a camcorder, they often move onto avocational and even vocational applications. Here are just a few examples.

■ A camp counselor videotapes the daily experiences of a group of scouts and sells the videotapes to parents.

■ After doing a creative job of videotaping his sister's wedding, an enterprising young man starts his own business producing videotapes of weddings.

■ A law student earns money by taking video depositions for law firms.

■ A young woman makes money by producing videotapes of college graduations and selling them to parents.

■ Another woman produces videotapes of various types of athletic competition and sells them to contestants.

■ A college student with an interest in sports videotapes segments from athletic events at neighboring schools and sells them to a local TV station.

■ Another college student becomes a stringer (a free-lance agent) for area TV stations, selling them Hi8 footage of local news events.

■ A husband and wife team travel the world recording its people and places. The footage is edited and sold to video libraries around the United States to be used as "stock footage" in productions (Figure 15.5).

These are just a few examples of the burgeoning possibilities in private video production. With the advent of comparatively inexpensive camcorders, including PC-based video editing and special-effects equipment, video production is no longer reserved for those who can invest hundreds of thousands of dollars in production equipment. We seem to be "democratizing video." Anyone with sufficient motivation to get an idea across can commit it to video and go in search of an audience. Although many people will be using video in private and avocational applications, others are interested in making television a full-time career.

CAREERS

Carving out a successful career in a competitive field like television takes some very special talents. Of course, you can't even start developing your professional credentials until you land that first job. What does it take to get off to a good start and become successful? The final part of this chapter is devoted to answering this question.

The author has been involved in television for several decades: as an announcer and so-called "TV personality," as a producer-director of thousands of hours of TV programming (much of it live), and as a teacher. In the latter capacity he has watched some of his students work themselves up through the ranks to become executive producers of major TV series. Others, who found the competition too

Figure 15.5 Stock footage is an important resource in video production. Thousands of subject areas are available—even an open door signifying an entrance to a bright future. Although a fee has to be paid for the right to use the footage, considerable money can still be saved over having to send out a crew to a location to shoot original footage, especially if that location is hundreds or thousands of miles away.

stiff, gave up their career goals, and found employment elsewhere. What has made the difference? Probably seven factors:

1. *Motivation*   In any competitive field you must really want to make it. This type of motivation cannot waver from week-to-week or month-to-month, but is characterized by a consistent and single-minded dedication.

2. *Personality*   Although this is a vague term, it encompasses several things. First, since television is typically a collaborative effort, it means an ability—even an unselfish desire—to work with others to accomplish production goals. Included in this category is *attitude,* another term that has many definitions. But in this context it refers to the general demeanor of individuals, how they accept assignments, whether they are pleasant to be around and to work with, and how well they accept suggestions or criticism. Since there is often considerable pressure in TV production, employers look for people who can cope with stress and remain cooperative. "Thin skinned" individuals, who can't detach themselves from their work and take constructive criticism, are in for a bumpy ride.

3. *Knowledge and skills*   Employers seek out those who know how to do things, how to solve problems, and how to make the technology work to its best advantage. "Nice but incompetent," is not a phrase we want to hear about ourselves. We would much rather be told, "Well, I know if anybody can make this fly, you can!"

4. *Creativity*   People have been trying to define this concept for centuries. It involves looking at things in new ways, and then (in TV production) helping the audience to see and experience them in new ways. In Hollywood there's a saying that an "original idea" for a story is one that hasn't been used for at least six months. How many movies have you seen that follow the theme: boy meets girl; boy loses girl; and boy wins girl back again? Although the idea may be hackneyed, we continue to be entertained by this basic love-story concept because the idea is regularly played out in new, creative, and interesting ways as well as with interesting new stars. If the book of Proverbs is right and there is nothing new under the sun, then it becomes a matter of presenting old concepts in creative new ways. In drama, it may mean unexpected and unpredictable twists. In traditional production, it may mean creative new camera angles, effects, or editing techniques. One thing is certain: the more thoroughly you understand the medium, the production equipment, and the full range of production techniques available to you, the better chance you will have in using the medium in creative new ways that will hold, inform and entertain an audience.

5. *Willingness to sacrifice for your goals*   Since television, especially broadcast television, is highly competitive, the supply of job applicants normally exceeds the number of job openings, and starting salaries are often low. Faced with this situation, many students quickly abandon dreams of making a success in television and opt for better-paying jobs.

Those who are willing to stick with it and "pay their dues" often not only end up making more money than those who dropped out of the competition, but find themselves working in a field that, for them, may be much more exciting and satisfying than any other. For many people, doing something they really enjoy throughout their lives is more important than making more money at a profession that they dread to face each morning.

There are also certain sacrifices when it comes to life-style. If your main goal is to have a predictable, 9-to-5 job with optimum stability, broadcasting will not be your first choice. TV production, especially news and documentary work, can have unpredictable hours. In doing documentary work you may be away from home for days or weeks at a time. In news, you may be called out on a story at any hour of the day or night. Although some may find this lack of routine exciting, others feel—quite accurately—that it gets in the way of a stable family life. (If you go into one of these areas, you may want to look for an understanding spouse, one who is sympathetic—even enthusiastic—about your goals. News and documentary work have definitely taken a toll on the institution of marriage.)

6. *An aptitude for working with words and pictures*   Great composers have an ability to "hear" music in their heads, even before it is written on paper. Television writers, directors, and artists must have the same kind of aptitude, an ability to visualize their ideas.

Although television is visual, it is also very much word-based. We have to clearly and succinctly communicate ideas in the form of proposals, scripts, and instructions to cast and crew. When an aspiring television student approached David Brinkley in a swank restaurant and boldly asked his advice on the key to success in television news, Brinkley, who by that time had spent more than 40 very successful years in news, reportedly put down his fork, considered the question, and said, "Three things. First, learn to write; second, learn to write; and third, learn to write."

We should also add *reading* to this list. Since TV is a profession that deals in ideas, you must become an avid reader. Current events inform you of ideas that will soon find their way into productions. The *trades* (professional publications) keep you abreast of the latest technology in your field and how it's being applied in current production work. In short, read! Keep up with what's going on.

7. *Reliability and an ability to meet deadlines* The most important "instrument" in broadcasting is the clock. If you can't be relied on to get the job done within the assigned time, your chances of getting future assignments will rapidly diminish and, eventually, cease to exist.

A newscast that's finished a minute after air time is worthless; a production that's finished late will, at the very least, incur added production expenses. The availability of crew members, production equipment and facilities are generally tightly scheduled. A camera operator or on-air personality may not be available tomorrow for what you didn't finish today. Satellite or studio time may not be available a few minutes after your scheduled time to finish.

To avoid costly overtime expenses in one production facility, engineers were instructed to shut down all equipment precisely at the end of the time allotted for the production, even though completion may be only minutes away. Late starts, the need to re-do segments, etc., had to somehow be made up by the director before the end of the time allotted for the production. Before learning to plan ahead and stay within the established time limits, more than one director has seen all the screens in the control room suddenly go black when time ran out.

Collecting Evidence of Competency

Each year hundreds of young people who have just finished a degree in broadcasting or telecommunication appear in front of prospective employers. For each job opening, several candidates who are lucky enough to get through the initial screening will be interviewed. Only one will get the job.

Preparation for landing a job in television must start long before graduation. Specifically, we're talking about such things as work experience, internship experience, and a solid resumé, which will probably include a resumé reel (a videotape) of some of your best work.

Work Experience

On-the-job training is costly to an employer. The inevitable mistakes that occur during the learning process are also costly. Employers would rather play it safe (their reputations are on the line too) and place in jobs people who have already proven themselves in some way. For this reason, *experience* is ranked at the top of desirable qualifications. Although not everyone will be fortunate enough to spend one or more summers working at a local TV station, for those who are able to wrangle jobs, even part-time jobs, employment prospects will be better.

Students often ask, "I worked several summers at a fast-food restaurant (or doing other work unrelated to television); should I put that on my resumé?" The answer is, "yes," unless you can fully "feather out" a one-page resumé with significant professional experience. Showing an employer that you have already held a job indicates that you've learned to deal with job responsibilities and deadlines, as mundane as you think they might have been.

Internships

The second factor that prospective employers look for is internship experience, which shows not only that applicants are probably serious about the field, but that they have already "gotten their feet wet." Internship experience also indicates that the school-to-job transition will probably be easier.

From the students' point of view, not only do internships offer valuable, on-the-job experience, but they provide important professional contacts. By keeping in touch with people working in the field you will often know of job openings far in advance of seeing the ads in professional publications.

College Experience

Although not as impressive as "real world" experience, when listing your experience on your resumé, don't overlook what you have done in college. Have you produced or directed a TV show, or a series? Have you hosted one or more productions? Have you won any awards for productions? Keep these things in mind as you move through the curriculum; they may eventually set you apart from other applicants.

Resumés

When you first apply for a job in television you will probably be represented solely by a cover letter and a one-page resumé. Without dwelling on such totally essential things as good writing, organization, etc., let's just say that your resumé has to be strong enough to outshine the competition and get you in for an interview.

In many professional media areas—advertising, public relations, journalism, and television—you will typically be asked for some sort of proof of what you can do. (As sincere as they might be, good intentions don't carry too much weight by themselves.) In television this generally translates into a "resumé reel" of your best work. (You will probably be continually updating your resumé reel all of your professional life.)

While in production classes, be sure to save particularly good examples of your work. Before graduation—after which you may lose access to production equipment—you can assemble your best segments into a short resumé reel. (Today, it would probably be more accurate to change "resumé reel" to "1/2-inch resumé cassette.") In putting together your reel, don't save the best for last. Those reviewing a stack of resumé reels often don't take the time to view more than an opening cut. Lead off strong and finish strong, and include only your most professional-looking work.

Looking for Work in All the Right Places

Many large media corporations publish monthly bulletins of jobs. In addition there are computer bulletin-board services that list jobs in multiple-media areas. There are also several media employment services or agencies. Your school's placement service may have information on these. *Broadcasting Magazine,* as well as several other broadcast-related publications, carries regular ads for jobs.

As a last resort you can use the "shotgun approach" of sending out unsolicited resumés to selected TV stations and production facilities. Check the latest edition of a reference like the *Broadcasting and Cable Yearbook* for information on a facility you are interested in. You will find key personnel listed, including the name of the personnel manager or department head. If you do get called for an interview, make sure to do your "homework"; know everything possible about the facility.

Finally, learn to handle rejection without dejection. While you are striving to break into this competitive field, you'll probably be competing with many applicants who have similar qualifications. Many candidates give up hope and drop out along the way. Maybe that's just as well. If you can stay optimistically persistent, and keep pursuing every possibility, the chances are good that eventually you will end up being "the right person, at the right place, at the right time."

Once you get into the field you'll know that you are in the company of others like yourself—men and women who have demonstrated that they have what it takes to be successful in a competitive, rewarding, and oftentimes very exciting profession.

GLOSSARY

Note: Some terms can be found under their abbreviations. For example, electronic field production *can be found under its common designation,* EFP.

8mm; video 8 The smallest consumer videotape format in general use. The cassettes are about the size of a standard audiocassette tape. The higher-quality *Hi8* version is often used as a *prosumer format.*

A and B rolls; A-B rolls Refers to use of two videotapes in recording a single-camera segment. During editing the audio and/or video from the B-roll (generally consisting of cutaways and insert shots) is inserted over the primary A-roll footage.

above-the-line; above-the-line personnel Budgetary division focusing on non-technical, creative expenses. Included are the producer, director, writer and the on-camera talent. See also *below-the-line.*

acquisition format A small, convenient, inexpensive VCR format used to acquire footage that later will be copied to a higher-quality format before editing. This procedure minimizes generational loss during the editing procedure.

actor A male or female who assumes a role in a dramatic production.

A/D converter See *analog-to-digital converter.*

additive color Process used in color television in which colored light is combined in various proportions to create a full spectrum of colors.

AGC (automatic gain control) Circuit that automatically maintains a preset audio or video level. Although convenient, the use of AGC circuits does not achieve the best results in some situations.

amplitude The strength of a video or audio signal.

analog-to-digital converter (ADC) The process of converting an analog signal to digital data (also called A/D converter).

animation The process of taking a series of still frames of slightly different drawings or objects that, when presented at normal film or video speeds, gives the illusion of motion. Typically, two or three frames of the drawing or object are photographed before changes are made and new frames are photographed.

announcer (ANNCR) An individual who (generally off camera) provides narration for a production; script abbreviation for announcer.

approximate color consistency The human ability to visually correct for changes in color temperature. For example, a white piece of paper will appear white under both daylight and incandescent light even though the actual color will vary by more than 2,000° K.

ASCAP (American Society of Composers, Authors and Publishers) A trade guild that protects the publication and performance rights of composers, authors and publishers.

aspect ratio The numerical ratio of picture width to height. The standard broadcast aspect ratio is 4 × 3.

assemble editing In contrast to *insert editing,* an editing process whereby a new video or audio sequence is consecutively added to a previously edited scene, complete with the associated control track.

assignment editor The individual in a broadcast newsroom who has the responsibility of assigning news and ENG stories to specific reporters.

associate producer An individual delegated certain producing responsibilities by the producer or executive producer.

atmosphere introduction Beginning a video segment with a scene or series of scenes intended to establish the conditions, habitat, environment, spirit, or climate of the central subject matter.

audio board A basic desktop control center used to switch, mix and control audio levels for a variety of audio sources. See *audio console.*

audio compressor Audio-processing circuit that reduces dynamic range by simultaneously raising low audio levels and lowering high levels so that a higher average level is achieved.

audio console An electronic mixing and switching device that controls audio sources during a production.

audio director See *audio technician.*

audio expander An electrical circuit that increases the dynamic range of an audio signal.

audio limiter An electronic device intended to restrict the maximum amplitude of a signal.

audio mixer A device that allows the simultaneous combining and blending of several sound inputs into one or two outputs.

audio sweetening A postproduction process designed to correct problems in audio as well as to enhance and supplement audio tracks.

audio technician A person who is in charge of some phase of audio; generally, a person who operates an audio board.

B-roll See *A- and B-rolls.*

back light Light directed from behind and above the subject used to separate and add dimension to a scene. Slightly stronger than front light.

balanced line In contrast to an *unbalanced line,* an audio cable based on three conductors. Balanced lines are preferable in high-quality applications.

barn door Side and/or top flaps that attach to front of light and shape the light beam. Commonly used with a Fresnel light.

beam splitter A prism or dichroic mirror device used behind a color TV camera lens to divide the light into the three primary colors.

below-the-line Production costs associated with technical rather than creative services.

below-the-line personnel Generally speaking, personnel associated with the technical aspects of production. See also *above-the-line personnel.*

Betacam A broadcast-quality format developed by Sony and used in several types of camcorders.

bit speed Speed at which units of digital information can be transmitted from one point to another.

blanking a tape Recording black, sync and a control track on a videotape. The process of creating a blanked tape. Also called blacking a tape.

BMI (Broadcast Music Incorporated) An organization that handles permissions and licenses for music used in productions and broadcasting.

border merger In composition, cutting off subject matter at the edge of a frame at an inappropriate or awkward point. Thus, significant subject matter merges with or is cut off by the edge of the frame.

broadcast quality Equipment or production that conforms to the highest-quality technical standards. Originally, the Federal Communications Commission established many of these standards.

budgeting Process of determining costs for a production.

burned-in time-code As opposed to *keyed-in time-code,* SMPTE/EBU time-code numbers that are a permanent part of the corresponding video.

cam head A type of pan head for a camera mount commonly associated with studio cameras. Pan and tilt actions are controlled by variable-drag adjustments.

camcorder An all-in-one *cam*era and re*corder.*

camera control unit (CCU) A device containing electronics and controls used for setting up and adjusting the video from one or more cameras.

camera jib Remotely operated, crane-like camera mount that can typically move a camera from floor or ground level to a height of 10 or more feet.

camera operator Person responsible for operating a camera, generally under the command of a director.

canted camera Camera angle achieved by turning the camera slightly to one side causing the subject matter to run up or down hill. Result is also referred to as *Dutch angle.*

canted shot A *Dutch angle.* A shot in which the subject matter is tilted (rotated) in one direction or the other so that it moves diagonally across the frame.

card puller An individual responsible for holding a stack of cue cards for on-camera talent and pulling each one when the content is finished.

cart machine; cartridge machine An audio recording and playback system that makes use of a continuous loop of 1/4-inch audiotape in a plastic cartridge. Both analog and digital versions are available.

catadiatropic lens; cat lens A telescopic lens that uses an internal mirror to reduce the physical length of the lens.

CCD (charge-coupled device) A solid-state camera imaging device that has a number of advantages over camera tubes.

CG (character generator) A device that electrically creates letters and symbols for TV titles and other graphic displays.

chip; chip camera A video camera that uses one or more CCDs as imaging devices. (In appearance they resemble a computer chip.)

clip In the context of this chapter, to cut off video levels above a certain point in order to stay within a set contrast ratio. This problem commonly results in "chalky whites."

clip-on A personal microphone that can be clipped onto clothing.

coherence A descriptive dimension of light that characterizes its hardness or softness. The harder a light source is, the more coherence it is said to have. Professional photographers refer to coherence as light *quality*.

color burst The color timing information contained in the TV signal.

commercial appropriation A legal aspect of invasion of privacy relating to the unauthorized use of the name or likeness of a well-known individual for the personal or economic gain of a third party.

composition The controlled ordering of elements in a scene, designed to provide the strongest artistic arrangement and the most effective communication of a central idea.

compress; compression A technique used to reduce the size of a digital audio or video signal by extracting redundant information. This material is restored when the signal is played back. Some "lossy" compression techniques sacrifice detail and introduce undesirable artifacts into the signal.

condenser microphone A microphone that detects sound by amplifying changes in electrical capacitance between two closely spaced plates.

confidence heads VCR audio and video playback heads that immediately play back signals after they are recorded. In this way, signals can be monitored for quality as recordings are being made.

consortium A partnership of a number of TV stations or productions facilities that exchange programming or services. They are generally linked by satellites.

consumer format Unofficially recognized as the lowest quality standard for audio and video equipment, one that is intended for home rather than professional applications.

consumer quality One of several unofficial classifications of video and audio equipment quality. Consumer quality ranks below industrial and broadcast quality.

contact mic A type of microphone that picks up sound by direct physical contact with an object, generally a musical instrument.

continuity editing An editing structure that emphasizes a logical or temporal sequence.

continuity secretary An individual responsible for (among other things) seeing that visual elements remain consistent between takes in single-camera production. Without close watch, specific attributes of wardrobe, jewelry, or the setting, can change in the interval between takes, which sometimes can stretch over hours, weeks, or even months.

control track The portion of a videotape signal consisting of timing pulses associated with video fields and frames. Used in editing and maintaining playback synchronization.

control-track editing Equipment that uses an electronic count of control-track pulses rather than SMPTE/EBU time-code numbers for its cueing and editing functions.

convertible camera A video camera that can be quickly switched between use in the studio and in the field.

cover shot An establishing wide-angle or long shot of a set used both to establish the relationships between subject matter in a scene and to momentarily cover problems with lip sync or mismatched action.

CU A close-up shot.

cut The instantaneous changing from one shot to another. The term also refers to the removal of scenes in a script or production.

cutaway The use of a shot that is not part of the primary action but that is relevant to it and occurs at the same time. In an interview a cutaway is commonly used to show the interviewer's reaction to what is being said.

DAT (digital audio tape) A high-quality audio recording format that uses rotating heads and a tape cartridge containing 3.81-mm metal particle tape. Standard DAT contains a copy protection scheme; RDAT is a professional format that allows for copying.

DBS (direct broadcast satellite) A satellite or satellite system designed for home television reception. Typically, special receiver units are sold or leased to consumers.

decibels (dB) Unit of sound amplitude or loudness. One decibel is 1/10 of a bell. The designation dBm is used as an electrical measure of sound amplitude when a power of one milliwatt is the reference level.

dedicated editor As opposed to a computer-based editing system, which, depending on software, can be used for numerous tasks, an editing system designed to do only one thing: editing.

defamation A legal term relating to the utterance of slanderous words, especially false and malicious words, that injure a person's reputation.

defamation per quod As opposed to *defamation per se,* statements that are deemed slanderous or libelous only when supplemental (generally, widely-known information) is considered along with the statement in question.

defamation per se A legal term relating to the utterance of slanderous words, especially false and malicious words, that injure a person's reputation. As opposed to *defamation per quod,* statements which are deemed slanderous or libelous "on their face," i.e., without the need for information.

depth of field The range of distance in sharp focus along the lens axis.

desktop editing An audio or video editing system based on a personal computer application. See also *dedicated editor.*

dichroic mirror A mirror/filter that reflects only certain wavelengths or colors and allows others to pass. A combination mirror and filter positioned behind a color TV-camera lens that separates the three primary colors in a picture and directs them into three CCDs.

diffusion In lighting, the use of a diffusion device or material to soften light. Diffusers are also used in conjunction with camera lenses to soften images.

digital Betacam A high-quality professional videotape format that records signals in digital form.

digital stabilization A system for (within limits) canceling unwanted camera movement by electronically "floating" a frame within a larger CCD image area. See also *optical image stabilization.*

dimensional mergers A composition problem often caused by lighting or tonal contrast problems whereby objects at different distances in a scene merge together and cannot be adequately distinguished.

diopter correction A magnifying lens system used in conjunction with a camera viewfinder, which (within limits) eliminates the need for eyeglasses when using the camera.

director Person in charge of coordinating production elements before and during a production. Typically, the director "calls the shots" during a production.

disc-based camcorder A camcorder based on a recordable videodisc rather than videotape.

diversity receivers Using two or more electronically coordinated receivers with an RF mic to reduce interference from such things as multipath reception.

docudrama A dramatic production based on factual events or an actual situation.

documentary approach A reality-based approach to production content, generally on a specific topic, that more closely follows a news presentation format than a dramatic format.

double system recording Recording audio on a separate (generally synchronized) audio recorder rather than directly on the videotape used during the production. Since the number of audio tracks in a camcorder is limited, this technique allows for separately recording numerous sources of audio and mixing them as desired during postproduction.

dramatic format A script format associated with film and teleplays.

dress rehearsal A camera rehearsal. Final rehearsal with final facilities, sets and wardrobe. Often videotaped.

dropout A momentary loss of a picture signal during tape playback.

dry rehearsal Rehearsal without production facilities, generally done outside the studio, right after the camera blocking phase.

dual-redundancy The use of two identical condenser microphones on a subject, one intended as a backup in case the primary mic goes out.

Dutch angle A canted shot in which the subject matter appears titled (normally running up or down hill) on the screen.

dynamic composition Guidelines for composition, which apply primarily to the temporal or sequential elements in scenes.

dynamic mic A rugged type of microphone that uses a moving coil as a transduction device.

dynamic range The range between the weakest and loudest sounds that a particular piece of equipment can effectively reproduce.

ECU Extreme close-up; generally a head shot.

edit The recording of one or more videotaped sources onto a second tape. Also, any point on a videotape where the audio or video content has been modified through editing.

edit controller A device from which two or more editing machines are controlled during the editing process. The device used to program and control the editing process.

edit decision list A time-code listing of segments in a production; generally, those segments that will be used in creating the final edited version of a production.

edit recorder The destination VTR that records the source tapes onto the edited master during the editing session.

edited master The final tape created during the editing process.

editing workstation A complete computer-controlled, desktop system used to edit audio and/or video productions.

editor The term refers both to the individual person responsible for editing and a device by which videotape editing is done.

EDL (edit decision list) A handwritten listing or computer printout of time-code numbers associated with selected scenes.

EFP (electronic field production) The use of portable video equipment for taping on location.

ENG coordinator The individual under the assignment editor and news producer responsible for integrating the resources of the technical and news personnel in a TV newsroom.

essential area See *safe action area, safe title area.*

establishing shot A wide shot meant to orient the audience to an overall locale and the relationship between scene elements.

executive producer The individual primarily in charge of the financial aspects of a production and who may also make major creative decisions.

EXT Script designation for exterior. Exterior and interior (*INT*) designations are used to describe scenes in film-style scripts.

f-stop Lens aperture. The number attained by dividing the focal length of a lens by its aperture. Indicates the amount of light passing through the lens and, subsequently, exposure.

F/X Special audio or video effects.

fader A volume control or potentiometer used to control the amplitude of an electrical signal.

fair use act Leglislation that attempts to define the conditions under which copyrighted materials can be legally used without permission from the copyright holder.

field One-half of a complete television picture or frame. One complete vertical scan of a video image.

field producer The individual responsible for coordinating production for one or more production segments done away from the studio.

file server *Media server;* video server. A high-capacity, computer-based recording device that can be concurrently used by a number of computer terminals for the recording, editing and retrieval of audio and video segments in a production facility.

filter frame Holder used on the front of a light or a camera to hold colored gels, filters, diffusers, etc.

first draft The first (often rather rough) version of a script.

fish-eye lens An extreme wide-angle lens.

flag An opaque piece of material placed in front of a light used to block a portion of the beam.

floor manager Person in charge of the studio during production.

floor person *Stage manager.* The person responsible for coordinating the activities of talent and personnel in a studio or production setting.

fluid head The pan head of choice for EFP cameras because its internal parts move through a heavy liquid, making very smooth pans and tilts possible.

flyaway units A portable satellite up-link commonly used in electronic news gathering.

focal length Traditionally, the distance from the optical center of a lens to the *focal plane* (target) when the lens is focused on an object at infinity.

focal plane The point behind and perpendicular to a camera lens where a sharp image will appear. This is the target point of a camera CCD where the image is formed.

fog filter An optical filter that fits over a camera lens and creates the illusion of fog.

follow focus Shifting camera focus to accommodate subject movement.

foot-candle The measure of light intensity used in non-metric countries. The number of lumens per square foot.

form The basic design, genre and logical construction of a script, such as lecture, panel discussion, drama, variety show, news program, demonstration, or animated sequence.

frame A complete TV picture of (in NTSC) 525 horizontal lines. In the NTSC system frames are composed of two scanned fields of 262.5 lines each.

frequency Sound wave repetition rate in hertz or cycles per second. In electronics, the number of times a signal changes from positive to negative (or vice versa) per second.

friction head Camera mounting head that locks its movement through the action of adjustable friction between moving parts. Sometimes counterbalanced by a strong spring.

front-screen projection As opposed to rear-screen projection, an image projected on the camera side of a light-reflecting screen.

fully scripted show A script for a production in which all dialogue is fully written out.

gain selector switch A multipositing selector switch on a camcorder that controls the level of video gain (boost).

gear head A camera pan head in which gears are used to achieve smooth, controlled pans and tilts. Primarily used in motion picture and single-camera HDTV work.

geosynchronous satellite A satellite that orbits at the same speed as the earth and, therefore, stays in the same place in the sky.

giraffe A medium-sized microphone boom that extends about 15 feet and is mounted on a rolling tripod base.

goal In script writing, the goal relates to what the writer wants the audience to experience, feel or gain.

graphic equalizer A series of adjustable frequency filters designed to vary the amplitude of specific parts of the audio spectrum.

hard-copy prompter A talent prompting device (Teleprompter) in which the words are printed on a long roll of paper and picked up by a video camera, rather than originating from computer memory. See also *soft-copy prompter.*

head clog A loss of video signal resulting from dirt in the microscopic gap of a video head.

hertz Cycles-per-second interval associated with aural or electrical energy.

Hi8 An *8mm* videotape format developed by Sony that is of higher quality than the standard 8mm format. Often used as an *acquisition format.*

high-key Lighting characterized by minimal shadows and a low key-to-fill ratio.

IFB (interrupted feedback system) A small earpiece worn by talent that carries program sound or (when interrupted) instructions from a director.

image editor A software-based approach or system used in manipulating images.

image stabilizer A device that is part of a camera lens or camera mount that reduces or cancels vibration or moderate movement. Often used when a camera is hand-held or mounted in a moving vehicle.

incident light meter As opposed to a *reflected light meter,* a device that measures the amount of light falling on a subject.

industrial An audio and video equipment quality designation that falls between *broadcast quality* and *consumer* quality. This category is also referred to as *prosumer.*

insert editing As opposed to *assemble editing,* an editing process that inserts video and audio information over an existing control track.

insert shot A close-up shot of something within the basic scene that is used to show features or details.

institutional video Television production not intended for a mass audience or for general broadcast. Includes most corporate, educational and medical productions.

INT A script designation for an interior scene.

intercom See *PL.*

interlaced The scanning process that combines the odd and even fields to produce a full video frame.

interview format The use of a basic interview as the basis of production or program segment.

intro Introduction. The beginning or introductory portion of a production or production segment.

intrusion A legal term relating to the uninvited, unwarranted or illegal invasion of privacy.

iris An adjustable diaphragm that controls the amount of light passing through a lens.

jam sync Regenerating original time-code when a tape is copied to compensate for losses that could make the code unusable.

key An electronic effect in which a video source is electronically inserted into background video.

keyed-in time-code As opposed to burned-in time-code, which is a permanent part of the video, a process of temporarily superimposing time-code numbers over video footage.

kicker light A light typically placed between the back light and the fill lights. Sometimes used to simulate the light from a window or table lamp behind a subject.

lavaliere; lav mic A small, personal microphone clipped to clothing or suspended from a cord around the neck.

leading lines In composition the use of either visible or implied lines within a scene to direct the eye to a specific location, generally to the scene's center of interest.

lecture format A production- or program-segment approach that features an individual communicating information directly to a camera—in somewhat the same manner as a teacher addresses a class.

lens coating An ultrathin coating on glass surfaces designed to reduce surface reflection and increase light transmission.

lens extender An auxiliary lens used within, or as an attachment to, a camera lens, that increases focal length. A 2× extender doubles the focal length.

lens hood A device used on the front of a lens to shield it from the image-degrading effects of strong sidelight.

lens shade Lens hood. A round or rectangular black hood that fits over the end of a camera lens to shield the lens from strong sidelight or inclement weather.

lens speed The f-stop that transmits the maximum amount of light for a specific lens. The smallest f-stop number.

letterbox Term used for one method of adapting a 16 × 9 aspect ratio to 4 × 3, which results in a black or patterned bar at the top and bottom of the 4 × 3 image. Since this technique does not involve altering original images or scenes in any way, it is considered the "most honest" form of conversion.

libel A legal term relating to a published (or sometimes a broadcast) statement that tends to subject someone to public ridicule or contempt or to injure the person's reputation.

lighting director An individual responsible for the planning, design and setup of lights for a production.

lighting plot A detailed drawing, generally to scale, showing the placement of each light in relation to talent positions and scenic elements.

lighting ratio The relationship between the key and fill lights. Typically 2:1 for color and 3:1 for black and white television.

linear editing As opposed to *random access editing,* an editing approach that requires edits to be entered and done in the sequence required for the final edited version. Each segment has to be found, cued and then re-corded in sequence, which necessitates the stopping of both tapes as each segment is located and cued.

location manager The individual responsible for coordinating the concerns associated with using a specific location for a production.

low-key Lighting characterized by a high key-to-fill ratio resulting in predominant shadow areas. Typically used for night scenes in dramatic productions.

LS In scripts an abbreviation for long shot.

luminance The black-and-white aspect of a television signal. Also called the *Y-signal.* When part of a composite color signal, the luminance signal consists of 0.30 red, 0.59 green and 0.11 blue.

lux Unit of light intensity used in metric countries. One *foot-candle* is equal to 10.74 lux.

M-II A second generation improvement on the basic *M-format* discussed below.

M-format A professional videotape format based on a cassette with ½-inch videotape. Originally developed by RCA and Panasonic, the cassette resembles a standard VHS cassette.

macro setting A zoom lens setting that allows for extreme close-ups of subjects.

makeup person The individual responsible for applying makeup to persons appearing on camera.

master control An audio and video control center that is the final switching point before signals are sent to the television transmitter.

master scene script style An approach to script writing where only the basic scenes are described. Decisions on the various shots within the scenes are not outlined in the script and are left to the discretion of the director.

master shot A wide, all-inclusive shot of a scene that establishes major elements. Often in single-camera, film-style production, action and dialogue are taped from the master-shot perspective before the closer insert shots are done.

matte box An adjustable square box, typically constructed with bellows, that goes on the front of a camera and acts as a lens shade, and filter and matte holder.

maximum aperture The f-stop that allows the maximum light through a lens. Equal to the *lens speed,* or the smallest f-stop number.

MCU Script designation for medium close-up.

media server *File server;* video server. A high-capacity, computer-based recording device that can be concurrently used by a number of computer terminals for the recording, editing and retrieval of audio and video segments in a production facility.

MS (medium shot) Object seen from a medium distance. Normally covers framing between a long shot and a close-up.

mic Microphone; the device that detects sound and changes it into electrical energy.

microphone boom/grip operator The individual in charge of holding a mic, or operating a mic boom on a location.

MIDI (music instrument digital interface) A standardization system allowing various pieces of digital audio equipment, including computers, to work together.

MLS Script designation for medium long shot.

monopod A one-legged camera support.

montage editing Although the term as used in early film work had a different meaning, today montage editing refers to a rapid, impressionistic sequence of disconnected scenes linked by a variety of transition devices that are designed to communicate feelings or experiences. A montage does not tell a story by developing an idea in a logical sequence.

morphing A visual—generally computer-generated—effect in which a person or object is progressively transformed into another person or object.

MPEG-2 A sophisticated digital video-signal-compression technique capable of compressing and decompressing a signal in real time. See *compression.*

MS Script designation for medium shot.

multimedia CD A compact disc that contains both audio and video data.

multistandard A device capable of reproducing two or more broadcast standards.

neutral density (ND) filter A filter that reduces the light coming into a camera lens without altering its color.

news director The individual in charge of a newsroom or a news operation.

news producer Although responsibilities vary widely, producers are generally under the news director and in charge of specific newscasts. Producers often write basic transitional news copy.

night vision module A light multiplying device that makes it possible to get video images under extremely low light conditions.

noise Any background interference in video or audio signals. Typically manifested as hiss or hum on sound tracks, and as snow or graininess in video.

non-diversity receiver For wireless mics, a radio frequency receiver that uses one receiving antenna (in contrast to a diversity receiver that uses two or more antennas).

non-interlaced As opposed to an *interlaced,* odd-even field approach to scanning a video image, a technique that reproduces all of the lines sequentially.

non-volatile memory Computer memory that is not lost when electrical power is shut off.

off-line editing Editing or making editing decisions from a copy (work print) of an original videotape. Once off-line editing decisions are made, they are used in *on-line editing* to create the final edited master from the original videotape footage.

on-air director The technical director. Primarily responsible for video switching during a production.

on-line editing Using the original videotape in making the final edited master.

one-inch A broadcast quality, reel-to-reel videotape format. Originally, two, one-inch formats were in wide use: type B and *type C.*

optical image stabilization An approach to reducing or eliminating undesirable camera movement based on shifting the alignment of optical elements in the lens path in response to camera movement. Generally considered superior to electronic stabilization.

OS-shot A shot taken over the shoulder of one person, focusing on the face of a second person.

OSV A script designation for an off-screen voice.

package A completed news segment containing all needed audio and video components, ready for insertion (rolling into) a news production.

PAL (phase alternate line) The TV color standard used in most of western Europe and other parts of the world, including Australia, India, China, Argentina, Brazil and most of Africa.

pan handle The handle attached to the pan head of a camera that enables the cameraperson to pan or tilt the camera.

pan head Device connecting the camera to the camera mount, which allows the camera head to be tilted vertically and to be panned horizontally.

pan pot An attenuator-based device that can "place" a sound to varying degrees in a left or right stereo channel by raising or lowering the volume of the sound.

pan-and-scan A type of aspect ratio conversion whereby the smaller area of a new display is electronically moved left and right across the original source's wider area aspect ratio in order to follow action occurring at the sides of the original picture.

parallel cutting; parallel stories Cutting back and forth between two or more related stories in a dramatic production.

PC-based editing A software-based audio or video editing system based on a personal or desktop computer.

performer On-camera talent. A person who appears on camera in non-dramatic productions.

period piece A dramatic production that takes place during a specific historic, time period.

phantom power supply As opposed to using a battery source of power, an external source of power for a condenser mic. Generally, the power is fed through the mic cable from an audio board.

phase cancellation Interference resulting in reduced audio levels caused by a sound source being picked up by two microphones.

pixel point On a video screen, the smallest point that can be addressed and controlled.

PL (private line, phone line, production line) Wired or wireless headset intercommunication link between production personnel.

polarizing filter A filter (often adjustable) that reduces or eliminates reflections from glass, water and shiny surfaces. Also used to dramatically intensify contrast between the sky and clouds.

pop filter A screen, placed over a microphone, that reduces the effect of speech plosives and wind.

postproduction phase The final phase in a production, including follow-up and evaluation. Typically, postproduction is mainly seen as the editing phase.

POV (point of view) A shot from an angle that approximates what a designated actor is seeing at a particular moment.

preproduction The all-important, initial planning phase in production. All work that precedes actual production.

prime lens A fixed-focal-length lens.

prism block Beam splitter. The device that splits a full-color image from the camera lens into its color components; typically, in a professional camera, red, blue and green.

producer The creator and organizer of television shows, usually in charge of financial matters.

producer-director An individual who takes on the role of both producer and director in a production. The individual with the primary responsibility for guiding the production through all production phases.

production assistant An assistant to a producer or director can be assigned responsibilities for a wide variety of production details, including script changes, personnel issues, talent coordination, logistical arrangements, etc.

production outline A preproduction outline of the basic elements or steps involved in doing a specific production.

production phase As opposed to the preproduction and postproduction phases, the interval during which the actual video and audio are recorded or (in the case of a live production) broadcast.

program proposal A treatment. Outline of the basic elements of a proposed production. Often used to interest investors or talent in the production.

progressive scanning See *non-interlaced* scanning.

prompter Teleprompter. An electrical device for displaying a script that can be read by talent during a production.

prosumer Combining the terms "professional" and "consumer," a term denoting an equipment quality standard between the two classifications.

proximity effect The exaggeration of low-frequency response associated with most microphones when they are used at very close distances. Some microphones have built-in adjustments that can compensate for proximity effect.

public domain (PD) A creative work that can be used without charge because it is not copyrighted or because the copyright has expired.

PZ; PZM A type of microphone that relies on sound reflected from a flat surface.

quad mic; quadraphonic mic A type of microphone that can detect sound from nearly a 360-degree sound perspective. See *quadraphonic sound*.

quadraphonic sound A system of sound reproduction that goes beyond stereo and attempts to record and playback a 360-degree sound perspective. See *quad mic*.

quality Light coherence. A dimension of light relating to its hardness or softness.

quantization Related to the process of converting an analog signal to a digital signal. The accuracy resolution is dependent on the total number of bits in the final digital word.

rack focus Shifting focus from one object to another, generally in response to a shifting point of interest in a scene.

random access editing Non-linear editing. The ability of an editing playback system to find and cue successive, non-sequential segments in an editing session before they are needed, making it possible for a sequence of edits to be previewed and assembled in real time and in any order.

range extender An optical attachment to a lens (or an internal device) that increases focal length.

RDAT In contrast to the consumer version, a professional version of a Digital Audio Tape system that allows for recording.

reaction shot A cut to a performer's face that registers a response. Generally a close-up of someone reacting to the central dialogue or action.

rear screen projection A technique of optically projecting images behind talent to simulate settings. Rather than projecting the images onto the front of the screen, the images are projected from the back side of a translucent screen.

reference black The darkest portion of the video picture, generally with a reflectance value of 3 percent.

reference white The whitest portion of the video picture, generally with a reflectance value of 60 percent or above.

reflected light meter A device that measures the amount of light being reflected off of subject matter. Although commonly used in cameras, it is not as accurate as an *incident light meter.*

rehearsal A practice phase in which the talent and production personnel run though a production to detect problems and smooth out performance.

rendering A phase of image development in which a computer calculates and generates image attributes to "fill in" information needed to create a fully formed image or sequence of images.

resolution The ability of the camera system to distinguish and reproduce fine detail.

resolution chart A test pattern (used to set up and check a camera) that shows camera sharpness and the condition of the camera system.

RF mic Radio frequency mic. A combination microphone and miniature broadcast transmitter, which eliminates the need for microphone cables. See *wireless microphone.*

room tone The ambient sound present in a room recorded during original taping and used during editing to add needed intervals of "silence" between edits. It is important in maintaining the audio atmosphere existing at a location.

rule of thirds A guideline in composition based on placing the center of interest at or near the intersecting points of two, equally spaced horizontal and two, equally spaced vertical lines in the image area.

S-VHS (super VHS) A videotape format based on VHS, but with a wider luminance bandwidth, that has a potential horizontal resolution of more than 400 lines. Allows component recording and playback without cross-luminance or cross-color artifacts.

safe action area Also called *essential area.* The inner 90 percent of the video frame. Since the outer 10 percent of a broadcast picture is typically cut off by over scanning, this area is considered safe for most subject matter. See also *safe title area.*

safe area See *safe action area* and *safe title area.*

safe title area The inner 80 percent of the video raster or frame. Since the outer 20 percent of a broadcast picture is cut off by some home receivers, this area is considered safe for essential subject matter such as titles and text. See also *safe action area.*

sampling Digital representation of an analog sound or video signal made at precise intervals of time. Also digitally recording sounds or short musical segments from live or prerecorded sources. Once a sound is sampled, it can be endlessly modified. Sampling is used in *MIDI-*based sound creation systems.

saturation The purity of a color or its freedom from black or white.

scale The minimum fees prescribed by unions for television talent.

scheduling Breaking down scenes and shots into a convenient and cost-efficient sequence to create a production timetable.

scoop A floodlight (often used as a fill light) that has a deep, diffuse, and generally elliptical reflector.

screenplay A film-style script for a production.

scrim A spun-glass material placed over the front of a light to reduce intensity.

script The written blueprint for a production.

SECAM (Systèm Électronique Couleur Avec Mémoire) A broadcast standard used in France and the Soviet Union.

second unit A video or film production team responsible for doing supplementary scenes.

SEG See *special effects generator.*

segment producer A producer who takes charge of a specific production segment, generally a segment of a newscast.

selective focus Using limited depth of field to make sharp only one plane of focus in a scene, thereby forcing an audience to concentrate on that area.

semi-dramatic format A production containing dramatic scenes with actors.

semi-scripted show In contrast to a *fully scripted show,* that contains all the elements and written dialogue, a semi-scripted show contains only the beginning, the end, and a basic outline of the show.

servo-controlled An electronically controlled mechanical device, generally within a tape machine, that uses electronic feedback to maintain a desired and accurately controlled speed.

servo zoom A lens that uses a motor-driven mechanism to alter focal length.

set designer An individual who handles the initial phases of creating a production setting.

setup (1) In single-camera, film-style production, a single-camera position from which one or more segments in a scene are done; (2) on a waveform monitor, the pedestal or black level baseline dividing reference that is black from the blanking and synchronizing pulses.

sets Scenery and properties supporting the suggested locale, idea, and mood of a production.

SFX Special audio or video effects.

shading To adjust the chroma and video levels on a video camera. Often, an on-going process that takes place throughout the broadcast or taping of a production.

shield law In many states, a law that keeps a news reporter from having to reveal confidential sources of information.

shift register An electronic memory bank associated with CCDs; holds a charge before being read out by the system's scanning process.

shock mount A rubber or spring-based microphone holder, which reduces or eliminates the transfer of sound or vibration to the mic.

shock value An element in news value based on the amount of amazement, surprise, horror or scandal represented by a story.

shoot-and-protect A term that relates to the need to keep the full HDTV 16:9 aspect ratio free of extraneous subject matter, even if it is reproduced in a 4×3 ratio. In this case action should be confined to the smaller area (the shoot range), but the larger area (the protect range) must be free of microphone booms, lights and other distracting elements.

shooting ratio The amount of tape recorded relative to the amount of tape actually used.

shot box A control that can electronically present various zoom speeds and focal lengths for a zoom lens. Preset positions are activated by push buttons.

shot Individual production setup. A video segment that will later be combined with other shots in a meaningful sequence.

shot-by-shot script style As opposed to the *master scene script style,* which outlines only general scenes, the shot-by-shot script style lists each individual shot.

shotgun mic A highly directional microphone capable of picking up sound over a great distance.

shoulder mount; shoulder brace A support for a video camera that rests on both the shoulder and the body.

shutter speed In CCD cameras, the time allowed for the exposure to build. "Normal" is 1/60 second, or the maximum time it takes for one complete video frame. Higher shutter speeds (up to 1/10,000 second) are used to decrease or eliminate blur with rapidly moving action. The principle of CCD shutter speeds is comparable to shutter speeds in still film cameras.

single system recording As opposed to *double system recording,* the process of recording both sound and video on the same videotape.

skew control On a videotape machine, a playback control that adjusts videotape tension and the length of the video tracks read from the videotape. Improper skew adjustment results in various picture aberrations.

slander Uttering false statements deemed harmful to another person's character or reputation.

slate A small blackboard-type visual that is photographed at the beginning of a scene; identifies the scene in terms of basic production information such as the date, scene, take, director, etc.

slate person The individual responsible for setting up and displaying basic production information marking the beginning of each take in a production.

smart card A credit-card sized device that records digital information related to camera setup. After information is recorded on the card from one camera, the card can be inserted into other cameras and the information instantly transferred, thus ensuring technical consistency.

SMPTE (Society of Motion Picture and Television Engineers) A professional engineering society responsible for establishing technical standards in film and television. The SMPTE is the largest such society in the world.

SMPTE/EBU time-code A digital electronic signal recorded on a video or audio tape that provides a precise time-based numbering system together with other information. Also called address track. The name designates a standard agreed on by the Society of Motion Picture and Television Engineers and the European Broadcast Union.

snap zoom A very rapid zoom from a wide-angle into a close-up of some person or object; the effect is intended to achieve a dramatic effect.

snow A rapidly moving grainy effect in video caused by little or no picture information.

SOF (sound-on-film) A film that includes a soundtrack.

soft-copy prompter A camera prompting device that uses a video display, as opposed to a *hard-copy prompter,* which uses paper.

soft focus See *diffusion.*

softlight A floodlight producing an extremely soft and virtually shadowless light.

software-based editor In contrast to a dedicated editing system, a PC-based editing system that uses a computer software program as an operational basis.

SOT (sound-on-tape) videotape that includes a sound track.

sound bite Videotape segment in which the corresponding audio remains intact and in lip-sync with the video.

sound effects Studio-created sounds to give the illusion of real-life sounds.

source machine In videotape editing, the machine(s) that contain the original footage to be edited onto the edited master.

special effects Video effects. A wide range of electronic video transitions and methods of combining video sources including wipes, keys, mattes and inserts.

special effects generator (SEG) A video-mixing device that allows switching between several cameras and a variety of special effects, such as dissolves, fades, inserts and wipes.

spectral (or specular) highlights Bright reflections from shiny subject matter that often cause spikes on a waveform monitor and video brightness range problems.

spot meter A reflected light meter with an extremely narrow angle of acceptance (often about 5 degrees) designed for accurate light readings at a distance.

stagehand An assistant who can be assigned a wide variety of studio responsibilities including setting up and moving sets, props and equipment.

stage manager See *floor manager, floor person.*

staging The re-enactment of an event for the purposes of video production. In doing news, staging refers to the sometimes questionable re-enactment of a happening for the purposes of a news story. Also, a temporary structure used as a production setting.

stand-alone monitor A high-quality video monitor (display device), without an RF tuner, which is commonly used to monitor video from one or more cameras in the field.

standards converter A device for converting signals from one broadcast standard to another.

stand upper; stand-up An on-location shot of a reporter talking to the camera, often used to introduce or conclude a news piece.

star filter An optical filter that has finely etched criss-crossing lines on the surface; creates fingers of light around bright lights and spectral reflections.

static composition Elements and guidelines of composition related to still images. See also *dynamic composition.*

status indicators The collection of various lights, patterns and alphanumeric characters, visible in and around a video camera viewfinder, that shows the operating condition of the camera, recorder and battery.

Steadicam A brand-name for body camera mounts that use a system of counterbalanced springs to keep a camera reasonably steady, even when the camera operator is walking or running.

stereo mic A microphone containing two sound-sensitive elements designed and arranged in such a way as to reproduce a stereo sound perspective.

stereo separation The degree to which left and right stereo channel information is perceived as being distinct and separate.

stereo synthesizer An electronic circuit that modifies a monophonic audio signal to simulate stereo.

stock footage Scenes from a film or tape library that show common, generally exterior scenes, which, for a fee, can be used in a production. Such scenes eliminate the time and expense involved in reshooting or re-creating the footage.

storyboard A series of rough drawings of the basic shots or scenes in a planned production. They normally include a brief written description of the associated action and audio.

strike To take down and remove scenery after a production.

striped filter Microscopic vertical stripes on the surface of a color CCD imaging device designed to break up the picture into two basic color components. Serves the same basic function of dichroic mirrors in three-CCD or three-tube cameras.

studio floor plan A scale drawing of a studio area showing where scenery and props (and sometimes lights and cameras) are to be placed.

subjective shot A camera perspective that simulates (or is made to represent) the perspective of one of the actors.

subtractive colors Typically, magenta, cyan and yellow. Any three colors, which when mixed together, filter each other out and produce black. Basically the opposite of the *additive color process.*

subtractive primaries Magenta, cyan, and yellow. Used in color printing, paints and pigments. When mixed, they act as filters for a white light source, subtracting specific colors and leaving a dominant color.

sun gun A small, battery-powered light mounted on a film or video camera. Sometimes called a headlight.

super (superimposition) A double-exposure effect. The simultaneous showing of two pictures in the same area of a video screen.

supercardioid A moderately directional microphone response pattern.

superconductors A general classification of experimental conductors that exhibit zero or near-zero resistance to the passage of an electrical current.

superimposition See *super.*

supplementary lenses Used with a video camera lens, an optical attachment that alters the optical characteristics of the lens. Three general categories are used: those that enable a camera lens to focus on objects at very short distances, those that increase the effective focal length of the lens (creating a telephoto effect), and those that decrease effective focal length (providing a wide-angle effect).

surround-sound A system of sound recording and reproduction that goes beyond stereo in its dimensional perspective and approximates quadraphonic sound.

sweetening The postproduction addition of sound effects, laughter, music, etc., to a production sound track. Various problems in audio are also corrected during sweetening.

switchback A camera shot that returns to the central action after a cutaway.

switcher The main production video control device capable of handling and manipulating numerous sources of video and selecting which video source is recorded or goes on the air.

sync; synchronization The basic synchronizing pulse in video. The crucial timing signal that keeps various pieces of video equipment electronically coordinated.

sync generator An electronic device that generates the variety of timing pulses needed to keep the video equipment synchronized.

synchronization license A step in obtaining clearance to use a copyrighted work; grants a producer permission to use the music for a specific period.

synthesized music Music created entirely by electronic means without the use of traditional musical instruments.

synthesized stereo An approach to creating a simulated stereo effect from one or more monophonic audio signals.

synthesizer An electronic device with associated software used to create sound effects.

t-stop As opposed to relying on a simple mathematical ratio, an iris setting that designates the actual amount of light going through a lens. T-stops are more accurate than f-stops, which do not take into consideration light losses within the lens.

table reading The initial rehearsal phase in which the talent and key production personnel sit around a table and read through (and discuss) a script.

take A single shot. In single-camera production a specific shot often requires several takes before it meets the approval of the director.

talent Individuals who perform in front of a camera.

talent release Model release. A form signed by a person appearing in a videotape; grants legal permission to a production agency to broadcast the segment under specified terms.

tally light The red light on a video camera that indicates the camera is on the air or that videotape is recording.

tape format Any of several tape widths and recording methods, such as Digital Betacam, *S-VHS,* or D-5, used in video recording systems.

tapeless workstation An audio or video editing console or *workstation* that typically uses computer disks as a recording medium.

target The light-sensitive front surface of a television camera imaging device. It coincides with the focal plane of the lens.

target audience The intended audience for a production.

TBC (time base corrector) An electronic device that stabilizes the scanning and timing pulses in video; commonly used to bring technical attributes of the video from small field cameras and recorders up to broadcast quality.

technical continuity problem Any one of several types of unintentional changes in video or audio quality. Examples are unintended changes in color balance or changes in audio levels during the course of consecutive shots.

technical director (TD) The individual who operates the control-room switcher and is in charge of various technical aspects of a production.

telephoto lens A lens that seemingly brings subject matter closer to the camera. A prime lens with a focal length of more than twice the camera's normal focal length.

teleplay A script for a dramatic video production.

TelePrompTer Originally, a brand name for a camera prompter. A device used by on-air talent that rolls an image of a script across a screen near the camera lens.

television production The process of creating television programming.

test pattern Any number of standardized electronic patterns or camera charts intended to evaluate specific video qualities such as linearity and resolution.

test tone A zero-decibel tone used as a reference standard.

thematic editing See *montage editing.*

3-D animation Building a 3-D computer model of an object on a video screen and thereafter being able to rotate the object in several directions.

three-shot A video picture containing three individuals.

tighten up To zoom in or dolly in on a subject.

tilt A camera move from the pan head involving moving the lens up and down along the camera's vertical y-axis

tilting The process of creating the opening and closing credits of a production; sometimes refers to process of creating subtitles for dialogue.

time-base The timing component of a video signal, particularly the horizontal and vertical sync pulses.

time-base corrector An electronic device commonly used in VCRs and editing systems; stabilizes video signals. See *time-base*.

time-code *SMPTE/EBU time-code.* A series of eight numbers identifying the hours, minutes, seconds and frames related to a specific video frame on a tape.

time-code generator A device that supplies an electronic SMPTE/EBU time-code signal to recording equipment.

time-lapse photography Significantly slowing down the frame rate of motion photography so that events that may take minutes, hours, or even days, can be shown and observed within seconds.

time line A linear representation on a computer screen of the various audio and video elements to be combined in an editing session. Typically, changes in a sequence are as simple as "grabbing" an audio or video segment on the time line with the mouse or pointing device and dragging it to a different point along the line.

time-and-motion study Similar to *time-lapse photography* except that the condensation of time is designed to allow researchers to analyze (generally human) actions over a period of time in an effort to minimize wasted or inefficient movement.

timeliness A measure of newsworthiness relating to how recent or new the developments in a story are.

timing The total length of a production, including time allotted to the individual scenes and program components.

titillation component A measure of newsworthiness relating to the sexual or sensual components of a story.

toe In television the bottom portion of a gray-scale gamma curve representing the reference black and the darker portions of the gray scale.

tonal compression Commonly, a darkening of skin tones associated with either underexposure, or exceeding the optimum contrast ratio of a video system. The inability of a video system to differentiate between different gray scale reflectance values.

tonal mergers An undesirable visual blending of different objects in such a way that they cannot be clearly distinguished.

touch-screen system Computer function selection approach where a finger can be used to touch options on a computer screen to initiate actions.

trace capability The ability of some editing systems to retain and display the original time-code references on footage after the codes have been changed during later stages of editing. This capacity can be important in going back to original footage and locating needed segments.

tracking An adjustment to the playback heads of a videotape machine to make them match the phase of recording heads. Sometimes the adjustment is necessary because the tape was recorded on another machine. Tracking problems cause video breakup and aberrations at the top or bottom of the picture.

tracking shot A dolly shot that follows a moving subject or moves with respect to a stationary subject.

trade libel A false or grossly misleading statement that damages a business or product.

trades Publications intended to serve the special interests of specific segments of the television and film community.

transmitter In television, an electronic device that modulates the audio and video signals onto a carrier wave for broadcast.

transponder A combination transmitter and receiver; commonly used in satellite transmission and reception.

traveling shot A moving camera shot.

treatment A summary of a film or video script that includes a description of the characters and the story plot. Often samples of action or dialogue are included.

treble Sounds representing the higher audio frequencies, generally from about 4,000 hertz and up.

triangular lighting Formula lighting; three-point lighting. The commonly used triangular arrangement of key, back, and fill lights for lighting a subject.

triax A coax-type video cable with three conductors.

trim control On an editor, a control that makes it possible to add or delete a specified number of frames to an edit point.

tripod head See *pan head.*

tripod Three-legged camera mount. Sometimes wheels are attached to facilitate camera movement.

truck A left or right movement of the camera along with its mount.

truth A legal defense against libel or slander. If the truth of a statement can be proven, it cannot be considered slanderous or libelous.

tungsten-halogen light Quartz lights; the most frequently used type of studio and on-location light. They get their name from the tungsten element that is encased within a quartz envelope filled with halogen gas.

TV black The blackest part of a TV picture, generally 3 percent reflectance.

TV receiver TV set. Video display device that has the capability of tuning in video channels, demodulating them and reproducing audio and video.

TV white The whitest part of a TV picture, generally 60 percent or more reflectance.

two-shot A picture showing two individuals.

two-way barn doors Flaps attached by hinges to two sides of a spotlight, intended to mask off and shape the beam.

type-C videotape machine An approach to 1-inch videotape recording used in NTSC countries. A complete television picture is recorded with each helical scan of the tape heads.

U-matic Trade name for the 3/4-inch tape format invented by Sony.

ultradirectional mic A microphone with a highly directional response pattern.

ultraviolet (UV) filter Transparent filter that absorbs UV wavelengths. Used to help penetrate haze and give clearer video of distant views. Also used over a lens simply to protect the surface of the lens.

umbrella reflector A white or silver umbrella with a bright light placed near the center used for creating soft light.

unbalanced line Audio sources (associated with non-professional equipment) that rely on two-conductors. Unbalanced lines tend to be susceptible to hum and electronic interference. See also *balanced line.*

underexposure An inadequate amount of light from the lens being transmitted to the camera's target resulting in a dark picture; specifically, a loss of shadow detail and a compressed gray scale.

unicam Camcorder. A combination all-in-one camera and recorder.

unidirectional microphone A microphone with a cardioid pattern of sensitivity that is primarily responsive to sound coming from one specific direction.

unipod A camera support consisting of a single, adjustable leg. See *monopod.*

up-link A ground-to-satellite transmitter link.

user bits Additional digital information that can be recorded within the SMPTE/EBU time-code; a limited number of user bit letters or numbers can be entered to register reel number, date scene, take, etc.

Variable-focal-length lens See *zoom lens.*

VCR Videocassette recorder.

vector graphics system A graphic 3-D modeling electronic graphics approach in which the appearance of three-dimensions is created by rotating or moving the subject matter. The moving perspectives are automatically calculated and created by the software involved.

vectorscope A CRT instrument that displays the phase and saturation of the primary and secondary video colors; used to align cameras and equipment.

velocity mic Ribbon mic; a type of microphone that uses a thin metallic ribbon suspended within a magnetic field. Although useful in an announcer's booth, this type of mic has limited use in the field.

vertical blanking interval A period in which the electron beam in display is blanked out while it travels from the bottom of the screen to the top.

vertical fader Linear fader. As opposed to a rotary fader, level-controlling device that is based on sliding a controller along a straight line.

vertical interval Synonymous with *vertical blanking*.

vertical sync Pulses that define the end of one television field.

VHS (video home system) A consumer-oriented videotape format using 1/2-inch tape housed in a cassette.

VHS-C A compact version of VHS.

video 8 Videocassette format that uses 8mm tape in a cassette. See also *8mm video* and *Hi8*.

videocassette A plastic videotape housing containing both a supply and take up reel.

video digital effects Electronic special effects that make it possible to alter video in a variety of ways, such as compressing, flipping and reversing polarity.

videodisc Video storage medium that uses thin circular plates, and translucent plastic, on which video, audio and various control signals are encoded along a spiral track. Optical disc systems use a laser beam to read the surface of the disc.

video field production Non-studio video production.

video gain switch On a camera or CCU, a selector switch that increases the gain or amplitude of a video signal—generally at the expense of some video quality. Used to compensate for the lack of light.

video head The small signal-to-tape transfer device responsible for recording the video signal in a VTR. Video heads are mounted on a head wheel that rotates at a high rate of speed in relation to the videotape.

video monitor A high-quality television display device, generally without a tuner or audio circuitry.

video noise See *noise*.

video server A centralized, computer-based unit typically with numerous hard disks used for storing, editing and retrieving audio and video segments within a production facility. Also referred to as a media server.

video switcher See *switcher*.

viewfinder A viewing screen built into a video camera enabling the operator to monitor the images being recorded. Most electronic viewfinders also allow the playback and review of recorded material.

vision How the tools of the trade are used to translate the goal of a production into an audio and visual experience for the viewer. The vision component of production should be unique in that it springs from the dictates of personal perspective and viewpoints.

visual effects Special effects. A wide range of electronic video transitions and methods of combining video sources. Included are wipes, keys, mattes and inserts.

VITC (vertical interval time-code) A system of recording NTSC/EBU time-code in the vertical interval of the video signal.

VL bayonet mount A standardized lens mount system used on many video camcorders.

VLS A script designation for very long shot.

voice recognition A computer system that can recognize certain voice commands and respond appropriately.

VO (voice-over) Speech heard over related video, without the person talking being seen on the screen.

volatile memory Digitized information stored in a computer or microprocessor that remains only as long as there is electrical power.

VTR Videotape recorder.

VTRO Videotape recorder operator.

VU meter An instrument (meter) that measures the loudness of sound in terms of decibels and percentage of modulation.

VU (volume unit) Unit of measure for audio level or signal strength.

W-VHS A wide-screen version of the VHS videotape format that is based on a 16 × 9 aspect ratio instead of a 4 × 3 aspect ratio; introduced in 1994.

walk-through A rough rehearsal in which no cameras are used; generally the actors walk from place to place and check their actions without speaking any dialogue.

wardrobe person Individual responsible for selecting and supplying clothes and accessories for talent.

waveform monitor A type of oscilloscope or CRT that displays the amplitude of a video signal and its sync.

wedge mount Mounting device enabling cameras to be rapidly mounted and dismounted from cameras, pedestals or tripods.

white balancing Electronically adjusting a camera's chroma channels for a light source so that white will be reproduced as true white. Most cameras can automatically white balance when the operator fills the screen with a white card and pushes a white balance button.

wide angle A lens or a scene that represents an angle of view significantly wider than normal. A wide-angle lens or shot is either a prime lens with a focal length significantly less (at least 25 percent less) than a normal lens, or a zoom lens used at a focal length significantly less than normal.

wide-angle converter An optical attachment to a lens that effectively decreases its focal length and makes possible a wider field of view.

wild sound; wild track Sound, generally background sound, recorded independently of the video and added during postproduction. Does not need to be synchronized with the video.

window burn; window dub An off-line copy of an original videotape that contains a permanent display of the SMPTE/EBU time-code in the video.

windscreen A small fabric or foam rubber cover for the top of a microphone that reduces or eliminates the sound of moving air or wind.

wipe Visual effect in which a moving line or pattern acts as a border as one video signal gradually replaces another. As one picture disappears another is revealed.

wireless microphone A microphone that has a built-in, low-power transmitter, or that is connected to a transmitter. Wireless microphones are commonly used when the use of a cord would create a problem. See also *RF mic.*

WORM (write once read many [times]) A videodisc system that permanently writes information onto a disk.

workstation A (generally dedicated) computer-based editing system for either audio or video.

writer In television and film the individual responsible for writing the production script.

WS Script designation for wide shot.

X-Y pickup A microphone configuration used in stereo recording in which two directional mics are mounted next to each other, one directed 45 degrees to the right and one 45 degrees to the left.

XCU Script designation for extreme close-up.

XLR connector Canon connector. A standard, three-prong professional audio connector.

XLS A script designation for extra long shot.

Y/C The separate processing of the luminance (Y) and chrominance (C) video signals.

Y; Y-signal The luminance or brightness part of a video signal.

yo-yo shots Repeated zooming in and out on subjects. An annoying effect associated with amateur video productions.

zebra stripes Black lines superimposed over specific areas of an image in the viewfinders of some cameras; used as an aid in making video level adjustments.

zoom lens A lens with a continuously variable *focal length* and angle of acceptance.

zoom ratio Numbers indicating zoom range for a lens. The mathematical ratio for a zoom lens derived by dividing its shortest focal length into its longest focal length.

zooming The process of varying the focal length and, therefore, the angle of view of a zoom lens.

Selected Bibliography

Announcing

Hyde, Stuart W. *Television and Radio Announcing.* 6th ed. Boston: Houghton Mifflin, 1991.

Keith, Michael C. *Broadcast Voice Performance.* Boston: Focal Press, 1989.

O'Donnell, Lewis B., and others. *Announcing: Broadcast Communicating Today.* 2d ed. Belmont, Calif.: Wadsworth, 1992.

Audio

Alkin, Glyn. *Sound Techniques for Video and TV.* 2d ed. Boston: Focal Press, 1989.

Alten, Stanley R. *Audio in Media.* 3d ed. Belmont, Calif. Wadsworth, 1990.

Baert, L., and others. *Digital Audio and Compact Disc Technology.* 2d ed. Newton, Mass.: Focal Press, 1992.

Clifford, Martin. *Microphones.* 3d ed. Blue Ridge Summit, Pa.: TAB Books, 1986.

Ford, Ty. *Advanced Audio Production Techniques.* Newton, Mass.: Focal Press, 1993.

Gross, Lynne, and David E. Reese. *Radio Production Worktext: Studio and Equipment.* Boston: Focal Press, 1990.

Hubatka, Milton C., and others. *Audio Sweetening for Film and TV.* Blue Ridge Summit, Pa.: TAB Books, 1985.

Huber, David Miles. *Audio Production Techniques for Video.* Indianapolis: Howard W. Sams, 1987.

Huber, David Miles. *Microphone Manual: Design and Application.* Indianapolis: Howard W. Sams, 1988.

Nisbett, Alec. *The Sound Studio.* 5th ed. Newton, Mass.: Focal Press, 1993.

O'Donnell, Lewis B. *Modern Radio Production.* 2d ed. Belmont, Calif.: Wadsworth, 1990.

Oringel, Robert S. *Audio Control Handbook: For Radio and Television Broadcasting.* 6th ed. Boston: Focal Press, 1989.

Pohlmann, Ken C. *Principles of Digital Audio.* 2d ed. Indianapolis: Howard W. Sams, 1989.

Prentiss, Stan. *AM Stereo and TV Stereo: New Sound Dimensions.* Blue Ridge Summit, Pa.: TAB Books, 1985.

Rumsey, Francis. *MIDI Systems and Control.* Newton, Mass.: Focal Press, 1994.

Rumsey, Francis. *Sound and Recording: An Introduction.* 2d ed. Newton, Mass.: Focal Press, 1994.

Rumsey, Francis. *Stereo Sound for Television.* London, Boston: Focal Press, 1989.

Sweeney, Daniel. *Demystifying Compact Discs: A Guide to Digital Audio.* Blue Ridge Summit, Pa.: TAB Books, 1986.

Thom, Randy. *Audio Craft: An Introduction to the Tools and Techniques of Audio Production.* 2d ed. Washington, D.C.: National Federation of Community Broadcasters, 1989.

Watkinson, John. *The Art of Digital Audio.* 2d ed. Newton, Mass.: Focal Press, 1994.

Watkinson, John. *R-DAT.* Newton, Mass.: Focal Press, 1991.

White, Ray. *TV News: Building a Career in Broadcast Journalism.* Boston: Focal Press, 1990.

Electronic Field Production

Bernard, Robert. *Practical Videography: Field Systems and Troubleshooting.* Boston: Focal Press, 1990.

Compesi, Ronald J., and Ronald E. Sherriffs. *Video Field Production and Editing.* 3d ed. Boston: Allyn & Bacon, 1994.

Gross, Lynne S., and Larry W. Ward. *Electronic Movie-Making.* 2d ed. Belmont, Calif.: Wadsworth, 1994.

Medoff, Norman J., and Tom Tanquary. *Portable Video ENG and EFP.* White Plains, N.Y.: Knowledge Industry Publications, 1986.

Quinn, Gerald V. *The Camcorder Handbook.* Blue Ridge Summit, Pa.: TAB Books, 1987.

Ratcliff, John, and N. Papworth. *Single Camera Stereo Sound.* Newton, Mass.: Focal Press, 1992.

Ward, Peter. *Basic Betacam Camerawork.* Newton, Mass.: Focal Press, 1994.

Graphic and Scenic Design

Byrne, Terry. *Production Design for Television.* Newton, Mass.: Focal Press, 1993.

Blythe-Lord, Robin. *Captions and Graphics for Low Budget Video.* Newton, Mass.: Focal Press, 1992.

Merritt, Douglas. *Graphic Design in Television.* Newton, Mass.: Focal Press, 1993.

Millerson, Gerald. *TV Scenic Design Handbook.* Newton, Mass.: Focal Press, 1989.

Olson, Robert. *Art Direction for Film and Video.* Newton, Mass.: Focal Press, 1993.

Issues in Television Production

Christians, Clifford G., and others. *Media Ethics: Cases and Moral Reasoning.* 2d ed. New York: Longman, 1987.

Creech, Kenneth C. *Electronic Media Law and Regulation.* Newton, Mass.: Focal Press, 1992.

Fore, William F. *Television and Religion: The Shaping of Faith, Values and Culture.* Minneapolis: Augsburg, 1987.

Frankl, Razelle. *Televangelism: The Marketing of Popular Religion.* Carbondale: Southern Illinois University Press, 1987.

Hoover, Stewart M. *Mass Media Religion: The Social Sources of the Electronic Church.* Newbury Park, Calif.: Sage, 1988.

Limburg, Val E. *Electronic Media Ethics.* Newton, Mass.: Focal Press, 1994.

Orlik, Peter B. *Critiquing Television and Radio Content.* Boston: Allyn & Bacon, 1988.

Rivers, William L. *Ethics for the Media.* Englewood Cliffs, N.J.: Prentice-Hall, 1988.

Rosen, Phillip T., ed. *International Handbook of Broadcasting Systems.* Westport, Conn.: Greenwood Press, 1988.

Law

Carter, T. Barton, and others. *The First Amendment and the Fifth Estate: Regulation of Electronic Mass Media.* 2d ed. Westbury, N.Y.: Foundation Press, 1989.

Dannay, Richard. *How to Handle Basic Copyright and Trademark Problems.* New York: Practicing Law Institute, 1990.

Dennis, Everette E., and others, eds. *Media Freedom and Accountability.* New York: Greenwood Press, 1989.

Francois, William E. *Mass Media Law and Regulation.* 4th ed. New York: Wiley, 1986.

Franklin, Marc A. *Cases and Materials on Mass Media Law.* 3d ed. Mineola, N.Y.: Foundation Press, 1987.

Henn, Harry G. *Copyright Law: A Practitioner's Guide.* 2d ed. New York: Practicing Law Institute, 1988.

Ingelhart, Louis Edward. *Press Freedoms.* Westport, Conn.: Greenwood Press, 1987.

Introduction to Copyright and Trademark Law 1987. New York: Practicing Law Institute, 1987.

Labunski, Richard. *Libel and the First Amendment: Legal History and Practice in Print and Broadcasting.* New Brunswick, N.J.: Transaction Books, 1987.

Lawrence, John Shelton, and Bernard Timberg, eds. *Fair Use and Free Inquiry: Copyright Law and the News Media.* 2d ed. Norwood, N.J.: Ablex, 1989.

Leibowitz, Matthew L., and Sanford H. Bohrer. *Broadcasting and the Law News Handbook.* Miami: Broadcasting and the Law, 1988.

Leibowitz, Matthew L., and John M. Spencer. *Broadcasting and the Law Political Handbook.* Miami: Broadcasting and the Law, 1988.

Meeske, Milan D., and R. C. Norris. *Copyright for the Electronic Media: A Practical Guide.* Belmont, Calif.: Wadsworth, 1987.

Nelson, Harold L., and others. *Law of Mass Communications: Freedom and Control of Print and Broadcast Media.* 6th ed. Westbury, N.Y.: Foundation Press, 1989.

Pember, Don R. *Mass Media Law.* 4th ed. Dubuque, Iowa: Brown, 1987.

Powe, Lucas A., Jr. *American Broadcasting and the First Amendment.* Berkeley: University of California Press, 1987.

Zuckman, Harvey L., and others. *Mass Communications Law in a Nutshell.* 3d ed. St. Paul: West, 1988.

Lighting

Brown, Blain. *Motion Picture and Video Lighting.* Newton, Mass.: Focal Press, 1993.

Carlson, Verne, and Sylvia Carlson. *Professional Lighting Handbook.* 2d ed. Boston: Focal Press, 1991.

Ferncase, Richard K. *Basic Lighting Worktext for Film and Video.* Newton, Mass.: Focal Press, 1992.

Ferncase, Richard K. *Film and Video Lighting Terms and Concepts.* Newton, Mass.: Focal Press, 1994.

Fitt, Brian, and Joe Thornley. *The Control of Light.* Newton, Mass.: Focal Press, 1993.

Fitt, Brian, and Joe Thornley. *Lighting by Design.* Newton, Mass.: Focal Press, 1993.

LeTorneau, Tom. *Lighting Techniques for Video Production: The Art of Casting Shadows.* White Plains, N.Y.: Knowledge Industry Publications, 1986.

Malkiewicz, Kris. *Film Lighting.* New York: Prentice-Hall, 1986.

Millerson, Gerald. *Lighting for Video.* 3d ed. Newton, Mass.: Focal Press, 1991.

Sweet, Harvey. *Handbook of Scenery, Properties, and Lighting.* Vol. 1, *Scenery and Props.* Boston: Allyn & Bacon, 1990.

News and Electronic Journalism

Atkins, Gary, and William Rivers. *Reporting With Understanding.* Ames: Iowa State University Press, 1987.

Becker, Lee B., and others. *The Training and Hiring of Journalists.* Norwood, N.J.: Ablex, 1987.

Biagi, Shirley. *Newstalk 2: State-of-the-Art Conversations With Today's Broadcast Journalists.* Belmont, Calif.: Wadsworth, 1987.

Block, Mervin. *Writing Broadcast News—Shorter, Sharper, Stronger: A Professional Handbook.* Chicago: Bonus Books, 1987.

Bohrer, Sanford L., and others. *News Handbook.* Miami: Broadcasting and the Law, 1988.

Boyd, Andrew. *Broadcast Journalism: Techniques of Radio and TV News.* 2d ed. Newton, Mass.: Focal Press, 1992.

Cohen, Akiba A. *The Television News Interview.* Newbury Park, Calif.: Sage, 1987.

Fensch, Thomas. *Sportswriting Handbook.* Hillsdale, N.J.: Lawrence Erlbaum Associates, 1988.

Fink, Conrad C. *Media Ethics: In the Newsroom and Beyond.* New York: McGraw-Hill, 1988.

Goald, Robert S. *Behind the Scenes at Local News.* Newton, Mass.: Focal Press, 1994.

Goedkoop, Richard J. *Inside Local Television News.* Salem, Wis.: Sheffield, 1988.

Goodwin, H. Eugene. *Groping for Ethics in Journalism.* 2d ed. Ames: Iowa State University Press, 1987.

Hall, Mark W. *Broadcast Journalism: An Introduction to News Writing.* 3d ed. New York: Hastings House, 1986.

Hewitt, John. *Air Words: Writing for Broadcast News.* Mountain View, Calif.: Mayfield, 1988.

Hitchcock, John R. *Sportscasting.* Newton, Mass.: Focal Press, 1991.

Hosley, David H., and Gayle K. Yamada. *Hard News: Women in Broadcasting Journalism.* Westport, Conn.: Greenwood Press, 1987.

Hough, George A. *News Writing.* 4th ed. Boston: Houghton Mifflin, 1988.

Irvine, Robert B. *When You are the Headline: Managing a Major News Story.* Homewood, Ill.: Dow Jones-Irwin, 1987.

Kessler, Lauren, and Duncan McDonald. *When Worlds Collide: A Journalist's Guide to Grammar and Style.* 2d ed. Belmont, Calif.: Wadsworth, 1988.

Klaidman, Stephen, and Tom L. Beauchamp. *The Virtuous Journalist.* New York: Oxford University Press, 1987.

MacDonald, R. H. *A Broadcast News Manual of Style.* New York: Longman, 1987.

Mencher, Melvin. *Basic News Writing.* 3d ed. Dubuque, Iowa: Brown, 1989.

Musburger, Robert B. *Electronic News Gathering: A Guide to ENG.* Newton, Mass.: Focal Press, 1991.

Olen, Jeffrey. *Ethics in Journalism.* Englewood Cliffs, N.J.: Prentice-Hall, 1988.

Papper, Robert A. *A Broadcast News Writing Stylebook.* Delaware: Ohio Wesleyan University, 1987.

Paisner, Daniel. *The Imperfect Mirror: Inside Stories of Television Newswomen.* New York: Morrow, 1989.

Shook, Frederick. *Television Field Production and Reporting.* New York: Longman, 1989.

Stephens, Mitchell. *Broadcast News.* 2d ed. New York: Holt, Rinehart and Winston, 1986.

Stepp, Carl Sessions. *Editing for Today's Newsroom: New Perspectives for a Changing Profession.* Hillsdale, N.J.: Erlbaum, 1989.

Stewart, Charles J., and William B. Cash, Jr. *Interviewing Principles and Practices.* 5th ed. Dubuque, Iowa: Brown, 1988.

Strentz, Herbert. *News Reporters and News Sources: Accomplices in Shaping and Misshaping the News.* 2d ed. Ames: Iowa State University Press, 1989.

White, Ray. *TV News: Building a Career in Broadcast Journalism.* Newton, Mass.: Focal Press, 1990.

Yorke, Ivor. *Basic TV Reporting.* Newton, Mass.: Focal Press, 1990.

Yorke, Ivor. *The Technique of Television News.* 2d ed. Boston: Focal Press, 1987.

Zousmer, Steven. *TV News Off-Camera: An Insider's Guide to Newswriting and Newspeople.* Ann Arbor: University of Michigan Press, 1987.

Postproduction

Anderson, Gary H. *Video Editing and Post-Production: A Professional Guide.* 2d ed. White Plains, N.Y.: Knowledge Industry Publications, 1988.

Anderson, Gary H. *Electronic Post-Production: The Film to Video Guide.* White Plains, N.Y.: Knowledge Industry Publications, 1986.

Browne, Steven E. *Videotape Editing: A Postproduction Primer.* 2d ed. Boston: Focal Press, 1993.

The Complete Guide to Videotape Editing. Level One, VTV Productions. Los Angeles: Sony Institute of Applied Video Technology, 1988.

Dancyger, Ken. *The Technique of Film and Video Editing.* Newton, Mass.: Focal Press, 1993.

Kerner, Marvin M. *The Art of the Sound Effects Editor.* Boston: Focal Press, 1989.

Mott, Robert L. *Sound Effects: Radio, TV and Film.* Boston: Focal Press, 1990.

Ohanian, Thomas D. *Digital Nonlinear Editing.* Newton, Mass.: Focal Press, 1993.

Ratcliff, John. *Timecode: A User's Guide.* Newton, Mass.: Focal Press, 1993.

Schneider, Arthur. *Electronic Post-Production: Terms and Concepts.* Newton, Mass.: Focal Press, 1990.

Schneider, Arthur. *Electronic Post-Production and Videotape Editing.* Boston: Focal Press, 1989.

The Video Post-Production Survival Kit, The Producers Group. Los Angeles: Sony Institute of Applied Video Technology, 1988.

Weynand, Diana. *Computerized Videotape Editing.* Woodland Hills, Calif.: Weynand Associates, 1983.

Producing and Directing

daSilva, Raul. *Making Money in Film and Video.* 2d ed. Newton, Mass.: Focal Press, 1992.

DiZazzo, Ray. *Directing and Corporate Video.* Newton, Mass.: Focal Press, 1993.

Gates, Richard. *Production Management for Film and Video.* Newton, Mass.: Focal Press, 1992.

Lindheim, Richard D., and Richard A. Blum. *Inside Television Producing.* Newton, Mass.: Focal Press, 1991.

Maier, Robert G. *Location Scouting and Management Handbook: Television, Film, and Still Photography.* Newton, Mass.: Focal Press, 1994.

Millerson, Gerald. *Effective TV Production.* 3d ed. Newton, Mass.: Focal Press, 1993.

Richards, Ron. *A Director's Method for Film and Television.* Newton, Mass.: Focal Press, 1992.

Wiese, Michael. *Film and Video Financing.* Newton, Mass.: Focal Press, 1991.

Wiese, Michael. *Independent Film and Videomaker's Guide.* 2d ed. Newton, Mass.: Focal Press, 1990.

Production, General

Aldridge, Henry B., and Lucy A. Liggett. *Audio/Video Production: Theory and Practice.* Englewood Cliffs, N.J.: Prentice-Hall, 1990.

Armer, Alan A. *Directing Television and Film.* 2d ed. Belmont, Calif.: Wadsworth, 1990.

Bermingham, Alan, and others. *The Video Studio.* 2d ed. Newton, Mass.: Focal Press, 1990.

Blum, Richard A. *Working Actors: The Craft of Television, Film and Stage Performance.* Boston: Focal Press, 1989.

Blumenthal, Howard J. *Television Producing and Directing.* New York: Barnes & Noble, 1987.

Bordwell, David, and Kristin Thompson. *Film Art: An Introduction.* 3d ed. New York: McGraw-Hill, 1990.

Burrows, Thomas D., and others. *Television Production: Disciplines and Techniques.* 5th ed. Dubuque, Iowa: Brown, 1992.

DiZazzo, Raymond. *Corporate Television: A Producer's Handbook.* Boston: Focal Press, 1990.

Fielding, Ken. *Introduction to Television Production.* New York: Longman, 1990.

Gayeski, Diane. *Corporate and Instructional Video.* 2d ed. Englewood Cliffs, N.J.: Prentice-Hall, 1991.

Hausman, Carl. *Institutional Video.* Belmont, Calif., Wadsworth, 1991.

Jarvis, Peter. *A Production Handbook: A Guide to the Pitfalls of Programme Making.* Newton, Mass.: Focal Press, 1993.

Kallenberger, Richard H., and George D. Cvjetnicanin. *Film Into Video: A Guide to Merging the Technologies.* Newton, Mass.: Focal Press, 1994.

Kehoe, Vincent J. R. *The Technique of the Professional Make-up Artist for Film, Television, and Stage.* Boston: Focal Press, 1985.

Kuney, Jack. *Take One: Television Directors on Directing.* Westport, Conn.: Greenwood/Praeger, 1990.

Lewis, Colby, and Tom Green. *The TV Director/Interpreter.* rev. ed. New York: Hastings House, 1990.

Merritt, Douglas. *Television Graphics—From Pencil to Pixel.* New York: Van Nostrand Reinhold, 1987.

Millerson, Gerald. *TV Scenic Design Handbook.* Boston: Focal Press, 1989.

Millerson, Gerald. *Video Camera Techniques.* 2d ed. Newton, Mass.: Focal Press, 1994.

Millerson, Gerald. *Video Production Handbook.* 2d ed. Boston: Focal Press, 1992.

Rabiger, Michael. *Directing the Documentary.* Boston: Focal Press, 1987.

Rowlands, Avril. *Continuity in Film and Video.* 2d ed. Boston: Focal Press, 1989.

Rowlands, Avril. *The Continuity Handbook: for Single Camera Shooting.* Newton, Mass.: Focal Press, 1994.

Rowlands, Avril. *The Production Assistant in TV and Video.* Boston: Focal Press, 1987.

Smith, David L. *Video Communication.* Belmont, Calif.: Wadsworth, 1991.

Watkinson, John. *The Art of Digital Video.* 2d ed. Newton, Mass.: Focal Press, 1993.

Watkinson, John. *The Digital Videotape Recorder.* Newton, Mass.: Focal Press, 1994.

Watkinson, John. *An Introduction to Digital Video.* Newton, Mass.: Focal Press, 1994.

Utz, Peter. *Video User's Handbook.* 3d ed. New York: Prentice-Hall, 1989.

Whittaker, Ron. *Television Production.* Mountain View, Calif.: Mayfield, 1993.

Wurtzel, Alan and Stephen R. Acker. *Television Production.* 3d ed. New York: McGraw-Hill, 1989.

Zaza, Tony, *Widescreen Film and Video Handbook.* Newton, Mass.: Focal Press, 1994.

Zettl, Herbert. *Sight-Sound-Motion: Applied Media Aesthetics.* 2d ed. Belmont, Calif.: Wadsworth, 1990.

Zettl, Herbert. *Television Production Handbook.* 5th ed. Belmont, Calif.: Wadsworth, 1992.

Zettl, Herbert. *Video Basics.* Belmont, Calif.: Wadsworth, 1995.

Satellites, Cable and Fiber Optics

Baldwin, Thomas F., and D. Stevens McVoy. *Cable Communication.* 2d ed. Englewood Cliffs, N.J.: Prentice-Hall, 1988.

Binkowski, Edward S. *Satellite Information Systems.* Boston: G. K. Hall, 1988.

Dalgleish, D. I. *An Introduction to Satellite Communications.* London: Institute of Electrical Engineers, 1989.

Eastman, Susan Tyler, and others. *Broadcast/Cable Programming: Strategies and Practices.* 3d ed. Belmont, Calif.: Wadsworth, 1989.

Garay, Ronald. *Cable Television: A Reference Guide to Information.* Westport, Conn.: Greenwood Press, 1988.

Hecht, Jeff. *Understanding Fiber Optics.* Indianapolis: Howard W. Sams, 1989.

Killen, Harold B. *Digital Communications With Fiber Optics and Satellite Applications.* Englewood Cliffs, N.J.: Prentice-Hall, 1988.

Long, Mark, comp. *World Satellite Almanac.* 2d ed. Indianapolis: Howard W. Sams, 1987.

Maral, G., and M. Bousquet. *Satellite Communications Systems.* New York: Wiley, 1986.

Mobilizing the Future: The Evolution of Mobile Satellite Services. Washington, D.C.: Television Digest, 1988.

Prentiss, Stan. *Satellite Communications.* 2d ed. Blue Ridge Summit, Pa.: TAB Books, 1987.

Wood, James. *Satellite Communications and DBS Systems.* Newton, Mass.: Focal Press, 1992.

The World Satellite Directory. Potomac, Md.: Phillips, 1990.

Writing, General

Armer, Alan A. *Writing the Screenplay: TV and Film.* Belmont, Calif.: Wadsworth, 1988.

Berman, Robert A. *Fade In: The Screenwriting Process.* Stoneham, Mass.: Focal Press, 1988.

Fensch, Thomas. *Writing Solutions: Beginnings, Middles & Endings.* Hillsdale, N.J.: Erlbaum, 1989.

Hilliard, Robert L. *Writing for Television and Radio.* 5th ed. Belmont, Calif.: Wadsworth, 1991.

Johnson, Mary C. *The Scriptwriter's Journal.* Newton, Mass.: Focal Press, 1994.

Kessler, Lauren, and Duncan McDonald. *Mastering the Message: Media Writing With Substance and Style.* Belmont, Calif.: Wadsworth, 1989.

Maloney, Martin, and Paul Max Rubenstein. *Writing for the Media: Film, Television, Video and Radio.* 2d ed. Englewood, Cliffs, N.J.: Prentice-Hall, 1988.

Mehring, Margaret. *The Screenplay: A Blend of Film Form and Content.* Newton, Mass.: Focal Press, 1990.

Morley, John. *Scriptwriting for High-Impact Videos.* Belmont, Calif.: Wadsworth, 1992.

Orlik, Peter B. *Broadcast Copyrighting.* 4th ed. Boston: Allyn & Bacon, 1990.

Rosenthal, Alan. *Writing Docudrama: Dramatizing Reality for TV and Film.* Newton, Mass.: Focal Press, 1994.

Rubenstein, Paul Max, and Martin Maloney. *Writing for the Media: Film, Television, Video and Radio.* 2d ed. Englewood Cliffs, N.J.: Prentice-Hall, 1988.

Stovall, James Glen. *Writing for the Mass Media.* 2d ed. Englewood Cliffs, N.J.: Prentice-Hall, 1990.

Swain, Dwight V. *Film Scriptwriting: A Practical Manual.* 2d ed. Boston: Focal Press, 1988.

Van Nostran, William. *The Scriptwriter's Handbook.* White Plains, N.Y.: Knowledge Industry Publications, 1989.

Walters, Roger L. *Broadcast Writing.* New York: Random House, 1988.

Walters, Roger L. *Broadcast Writing: Principles and Practice.* New York: Random House, 1988.

Wolff, Jurgen. *Successful Sitcom Writing.* New York: St. Martin's Press, 1988.

Zaza, Tony. *Script Planning: Positioning and Developing Scripts for TV and Film.* Newton, Mass.: Focal Press, 1992.

INDEX